Residential Real Estate Transactions

THIRD EDITION

JoAnn Kurtz, LLB
Joan Emmans, BA, LLB
Arlene Blatt, LLB

2009
Emond Montgomery Publications Limited
Toronto, Canada

Emond Montgomery Publications Limited
60 Shaftesbury Avenue
Toronto ON M4T 1A3
http://www.emp.ca/college

Printed in Canada.

Forms reproduced with the permission of Dye & Durham, a division of The Cartwright Group Ltd.

We acknowledge the financial support of the Government of Canada through the Book Publishing Industry Development Program (BPIDP) for our publishing activities.

Acquisitions and developmental editor
Peggy Buchan

Marketing manager
Christine Davidson

Sales manager, higher education
Dave Stokaluk

Copy and production editor
Nancy Ennis, WordsWorth Communications

Proofreader
David Handelsman, WordsWorth Communications

Indexer
Paula Pike, WordsWorth Communications

Cover designer
John Vegter

Library and Archives Canada Cataloguing in Publication

Kurtz, JoAnn, 1951–
Residential real estate transactions / JoAnn Kurtz, Joan Emmans, Arlene Blatt. — 3rd ed.

Includes bibliographical references and index.
ISBN 978-1-55239-281-2

1. Vendors and purchasers — Ontario — Textbooks.
I. Emmans, Joan II. Blatt, Arlene III. Title.

KE729.K87 2009 346.71304'36 C2009-900612-X

To Ely, Max, Jacob, and Danny.

To Andrew, Karyn, Kaitryn, and Rudy.

To Jeffrey, Jordan, and Matthew.

Contents

List of Figures

Introduction

Residential real estate purchases and sales form a big part of the business of many law firms. Real estate is an area of practice in which lawyers rely heavily on the help of law clerks, legal assistants, and legal secretaries. This book begins by giving students and law clerks an overview of legal concepts and principles of residential real estate law. It then proceeds to take them step by step through a standard residential real estate transaction. Included are the forms and precedents that they need to perform the routine tasks involved in the purchase and sale of a residential property. The book ends with discussions about more complex transactions, namely, the purchase of a new home, a condominium, a rural property, and a property being sold under power of sale.

The book deals primarily with the procedures to be followed by a law clerk working for a law firm that is acting for a purchaser, although there is a chapter that summarizes the real estate transaction from the perspective of a law firm acting for a vendor.

The procedures and precedents provided in this book are meant to be a guide only. Every lawyer or law firm has a certain way of doing things. As a law clerk, you must always follow your firm's practices and procedures.

Acknowledgments

We would like to thank the following people and organizations for their help in writing this book: Jan Oldreive of Toronto and Ken Goodbrand of Stouffville, who answered our questions; the Ontario Real Estate Association, and in particular Bob Kinnear, who provided us with copies of the association's standard form agreement of purchase and sale; and the staff at the Registry Office in Newmarket.

For the second edition, we would like to thank the following people and organizations for their help in updating the text and forms: Stephen Bitton, Ken Goodbrand, Barbara LaVieille, and Judy Wolf, who answered our questions and provided some precedents; the Ontario Real Estate Association, and specifically Leslie Alton, who provided us with agreements of purchase and sale; and Nancy Reason and Leah Daniels of the Law Society of Upper Canada, who gave us information about the document registration agreement.

For the third edition, we would like to thank Judy Wolf for answering our questions and Les Alton of the Ontario Real Estate Association for providing us with updated agreements of purchase and sale.

PART I

Introduction

CHAPTER 1

Overview of the Residential Real Estate Transaction

Before learning the specific steps and procedures of a residential real estate transaction, you must understand the stages of the transaction and the purpose of each stage.

In a residential real estate purchase, it is necessary to

- open and organize a file;
- review the agreement of purchase and sale;
- review the plan of survey of the property;
- search the title to the property;
- conduct other relevant searches;
- discuss with the client the advantages and disadvantages of title insurance;
- advise the client on how to take title to the property;
- prepare or review all of the necessary documents;
- prepare for the closing, including the execution of documents by the client;
- close the transaction and register the documents;
- notify utilities and government offices of the change in ownership; and
- provide the client with a reporting letter and opinion as to title.

Some of these tasks are performed by a law clerk; others may be done only by a lawyer.

These tasks have changed a great deal in recent years because the province of Ontario is in the process of automating its land registration system. Eventually, the title records of all properties in the province will be stored electronically in databases that are part of the Province of Ontario Land Registration and Information System or "POLARIS." The conversion from a paper system to the electronic one is being implemented gradually across the province. In those areas where automation is complete and electronic registration is mandatory, law firms are able to access POLARIS online from their office computers to conduct searches and register documents using software known as "Teraview."

THE STAGES OF A REAL ESTATE TRANSACTION

Let's take a closer look at the stages of a real estate transaction.

The Offer

offer
proposal from one person to another that, when accepted, becomes a contract

offeror
person who makes an offer

offeree
person to whom an offer is made

counteroffer
offer tendered by the original offeree as an alternative to the original offer; also known as a sign-back

sign-back
offer whereby the original offeree changes some of the terms in the original offer, initials the changes, then submits it to the original offeror

agreement of purchase and sale
contract created once an offer of purchase and sale has been accepted

vendor
seller of the property

purchaser
buyer of the property

closing date
day on which a real estate transaction is completed and title is transferred

execution
signing of a document; also a short name for a writ of execution or a writ of seizure and sale

A real estate purchase starts with the making of an **offer** — usually by the purchaser to purchase a particular property. Even though an offer to purchase should be reviewed by a lawyer before the purchaser signs it, usually it is not. Instead, it is prepared by a real estate agent, signed by the purchaser as the **offeror**, and presented by the agent to the vendor as the **offeree**. The standard form of offer is set up to allow the offeree to accept the offer by signing it. Instead of accepting the offer, the offeree may reject it or sign it back — that is, amend it in some way and present it back to the original offeror as a **counteroffer**. If there is a **sign-back**, the original offeror may accept it, reject it, or sign it back yet again. Once the offer is accepted, it becomes a contract referred to as the **agreement of purchase and sale**.

The Agreement of Purchase and Sale

The work of the law firm usually starts when it receives a copy of the signed agreement of purchase and sale.

The parties to the agreement of purchase and sale are the **vendor** and the **purchaser**. The vendor agrees to transfer title to the property to the purchaser on the **closing date** in return for the payment of a specified amount. The purchaser agrees to accept title and to pay that sum of money. The agreement sets out the terms on which and the manner in which title is to be transferred. *It does not transfer title.*

The residential real estate transaction covers the time from the **execution** or signing of the agreement of purchase and sale to, and in fact beyond, the actual transfer of title on closing. During this time, it is the role of the purchaser's lawyer to make sure that the title transferred on the closing date is exactly the same as the title the vendor promised to deliver. It is the role of the vendor's lawyer to make sure that the vendor is in a position to transfer title.

The purchaser's lawyer makes sure that proper title is transferred by conducting a number of searches and by making various inquiries. The vendor's lawyer must anticipate and respond to questions raised by the purchaser's lawyer and clear up, where possible, any matters that are contrary to the agreement of purchase and sale.

The Survey

When clients buy a house, they are actually buying land and the buildings that happen to be located on it. It is therefore important to make sure that

- the house and other structures are located wholly within the property lines of the land being purchased;
- neighbours' buildings are not located on the land;
- the parcel of land is as big as the client has been led to believe;
- any fences are located on the lot lines; and

- the size and location of the house and other buildings satisfy zoning requirements.

You can be sure of these matters only if there is a **plan of survey** of the property being purchased. A plan of survey is prepared by an Ontario land surveyor, based on a physical examination of the property. The surveyor then prepares a schematic sketch showing the boundaries of the property and the location of fences, structures, and rights of way.

plan of survey
schematic sketch showing boundaries of property and location of all fences, structures, and rights of way

The Title Search

The agreement of purchase and sale usually states that the property's title is to be transferred to the purchaser free of **encumbrances**, except those specified in the agreement. For example, there may be an exception for a mortgage that the purchaser has agreed to assume.

encumbrances
charges, claims, liens, or liabilities attached to a property

It is up to the purchaser (or the purchaser's lawyer) to satisfy himself or herself that the title to the property delivered on closing is the title that was promised. The purchaser's lawyer will search the title to the property to confirm that the vendor is the owner of the land and to look for any encumbrances against the property. If the search of title reveals any encumbrances that are not supposed to be there, the purchaser's lawyer will require the vendor's lawyer to correct these title defects by the time of closing. For example, if there is a mortgage registered on title that the purchaser has not agreed to assume, the purchaser's lawyer will require the vendor's lawyer to have the mortgage discharged. If there are any defects that the vendor cannot clear up, the purchaser may be entitled to end the deal and get the **deposit** back.

deposit
part of the purchase price prepaid when the contract is entered into and applied against the purchase price

The vendor's lawyer must make sure that title to the property conforms to the agreement. If it does not, it is the lawyer's job to "fix" the title by the time of closing. For example, the lawyer may have to arrange to discharge any outstanding mortgage that the purchaser did not agree to assume.

Other Searches and Inquiries

A number of other matters that affect title to the land are dealt with in the agreement of purchase and sale and must be confirmed by conducting various searches and inquiries.

BUILDING AND ZONING CONSIDERATIONS

Is the property zoned to allow the purchaser's intended use? Do the size and location of the buildings on the property conform with relevant bylaws? Are there outstanding work orders against the property? You must contact the municipal building and zoning departments for the answers to these questions, and they can be answered fully only if you provide the departments with a copy of the survey.

PUBLIC UTILITY ACCOUNTS

Certain unpaid utility accounts can be added to the municipal tax bill and become a lien on the land. These include water, sewage, and sometimes hydro. Therefore, you must contact any public utilities provided by the municipality to find out the status of the accounts.The vendor must pay any outstanding balances by closing.

REALTY TAXES

Realty tax arrears also constitute a lien on the land. Accordingly, you must contact the municipality to ensure that the vendor has paid all taxes owing up to the closing date.

WRITS OF EXECUTION

You must contact the sheriff of the relevant judicial district to ensure there are no outstanding writs of execution, also called writs of seizure and sale (outstanding judgments). Such writs constitute a lien against the land.

OTHER INQUIRIES

Depending on the nature of the property, you may have to make additional inquiries of municipal, provincial, or federal government departments. For example, if the property is rural, you would inquire whether the well water and the septic system meet government standards.

Title Insurance

In Ontario, in recent years, title insurance has become an increasingly popular option for purchasers of property, as well as for the lawyers representing them. A purchaser may buy title insurance for the property instead of relying on a lawyer's opinion that the purchaser has good title to the property. Without a title insurance policy, the lawyer must make sure that there are no problems with the title by conducting searches and making letter inquiries, all of which cost money — sometimes a significant amount.

Under a title insurance policy, the insurer "insures over" certain problems that might arise on title. Title insurers assume the risk of some of the potential problems that some of the searches or answers to letters might disclose, thus saving the purchaser the cost of the searches. Some policies protect the buyers from problems that an up-to-date survey might disclose, such as an encroachment by a neighbouring property. A purchaser may save several hundred or even several thousand dollars by not having to pay for a new survey. Title insurance also protects a buyer against post-closing events, such as a fraudulent mortgage being placed on the property.

Every title insurance policy has exceptions to coverage and specific requirements of the lawyer acting for the purchaser. It is up to the lawyer to discuss with the client the policies available and whether or not the client wishes to purchase title insurance. Under rule 5.01 of the *Rules of Professional Conduct* governing lawyers (see chapter 2, The Role of the Law Clerk), this is a task that cannot be delegated to a law clerk.

Taking Title

The lawyer will also talk to the client about how ownership of the property will be taken — in one name alone or with another person, either as tenants in common or as joint tenants. Again, this is something only a lawyer should do.

Document Preparation and Review

The vendor's lawyer prepares the transfer, which the purchaser's lawyer reviews before closing. The vendor's lawyer also prepares a **statement of adjustments**. This is a statement that determines the exact amount to be paid on closing by calculating various credits and debits against the purchase price as set out in the agreement of purchase and sale. Adjustments are made for expenses such as taxes, utilities, and mortgage payments that the vendor paid in advance. If the vendor has paid more than his or her share of the expense, the purchaser will have to compensate the vendor for that overpayment. If the vendor has not paid enough, the unpaid portion will be subtracted from the purchase price because the purchaser will ultimately have to pay the expense. For example, suppose a purchase is closing on September 15 and the vendor has paid the realty taxes for the entire year. The vendor is responsible for the payment of taxes only until the date of closing. Taxes will therefore be prorated to the date of closing, and the purchaser, in addition to the purchase price, will have to reimburse the vendor for that overpayment.

statement of adjustments
statement that outlines the various credits and debits against the purchase price and specifies the exact amount to be paid on closing

Although the vendor's lawyer prepares the statement of adjustments, the purchaser's lawyer reviews it. You must have the information required to verify all amounts that appear. You must also know how to calculate the various adjustments.

In addition to the transfer and statement of adjustments, other documents must be prepared in order to close the deal. These documents include directions, undertakings, supplementary agreements, declarations of possession, and affidavits.

Preparation for Closing

In preparation for closing, some documents must be signed by the purchaser and others by the vendor. If the conveyancing documents are being registered electronically, they are not actually signed by the parties. Instead, the parties sign an acknowledgment and direction, authorizing their respective lawyers to sign and release the documents electronically on their behalf. The lawyers must explain all the documents to their clients before having the clients sign them. The vendor's lawyer will calculate how much money is required to complete the transaction (the **balance due on closing**), decide to whom the money should be paid, and give that information to the purchaser's lawyer. The purchaser's lawyer will tell the purchaser how much money is needed in order to close. The purchaser's lawyer will receive the closing funds from the purchaser and any lenders involved, and ensure that they are payable as the vendor directs. Both lawyers must finalize arrangements for the actual closing of the transaction.

balance due on closing
exact amount the purchaser pays to the vendor when the real estate deal closes

escrow closing
exchange and holding of funds, keys, and documents by the lawyers pending registration of the electronic documents

The Closing

The lawyers do not physically meet for electronic closings. Rather, they follow an **escrow closing** procedure set out in the **document registration agreement** (DRA), which the lawyers sign prior to the closing. They courier to each other any materials required for closing. When the vendor's lawyer is satisfied that he or she has received all that is required, he or she releases, through Teraview, the transfer for registration. When the purchaser's lawyer is satisfied that he or she has received all that is required, he or she signs on to Teraview, checks to make sure that title to the property

document registration agreement
agreement entered into by the lawyers for the parties dealing with the procedures for electronic registration and the escrow closing arrangement

has not changed since the title search was done, and then registers the transfer and mortgage, if any.

If the closing is not electronic, the lawyers for the parties (or their agents) meet, usually at the appropriate land registry office. At that time, the vendor's lawyer gives a key and all the necessary documents, including the transfer, to the purchaser's lawyer. The purchaser's lawyer gives the vendor's lawyer the closing funds. The purchaser's lawyer does a subsearch of title to make sure that the state of the title has not changed since the search of title was completed. If satisfied that there have been no changes, the purchaser's lawyer registers the transfer/deed of land and mortgage, if any.

Post-Closing Requirements

After the closing, the lawyers will notify the relevant offices, such as the municipal assessment department, utility companies, and any mortgagees, of the change in title. The vendor's lawyer will pay any outstanding real estate commission and pay off any liens, expenses, or mortgages that were to be discharged. The balance of the proceeds will be paid to the vendor. Both lawyers must follow up on any undertakings given on closing, prepare reporting letters to their clients, and submit their statements of account.

REVIEW QUESTIONS

1. What is POLARIS?
2. What is Teraview?
3. How does a real estate purchase start?
4. Who are the parties to the agreement of purchase and sale?
5. What do the parties to the agreement of purchase and sale agree to do?
6. Does the agreement of purchase and sale transfer title?
7. What is the role of the purchaser's lawyer in a residential real estate transaction?
8. What is the role of the vendor's lawyer?
9. What is a plan of survey, and what purpose does it serve in a real estate transaction?
10. Why does the purchaser's lawyer search the title to the property?
11. What are some of the other searches or inquiries that the purchaser's lawyer might conduct?
12. How does title insurance save a purchaser money?
13. Who prepares the transfer?
14. What is a statement of adjustments, and who prepares it?
15. What is the procedure for an electronic closing?
16. How does a non-electronic closing take place?

CHAPTER 2

The Role of the Law Clerk

Now that you have an understanding of the various stages of a real estate transaction, let's look at your role in this process.

PROFESSIONAL EXPECTATIONS OF THE LAW CLERK

You are expected to know the routine procedures in a real estate transaction. If a routine question arises in the course of the file, you should know the answer or be able to find it. At the same time, if anything out of the ordinary arises, you must notify the lawyer handling the file.

Your job will include opening and organizing a real estate file. All files have deadlines, and you must be able to determine what those deadlines are and to make sure you meet them. The law firm will expect you to obtain routine documents from third parties and to extract the information you need from these documents.

There are certain standard elements and principles that apply to all real estate transactions, and you are expected to be familiar with them. However, each law firm or individual lawyer will have a certain way of doing things, so, in addition to knowing the standard procedures, you must also know the procedures and forms used by the firm you work for.

ERRORS AND OMISSIONS CONSIDERATIONS

All lawyers have errors and omissions insurance to protect themselves and their clients in case they are negligent in performing their clients' work. This insurance coverage is required by the **Law Society of Upper Canada** (**LSUC**), the professional body that governs lawyers in Ontario, and is provided by the **Lawyers' Professional Indemnity Company** (**LAWPRO**). In 2003 real estate claims accounted for 26 percent of claims reported to LAWPRO and 23 percent of claims paid. Real estate claims have decreased significantly in recent years, largely because of the impact of title insurance.

When you work as a law clerk, the law firm is responsible for all the tasks that you perform. If you make a mistake that results in a loss to a client, the law firm is responsible to the client for that loss, and the firm's errors and omissions insurance will probably cover any claim. Despite this coverage, lawyers are still concerned

Law Society of Upper Canada (LSUC)
professional body governing the activities of lawyers in Ontario

Lawyers' Professional Indemnity Company (LAWPRO)
insurance company controlled by the Law Society of Upper Canada that insures lawyers against errors and omissions and administers TitlePLUS, a title insurance product

about mistakes and negligence claims. Errors are still very expensive to a lawyer. A mistake may cost the lawyer the client and whatever future fees that client would pay. A mistake also takes time to correct. Since lawyers charge based on time, the time spent correcting a mistake represents lost revenue, and although lawyers are insured, they must pay the deductible portion of the claim. Depending on the law firm's insurance coverage, the deductible portion can be as high as $25,000, and insurance premiums will increase if claims are made.

It is therefore very important that you avoid making mistakes that could give rise to an insurance claim. You can do so by following standard office procedures and by not overstepping the bounds of your assigned responsibilities. You should follow all instructions exactly as given and document all steps you take and conversations you have — especially conversations with clients. You should not volunteer to make decisions that are not yours to make, and you should try to avoid being placed in situations where you may be called upon to do so. You should always refer questions on these matters to the lawyer handling the file. If the lawyer will be away from the office during important times, you should make sure that another lawyer is available in the event of an emergency. You should also keep an eye out for mistakes made by others. If you notice something questionable in the file, bring it to the lawyer's attention. You may save the lawyer from a possible negligence claim.

PROFESSIONAL CONDUCT LIMITATIONS

The legal profession is governed by statute, and statute law determines, among other things, the educational and other qualifications required before a person may be licensed to practise law in Ontario. The *Law Society Act* also establishes the Law Society of Upper Canada as the professional body that governs the conduct of lawyers in Ontario.

The Law Society of Upper Canada sets *Rules of Professional Conduct* and *By-Laws*, which lawyers in Ontario are required to follow. Failure to follow these rules may result in disciplinary proceedings being brought against the lawyer. If a lawyer is found guilty of a breach of the *Rules of Professional Conduct* or *By-Laws*, a range of penalties, including disbarment, is available. Even though a law clerk is not subject to disciplinary proceedings, it is still important for you to know and follow these rules. There are two rules that are relevant to the role of a law clerk in a real estate transaction:

- confidentiality; and
- supervision and delegation.

Confidentiality

Rule 2.03(1) requires lawyers to keep all information from and about a client strictly confidential:

> A lawyer at all times shall hold in strict confidence all information concerning the business and affairs of the client acquired in the course of the professional relationship and shall not divulge any such information unless expressly or impliedly authorized by the client or required by law to do so.

The commentary to the rule sets out the rationale for the rule as follows:

> A lawyer cannot render effective professional services to the client unless there is full and unreserved communication between them. At the same time, the client must feel completely secure and entitled to proceed on the basis that, without any express request or stipulation on the client's part, matters disclosed to or discussed with the lawyer will be held in strictest confidence.

The following excerpt from the commentary to the rule clarifies the care that lawyers are expected to take in protecting client confidentiality:

> A lawyer should avoid indiscreet conversations, even with the lawyer's spouse or family, about a client's affairs and should shun any gossip about such things even though the client is not named or otherwise identified. Similarly, a lawyer should not repeat any gossip or information about the client's business or affairs that is overheard or recounted to the lawyer. Apart altogether from ethical considerations or questions of good taste, indiscreet shop-talk between lawyers, if overheard by third parties able to identify the matter being discussed, could result in prejudice to the client. Moreover, the respect of the listener for lawyers and the legal profession will probably be lessened.

Law firms expect the same level of behaviour from their law clerks.

Supervision and Delegation

Rule 5 of the *Rules of Professional Conduct* and by-law 7.1 deal with the relationship between lawyers and their students, employees, and others. Rule 5.01 is entitled "Supervision" and discusses the responsibilities of a lawyer who delegates tasks to a non-lawyer. It also sets out what tasks a lawyer may and may not delegate.

Subrule 5.01(2) provides that direct supervision by a lawyer is required. It states as follows:

> A lawyer shall, in accordance with the *By-Laws*,
>
> (a) assume complete professional responsibility for all business entrusted to him or her and
>
> (b) directly supervise staff and assistants to whom particular tasks and functions are delegated.

The commentary to the subrule makes it clear that a lawyer may delegate work to a law clerk who "has received specialized training or education and is competent to do independent work under the general supervision of a lawyer." The lawyer must supervise the work, and the lawyer must maintain a direct relationship with the client. The extent of supervision will depend on the type of legal matter and the experience of the law clerk. The lawyer is responsible for educating the law clerk concerning the duties assigned to the law clerk and supervising the manner in which the duties are carried out. The lawyer must review the law clerk's work at sufficiently frequent intervals to ensure that the work is completed properly and on time.

The commentary specifically addresses real estate transactions and provides that a lawyer may permit a law clerk to attend to all matters of routine administration, to assist in more complex transactions, to draft statements of account and routine documents and correspondence, and to attend at registrations.

A lawyer may not, however, delegate to a law clerk ultimate responsibility for

- review of a title search report;
- review of documents before signing;
- review and signing of a letter of requisition;
- review and signing of a title opinion; and
- review and signing of a reporting letter to the client.

In addition, in transactions using electronic registration, only a lawyer may sign for completeness of any document that requires "compliance with law" statements. (See chapter 21, Document Preparation.)

Since the *By-Laws* apply to both lawyers and paralegals, they use the term "licensees," rather than "lawyers." By-law 7.1 sets out the requirements for licensees with respect to tasks being done by non-licensees, such as law clerks.

Section 4(1) of by-law 7.1 indicates that licensees must assume complete professional responsibility for the practice of law with respect to clients' affairs, and must directly supervise all non-licensees who are assigned work relating to those clients' affairs.

Section 4(2) of by-law 7.1 sets out the licensee's specific responsibilities, including the ones that apply to law clerks, which are as follows:

- the licensee shall not permit a non-licensee to accept a client on the licensee's behalf;
- the licensee shall assign to the non-licensee only tasks that the non-licensee is competent to perform;
- the licensee shall ensure that the non-licensee does not act without the licensee's instruction;
- the licensee shall review a non-licensee's performance of the tasks assigned to him or her at frequent intervals;
- the licensee shall ensure that the tasks assigned to a non-licensee are performed properly and in a timely manner;
- the licensee shall assume responsibility for all tasks performed by a non-licensee, including the preparation of all documents; and
- the licensee shall ensure that a non-licensee does not act finally in respect of a client's affairs.

Section 5 of by-law 7.1 indicates that a non-licensee cannot, *without prior express authorization from the licensee*,

- give or accept an undertaking on behalf of the licensee;
- act on behalf of the licensee in routine matters before an adjudicative body; or
- take clients' instructions.

A non-licensee cannot negotiate with a third party on behalf of a client without the client's consent (and permission from the licensee), and the licensee must approve the results of any such negotiations.

Section 6 of by-law 7.1 sets out tasks that cannot be performed by a non-licensee. They include

- giving legal advice;
- appearing before an adjudicative body, except as provided in section 5;
- negotiating with third parties, except as provided in section 5;
- signing correspondence, other than that of a routine administrative nature;
- forwarding documents (other than routine ones) to clients, without prior review by the licensee; and
- using the licensee's personalized specially encrypted diskette to access the system for the electronic registration of title documents.

Subrule 5.01(5) covers delegation with respect to title insurance in real estate matters. A lawyer may not permit a non-lawyer to

- provide advice to a client with respect to any insurance, including title insurance, without supervision;
- present insurance options or information regarding premiums to a client without supervision;
- recommend one insurance product over another without supervision; or
- give legal opinions regarding the insurance coverage obtained.

Subrules 5.01(3) and (4) deal with electronic registration of title documents. Under the e-reg system, every user is issued a specially encrypted diskette and password. The combination of the diskette and password identifies the user and controls access to the system. In order to maintain and ensure the security of the diskette, subrule 5.01(3) provides that a lawyer shall not disclose his or her password to anyone else or permit anyone else, including a non-lawyer employee, to use the lawyer's diskette. Subrule 5.01(4) requires the lawyer to ensure that any non-lawyer employed by the lawyer does not disclose his or her password to anyone else or permit anyone else to use the non-lawyer's diskette.

If the rules with respect to delegation are contravened, the instructing lawyer, not the law clerk, is subject to disciplinary proceedings. Even so, it is still important for you to understand and follow these provisions. You should never unilaterally, without the knowledge of the instructing lawyer, undertake work contrary to the provisions of rule 5.01. Subrule 5.01(2)(a) states that the lawyer handling the file is responsible for all work you perform. As a result, disciplinary proceedings could be brought against the lawyer because of your conduct, and, consequently, your future at the law firm would not be very bright.

What about a situation in which the lawyer handling the file contravenes by-law 7.1 by assigning work to you that only a lawyer should undertake? This can put you in an awkward and uncomfortable situation. On the one hand, it is difficult, if not impossible, to refuse to follow your employer's instructions. On the other hand, even though it is the lawyer and not you who would be disciplined by the Law Society of Upper Canada, you may still be blamed. Your best approach in such a situation is to carry out the assigned tasks while always referring the work back to the instructing lawyer for review, and to document this referral by memo. For example, if the lawyer handling the file directs you to review a title search, to decide on the appropriate requisitions to be made on title, and to draft a requisition letter, you should return the title search and draft requisition letter to the lawyer with a memo, a copy of which is placed in the file, stating that the material is being returned to the lawyer for review.

If the lawyer tries to delegate a task to you that "lawyers themselves may not do," serious misconduct may well be involved, and, depending on the particular situation, you should probably refuse to perform the task.

To summarize,

- a law clerk should be aware of the provisions of rule 5.01 of the *Rules of Professional Conduct* and by-law 7.1;
- a law clerk should never unilaterally, without the knowledge of the instructing lawyer, undertake work in contravention of the provisions of rule 5.01 or by-law 7.1;
- if a law clerk is assigned work that a lawyer is required to undertake, the law clerk should perform the work but should refer it back to the instructing lawyer for review and should document the referral by memo; and
- if a law clerk is assigned work that would be improper for a lawyer to undertake, in most circumstances, the law clerk should refuse to perform the work.

Conflict of Interest

The *Rules of Professional Conduct* also address the issue of conflict of interest in the real estate area. Under rule 2.04, a lawyer is required to avoid conflicts of interest. Generally, a lawyer should not act for both the purchaser and the vendor in a real estate transaction. Subrule 2.04(11) specifically prohibits a lawyer from representing a lender and a borrower in mortgage loan transactions. However, subrule 2.04(12) provides that a lawyer may act for both lender and borrower if the lender is a bank, trust company, insurance company, credit union, or finance company that lends money in the ordinary course of its business.

REFERENCES

Law Society Act, RSO 1990, c. L.8.

REVIEW QUESTIONS

1. Why do lawyers have errors and omissions insurance, and who provides it?
2. Who is responsible for the mistakes made by a law clerk?
3. What are the *Rules of Professional Conduct*?
4. What do the *Rules of Professional Conduct* provide with respect to confidentiality?
5. Pursuant to the *Rules of Professional Conduct* and the *By-Laws*, to whom and in what circumstances may a lawyer delegate work?
6. Under the *Rules of Professional Conduct* and the *By-Laws*, what may a lawyer permit a law clerk to do in a real estate transaction?
7. Under the *Rules of Professional Conduct* and the *By-Laws*, what may a lawyer not delegate to a law clerk in a real estate transaction?
8. What may a lawyer not permit a law clerk to do with respect to title insurance?
9. What are the main points for a law clerk to keep in mind, in light of the provisions of the *Rules of Professional Conduct* and the *By-Laws* with respect to delegation?
10. Summarize the provisions of the *Rules of Professional Conduct* regarding conflicts of interest in real estate transactions.

PART II

Overview of Real Estate Law

CHAPTER 3

Estates and Interests in Land

The legal term for land is **real property**. This term is used to describe land and everything attached to it, including

real property
land, including everything that is attached to it

- minerals below the surface of the land;
- airspace above the land;
- buildings placed on the land; and
- **fixtures** on the land — **personal property** that has become attached, or affixed, to the land.

fixtures
chattels that have become attached or affixed to the real property

personal property
chattels; property that is not real property

The law that deals with real property dates back to feudal times in England, and much of the terminology still in use today dates back to that time. In feudal times, the King of England owned all land and granted some of his subjects **estates** in land in return for their service and allegiance. The king had the right to take back the land if a subject **forfeited** it, for example, by committing treason.

estate
interest in land that provides the right to exclusive possession

forfeit
lose the right

The English law of real property was brought to Ontario, and today the Crown is still the ultimate owner of all land. Therefore, the government controls the use, disposition, and development of all land in Ontario.

Because the Crown is the ultimate owner of all land, and because land is permanent and immovable, owning land is different from owning other kinds of property. Land ownership is more like "possession" of land, together with rights and obligations that are recognized and enforced by law. Indeed, individuals don't own *land*; rather, they own estates or **interests** in land. The rights that people have with respect to their land will depend on the estate or interest they have.

interests
rights to land that are not estates and do not confer a right to exclusive possession of the land

In this chapter we will look at

- estates in land;
- other interests in land;
- possessory interests in land;
- fixtures; and
- title to land.

ESTATES IN LAND

exclusive possession sole possession of the land; denial of possession to all others

An estate in land is an interest in land that gives the owner the right to **exclusive possession** of the land. There are three types of estates in land:

- the fee simple estate;
- the life estate; and
- the leasehold estate.

Fee Simple Estate

The fee simple estate is the greatest interest in land that an individual can have. The land is still owned by the Crown (the government), which grants the fee simple estate to the first "owner" by way of **Crown patent**.

Crown patent grant of land by the Crown (the government) to the first owner

In theory, the fee simple estate extends physically upward into the sky and downward to the centre of the earth. In fact, there are limitations in both directions. A landowner cannot sue the owner of an airplane flying overhead for trespass. However, the owner could sue the owner of a neighbouring property who makes permanent use of the first owner's airspace, for example, by building a structure that hangs over the property. With respect to rights below the surface, most Crown patents do not include oil and mineral rights, which are reserved for the Crown.

fee simple the right to exclusive possession and the right to dispose of the land for an indefinite period of time

A person who has the **fee simple** estate (called the owner in fee simple) has the right to exclusive possession of the land and the right to dispose of the land for an infinite period of time. That person is considered to be the true owner of the land and has all the rights associated with land ownership. These rights include the right to

- grant the fee simple estate to someone else (by sale or gift);
- grant a life estate in the property;
- grant a leasehold estate in the property (rent the property); and
- convey the property by inheritance (with or without a will).

escheat reversion of property to the Crown

expropriation reacquisition of land, with compensation, by the Crown for public purposes

If the owner in fee simple dies without leaving a will and has no surviving heirs or relatives, the land will **escheat**, or revert to the Crown. The Crown may reacquire the land by way of **expropriation**. The acquisition must be for public purposes (for example, a road widening or new highway), and the owner is compensated for the value of the land.

Life Estate

life estate right to exclusive possession of the property for the length of a particular lifetime

A **life estate** grants to the owner the right to exclusive possession of the property for the length of a particular lifetime (usually, but not always, that of the owner of the life estate). A life estate runs for an indefinite period of time — we know it will end, but we don't know when. On the death of the person to whose life the life estate is tied, the life estate ends and the property reverts to the person who holds the estate in fee simple.

The owner of the fee simple estate can convey the fee simple to another person and reserve a life estate, keeping the use of the property until death. Also, the owner in fee simple can convey a life estate to one person and the fee simple estate to yet another. For example, in a will, a husband can leave a life estate in his home to his wife and the fee simple estate to his son upon the wife's death. Life estates are most commonly conveyed to family members.

Once a life estate is created, the owners of the life estate and the fee simple estate both have legal, though different, rights to the same property. For example, assume that Sam has a life estate in a parcel of land and David has the fee simple estate. Sam is entitled to exclusive possession of the property during his lifetime. As soon as Sam dies, the life estate ends, and David will obtain full rights to the property. Even though David holds the fee simple estate, his estate is limited by Sam's life estate. In other words, David is entitled to possession of the property only when Sam dies and the life estate ends. Sam, on the other hand, must use the land in a reasonable manner and must not **commit waste** on the land. For example, he must not tear down buildings or destroy trees.

commit waste
destroy, abuse, or make permanent undesirable changes to a property

The person with the fee simple estate in land may grant successive life estates in that same parcel of land. For example, assume that David grants a life estate first to Bob, then to Chuck, and then to Don. When Bob dies, Chuck gets a life estate in the property. When Chuck dies, Don gets a life estate in the property. When Don dies, David will regain full ownership and possession of the property, assuming he is still alive. If he is dead, David's heirs will inherit the property.

The owner of a life estate in land may grant the right to possession of the land to someone else, but that right to possession will end when the life owner dies. For example, assume that David is the owner in fee simple of a property that has a townhouse. He grants Sam a life estate in the property. Sam, who does not wish to live there, in turn grants Alice the right to exclusive possession of the townhouse. As soon as Sam dies, the life estate ends, and the right to possession reverts to David.

Leasehold Estate

A **leasehold estate** grants the right to exclusive possession of the property for a specified period of time in return for the payment of rent. This estate creates a landlord–tenant relationship between the parties.

leasehold estate
right to exclusive possession of property for a specified period of time in return for the payment of rent

For example, assume that David has the fee simple estate in a townhouse property and grants a leasehold estate to Sam. Both Sam and David will have legal rights to the same property. Sam is entitled to exclusive possession of the property during the term of the leasehold agreement and must pay rent to David. David is entitled to regain possession of the property only when the lease terminates.

OTHER INTERESTS IN LAND

There are interests in land that are not estates in land. These interests do not confer on their owners a right of exclusive possession to the land.

Easements

easement
right to use a portion of someone else's land for a specific purpose, without requiring the owner's permission

right of way
right to use a portion of another's land for access purposes

servient tenement
land over which an easement runs

dominant tenement
land that benefits from an easement

An **easement** is the right to use a portion of someone else's land for a specific purpose, without requiring the owner's permission each time. An easement is often referred to as a **right of way**.

For example, assume that Sam has a garage at the back of his townhouse but does not own the driveway. The land on which the driveway is situated is owned by his neighbour, Bob. Sam would need an easement interest in Bob's land to be able to use the driveway to get to his garage. If Bob grants Sam an easement, Sam will be entitled to use the easement only for access to the garage. He is not entitled to park his car in the driveway, thereby obstructing the easement.

The land that supplies the easement is called the **servient tenement** and the land that benefits from the easement is called the **dominant tenement**. The servient tenement and the dominant tenement must each be owned by different people for an easement to exist. In the previous example, Bob's land is the servient tenement and Sam's townhouse property is the dominant tenement.

An easement interest attaches to the land, not the owner. If Sam sells his townhouse to Susie, she will acquire the easement over Bob's land, giving her the right to use the driveway to gain access to the garage. Similarly, if Bob sells his land to Betty, she gets the land subject to the easement in favour of Sam and cannot block the driveway.

express grant
creation of an easement by written document from the owner of the servient tenement to the owner of the dominant tenement

prescription
means by which an interest is acquired in another's land after a period of open and uninterrupted use

easement implied by law
creation of an easement when the only way to gain access to a property is by crossing over another property

Easements are usually created when the owner of the servient tenement grants an easement to the owner of the dominant tenement. This is called an **express grant**. They can also be created by **prescription** — if the easement is used over a period of 20 years. For a more complete discussion of easements by prescription, see below under the heading "Possessory Interests in Land." An easement can also be **implied by law** when the only way to get access to a property or a main road is by crossing over another person's property.

Utility companies commonly have easement rights over landowners' property so that they can service and maintain their utility lines.

Neighbours whose houses are very close together may have the right to enter upon the neighbouring property to facilitate maintenance and repair work. For example, an owner may need to place a ladder on a neighbour's property to access a roof.

Restrictive Covenants

restrictive covenant
promise by an owner of land to refrain from doing something on the property

A **restrictive covenant** imposes limitations on the use of the property. It is typically a promise by an owner to refrain from doing something on the property — for example, putting up an outdoor clothes line. A restrictive covenant attaches to the land and therefore will bind subsequent owners of the property. In order to be enforceable, the restriction must be reasonable in nature and cannot be contrary to public interest.

Builders often use restrictive covenants in subdivision developments to maintain control over the appearance of homes. They may, for example, impose a restriction on property owners from painting their front doors red or from installing satellite dishes.

Mineral Rights

Most Crown patents do not convey mineral rights but retain them for the benefit of the Crown. The Crown can transfer the mineral rights to a person other than the owner of the fee simple estate. When a person acquires mineral rights in the land of another person, that interest is called a **profit à prendre**.

profit à prendre
interest created when mineral rights are acquired in the land of another person

Riparian Rights

Riparian rights are the rights of an owner of land to a watercourse that runs through, or is adjacent to, the property. The owner of the land has the right to the use and flow of the water but cannot interfere with the flow of the water to downstream users.

riparian rights
rights to the use of a watercourse running through or adjacent to the property

POSSESSORY INTERESTS IN LAND

The various interests in land are generally acquired when the owner of the interest expressly grants it to another person. It is possible, however, for a person to acquire an interest in land by simply using the land over an extended period of time. In such a case, the interest is said to have been acquired by **possession**, by **adverse possession**, or by prescription. It is possible to acquire, by possession,

- the fee simple estate in a property;
- an easement over a property; or
- the right to an encroachment over a property.

This type of interest can be acquired only in the Registry system (discussed in chapter 5, Land Registration Systems).

possession
control or occupancy of land regardless of ownership

adverse possession
valid title to land through open, visible, and uninterrupted possession of that property, without the owner's permission, for a period of at least 10 years

Fee Simple Estate

A person who does not own land can acquire the owner's fee simple estate by treating the land as his or her own over a period of time. If a person exercises exclusive possession over another person's property **adversely** (without the owner's permission), openly, and continuously, the original owner's interest in the land will be **extinguished** after 10 years of uninterrupted use, and the person who has used the land will obtain the fee simple estate.

For example, assume that Ellen maintains a vegetable garden on land that is owned by Brenda. Ellen takes care of the garden for many years. Brenda never tends to the garden and never uses the property. Although Brenda knows about the garden on her land, she does not consent, nor does she do anything to stop it. After 10 years, Ellen will acquire a valid claim to the land by adverse possession, and Brenda will lose the right to regain possession of the land.

The period of possession must be continuous and undisputed. If the true owner of the land regains possession at any time during the 10 years, the time period stops running.

Note that it is not possible to acquire possessory title to land that is registered in the Land Titles system. For a discussion of the Land Titles system, see chapter 5.

adversely
without the owner's permission

extinguish
bring to an end

Easements

It is possible to acquire an easement interest by prescription if the following conditions are met:

- The easement has been used openly and continuously for at least 20 years (there can be different owners during this period).
- The owner of the servient tenement knows that the easement is being used.
- The owner of the servient tenement has not consented to the use of the easement.
- The owner of the servient tenement has not received any payment for the use of the land.

In the case of an easement by prescription, the easement is imposed by law on the owner of the servient tenement. The owner of the servient tenement is entitled to prevent the use of the property, at any time during the 20-year period, and thus prevent the creation of the easement, in which case the time period could start to run again.

Encroachments

encroachment building or structure intruding upon someone else's land

An **encroachment** is any building or structure that intrudes upon someone else's property. A common example is the overhang of a roof or eaves of a building that is situated too close to the property line. Another example is a shed or fence that ends up being partly or wholly built on the land of a neighbour. This second example will give rise to a claim for adverse possession if the structure remains for a period of 10 years. The original owner will no longer be able to demand the removal of the encroaching structure.

FIXTURES

Fixtures are items of personal property that are permanently or constructively attached to real property and become part of the real property. Unless specifically excluded from the sale of the property, fixtures must be left behind by vendors when they move out. The rules for determining whether or not certain items have become attached to the land or to the building are very confusing. Some of the factors are

annexation attachment

- the degree of **annexation** (attachment) to the land;
- the ability to remove the fixture without causing serious damage to it or to the land or building to which it is attached; and
- the use of the fixture.

TITLE TO LAND

In real estate law, **title** is another word for ownership. A person who holds the fee simple estate in a property is said to have title to that property. This person is known as the owner of the property.

title
legal right to the ownership and possession of property; evidence showing such a right

Property can be owned by one person alone, or by two or more people together. When two or more people own property together, they can hold title either as joint tenants or as tenants in common. Do not be confused by the term "tenants." These people are owners and not to be confused with people who pay rent to landlords.

Holding Title as Joint Tenants

When two or more people hold title to property as **joint tenants**, each person has an equal interest in the property and an undivided interest in the entire property (as opposed to an exclusive right to part of the property). All of the joint tenants must receive their interests in the property at the same time, in the same deed. If one joint tenant conveys his or her interest in land, the joint tenancy is severed, and the person who receives the interest will be a tenant in common (see below) with the other owner or owners.

joint tenants
two or more people owning property where on the death of one, the survivors inherit the deceased's share

The key characteristic of a joint tenancy is the **right of survivorship**. When one joint tenant dies, the deceased's interest automatically **vests** in the surviving joint tenant or tenants. In other words, the other joint tenant or tenants receive the deceased's share. Because of the right of survivorship, a person holding title as a joint tenant cannot transfer that share or interest in the property by will. Such a provision, if included in a will, would be inoperative (invalid).

right of survivorship
automatic vesting of an interest in the surviving joint tenant or tenants when one joint tenant dies

vest
to provide an immediate right to present or future ownership or possession

For example, assume that Bob, Brian, and Brenda own a property as joint tenants. Each of them has a one-third interest in the property, which gives each of them rights to the entire property. If Bob dies, his interest automatically vests in Brian and Brenda, as joint tenants, who now each have a one-half interest in the property. If Brian dies, his interest vests in Brenda, who becomes the sole owner of the property.

Holding Title as Tenants in Common

When two or more people hold title as **tenants in common**, there is no right of survivorship and the interests do not have to be equal. For example, one tenant in common can own three-quarters of the property while the other tenant in common owns one-quarter. While the interests of each tenant may not be equal, each tenant still has an undivided interest in the entire property (as opposed to an exclusive right to part of the property). Each tenant in common may transfer the individual interest in the property to a third party or dispose of it by will.

tenants in common
two or more people owning property where on the death of one, the deceased person's share passes to his or her heirs rather than the other owners; no right of survivorship

For example, assume that Bob and Brian own a property as tenants in common. They can each have a 50 percent interest in the property, or Bob may have a 75 percent interest and Brian a 25 percent interest. If Bob dies, his interest in the property becomes part of his estate and passes to his heirs by will or intestacy. If Bob sells his interest to David, Brian and David will own the property as tenants in common.

The Partition Act

When two people own property, one owner may want to sell the property while the other may not. While it is legally possible for a part owner of property to sell only that person's interest in the land, in practice it is difficult to find a buyer who wants to own land as a tenant in common with a stranger. If the owners can't agree whether to sell the property, one owner can seek a court order under the *Partition Act* to force the sale of the entire property.

REFERENCES

Partition Act, RSO 1990, c. P.4.

REVIEW QUESTIONS

1. What does real property include?
2. What is a fixture?
3. What happens when a landowner dies without heirs to inherit his or her land?
4. What is meant by the term "fee simple"?
5. What is a life estate?
6. When does a life estate end?
7. What is a leasehold estate?
8. What is an easement?
9. For an easement to exist, there must be a dominant and a servient tenement. Explain the meaning of these two terms.
10. How is an easement created?
11. What is a restrictive covenant?
12. What are riparian rights?
13. What happens if a person exercises exclusive possession of another person's property without the owner's permission, openly and continuously for over 10 years?
14. Provide an example of an encroachment.
15. In real estate law, what does the term "title" mean?
16. What happens when one joint tenant dies?

DISCUSSION QUESTIONS

1. It is said that "individuals don't own land." Explain.
2. Senior Sam owns real property. He would like his wife to be able to live on the property until she dies but wants his son to inherit it. What should he do?
3. Explain the difference between taking title as joint tenants and as tenants in common.

CHAPTER 4

Legal Descriptions

Documents creating an interest in land describe the property by using a **legal description**, not the property's municipal address. Rather than using the street number and name, the legal description of a property describes the property with reference to recorded maps, surveys, or plans of the land. All land in Ontario has a legal description. Land registry systems record the documents that create an interest in land by using the legal description of the property.

legal description
description of land that is used in documents creating an interest in land; describes the land with reference to recorded maps, surveys, or plans

ORIGINAL DIVISION OF LAND IN ONTARIO

It is helpful to know how land in Ontario was originally divided to better understand legal descriptions and Ontario's land registration system.

In the 18th century, the Crown hired land surveyors to identify and record all the land in the province. The surveyors divided the province first into counties and then into townships. They then created east–west road allowances in each township to provide access to the main roads. The surveyors used a measuring tool called a "gunters chain," which is the equivalent of 66 feet (approximately 20.1 metres). Each road allowance was one chain, and the distance between road allowances was 100 chains, or 6,600 feet (1¼ miles, or approximately 2 kilometres). The creation of the road allowances resulted in the formation of areas of land called **concessions**. By this method, the townships were laid out into a grid pattern as illustrated in figure 4.1. (Note: The illustrations in figures 4.1 to 4.7 are not to scale.)

concession
large parcel of land created during the original division of land in Ontario resulting from the creation of east–west road allowances in a township

FIGURE 4.1 Division of Land into Concessions

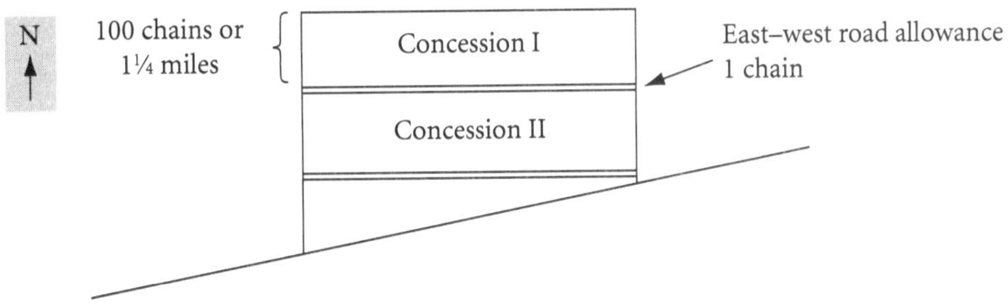

This kind of layout made it possible to identify a parcel of land by referring to its location in a particular county, township, and concession. For example, a property is located in Concession I, in the Township of Nottawasaga, in the County of Simcoe.

Next, the surveyors mapped out north–south road allowances within the concessions. These road allowances were surveyed in a similar manner to the east–west road allowances: the distance between them was 100 chains (1¼ miles), and each road allowance was one chain wide. The intersection of the north–south road allowances with the east–west road allowances created squares of 1,000 acres each — enormous parcels of land. See figure 4.2.

FIGURE 4.2 Division of Concessions by Road Allowances

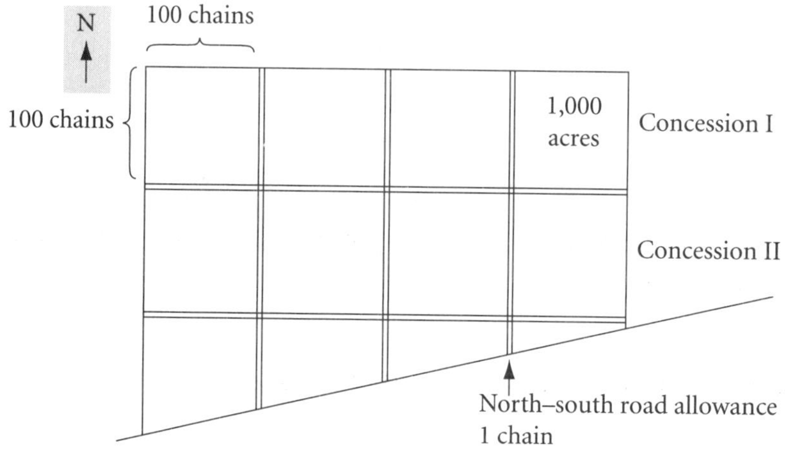

lot
200-acre parcel of land created during the original division of land into concessions; also, a parcel of land created by a plan of subdivision

The 1,000-acre squares were divided into **lots** by surveying additional boundary lines. Each lot was 20 chains × 100 chains, or 200 acres, and was assigned a concession lot number. Most original Crown patents were grants of either the whole or half of one of these concession lots. Figure 4.3 illustrates this further division.

FIGURE 4.3 Division of Concessions into Lots

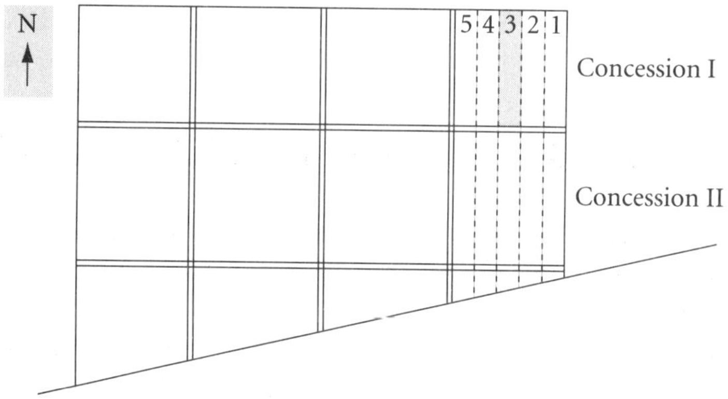

As a result, it became possible to describe a parcel of land even more precisely by referring to the county, township, concession number, *and* lot number. For example, the shaded area in figure 4.3 can now be described as Lot 3, Concession I, Township of Nottawasaga, County of Simcoe.

In time, lots were further divided into even smaller parcels of land. The most common division was to halve them between the east–west road allowances, so that each half would have access to a road. This created a 100-acre parcel of land. Reference to the north or south half of the lot could now be added to the description of land situated within the lot, as illustrated in figure 4.4.

FIGURE 4.4 Division of Concession Lot into Half Lots

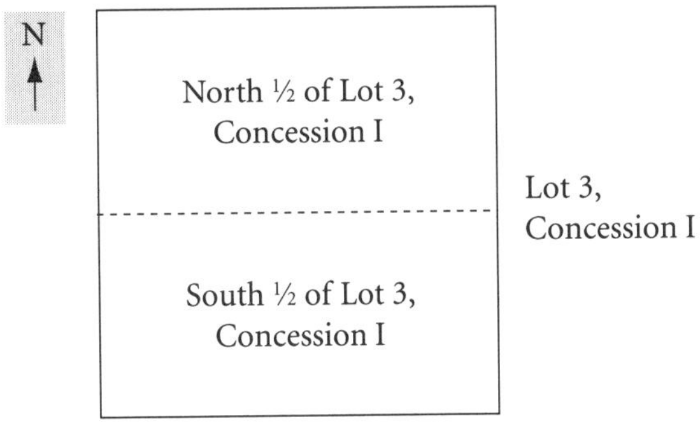

A further division could be made between the west and the east half of each part of the lot, which, again, would further narrow the description of land within that lot, as illustrated in figure 4.5.

FIGURE 4.5 Division of Concession Half Lot into Quarter

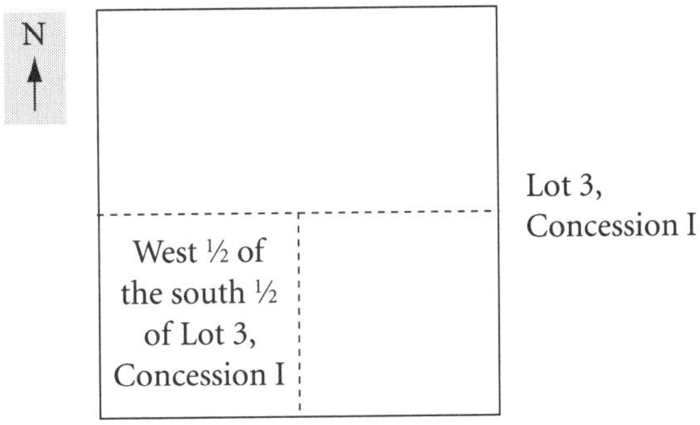

MODIFICATIONS TO THE ORIGINAL SYSTEM

Over time, **municipalities** — villages, towns, and cities — were formed within the townships. Once a municipality was incorporated, the land was described with reference to the municipality rather than the township.

municipality
form of urban organization including cities, towns, and villages

As some areas became more urbanized, large farm properties were divided into smaller lots for housing. Over time, the government instituted controls over the division of land by requiring a **plan of subdivision** whenever a concession lot is divided into smaller lots. Once a plan of subdivision is registered, the land is described with reference to the plan, rather than the concession lot.

plan of subdivision
registered plan illustrating the measurements and boundaries of all lots and streets created by the division of concession lots into many smaller lots

LEGAL DESCRIPTIONS

Legal descriptions have changed over time as Ontario has evolved from primarily a farming culture to an urban and suburban culture. Large parcels of farmland are divided into smaller parcels for housing. Today land in Ontario, depending on its size and location, may be described

- by reference to lot and concession;
- by reference to a registered plan of subdivision; or
- by reference to a reference plan.

By Reference to Lot and Concession

The original division of land into concessions and lots made it possible to describe all land with reference to something permanent. All land could be described by identifying the lot, concession, township, and county within which the land was situated.

It becomes more difficult to describe a parcel of land that is not exactly a whole, half, or quarter of a concession lot, such as the land represented by the shaded area in figure 4.6. You start by describing the part of the concession lot within which the parcel of land is situated — part of the east ½ of the south ½ of Lot 3, Concession I — but a further description is needed to clarify the boundaries of the shaded area.

FIGURE 4.6 Division of Concession Quarter Lots into Smaller Parcels

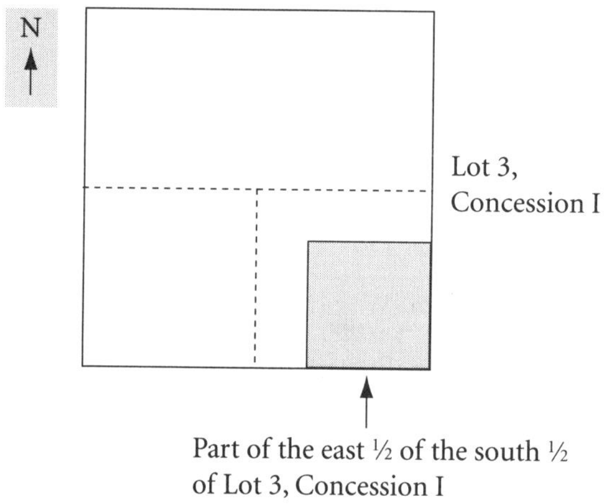

metes and bounds description
written description of the boundaries and dimensions of a parcel of land in relation to lot lines; enables a sketch of the parcel to provide a picture of the area of land

This additional description is called a **metes and bounds description**. It describes, in words, the boundaries and dimensions of a parcel of land in relation to lot lines. By following this written description, it is possible to sketch the outlines of the parcel to provide a picture of the area of land.

The legal description of the shaded area above would read as follows: Part of the east ½ of the south ½ of Lot 3, Concession I, Township of Nottawasaga, County of Simcoe, described as follows:

> Commencing at the southeast corner of Lot 3, Concession I;
>
> Thence north 200 feet along the easterly boundary line to a point;
>
> Thence west 200 feet, parallel to the southerly boundary line to point;
>
> Thence south parallel to the easterly boundary line 200 feet.
>
> Thence east 200 feet, along the southerly boundary line to the point of commencement.

All land in Ontario was originally described by reference to concessions and lots, together with a metes and bounds description, if necessary.

By Reference to a Registered Plan of Subdivision

As stated above, as certain areas became more urbanized, large farm properties were divided into smaller lots. Developers subdivided whole or parts of concession lots into many smaller residential or commercial lots for sale. In order to control the manner in which this development took place, the government of Ontario began to require developers to register a plan of subdivision showing the measurements and boundaries of all lots and streets created. For a discussion of the role of plans of subdivision in controlling the development of land, see chapter 8, Government Controls over the Use and Subdivision of Land. When a plan of subdivision is registered, it is assigned a number. Each lot on the plan is assigned a number as well.

The registration of the plan affects the legal description of the property. Suppose a developer purchases the parcel of land in figure 4.6 for the purpose of creating a subdivision. Before the plan of subdivision is registered, the property is described as part of the east ½ of the south ½ of Lot 3, Concession I, followed by the metes and bounds description. After the plan of subdivision is registered and assigned a number, the property is described by referring to the plan number. The entire parcel is now described as Plan 1234, and each separate lot within the plan of subdivision is described by its lot number. In figure 4.7, the shaded part of Plan 1234 is described as Lot 5, Plan 1234, Township of Nottawasaga, County of Simcoe.

FIGURE 4.7 Division of Part of a Concession Lot into Lots on a Plan of Subdivision

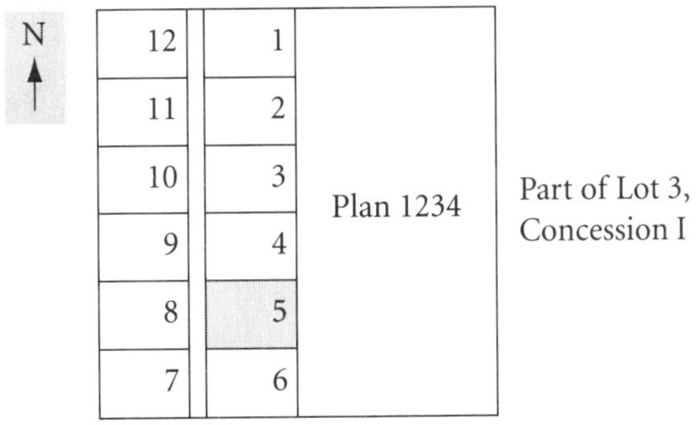

By Reference to a Reference Plan

A reference plan is prepared by a surveyor to illustrate in pictorial form boundaries of land that were previously described in words using a metes and bounds description. The three reasons for creating and registering a reference plan are

1. to replace a complicated metes and bounds description;
2. to illustrate the severance of a lot; and
3. to illustrate a parcel of land where an easement has been granted (often to municipalities).

REPLACING A METES AND BOUNDS DESCRIPTION

A reference plan may be required to replace a metes and bounds description that is so complex that there is a likelihood of error. In that case, a survey is prepared to clearly illustrate and mark the boundaries of the land in question. That survey is then registered as a **reference plan**. The reference plan is given a plan number preceded by the letter "R," which stands for "Reference Plan." Reference plans are often referred to as "R plans."

reference plan
registered survey prepared to illustrate the boundaries of a parcel of land

Once a reference plan is registered, the land can be described by simply identifying its part or parts on the reference plan. The complex metes and bounds description is no longer required.

SEVERING A LOT

A reference plan may be required when an owner severs and sells part of a parcel of land (without using a plan of subdivision). Severances often create irregular and complicated boundaries of land. The reference plan clearly illustrates that part of the land which is being severed, without the necessity of creating a new, complicated metes and bounds description.

CREATING AN EASEMENT

A reference plan may be required when an easement is created over property. The location of the easement on the original parcel of land can be easily depicted on a reference plan, and the land, together with the easement, can be more easily described by referring to the parts identified on the reference plan than by using a metes and bounds description.

Figure 4.8 reproduces Reference Plan 65R-3541, which is a reference plan of lots 88, 89, and 90 on subdivision Plan 65M-1879 (reproduced in figure 4.9). The plan was prepared to illustrate the severance of each of these lots as well as the creation of two easements affecting lots 89 and 90.

As the plan illustrates, each of the lots was severed into two parcels, each identified by a part number. Take a look at Lot 89. The northerly parcel comprises parts 3 and 4, and the southerly parcel comprises parts 5 and 6 on the reference plan. The plan also illustrates an easement affecting lots 89 and 90, in the form of a mutual driveway shared by the two parcels.

FIGURE 4.8 Reference Plan

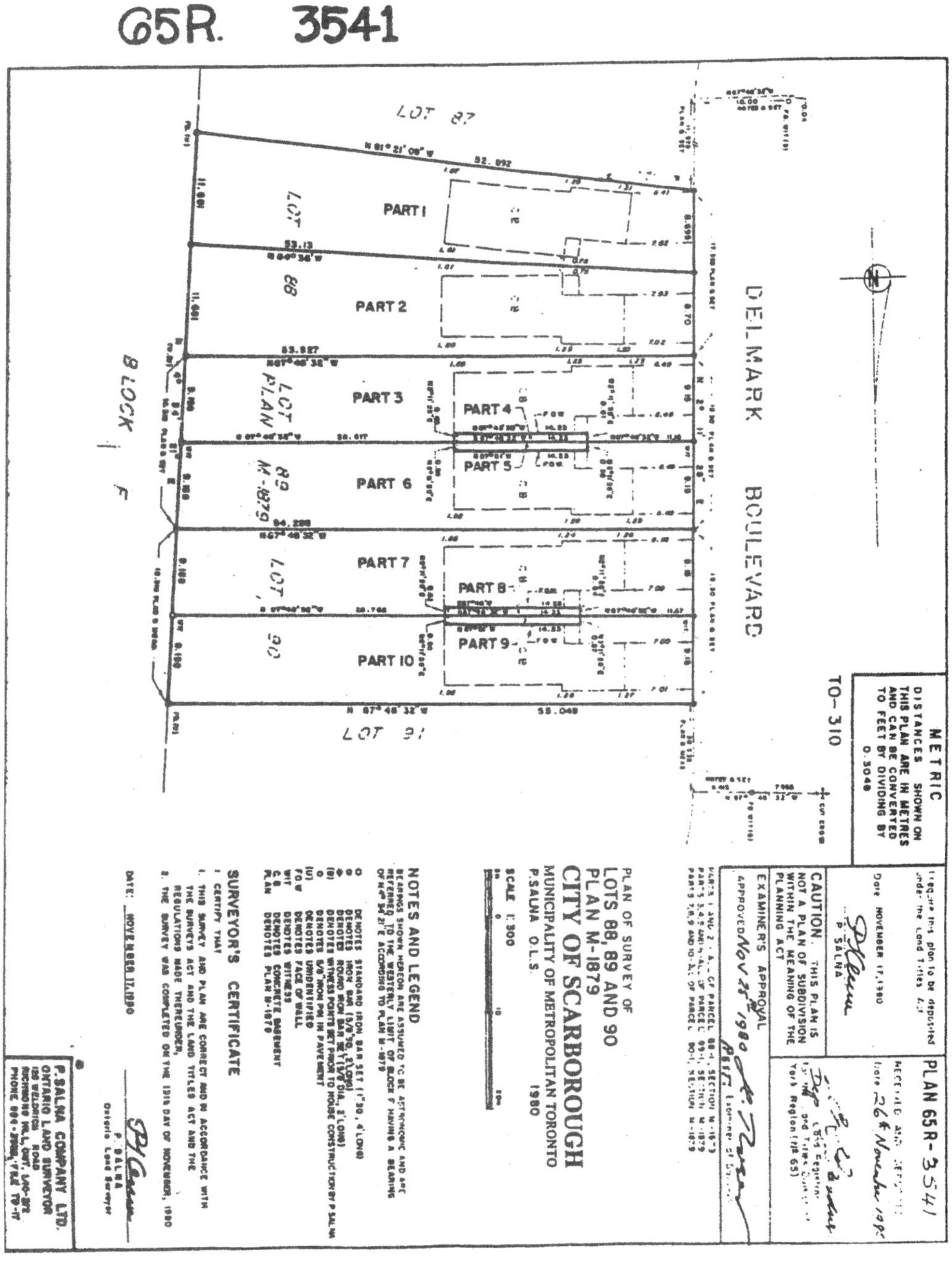

The legal description of the north half of Lot 89 reads as follows:

In the City of Scarborough, in the Municipality of Metropolitan Toronto and being composed of part of lot 89, Plan 65M-1879, designated as Parts 3 and 4 on Reference Plan 65R-3541 SUBJECT TO an easement over Part 4 on said plan in favour of the owner of Parts 5 and 6 of said plan and TOGETHER WITH an easement over Part 5 of the said plan.

It is much easier to describe the exact location and boundaries of the parcels and the easement by a "picture," as opposed to trying to describe them in words.

FIGURE 4.9 Plan of Subdivision

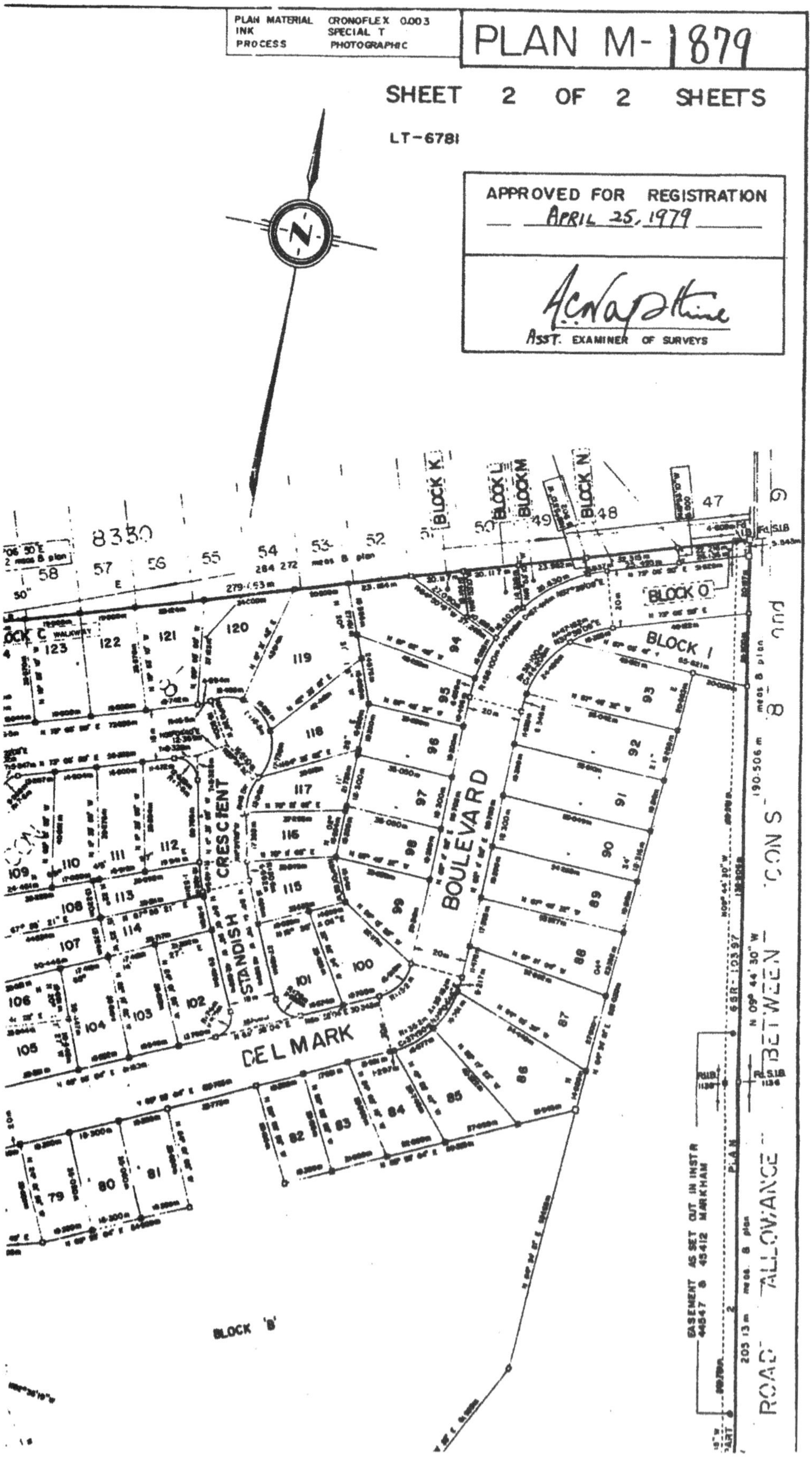

REVIEW QUESTIONS

1. How was land in Ontario originally divided?
2. What is a metes and bounds description?
3. What does a plan of subdivision illustrate?
4. When a plan of subdivision is registered, how is the property legally described?
5. When is a reference plan required?

CHAPTER 5

Land Registration Systems

Land registry systems record the consecutive ownership of land and other interests in land. Land registry systems evolved over time, and registration of interests in land is now mandatory. If an interest in land is not registered, a person who does not have actual notice of the unregistered interest may acquire an interest in the land in priority to the unregistered interest.

AN OVERVIEW

A land registration system provides an orderly and detailed system of recording all interests affecting land. Documents that create or dispose of an interest in land or otherwise affect the use of land are filed and assigned a registration number. Information about the registered document and the interest it has created is summarized into books and records to which the public has easy access.

The purpose of a land registration system is to provide protection regarding subsequent transactions with respect to the same land. It does so by

- establishing priority between competing claims against land; and
- providing public notice of interests in land.

Registration of a document merely provides notice of the existence of the document. It does not make the document legally effective.

Priority Between Competing Claims

Priority of claims is based on the date of registration of the document, not the date on which the document was signed. If two people claim to have an interest in the same land, the interest with the earlier registration date will prevail, regardless of the date on which the transaction was completed.

For example, assume that John Smith needs a loan. On Thursday morning he gets a loan from his bank and provides a signed charge/mortgage on his property in favour of the bank. The bank doesn't register the mortgage until Friday morning. In the meantime, on Thursday afternoon, John gets another loan from his Uncle Sam and also provides a signed mortgage on his property in favour of his uncle. His uncle registers his mortgage that same day. Uncle Sam's mortgage will have priority over the bank's even though it was signed *after* the bank's mortgage.

Public Notice of Interests in Land

Registration also offers protection regarding subsequent dealings with the same land by providing notice to the public of existing interests in land. Any person who deals with land is **deemed** to have notice of interests that are already registered against the land and takes the land subject to those interests. This is true even if the person has no personal or actual knowledge of the earlier interest in the land.

deemed
accepted as conclusive of a certain state or condition in the absence of evidence or facts usually required to prove that state or condition

An interest in land that is not registered does not get the same protection. An unregistered claim against land may be defeated by a subsequent registered interest in the same land if the person registering the subsequent interest had no actual notice of the prior claim.

For example, assume that Mr. Singh agrees to sell to Mr. Jones a parcel of land in five years in exchange for five yearly payments in the amount of $50,000 each. Mr. Jones does not register a notice of this agreement on title to the land. Three years later, Mr. Singh dies and his executor, not knowing of the agreement, transfers the land to Mr. and Mrs. Greenwald, who also have no knowledge of the agreement. Mr. and Mrs. Greenwald search the title records prior to the sale. According to the title records, Mr. Singh had title free and clear of any other claims. Once Mr. and Mrs. Greenwald register their deed, Mr. Jones's claim on the land will be extinguished, unless Mr. and Mrs. Greenwald *actually* knew of the existence of Mr. Jones's prior agreement (had actual notice of his interest). In the absence of actual notice to Mr. and Mrs. Greenwald, Mr. Jones's unregistered interest will be void as against Mr. and Mrs. Greenwald's interest in the property.

There are two systems of land registration in Ontario: the Registry system and the Land Titles system. All land in Ontario has been assigned to one of these two systems.

THE REGISTRY SYSTEM

Registry system
land registration system in Ontario governed by the *Registry Act*

The **Registry system** was the first land registration system in Ontario. It was established in 1795 and today is governed by the *Registry Act*. There is at least one land registry office per county and one office each for the cities of Toronto, Ottawa, and London. Until recently, these systems were entirely paper-based. All documents were filed for registration in the appropriate registry office, and all registered documents were recorded in an index book called an abstract book. On registration, a document was assigned a registration number, which was noted on the document along with the date of registration and the registrar's certificate as evidence of the registration.

Abstract Books

abstract book
book in the Registry system that records registered interests in land

Abstract books were organized by township. When land was first transferred by Crown patent, the land registrar in the geographic area where the land was situated opened a new page in the abstract book for each concession lot that had been patented. All registrations relating to that piece of land, starting with the Crown patent, are recorded on the appropriate page in the abstract book in order of registration, together with a brief summary of the document. The actual documents are filed in the office and are available for the public to examine (originally in paper form and later in paper form or on microfilm). For example, there will be an abstract book for the Township of Cavan, Concession III. Inside the abstract book there are separate pages for each of lots 1, 2, 3, and so on. If the concession is later subdivided by a registered plan of subdivision, then the registrar will create a new abstract book for the plan of subdivision, with a separate page for each lot within the plan.

If a lot has been severed into two or more parcels, information relating to all the different parts of the lot will continue to be entered on the same page for that lot. For example, assume that Lot 7, Plan 1234 has been severed into a west half and an east half. There will be an abstract book for Plan 1234 that contains a page for Lot 7. That page will contain entries for registered documents that deal with either half of the lot. People searching the title to Lot 7 will have to sort through the various entries and determine which entries are relevant to the half of the lot they are interested in.

Legal Descriptions

A document that is to be registered in the registry system must contain a legal description of the property. The legal description will refer first to the lot number and then to the number of the concession or plan of subdivision in which the lot is located. An example for a plan of subdivision would be Lot 5, Plan 1234, Township of Nottawasaga, County of Simcoe.

Effect of Registration

Section 74 of the *Registry Act* provides that registration of a document constitutes notice of the document to all persons claiming an interest in the land subsequent to registration. Registration, however, does *not* guarantee that a document is valid or legally effective. Under the Registry system, an individual acquiring an interest in land must both review the abstract book *and* examine all documents noted on title, to ensure that all the documents have the legal effect they purport to have.

Types of Documents

Many different kinds of documents have been registered over the years under the Registry system. These include

- documents that transfer ownership of land — called, at different times, **grants**, **deeds**, or **transfers**;
- documents that create a mortgage against land — called, at different times, mortgages or charges;
- documents related to mortgages — discharges of mortgage (or discharges of charge), agreements amending mortgage (or charge), and assignments of mortgage (or charge);
- **powers of attorney** — documents that authorize someone to deal with land on the owner's behalf;
- **bylaws** — laws passed by a municipality that affect land;

grant
document that transfers ownership of land

deed
document that transfers ownership of land

transfer
document that transfers ownership of land

power of attorney
document authorizing someone to deal with land or other property on the owner's behalf

bylaw (municipal)
law that is passed by a municipality

subdivision agreement agreement between a municipality and a builder setting out the terms under which the builder is allowed to subdivide the land

will document stating how a person's property will be dealt with upon death

deposit document registered on title that verifies or clarifies facts related to the title

- **subdivision agreements** — agreements between a municipality and a builder setting out the terms under which the builder is allowed to subdivide the land;
- documents dealing with the estates of owners — **wills** and certificates proving payment of inheritance taxes; and
- **deposits** — documents that verify or clarify facts related to the title to the property.

These documents will be discussed in more detail in chapter 13, Title Searching, and chapter 20, The Requisition Letter.

THE LAND TITLES SYSTEM

Land Titles system land registration system in Ontario governed by the *Land Titles Act*

The **Land Titles system** is the other system of land registration in Ontario. It was established in 1885 and is governed by the *Land Titles Act*. Unlike the Registry system, which simply provides a record of documents affecting title, this system provides a statement of title as a fact; the government guarantees the accuracy of title to land registered in the Land Titles system. The parcel register always reflects the current state of title. There are, however, a number of exceptions to the government's certification of title. For example, land in the Land Titles system is subject to

- provincial taxes, succession duties, and municipal taxes;
- rights of the Crown by authority of any statute; and
- *Planning Act* considerations.

The land registrar assumes responsibility for stating whether or not the title of the current registered owner is valid. If there is an error regarding title, a person wrongfully deprived of some estate or interest in land can request compensation from the **Land Titles Assurance Fund**, a fund established under the *Land Titles Act*.

Land Titles Assurance Fund fund established under the *Land Titles Act* to compensate a person wrongfully deprived of an estate or interest in land as a result of an error regarding title

parcel register book in the Land Titles system that records all registered interests in land

Parcel Register

In the Land Titles system, registrations are recorded in a book called the **parcel register**. Parcel registers are organized differently than abstract books under the Registry system. Each separately owned parcel of land is assigned its own page, whether it is a whole lot or a part of a lot, and all entries on that page relate only to that parcel of land. As each new registration is certified by the land registrar, the registrar either cancels earlier registrations by ruling them off or modifies them.

Documents in Land Titles are stored in a computer index and are available for public viewing on microfilm.

Legal Descriptions

A document that is to be registered in the Land Titles system must contain a legal description of the property. The legal description will refer to the parcel number and then the section number, in addition to the lot and plan number. If the parcel is a whole of a lot, the parcel number will be followed by "–1." If the parcel is a part of a lot, the parcel number will be followed by "–2," "–3," and so on. Plan of subdivision numbers start with the number of the Land Titles office in which the plan is registered, followed by the letter "M" for Master of Land Titles. Two examples are

- Parcel 4–1, Section 66M3456, being lot 4, Plan 66M3456, City of Toronto; and
- Parcel 2–3 Section 66M3456 (part of lot 2, Plan 66M3456), City of Toronto.

In both of the above examples, 66 is the number of the Toronto Land Titles Office. The first example is the description of a whole of a lot, and is indicated by the "–1" in the parcel number. The second example is the description of a part of a lot, as indicated by "–3" in the parcel number.

POLARIS

The province is nearing completion of a major revision to the way in which land is registered in Ontario. A project called **POLARIS** (Province of Ontario Land Registration Information System) began in 1975 with the overall objective of simplifying registration of documents and title searching.

POLARIS
Province of Ontario Land Registration Information System; computerized land information system

The *Land Registration Reform Act*, which was originally enacted in 1984 and came into effect on April 1, 1985, authorized the implementation of the POLARIS initiatives, which include

1. computerizing title records for each property in Ontario;
2. developing a property mapping system;
3. standardizing forms and procedures;
4. converting Registry system properties to the Land Titles system;
5. converting all paper documents to microfilm;
6. providing for electronic title searching and writ searching;
7. providing for the electronic registration of documents; and
8. integrating all land-related information and databases into one centralized, online land information system.

When the POLARIS initiatives are fully implemented, all land in Ontario will be registered under the Land Titles system, and the Registry system will no longer be used. All land records will be computerized in one centralized system, and all searches and registrations will be done online. The government intended to convert Registry system properties into the Land Titles system once they were mapped and automated. However, there are many properties that have been automated but have not yet been converted to the Land Titles system.

Even though the process is still under way, POLARIS has caused significant changes to the practices and procedures related to document preparation, registration, and title searching. As a result, before dealing with any property, it is necessary to ascertain the extent, if any, to which the property has been affected by POLARIS.

We will be looking at the following key aspects of POLARIS:

- computerization of land records;
- documents used under POLARIS;
- property mapping under POLARIS; and
- electronic land registration.

Computerization of Land Records

POLARIS consists of three databases:

1. Title Index database — This database replaces the paper abstract book (in the Registry system) and the parcel register (in the Land Titles system) with computer-generated title indexes.
2. Property Index database — This database provides a visual index map to all properties, and illustrates the property's position in relationship to adjoining properties. Each property is assigned a property identifier number (PIN). The PIN links the information in this database to the information in the Title Index database.
3. Central Image Storage database — This database contains images of all documents that have been registered, and allows online access to all registered documents.

POLARIS Documents

Prior to 1985, documents used to convey an interest in land were often extremely lengthy. Also, different documents were used, depending on whether the property was registered in the Land Titles or Registry system. POLARIS created five new forms to be used in both systems. These forms were standardized, shortened, and designed to accommodate any registered interest in land. The five forms are

- Form 1, Transfer/Deed of Land, used to register an ownership interest in the land (reproduced in figure 5.1);
- Form 2, Charge/Mortgage of Land, used to register a charge (mortgage) interest in the land (reproduced in figure 5.2);
- Form 3, Discharge of Charge/Mortgage, used to register a discharge of a charge interest in the land (reproduced in figure 5.3);
- Form 4, Document General, used to register any other type of instrument or interest that affects the use of the land (reproduced in figure 5.4); and
- Form 5, Schedule, used to register additional information that won't fit on any of the other forms (reproduced in figure 5.5).

These forms eliminated the requirement for personal and corporate seals, and the need for lengthy affidavits that previously accompanied documents affecting land. The truth of statements set out in each form is acknowledged when the form is signed.

Property Mapping Under POLARIS

Under POLARIS all properties in Ontario are being mapped. Property mapping allows for

- the determination of the number of properties in a given area;
- the creation of a unique identifying number for each property that will provide access to title records; and
- the visual identification of properties, their location, and the location of adjoining properties.

The province is first being divided into **blocks** identified by a five-digit **block number**. Block index maps illustrate the location of numbered blocks within a municipality. Blocks are then being further divided into **properties**, each identified by a unique four-digit **property number**. The combination of the block number and the property number creates a unique nine-digit **property identifier number (PIN)** for every property.

block
area of land created during the remapping of property under POLARIS

block number
five-digit number assigned to a block; the first part of the PIN

property
term used to describe area of land created by the division of blocks during the remapping of land under POLARIS

property number
four-digit number assigned to a property; the second part of the PIN

property identifier number (PIN)
unique nine-digit number for each property created by combining the block and property number for that property

e-reg
electronic registration

When a property is entered into POLARIS, the page in the abstract book or parcel register is stamped with a notation indicating the date of automation. Registrations that take place after that date are recorded on the computerized abstract only and can be accessed using the PIN.

Once a property is entered into POLARIS, title information is indexed according to the PIN and not according to the legal description of land. The legal description of the land remains unchanged, but title-related information can be accessed only by using the PIN and not the legal description.

Electronic Land Registration

After automating land registration records and converting Registry system properties to the Land Titles system, the final stage of POLARIS is electronic registration (or **e-reg**). It is intended to be a fully electronic and paperless registration system for properties in Land Titles.

Electronic registration is provided for in part III of the *Land Registration Reform Act*. Section 21 of the Act provides that an electronic document that creates, transfers, or otherwise disposes of an estate in land need not be in writing or signed. Electronic registration enables documents to be created, signed, exchanged between law offices, maintained, and registered, all in an electronic format. Documents are no longer registered by personally attending at the land registry office. They are registered electronically from a personal computer in a lawyer's office or from kiosks at the land registry office.

In addition, e-reg software allows lawyers and the public to conduct database searches and to view and print title indexes.

USING ELECTRONIC REGISTRATION THROUGH TERAVIEW

Teraview
software used to access the electronic land registration system in Ontario

The Ontario government licensed Teranet Inc. to create the electronic registration system for the government of Ontario. In order to use the electronic registration system, a lawyer must be a registered client of Teranet Inc. and purchase the **Teraview** software. Each registered user is given an individual diskette that allows that person to access the system. The diskette contains the user's electronic signature, which

- confirms to the system that the user is a lawyer;
- charges usage fees to the lawyer's specific account; and
- tracks the activities of the user.

In addition, the user is provided with a registered account name and a user name, to which the user assigns an individual pass-phrase. The use of these three items in combination at the time of signing onto the system ensures that no one other than the user will be charged for system usage. These security measures also prevent unauthorized access to the documents that the user is creating.

The user can authorize others to have access to the system to look at documents, to change and/or create documents, and to register documents. Certain functions, such as making **compliance with law statements** (statements in which a lawyer states that all necessary requirements have been met), can be performed only by qualified lawyers.

compliance with law statements
statements in which a lawyer confirms that all necessary legal requirements have been met

EXEMPTIONS FROM ELECTRONIC REGISTRATION

Documents that cannot be registered electronically must be submitted in paper form at the land registry office. Examples of such documents are plans, Crown grants, first applications under the *Land Titles Act*, and declarations and descriptions under the *Condominium Act, 1998*.

DOCUMENTS FOR ELECTRONIC REGISTRATION

The format of electronically registered documents is different from the paper forms under the *Land Registration Reform Act*. Special templates containing substantially the same information as POLARIS forms have been created for e-reg use.

The documents are prepared using the Teraview software, which provides an onscreen menu from which the user selects the form required. Once the user enters the PIN number of the property into the form, the system automatically loads the name of the present owner, the municipal address, and the legal description into the new document. If the user needs to include statements in the document, such as statements under the *Planning Act* or *Family Law Act*, the user selects them from a drop-down list of all possible statements. This process of carrying forward information and entering it into the document is called **pre-population**. It avoids the need for entering basic information already contained in the register. The system prompts the user to enter the names of new owners and any other new title information. The program will automatically warn the user if the user has left something out of a draft registration, such as a required statement. The system will allow for the registration of a document only after all mandatory information has been submitted.

pre-population
electronic process of copying information from a database into a document

Since e-reg documents are electronic, there is no paper document for a lawyer or client to sign. As a result, the system uses **digital signatures**. Participating lawyers are assigned a unique digital identifier comparable to a password or PIN, which serves as signature.

digital signature
unique digital identifiers comparable to a password or bank PIN used by lawyers when documents are registered electronically

IMPLEMENTING ELECTRONIC REGISTRATION IN ONTARIO

Electronic land registration was first introduced in 1999 as a pilot project. It was so successful that electronic registration of property in Land Titles is being implemented county by county across Ontario. As of June 2008, electronic registration is available in all of the province's 51 land registry offices, and is mandatory in 38 of them. As of April 2008, 92 percent of registrations are received electronically.

REFERENCES

Condominium Act, 1998, SO 1998, c. 19.

Family Law Act, RSO 1990, c. F.3.

Land Registration Reform Act, RSO 1990, c. L.4.

Land Titles Act, RSO 1990, c. L.5.

Planning Act, RSO 1990, c. P.13.

Registry Act, RSO 1990, c. R.20.

REVIEW QUESTIONS

1. What are two important features of a land registration system?
2. What is the most significant difference between the Registry system and the Land Titles system?
3. What information is recorded in the abstract book and the parcel register?
4. What is the effect of registration of a document?
5. How is priority determined between two competing interests in land?
6. List three initiatives of the POLARIS project.
7. What information do you require to access the computerized land records?
8. What is e-reg?
9. How are documents submitted if they are going to be registered electronically?
10. What is a digital signature?

FIGURE 5.1 Transfer/Deed of Land

Province of Ontario

Transfer/Deed of Land

Form 1 — Land Registration Reform Act

DYE & DURHAM CO. INC.—Form No. 970
Amended NOV. 1992

A

FOR OFFICE USE ONLY

New Property Identifiers — Additional: See Schedule ☐

Executions — Additional: See Schedule ☐

(1) Registry ☐ **Land Titles** ☐

(2) Page 1 of pages

(3) Property Identifier(s) Block Property — Additional: See Schedule ☐

(4) Consideration

Dollars $

(5) Description This is a: Property Division ☐ Property Consolidation ☐

(6) This Document Contains (a) Redescription New Easement Plan/Sketch ☐ (b) Schedule for: Description ☐ Additional Parties ☐ Other ☐

(7) Interest/Estate Transferred Fee Simple

(8) Transferor(s) The transferor hereby transfers the land to the transferee and certifies that the transferor is at least eighteen years old and that

Name(s)	Signature(s)	Date of Signature Y	M	D

(9) Spouse(s) of Transferor(s) I hereby consent to this transaction

Name(s)	Signature(s)	Date of Signature Y	M	D

(10) Transferor(s) Address for Service

(11) Transferee(s)

	Date of Birth Y	M	D

(12) Transferee(s) Address for Service

Planning Act — OPTIONAL

(13) Transferor(s) The transferor verifies that to the best of the transferor's knowledge and belief, this transfer does not contravene section 50 of the Planning Act.

Signature .... Date of Signature Y M D — Signature .... Date of Signature Y M D

Solicitor for Transferor(s) I have explained the effect of section 50 of the Planning Act to the transferor and I have made inquiries of the transferor to determine that this transfer does not contravene that section and based on the information supplied by the transferor, to the best of my knowledge and belief, this transfer does not contravene that section. I am an Ontario solicitor in good standing.

Name and Address of Solicitor — Signature .... Date of Signature Y M D

Affix Statement by Solicitor for Transferee(s) here if necessary

(14) Solicitor for Transferee(s) I have investigated the title to this land and to abutting land where relevant and I am satisfied that the title records reveal no contravention as set out in subclause 50 (22) (c) (ii) of the Planning Act and that to the best of my knowledge and belief this transfer does not contravene section 50 of the Planning Act. I act independently of the solicitor for the transferor(s) and I am an Ontario solicitor in good standing.

Name and Address of Solicitor — Signature .... Date of Signature Y M D

(15) Assessment Roll Number of Property	Cty.	Mun.	Map	Sub.	Par.

(16) Municipal Address of Property

(17) Document Prepared by:

FOR OFFICE USE ONLY

Fees and Tax	
Registration Fee	
Land Transfer Tax	
Total	

FIGURE 5.2 Charge/Mortgage of Land

Province of Ontario

Charge/Mortgage of Land

Form 2 — Land Registration Reform Act

DYE & DURHAM CFS POLARIS 1995

B

FOR OFFICE USE ONLY

New Property Identifiers — Additional: See Schedule ☐

Executions — Additional: See Schedule ☐

(1) Registry ☐ Land Titles ☐

(2) Page 1 of pages

(3) Property Identifier(s) Block Property — Additional: See Schedule ☐

(4) Principal Amount — Dollars $

(5) Description

(6) This Document Contains (a) Redescription New Easement Plan/Sketch ☐ (b) Schedule for: Description ☐ Additional Parties ☐ Other ☐

(7) Interest/Estate Charged

(8) Standard Charge Terms — The parties agree to be bound by the provisions in Standard Charge Terms filed as number and the Chargor(s) hereby acknowledge(s) receipt of a copy of these terms.

(9) Payment Provisions

(a) Principal Amount $	(b) Interest Rate % per annum	(c) Calculation Period	
(d) Interest Adjustment Date Y M D	(e) Payment Date and Period	(f) First Payment Date Y M D	
(g) Last Payment Date	(h) Amount of Each Payment Dollars $		
(i) Balance Due Date	(j) Insurance Dollars $		

(10) Additional Provisions

Continued on Schedule ☐

(11) Chargor(s) The chargor hereby charges the land to the chargee and certifies that the chargor is at least eighteen years old and that

The chargor(s) acknowledge(s) receipt of a true copy of this charge.

Name(s) Signature(s) Date of Signature Y M D

(12) Spouse(s) of Chargor(s) I hereby consent to this transaction.

Name(s) Signature(s) Date of Signature Y M D

(13) Chargor(s) Address for Service

(14) Chargee(s)

(15) Chargee(s) Address for Service

(16) Assessment Roll Number of Property Cty. Mun. Map Sub. Par.

(17) Municipal Address of Property

(18) Document Prepared by:

FOR OFFICE USE ONLY

Fees	
Registration Fee	
Total	

FIGURE 5.3 Discharge of Charge/Mortgage

Province of Ontario

DYE & DURHAM CO. INC.—Form No. 980
Amended NOV. 1992

Discharge of Charge/Mortgage

Form 3 — Land Registration Reform Act

C

FOR OFFICE USE ONLY

New Property Identifiers

Additional: See Schedule ☐

(1) Registry ☐ Land Titles ☐

(2) Page 1 of pages

(3) Property Identifier(s) Block Property

Additional: See Schedule ☐

(4) Description

(5) Charge to be Discharged

Registration Number

Date of Registration Y M D

(6) This is a

Complete Discharge ☐ Partial Discharge ☐ Final Partial Discharge ☐

(7) Description (cont'd.), Recitals, Assignments

Continued on Schedule ☐

(8) Chargee(s) I am the person entitled by law to grant the discharge and this charge is hereby discharged as to the land described herein.

Name(s)	Signature(s)	Date of Signature Y	M	D

Additional: See Schedule ☐

(9) Chargee(s) Address for Service

(10) Document Prepared by:

FOR OFFICE USE ONLY

Fees	
Registration Fee	
Total	

FIGURE 5.4 Document General

DYE & DURHAM CO. INC.—Form No. 985
Amended NOV. 1992

Province of Ontario

Document General

Form 4 — Land Registration Reform Act

D

FOR OFFICE USE ONLY

New Property Identifiers — Additional: See Schedule ☐

Executions — Additional: See Schedule ☐

(1) Registry ☐ Land Titles ☐

(2) Page 1 of pages

(3) Property Identifier(s) Block Property — Additional: See Schedule ☐

(4) Nature of Document

(5) Consideration — Dollars $

(6) Description

(7) This Document Contains: (a) Redescription New Easement Plan/Sketch ☐ (b) Schedule for: Description ☐ Additional Parties ☐ Other ☐

(8) This Document provides as follows:

Continued on Schedule ☐

(9) This Document relates to instrument number(s)

(10) Party(ies) (Set out Status or Interest)

Name(s)	Signature(s)	Date of Signature Y	M	D

(11) Address for Service

(12) Party(ies) (Set out Status or Interest)

Name(s)	Signature(s)	Date of Signature Y	M	D

(13) Address for Service

(14) Municipal Address of Property

(15) Document Prepared by:

FOR OFFICE USE ONLY

Fees and Tax	
Registration Fee	
Total	

FIGURE 5.5 Schedule

Province of Ontario

DYE & DURHAM CO. INC.—Form No. 990
Amended NOV. 1992

Schedule

Form 5 — Land Registration Reform Act

S

Page__________

Additional Property Identifier(s) and / or Other Information

FOR OFFICE USE ONLY

CHAPTER 6

Charges/Mortgages

Most people need to borrow money to finance the purchase of real property. When people use the real property as security for the loan, a mortgage or charge is created. Today, the terms "mortgage" and "charge" mean the same thing and are used interchangeably. Historically, however, the terms had different meanings.

"Mortgage" is a much older term and dates back to the 12th or 13th century. In Ontario, until the late 20th century, the term was used to mean a loan secured against land registered in the Registry system. A mortgage actually transferred the legal estate in land to the lender (called the **mortgagee**). The landowner/borrower (called the **mortgagor**) was entitled to remain in possession and have title restored when the debt was paid in full. The term "charge" was used to describe a loan secured against land registered in the Land Titles system. A charge did not transfer the legal estate to the lender (called the **chargee**), but, instead, created only an encumbrance on the legal estate of the landowner/borrower (called the **chargor**).

mortgagee
lender

mortgagor
borrower and owner

chargee
lender

chargor
borrower and owner

The *Land Registration Reform Act* eliminated the distinction between the two systems and created a charge/mortgage of land form to be used in both. The charge/mortgage of land has the same legal effect as a charge under the Land Titles system. When a charge/mortgage of land is registered, it conveys an interest (but not an ownership interest) in the land secured by the charge to the lender (chargee). The document also contains details of the loan, including all the provisions for its repayment. If the chargor doesn't pay or breaches other terms of the charge, the chargee can sell the property and use the proceeds to pay off the money owing.

THE PARTIES TO A CHARGE/MORTGAGE

The terminology can be confusing to anyone who is not familiar with this area of law. The chargor/mortgagor is the landowner who is borrowing the money, also referred to as the debtor. The chargee/mortgagee is the financial institution, company, or individual who lends the money, also referred to as the creditor. The chargor/mortgagor gives the charge/mortgage (the security interest in the land) to the chargee/mortgagee.

For example, assume that Alice borrows $100,000 from Best Bank and gives a charge on her property as security for the loan. Alice is the chargor, and Best Bank is the chargee. A search of title to Alice's property will show Alice as the owner and Best Bank as the holder of a charge interest in the amount of $100,000. Both Alice and Best Bank will have a registered interest in the property.

Most borrowers, lenders, and many lawyers still use the term "mortgage" and related terms in describing these transactions. However, the correct legal terms are charge, chargor, and chargee, and these are the terms that will be used in this chapter.

PRIORITIES BETWEEN CHARGES

It is possible for the owner of real property to grant successive charges to different lenders. If there are multiple charges registered against title, the order of registration determines the order of **priority** between the charges.

priority
rank or status of a registered interest in land as determined by the date of registration of that interest

For example, Steven arranges a new charge for $100,000 with Best Bank to help pay for his $300,000 house. Six months later, Steven arranges to borrow $50,000 from Generous Bank to help pay for renovations to the house. Steven can give another charge to Generous Bank as security for the loan. The charge in favour of Best Bank is called a **first charge**, and the charge in favour of Generous Bank is called a **second charge**. Best Bank's charge is said to have priority over Generous Bank's charge. Steven will have to make the loan payments on both charges in accordance with the payment schedules in the loan agreements. The priority of registration does not mean that Best Bank gets its loan paid off before payments begin to Generous Bank. However, if Steven ever defaults on the loan, the priority of registration determines the rights to **realize on the security** by selling the land. The proceeds of any sale will be used to pay Best Bank's charge first. Any money that is left over will be used to pay Generous Bank.

first charge
charge registered first and thus taking priority over subsequently registered charges

second charge
charge registered after the first charge and thus having subsequent priority to the first

realize on the security
seize and/or sell the charged property

TYPES OF CHARGES

There are a number of ways that a charge can arise in the purchase and sale of real property:

- The purchaser can arrange a **new charge** with a bank or other lender and use the borrowed money to pay for the property. If there is already a charge registered against the title to the property, the purchaser will agree with the vendor, in the agreement of purchase and sale, that the existing charge will be discharged prior to closing.
- The purchaser can agree to assume (take over) the existing charge and pay the vendor the purchase price less the amount of the charge (called an **assumed charge**).
- The purchaser can agree to borrow money for the purchase price from the vendor and give back to the vendor a charge on the property as security for the loan (called a **vendor take back charge** or **charge taken back**).

new charge
arrangement by the purchaser for a new loan by way of charge for the purchase of property

assumed charge
existing charge taken over by the purchaser, who pays the vendor the purchase price of the property minus the outstanding balance of the charge

vendor take back charge
charge created when the vendor of a property agrees to lend the purchaser money toward the purchase price and the purchaser gives the vendor a charge on the property as security for the loan

charge taken back
another name for vendor take back charge

New Charge

A new charge is used when the purchaser makes arrangements with a lender to borrow money by way of charge for the purchase of the property. For example, assume that Sam sells his home for $300,000. Bao wants to buy the home but only has $200,000. Bao has to borrow the additional funds needed from his bank and use the property as security for the loan. The bank will give Bao $100,000, and Bao will give the bank a charge on the property. Bao will have $300,000 to pay to Sam, and Sam will transfer title to Bao. Bao will be the owner of the property, but it will have a charge registered against title in the amount of $100,000 in favour of the bank.

Figure 6.1 illustrates the flow of money and property interests in a new charge transaction.

FIGURE 6.1 New Charge Transaction

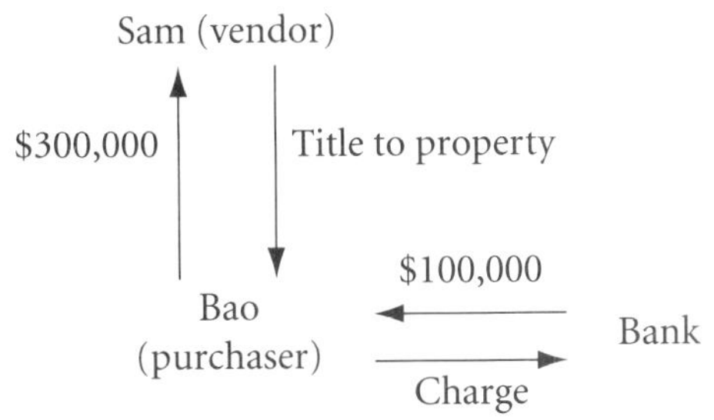

Assumed Charge

Instead of arranging a new charge, a purchaser may agree to assume an existing charge previously registered against title to the property. The purchaser will pay the vendor the purchase price minus the outstanding balance owing on the charge. The purchaser will take over the charge and make the future loan payments.

A purchaser may choose this option if the balance outstanding on the existing charge is close to the amount the purchaser needs to borrow, and the existing charge has favourable terms. For example, the interest rate payable on the charge may be lower than the current market rate. There are costs involved in arranging a new charge. New charges are discussed in chapter 23, Acting for the Mortgagee. Assuming an existing charge eliminates these expenses.

For example, assume that Sam is selling his home to Bao for $300,000. There is an outstanding charge in favour of Best Bank in the amount of $100,000; that is, Sam owes Best Bank $100,000. Bao agrees to assume this charge and pay Sam $200,000 (the amount of the purchase price less Sam's debt). In effect, Bao will replace Sam in the relationship with Best Bank and assume all of Sam's obligations under the charge. Figure 6.2 illustrates the flow of money and property interests in an assumed charge transaction.

FIGURE 6.2 Assumed Charge Transaction

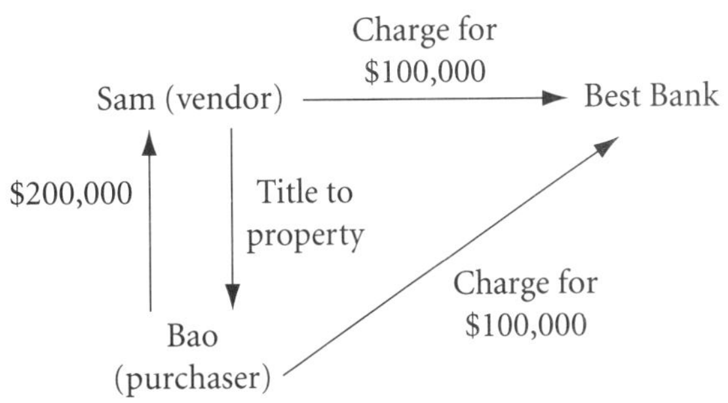

Vendor Take Back Charge

Sometimes a purchaser is unable to borrow money from traditional sources or to borrow enough money to purchase the property. If there are no other attractive offers, the vendor may agree to lend some money to the purchaser and take back a charge on the property. This type of charge is referred to as a vendor take back charge or charge taken back. It may be a first charge or a second or subsequent charge.

For example, assume that Sam is selling his property for $300,000. Bao is willing to pay $300,000 for the property but can come up with only $250,000. Sam can agree to accept payment of $250,000 at the time of the sale and, effectively, loan Bao the difference by taking back a charge on the property in the amount of $50,000. Figure 6.3 illustrates this type of charge transaction.

FIGURE 6.3 Vendor Take Back Charge Transaction

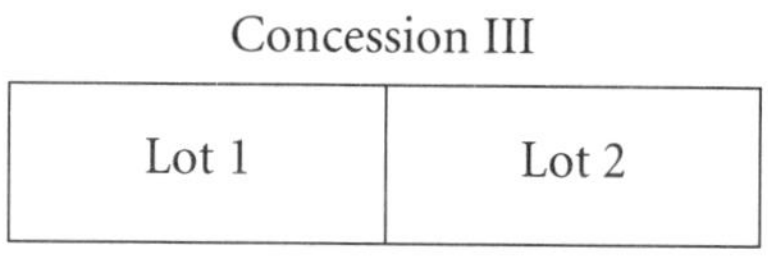

CHARGE TERMINOLOGY

There are a number of specialized terms used in discussing charges. The most important ones are discussed below.

Principal

principal
amount of money borrowed under a loan

The **principal** is the amount of money borrowed by the chargor (or loaned by the chargee) under the charge, which the chargor must repay.

Interest

interest
amount added to the principal amount of the loan in return for the right to obtain and use the money advanced

In addition to repaying the principal, the chargor must also pay **interest**. Interest is an amount added to the loan in return for the right to borrow and use the money advanced under the loan. The ability to collect interest provides an incentive to banks and other lenders to lend money, by allowing the lender to earn money on the amount loaned.

The amount of interest payable under a charge depends on the rate of interest and the intervals at which interest is calculated. Both of these factors are discussed below.

Interest Rate

The **interest rate** of a loan is calculated as an annual percentage of the amount of the loan. A charge can have a **fixed interest rate** or a **variable interest rate**. A fixed interest rate remains at the same percentage for the entire term of the charge. A variable interest rate fluctuates with changing market conditions.

interest rate
rate charged for the use of borrowed money, calculated as a percentage of the amount of the loan

fixed interest rate
rate of interest that remains the same for the term of the charge

variable interest rate
rate of interest that fluctuates with changing market conditions during the term of the loan

Calculation of Interest

Usually interest is not calculated as frequently as charge payments are made. Interest is often calculated yearly or half-yearly, while charge payments are typically made monthly. The frequency of the calculation affects the dollar amount of the interest payable: the more frequently interest is calculated, the more interest you end up paying.

For example, assume that you borrow $10,000 at an interest rate of 10 percent calculated yearly. Each year you will pay 10 percent of $10,000, or $1,000.

The following illustrates an interest calculation if, instead, interest is calculated half-yearly:

- You would owe interest after six months of $500 (yearly interest at 10 percent on $10,000, or $1,000, divided by 2).
- If the interest is not paid at that time, interest for the next six months is calculated on the new total owing of $10,500 (the original principal of $10,000 plus the interest for the first six months of $500). The interest for this six-month period is 10 percent of $10,500 divided by 2, or $525.
- The total interest payable for the year is $1,025, as compared to $1,000 in the example above.

This illustrates that you are paying interest on the interest owing after six months.

It is therefore not enough to pay attention only to the rate of interest in a charge. A lower rate of interest can be offset by frequent calculation of the interest at that rate.

Term

The **term** of the charge is the period of time within which the chargor has agreed to repay the loan in full. At the end of the specified term (also known as the **maturity date**), the chargor must either pay back the outstanding balance of the loan, or renew the charge for another term. Most charges have terms of five years or less. If the charge is renewed for another term, which is most often the case, the interest rate may change, depending on current market rates.

term
period of time within which the chargor has agreed to repay the loan in full

maturity date
date on which any outstanding balance of a charge is to be paid

Amortization Period

The **amortization period** of a charge is the total length of time it will take to pay off the charge in full following the monthly payment amounts in the charge. Most people borrow hundreds of thousands of dollars, and the term of most charges is 5 years or less. The monthly payments on such a large principal amount would be

amortization period
length of time it takes to repay a loan in full following the schedule of monthly payments in the charge

too much for most people to afford if they were calculated to repay the loan in full over such a short term. As a result, most charges are amortized over a much longer period of time than the term of the charge (usually 25 years).

If a charge has a 5-year term and a 25-year amortization period, the monthly payments of the charge are calculated as if there were 25 years to pay off the loan. At the end of the 5-year term, a very large amount of the principal will remain unpaid. This large final payment is called a **balloon payment**.

balloon payment final payment for the amount of principal that remains unpaid at the end of the term of a charge

For example, assume that Alice has arranged a charge with Best Bank in the amount of $200,000. The term of the charge is 5 years, and the loan has an amortization period of 25 years. The monthly payments are $1,413.56. If Alice were to make monthly payments of $1,413.56 for 25 years, the loan would be paid in full. Because the term is a much shorter period of time than the amortization period, at the expiration of the 5-year term, the balance outstanding on the loan will be $182,324.30. At this point in time, Alice will have to either make this balloon payment or, more likely, renew the charge for another term.

Charge Payments

Principal and interest payable under a charge are not paid in advance. If a loan is **advanced** (the loan money is given to the chargor) on the 1st of a month, charge payments are not due until the 1st of the following month. The interest paid at that time is for the use of the money during the preceding month. This contrasts with residential rental payments, which are usually payable on the 1st of each month for the use of the rented premises for that month.

advanced given or provided

Blended Payments

Blended payments combine principal and interest into equal monthly payments. Although the payment amount remains the same each month, part of each payment is applied toward the interest that has accumulated on the loan, and the remaining part is applied toward repaying the principal. Initially, a greater portion of each monthly payment is applied toward interest, rather than principal. Gradually, throughout the term of the loan, as more of the principal is repaid, the interest portion of each payment will decrease (because interest is paid only on the outstanding principal), and more of each payment will be applied toward repayment of the principal.

blended payment charge payment combining principal and interest into equal monthly payments

Non-Blended Payments

Non-blended payments do not combine principal and interest into equal payments. The amount of principal repaid each month is a fixed amount. In addition, interest is paid on the outstanding principal at the time. The amount of interest payable decreases as the loan is paid off, and so the total monthly payment changes each month.

Non-blended charge payments are usually higher and payable less frequently than blended payments. In addition, more principal will be paid off by the maturity date of the loan when payments are non-blended.

non-blended payment charge payment that does not blend or combine principal and interest into equal payments; the amount of principal repaid each month is a fixed amount and the amount of interest is calculated on the outstanding principal at the time

Amortization Schedule

An **amortization schedule** illustrates how blended payments are applied each month. It shows what part of each monthly payment is applied toward principal, what part is applied toward interest, and the principal balance outstanding on the charge after each payment is made. Figure 6.4 is an example of an amortization schedule for a loan amortized over a period of 25 years. Note how the interest portion of each payment decreases while the principal portion increases. Note also how little of the principal amount will be repaid after the first five years.

amortization schedule
schedule setting out the breakdown of each monthly blended payment between principal and interest and the remaining principal balance after each payment

Interest Adjustment Date

Charge payments are sometimes arranged to be payable on the 1st or 15th day of each month. Often the loan is advanced on a different day of the month. If all of the monthly payments are going to be equal, it is necessary to make an adjustment for interest that accumulates between the date the loan was advanced and the charge payment date for the following month. Assuming that charge payments are being made monthly, the **interest adjustment date** will be one month before the date of the first regular payment.

For example, assume that Ahmed borrows money on March 5 and arranges for monthly payments on the 1st of each month. The first monthly payment will be due not on April 1, but May 1. April 1 will be the interest adjustment date, and a separate payment will be made for interest accrued between March 5 and April 1. Often this interest amount is deducted from the amount advanced under the charge.

interest adjustment date
date on which an adjustment is made for interest that accumulates between the date the loan was advanced and the charge payment date for the following month; assuming that charge payments are being made monthly, this date will be one month before the date of the first regular payment

Closed Charge

A **closed charge** prohibits repayment of the loan before the expiry of the specified term. For example, assume that Bao borrows money from Best Bank, to be paid back in three years. Two years later, Bao wins the lottery and wants to pay off the charge. If the charge is closed, Best Bank can refuse early repayment. Best Bank does not want to lose the interest that it will receive during the last year of the loan. Best Bank might permit early repayment if Bao pays a penalty or **bonus interest** equal to the amount of interest that she would pay if the loan continued for its intended duration.

Closed charges typically have lower interest rates and longer terms than open charges.

closed charge
charge that prohibits repayment of the loan before the expiry of the term

bonus interest
penalty of interest for a period of time, for early payment of a loan

Open Charge

An **open charge** permits repayment of the loan before the expiry of the specified term. If the charge is fully open, the chargor can prepay the principal in any amount and at any time. Often the charge will be partially open, permitting repayment but only for a specified amount and only on certain dates. For example, the charge may permit the chargor to pay up to 15 percent of the principal on the anniversary date of the charge in each year. If the charge is fully or partially open, the chargor is not required to pay bonus interest.

Open charges typically have higher interest rates and shorter terms than closed charges.

open charge
charge that permits repayment of the loan before the expiry of the term

FIGURE 6.4 Amortization Schedule

Principal borrowed: $150,000.00 **Annual interest rate:** 7.00%
Regular payment amount: $1,060.17 **Term:** 5 years **Amortization period:** 25 years

Payment	Payment amount	Principal	Interest	Principal balance
1	1,060.17	185.17	875.00	149,814.83
2	1,060.17	186.25	873.92	149,628.58
3	1,060.17	187.34	872.83	149,441.24
4	1,060.17	188.43	871.74	149,252.81
5	1,060.17	189.53	870.64	149,063.28
6	1,060.17	190.63	869.54	148,872.65
7	1,060.17	191.75	868.42	148,680.90
8	1,060.17	192.86	867.31	148,488.04
9	1,060.17	193.99	866.18	148,294.05
10	1,060.17	195.12	865.05	148,098.93
11	1,060.17	196.26	863.91	147,902.67
12	1,060.17	197.40	862.77	147,705.27
13	1,060.17	198.56	861.61	147,506.71
14	1,060.17	199.71	860.46	147,307.00
15	1,060.17	200.88	859.29	147,106.12
16	1,060.17	202.05	858.12	146,904.07
17	1,060.17	203.23	856.94	146,700.84
18	1,060.17	204.42	855.75	146,496.42
19	1,060.17	205.61	854.56	146,290.81
20	1,060.17	206.81	853.36	146,084.00
21	1,060.17	208.01	852.16	145,875.99
22	1,060.17	209.23	850.94	145,666.76
23	1,060.17	210.45	849.72	145,456.31
24	1,060.17	211.67	848.50	145,244.64
25	1,060.17	212.91	847.26	145,031.73
26	1,060.17	214.15	846.02	144,817.58
27	1,060.17	215.40	844.77	144,602.18
28	1,060.17	216.66	843.51	144,385.52
29	1,060.17	217.92	842.25	144,167.60
30	1,060.17	219.19	840.98	143,948.41
31	1,060.17	220.47	839.70	143,727.94
32	1,060.17	221.76	838.41	143,506.18
33	1,060.17	223.05	837.12	143,283.13
34	1,060.17	224.35	835.82	143,058.78
35	1,060.17	225.66	834.51	142,833.12
36	1,060.17	226.98	833.19	142,606.14
37	1,060.17	228.30	831.87	142,377.84
38	1,060.17	229.63	830.54	142,148.21
39	1,060.17	230.97	829.20	141,917.24
40	1,060.17	232.32	827.85	141,684.92
41	1,060.17	233.67	826.50	141,451.25
42	1,060.17	235.04	825.13	141,216.21
43	1,060.17	236.41	823.76	140,979.80
44	1,060.17	237.79	822.38	140,742.01
45	1,060.17	239.17	821.00	140,502.84
46	1,060.17	240.57	819.60	140,262.27
47	1,060.17	241.97	818.20	140,020.30
48	1,060.17	243.38	816.79	139,776.92
49	1,060.17	244.80	815.37	139,532.12
50	1,060.17	246.23	813.94	139,285.89
51	1,060.17	247.67	812.50	139,038.22
52	1,060.17	249.11	811.06	138,789.11
53	1,060.17	250.57	809.60	138,538.54
54	1,060.17	252.03	808.14	138,286.51
55	1,060.17	253.50	806.67	138,033.01
56	1,060.17	254.98	805.19	137,778.03
57	1,060.17	256.46	803.71	137,521.57
58	1,060.17	257.96	802.21	137,263.61
59	1,060.17	259.47	800.70	137,004.14
60	1,060.17	260.98	799.19	136,743.16

RIGHTS AND OBLIGATIONS OF THE PARTIES

As previously discussed, a charge is a loan transaction in which the loan is secured by the transfer of an interest in the land. Both the chargor and the chargee have rights and obligations.

Chargor

The chargor has the right to

- remain in possession of the property during the term of the charge, as long as the chargor complies with the terms of the charge; and
- have the charge discharged when the principal amount and interest are paid in full.

The chargor has the obligation to

- make charge payments in full and on time;
- comply with all laws affecting the property (for example, if the property is zoned for office use only, the chargor cannot open a restaurant);
- maintain adequate insurance on the property;
- pay all realty taxes; and
- maintain the property in good condition so that its value does not decrease.

Chargee

The chargee has the right to

- have a charge interest in the property;
- receive the chargor's personal **covenant** (promise) to repay the loan; and
- receive principal and interest payments in accordance with the terms of the charge.

covenant
promise

The chargee has the obligation to

- leave the chargor in exclusive possession, as long as there is no breach of the terms of the charge; and
- execute a **discharge of charge** when the charge is paid in full.

discharge of charge
a document given by the chargee to the chargor confirming that the loan has been paid in full and extinguishing the chargee's interest in the property

CHARGE FORM

The charge form (reproduced in figure 5.2) sets out all of the payment provisions of the loan agreement. In addition, the paper or electronic charge contains the following information:

- the name(s) of the chargor(s);
- the name(s) of the chargee(s);
- certification that the chargor(s) is (are) at least 18 years old;
- the spousal status of the chargor(s) and statements ensuring compliance with the *Family Law Act* (if a chargor is married and the property being charged is the matrimonial home, the chargor's spouse must consent to the charge, even if the spouse is not an owner);
- acknowledgment by the chargor(s) of receipt of a true copy of the charge;
- the file number of the standard charge terms deemed to be included with the charge, if applicable (see below);
- the amount of insurance on the property being charged (coverage is usually for the full replacement value of the property or, at the very least, for the amount of the loan; the chargee will be entitled to the insurance proceeds in the event that the property is destroyed); and
- any additional provisions (such as prepayment provisions).

STANDARD CHARGE TERMS

Standard charge terms set out, in detail, the rights and obligations of the chargor and the chargee. The *Land Registration Reform Act* permits a chargee to file its own set of charge terms in the land registry office and incorporate those terms into every charge to which it is a party, instead of having to attach the terms to each one. Standard charge terms are assigned a number when filed, and by identifying the filing number in a charge, the provisions of the previously filed standard charge terms are incorporated into the charge. Figure 6.5, at the end of the chapter, is an example of a set of standard charge terms.

IMPLIED COVENANTS IN A CHARGE

Pursuant to section 7(1) of the *Land Registration Reform Act*, every charge is deemed to include the covenants contained in that Act, unless the charge incorporates a set of standard charge terms filed by the chargee. In that case, the implied covenants are excluded. The covenants contained in the Act deal primarily with the obligations of the chargor and are more limited in scope than the typical set of standard charge terms.

TRANSFERS BY CHARGEE AND CHARGOR

Chargees have the right to transfer their rights under the charge to a third party, and chargors have the right to sell the property notwithstanding the existence of the charge. A transfer by either party has an effect on the rights and obligations of the other.

Transfer by Chargee

A chargee may sell or assign the right to repayment of the loan to a third party. For example, assume Sam mortgaged his property to Charlie. If Charlie needs the money prior to the end of the term, he can transfer the charge to Alice, who will pay Charlie the principal amount oustanding. Sam will then make the monthly payments to Alice, and not to Charlie. Charlie does not need Sam's consent to the transfer, but Sam must be notified before he is required to make the payments to Alice.

Alice will take the charge subject to the state of accounts existing between Sam and Charlie at the time of the transfer. Alice should request that Sam sign an acknowledgment confirming the amount of principal and interest outstanding at the time of the transfer. This prevents Sam from later claiming that a lesser amount is due under the charge.

Transfer by Chargor

An owner of property that has a charge registered against it may sell or transfer the property without the consent of the chargee. If the purchaser does not ask to have the charge discharged, he or she will assume the charge subject to the state of accounts that exists between the vendor/chargor and the chargee at the time of the transfer.

The person who is assuming a charge should get an assumption statement from the chargee confirming the state of accounts between the original chargor and the chargee as of the date of the assumption. This prevents the chargee from later claiming that a greater amount is due under the charge.

The chargee cannot prevent the chargor from selling the property, but the charge is likely to contain a clause (called a **due on sale clause**) that permits the chargee to **accelerate** (demand immediate) full payment of the loan in the event that the chargee does not approve the new purchaser.

A chargor who transfers the property remains responsible on the covenant to repay the amount of the charge and may be sued by the chargee if the new owner defaults on the payments. The vendor/chargor can escape future liability only by obtaining a specific release from the chargee.

due on sale clause
provision in a charge permitting the chargee to accelerate full payment of the loan in the event that the chargor sells the property and the chargee does not approve the purchaser

accelerate
demand immediate payment

DISCHARGE OF CHARGE

When a charge has been paid in full, the chargor is entitled to receive a discharge of charge. Registration of a discharge extinguishes the chargee's interest in the property. Prior to making the final payment, the chargor should obtain a discharge statement from the chargee confirming the exact amount owing on the charge as of the anticipated payment date. (See figure 5.3.)

DEFAULT REMEDIES

default
breach of one or more of the obligations contained in the charge; most commonly, the failure to remit principal and interest payments when due

Default occurs when the chargor breaches one or more of the obligations contained in the charge. The most obvious and most common form of default is the failure to remit principal and interest payments when due.

Other breaches that can be classified as default include

- failure to arrange adequate insurance on the property;
- failure to pay property taxes; and
- failure to maintain the premises in a reasonable state of repair.

acceleration clause
clause permitting the chargee to demand immediate payment of the full amount of the loan in the event of default

Most charges contain an **acceleration clause** that permits the chargee to demand immediate payment of the full amount of the loan in the event of default. In most cases, the chargor will be unable to pay the amount owing and the chargee can then choose from one of the available default remedies.

The chargee can simply sue the chargor for payment of the debt secured by the charge and hope to recover on the judgment. Typically, however, the chargee will choose a remedy that involves realizing on (seizing) the secured property. The chargee may either

- sell the property through power of sale provisions contained in the charge;
- obtain title to the charged property by means of a foreclosure action; or
- sell the property pursuant to a judicial sale action.

In all cases, the chargee will also require an order for possession of the charged property in order to get vacant possession of the property.

There are many business matters and legal issues to consider when choosing the appropriate remedy. The main features of each remedy are discussed below.

Power of Sale

power of sale
power to exercise the remedy of sale in case of default under a charge

The **power of sale** (the power to exercise the remedy of sale) is generally contained in every charge and permits the chargee to sell the charged property and use the proceeds of the sale to repay the charge debt. The purchaser from a chargee exercising the power of sale acquires good title, free and clear of the chargor's interest in the property. Power of sale is the most commonly used remedy because it is relatively quick, inexpensive, and simple to implement.

notice of sale
document used in a power of sale setting out the particulars of the default and the amounts owing under the charge

The charge must be in default for at least 15 days before the chargee can start power of sale proceedings. The chargee then serves the chargor with a **notice of sale** setting out the particulars of the default and the amounts owing under the charge. The notice must also be served on

- the spouse of the chargor;
- all subsequent chargees;
- any execution creditors of the chargor;
- the solicitor for any construction lien claimants; and
- any other person with an interest in the charged property.

The notice must allow the chargor at least 35 days to either put the charge back into good standing (by paying off any arrears that are due) or completely pay off the loan. During this 35-day period, the chargee cannot take any steps to sell the property. For example, the chargee cannot advertise the property for sale or hire a realtor to sell the property. If the charge is still in default after the 35-day period expires, the chargee can then proceed to sell the property.

The chargor continues to have the right to put the charge back into good standing and **redeem** the property until the property is sold. However, as soon as an agreement of purchase and sale is signed, the chargor loses the right to redeem the property.

redeem
release or free land from a claim against it by paying the amount owing under the charge

Once the property is sold, the chargee is required to apply the proceeds to pay off the outstanding debt, including all costs incurred in the sale. The chargee is accountable to the chargor and the holder of any subsequent encumbrances for any surplus left over after paying the debt and expenses related to the sale. If the proceeds of sale are insufficient, the chargee can sue the chargor for the deficiency.

The person who buys the property under power of sale acquires good title to the property, provided the sale was properly conducted and all appropriate parties were duly served with the notice of sale.

Foreclosure

A judgment for **foreclosure** gives legal title of the property to the chargee and is obtained by court action commenced by the chargee. Once the chargee becomes the registered owner of the property, the chargee has the choice of keeping the property or selling it. The chargee is no longer accountable to the chargor or other subsequent encumbrancers, whose rights will have been extinguished by the final order for foreclosure. Similarly, the chargee is no longer accountable to the chargor in the event that the proceeds from a subsequent sale of the property are less than the amount of the debt.

foreclosure
court action whereby the chargee obtains legal title to the property after default by the chargor

The chargor and any subsequent chargee can defend the foreclosure action or request time to bring the charge back into good standing. They can also request that the property be sold instead of foreclosed. By requesting a sale, the chargor converts the foreclosure action into a judicial sale, as discussed below.

If the chargor requests time to pay but fails to do so within the time permitted by the court (usually six months), then the chargee can apply for a final order of foreclosure.

Judicial Sale

In a **judicial sale**, a court orders the sale of the property and oversees all matters related to the sale. The sheriff carries out the sale by tender or public auction under the authority of a writ of seizure and sale. A chargee can start an action for a judicial sale, but, more commonly, a judicial sale takes place when a chargor asks that a foreclosure action be converted to a judicial sale.

judicial sale
sale of charged property ordered and administered by a court

The proceeds from a judicial sale are applied first against the charge debt and any expenses of the sale. Any surplus will then be applied against the amount outstanding on any subsequent charges. In this way, the chargor is released from the claims of all other chargees to the extent that the sale money will cover those claims.

Possession

writ of possession court order giving the chargee the right to take possession of the property

chargee in possession chargee who takes possession of the charged property after default by the chargor

The remedy of possession does not involve a sale of the property but, instead, gives the chargee the right to take possession of the property after obtaining a **writ of possession** from the court. While in possession, the chargee is referred to as the **chargee in possession** and is obligated to maintain the property so that it does not deteriorate. If the property is vacant, the chargee can rent out the premises and apply the rental income to the outstanding debt. If there are tenants living on the property, they will be directed to pay their rent to the chargee in possession, and not to the chargor. This remedy is used in combination with whichever of the previous remedies the chargee has chosen.

REFERENCES

Family Law Act, RSO 1990, c. F.3.

Land Registration Reform Act, RSO 1990, c. L.4.

REVIEW QUESTIONS

1. What is a mortgage or charge?
2. Who is the chargor, and who is the chargee?
3. If there are multiple charges registered against title, how is the order of priority between the charges determined?
4. What is a vendor take back charge?
5. What is an assumed charge?
6. Charge payments include both principal and interest. Define each of these terms.
7. What is the difference between the term of the charge and the amortization period?
8. What information does an amortization schedule provide?
9. Assume that a charge payment is made that includes both principal and interest. Is this a blended or a non-blended payment?
10. Peggy arranges a charge on November 15. Her charge payments are due on the 1st of each month. What is the interest adjustment date?
11. What are standard charge terms?
12. What happens when a charge has been paid in full?
13. What are the remedies available to the chargee when the chargor breaches one or more of the obligations contained in the charge?

DISCUSSION QUESTIONS

1. A charge has a 5-year term and a 25-year amortization period. What will happen at the end of the term?
2. Anita has a closed charge with her bank. She has just won the lottery and wants to pay off the charge. Can she do this? Explain your answer.
3. In addition to making regular payments, what obligations does the chargor have?
4. Sheila wants to sell her home. She is concerned because there is an outstanding charge on the property. What are her rights?

FIGURE 6.5 Standard Charge Terms

Page 1

Dye & Durham Co. Inc, Form No. 301A

Land Registration Reform Act

SET OF STANDARD CHARGE TERMS

Filed by **Filing Date: October 14, 2004**

Dye & Durham Co. Inc. **Filing number: 200434**

The following Set of Standard Charge Terms shall be deemed to be included in every charge in which the set is referred to by its filing number, as provided in section 9 of the Act.

Exclusion of Statutory Covenants **1.** The implied covenants deemed to be included in a charge under subsection 7(1) of the *Land Registration Reform Act* as amended or re-enacted are excluded from the Charge.

Right to Charge the Land **2.** The Chargor now has good right, full power and lawful and absolute authority to charge the land and to give the Charge to the Chargee upon the covenants contained in the Charge.

No Act to Encumber **3.** The Chargor has not done, committed, executed or wilfully or knowingly suffered any act, deed, matter or thing whatsoever whereby or by means whereof the land, or any part or parcel thereof, is or shall or may be in any way impeached, charged, affected or encumbered in title, estate or otherwise, except as the records of the land registry office disclose.

Good Title in Fee Simple **4.** The Chargor, at the time of the execution and delivery of the Charge, is, and stands solely, rightfully and lawfully seized of a good, sure, perfect, absolute and indefeasible estate of inheritance, in fee simple, of and in the land and the premises described in the Charge and in every part and parcel thereof without any manner of trusts, reservations, limitations, provisos, conditions or any other matter or thing to alter, charge, change, encumber or defeat the same, except those contained in the original grant thereof from the Crown.

Promise to Pay and Perform **5.** The Chargor will pay or cause to be paid to the Chargee the full principal amount and interest secured by the Charge in the manner of payment provided by the Charge, without any deduction or abatement, and shall do, observe, perform, fulfill and keep all the provisions, covenants, agreements and stipulations contained in the Charge and shall pay as they fall due all taxes, rates, levies, charges, assessments, utility and heating charges, municipal, local, parliamentary and otherwise which now are or may hereafter be imposed, charged or levied upon the land and when required shall produce for the Chargee receipts evidencing payment of the same.

Interest After Default **6.** In case default shall be made in payment of any sum to become due for interest at the time provided for payment in the Charge, compound interest shall be payable and the sum in arrears for interest from time to time, as well after as before maturity, and both before and after default and judgement, shall bear interest at the rate provided for in the Charge. In case the interest and compound interest are not paid within the interest calculation period provided in the Charge from the time of default a rest shall be made, and compound interest at the rate provided for in the Charge shall be payable on the aggregate amount then due, as well after as before maturity, and so on from time to time, and all such interest and compound interest shall be a charge upon the land.

No Obligation to Advance **7.** Neither the preparation, execution or registration of the Charge shall bind the Chargee to advance the principal amount secured, nor shall the advance of a part of the principal amount secured bind the Chargee to advance any unadvanced portion thereof, but nevertheless the security in the land shall take effect forthwith upon the execution of the Charge by the Chargor. The expenses of the examination of the title and of the Charge and valuation are to be secured by the Charge in the event of the whole or any balance of the principal amount not being advanced, the same to be charged hereby upon the land, and shall be, without demand therefor, payable forthwith with interest at the rate provided for in the Charge, and in default the Chargee's power of sale hereby given, and all other remedies hereunder, shall be exercisable.

Costs Added to Principal **8.** The Chargee may pay all premiums of insurance and all taxes, rates, levies, charges, assessments, utility and heating charges which shall from time to time fall due and be unpaid in respect of the land, and that such payments, together with all costs, charges, legal fees (as between solicitor and client) and expenses which may be incurred in taking, recovering and keeping possession of the land and of negotiating the Charge, investigating title, and registering the Charge and other necessary deeds, and generally in any other proceedings taken in connection with or to realize upon the security given in the Charge (including legal fees and real estate commissions and other costs incurred in leasing or selling the land or in exercising the power of entering, lease and sale contained in the Charge) shall be, with interest at the rate provided for in the Charge, a charge upon the land in favour of the Chargee pursuant to the terms of the Charge and the Chargee may pay or satisfy any lien, charge or encumbrance now existing or hereafter created or claimed upon the land, which payments with interest at the rate provided for in the Charge shall likewise be a charge upon the land in favour of the Chargee. Provided, and it is hereby further agreed, that all amounts paid by the Chargee as aforesaid shall be added to the principal amount secured by the Charge and shall be payable forthwith with interest at the rate provided for in the Charge, and on default all sums secured by the Charge shall immediately become due and payable at the option of the Chargee, and all powers in the Charge conferred shall become exercisable.

Power of Sale **9.** The Chargee on default of payment for at least fifteen (15) days may, on at least thirty-five (35) days' notice in writing given to the Chargor, enter on and lease the land or sell the land. Such notice shall be given to such persons and in such manner and form and within such time as provided in the *Mortgages Act*. In the event that the giving of such notice shall not be required by law or to the extent that such requirements shall not be applicable, it is agreed that notice may be effectually given by leaving it with a grown-up person on the land, if occupied, or by placing it on the land if unoccupied, or at the option of the Chargee, by mailing it in a registered letter addressed to the Chargor at his last known address, or by publishing it once in a newspaper published in the county or district in which the land is situate; and such notice shall be sufficient although not addressed to any person or persons by name or designation; and notwithstanding that any person to be affected thereby may be unknown, unascertained or under disability. Provided further, that in case default be made in the payment of the principal amount or interest or any part thereof and such default continues for two months after any payment of either falls due then the Chargee may exercise the foregoing powers of entering, leasing or selling or any of them without any notice, it being understood and agreed, however, that if the giving of notice by the Chargee shall be required by law then notice shall be given to such persons and in such manner and form and within such time as so required by law. It is hereby further agreed that the whole or any part or parts of the land may be sold by public auction or private contract, or partly

FIGURE 6.5 Continued

Page 2 - SET OF STANDARD CHARGE TERMS Dye & Durham Co.Inc, Form No. 301
Filing Date:
Filing No.

one or partly the other; and that the proceeds of any sale hereunder may be applied first in payment of any costs, charges and expenses incurred in taking, recovering or keeping possession of the land or by reason of non-payment or procuring payment of monies, secured by the Charge or otherwise, and secondly in payment of all amounts of principal and interest owing under the Charge; and if any surplus shall remain after fully satisfying the claims of the Chargee as aforesaid same shall be paid as required by law. The Chargee may sell any of the land on such terms as to credit and otherwise as shall appear to him most advantageous and for such prices as can reasonably be obtained therefor and may make any stipulations as to title or evidence or commencement of title or otherwise which he shall deem proper, and may buy in or rescind or vary any contract for the sale of the whole or any part of the land and resell without being answerable for loss occasioned thereby, and in the case of a sale on credit the Chargee shall be bound to pay the Chargor only such monies as have been actually received from purchasers after the satisfaction of the claims of the Chargee and for any of said purposes may make and execute all agreements and assurances as he shall think fit. Any purchaser or lessee shall not be bound to see to the propriety or regularity of any sale or lease or be affected by express notice that any sale or lease is improper and no want of notice or publication when required hereby shall invalidate any sale or lease hereunder.

Quiet Possession

10. Upon default in payment of principal and interest under the Charge or in performance of any of the terms or conditions hereof, the Chargee may enter into and take possession of the land hereby charged and where the Chargee so enters on and takes possession or enters on and takes possession of the land on default as described in paragraph 9 herein the Chargee shall enter into, have, hold, use, occupy, possess and enjoy the land without the let, suit, hindrance, interruption or denial of the Chargor or any other person or persons whomsoever.

Right to Distrain

11. If the Chargor shall make default in payment of any part of the interest payable under the Charge at any of the dates or times fixed for the payment thereof, it shall be lawful for the Chargee to distrain therefor upon the land or any part thereof, and by distress warrant, to recover by way of rent reserved, as in the case of a demise of the land, so much of such interest as shall, from time to time, be or remain in arrears and unpaid, together with all costs, charges and expenses attending such levy or distress, as in like cases of distress for rent. Provided that the Chargee may distrain for arrears of principal in the same manner as if the same were arrears of interest.

Further Assurances

12. From and after default in the payment of the principal amount secured by the Charge or the interest thereon or any part of such principal or interest or in the doing, observing, performing, fulfilling or keeping of some one or more of the covenants set forth in the Charge then and in every such case the Chargor and all and every other person whosoever having, or lawfully claiming, or who shall have or lawfully claim any estate, right, title, interest or trust of, in, to or out of the land shall, from time to time, and at all times thereafter, at the proper costs and charges of the Chargor make, do, suffer and execute, or cause or procure to be made, done, suffered and executed, all and every such further and other reasonable act or acts, deed or deeds, devises, conveyances and assurances in the law for the further, better and more perfectly and absolutely conveying and assuring the land unto the Chargee as by the Chargee or his solicitor shall or may be lawfully and reasonably devised, advised or required.

Acceleration of Principal and Interest

13. In default of the payment of the interest secured by the Charge the principal amount secured by the Charge shall, at the option of the Chargee, immediately become payable, and upon default of payment of instalments of principal promptly as the same mature, the balance of the principal and interest secured by the Charge shall, at the option of the Chargee, immediately become due and payable. The Chargee may in writing at any time or times after default waive such default and any such waiver shall apply only to the particular default waived and shall not operate as a waiver of any other or future default.

Partial Releases

14. The Chargee may at his discretion at all times release any part or parts of the land or any other security or any surety for the money secured under the Charge either with or without any sufficient consideration therefor, without responsibility therefor, and without thereby releasing any other part of the land or any person from the Charge or from any of the covenants contained in the Charge and without being accountable to the Chargor for the value thereof, or for any monies except those actually received by the Chargee. It is agreed that every part or lot into which the land is or may hereafter be divided does and shall stand charged with the whole money secured under the Charge and no person shall have the right to require the mortgage monies to be apportioned.

Obligation to Insure

15. The Chargor will immediately insure, unless already insured, and during the continuance of the Charge keep insured against loss or damage by fire, in such proportions upon each building as may be required by the Chargee, the buildings on the land to the amount of not less than their full insurable value on a replacement cost basis in dollars of lawful money of Canada. Such insurance shall be placed with a company approved by the Chargee. Buildings shall include all buildings whether now or hereafter erected on the land, and such insurance shall include not only insurance against loss or damage by fire but also insurance against loss or damage by explosion, tempest, tornado, cyclone, lightning and all other extended perils customarily provided in insurance policies including "all risks" insurance. The covenant to insure shall also include where appropriate or if required by the Chargee, boiler, plate glass, rental and public liability insurance in amounts and on terms satisfactory to the Chargee. Evidence of continuation of all such insurance having been effected shall be produced to the Chargee at least fifteen (15) days before the expiration thereof; otherwise the Chargee may provide therefor and charge the premium paid and interest thereon at the rate provided for in the Charge to the Chargor and the same shall be payable forthwith and shall also be a charge upon the land. It is further agreed that the Chargee may at any time require any insurance of the buildings to be cancelled and new insurance effected in a company to be named by the Chargee and also of his own accord may effect or maintain any insurance herein provided for, and any amount paid by the Chargee therefor shall be payable forthwith by the Chargor with interest at the rate provided for in the Charge and shall also be a charge upon the land. Policies of insurance herein required shall provide that loss, if any, shall be payable to the Chargee as his interest may appear, subject to the standard form of mortgage clause approved by the Insurance Bureau of Canada which shall be attached to the policy of insurance.

Obligation to Repair

16. The Chargor will keep the land and the buildings, erections and improvements thereon, in good condition and repair according to the nature and description thereof respectively, and the Chargee may, whenever he deems necessary, by his agent enter upon and inspect the land and make such repairs as he deems necessary, and the reasonable cost of such inspection and repairs with interest at the rate provided for in the Charge shall be added to the principal amount and be payable forthwith and be a charge upon the land prior to all claims thereon subsequent to the Charge. If the Chargor shall neglect to keep the buildings, erections and improvements in good condition and repair, or commits or permits any act of waste on the land (as to which the Chargee shall be sole judge) or makes default as to any of the covenants, provisos, agreements or conditions contained in the Charge or in any charge to which this Charge is subject, all monies secured by the Charge shall, at the option of the Chargee, forthwith become due and payable, and in default of payment of same with interest as in the case of payment

FIGURE 6.5 Continued

Page 3 - SET OF STANDARD CHARGE TERMS
Filing Date:
Filing No.

Dye & Durham Co. Inc. Form No. 30

before maturity the powers of entering upon and leasing or selling hereby given and all other remedies herein contained may be exercised forthwith.

Building Charge **17.** If any of the principal amount to be advanced under the Charge is to be used to finance an improvement on the land, the Chargor must so inform the Chargee in writing immediately and before any advances are made under the Charge. The Chargor must also provide the Chargee immediately with copies of all contracts and subcontracts relating to the improvement and any amendments to them. The Chargor agrees that any improvement shall be made only according to contracts, plans and specifications approved in writing by the Chargee. The Chargor shall complete all such improvements as quickly as possible and provide the Chargee with proof of payment of all contracts from time to time as the Chargee requires. The Chargee shall make advances (part payments of the principal amount) to the Chargor based on the progress of the improvement, until either completion and occupation or sale of the land. The Chargee shall determine whether or not any advances will be made and when they will be made. Whatever the purpose of the Charge may be, the Chargee may at its option hold back funds from advances until the Chargee is satisfied that the Chargor has complied with the holdback provisions of the *Construction Lien Act* as amended or re-enacted. The Chargor authorizes the Chargee to provide information about the Charge to any person claiming a construction lien on the land.

Extensions not to Prejudice **18.** No extension of time given by the Chargee to the Chargor or anyone claiming under him, or any other dealing by the Chargee with the owner of the land or of any part thereof, shall in any way affect or prejudice the rights of the Chargee against the Chargor or any other person liable for the payment of the money secured by the Charge, and the Charge may be renewed by an agreement in writing at maturity for any term with or without an increased rate of interest notwithstanding that there may be subsequent encumbrances. It shall not be necessary to register any such agreement in order to retain priority for the Charge so altered over any instrument registered subsequent to the Charge. Provided that nothing contained in this paragraph shall confer any right of renewal upon the Chargor.

No Merger of Covenants **19.** The taking of a judgment or judgments on any of the covenants herein shall not operate as a merger of the covenants or affect the Chargee's right to interest at the rate and times provided for in the Charge; and further that any judgment shall provide that interest thereon shall be computed at the same rate and in the same manner as provided in the Charge until the judgment shall have been fully paid and satisfied.

Change in Status **20.** Immediately after any change or happening affecting any of the following, namely: *(a)* the spousal status of the Chargor, *(b)* the qualification of the land as a family residence within the meaning of Part II of the *Family Law Act*, and *(c)* the legal title or beneficial ownership of the land, the Chargor will advise the Chargee accordingly and furnish the Chargee with full particulars thereof, the intention being that the Chargee shall be kept fully informed of the names and addresses of the owner or owners for the time being of the land and of any spouse who is not an owner but who has a right of possession in the land by virtue of Section 19 of the *Family Law Act*. In furtherance of such intention, the Chargor covenants and agrees to furnish the Chargee with such evidence in connection with any of *(a)*, *(b)* and *(c)* above as the Chargee may from time to time request.

Condominium Provisions **21.** If the Charge is of land within a condominium registered pursuant to the *Condominium Act* (the "Act") the following provisions shall apply. The Chargor will comply with the Act, and with the declaration, by-laws and rules of the condominium corporation (the "corporation") relating to the Chargor's unit (the "unit") and provide the Chargee with proof of compliance from time to time as the Chargee may request. The Chargor will pay the common expenses for the unit to the corporation on the due dates. If the Chargee decides to collect the Chargor's contribution towards the common expenses from the Chargor, the Chargor will pay the same to the Chargee upon being so notified. The Chargee is authorized to accept a statement which appears to be issued by the corporation as conclusive evidence for the purpose of establishing the amounts of the common expenses and the dates those amounts are due. The Chargor, upon notice from the Chargee, will forward to the Chargee any notices, assessments, by-laws, rules and financial statements of the corporation that the Chargor receives or is entitled to receive from the corporation. The Chargor will maintain all improvements made to the unit and repair them after damage. In addition to the insurance which the corporation must obtain, the Chargor shall insure the unit against destruction or damage by fire and other perils usually covered in fire insurance policies and against such other perils as the Chargee requires for its full replacement cost (the maximum amount for which it can be insured). The insurance company and the terms of the policy shall be reasonably satisfactory to the Chargee. This provision supersedes the provisions of paragraph 15 herein. The Chargor irrevocably authorizes the Chargee to exercise the Chargor's rights under the Act to vote, consent and dissent.

Discharge **22.** The discharge of the Charge shall be prepared by the Chargee and all legal and other expenses for the preparation and execution of such discharge shall be borne by the Chargor.

Guarantee **23.** Each party named in the Charge as a Guarantor hereby agrees with the Chargee as follows:

(a) In consideration of the Chargee advancing all or part of the Principal Amount to the Chargor, and in consideration of the sum of TWO DOLLARS ($2.00) of lawful money of Canada now paid by the Chargee to the Guarantor (the receipt and sufficiency whereof are hereby acknowledged), the Guarantor does hereby absolutely and unconditionally guarantee to the Chargee, and its successors, the due and punctual payment of all principal moneys, interest and other moneys owing on the security of the Charge and observance and performance of the covenants, agreements, terms and conditions herein contained by the Chargor, and the Guarantor, for himself and his successors, covenants with the Chargee that, if the Chargor shall at any time make default in the due and punctual payment of any moneys payable hereunder, the Guarantor will pay all such moneys to the Chargee without any demand being required to be made.

(b) Although as between the Guarantor and the Chargor, the Guarantor is only surety for the payment by the Chargor of the moneys hereby guaranteed, as between the Guarantor and the Chargee, the Guarantor shall be considered as primarily liable therefor and it is hereby further expressly declared that no release or releases of any portion or portions of the land; no indulgence shown by the Chargee in respect of any default by the Chargor or any successor thereof which may arise under the Charge; no extension or extensions granted by the Chargee to the Chargor or any successor thereof for payment of the moneys hereby secured or for the doing, observing or performing of any covenant, agreement, term or condition herein contained to be done, observed or performed by the Chargor or any successor thereof; no variation in or departure from the provisions of the Charge; no release of the Chargor or any other thing whatsoever whereby the Guarantor as surety only would or might have been released shall in any way modify, alter, vary or in any way prejudice the Chargee or affect the liability of the Guarantor in any way under this covenant, which shall continue and be binding on the Guarantor, and as well after as before maturity of the Charge and both before and after default and judgment, until the said moneys are fully paid and satisfied.

(c) Any payment by the Guarantor of any moneys under this guarantee shall not in any event be taken to affect

FIGURE 6.5 Concluded

Page 4- SET OF STANDARD CHARGE TERMS Dye & Durham Co. Inc. Form No. 301A
Filing Date:
Filing No.

the liability of the Chargor for payment thereof but such liability shall remain unimpaired and enforceable by the Guarantor against the Chargor and the Guarantor shall, to the extent of any such payments made by him, in addition to all other remedies, be subrogated as against the Chargor to all the rights, privileges and powers to which the Chargee was entitled prior to payment by the Guarantor; provided, nevertheless, that the Guarantor shall not be entitled in any event to rank for payment against the lands in competition with the Chargee and shall not, unless and until the whole of the principal, interest and other moneys owing on the security of the Charge shall have been paid, be entitled to any rights or remedies whatsoever in subrogation to the Chargee.

(d) All covenants, liabilities and obligations entered into or imposed hereunder upon the Guarantor shall be equally binding upon his successors. Where more than one party is named as a Guarantor all such covenants, liabilities and obligations shall be joint and several.

(e) The Chargee may vary any agreement or arrangement with or release the Guarantor, or any one or more of the Guarantors if more than one party is named as Guarantor, and grant extensions of time or otherwise deal with the Guarantor and his successors without any consent on the part of the Chargor or any other Guarantor or any successor thereof.

Date of Charge **24.** The date of the Charge unless otherwise provided shall be the earliest date of signature by a Chargor.

Interpretation In construing these covenants the words "Charge", "Chargee", "Chargor", "land" and "successor" shall have the meanings assigned to them in Section 1 of the *Land Registration Reform Act* and the words "Chargor" and "Chargee" and the personal pronouns "he" and "his" relating thereto and used therewith, shall be read and construed as "Chargor" or "Chargors", "Chargee" or "Chargees", and "he", "she", "they" or "it", "his", "her", "their" or "its", respectively, as the number and gender of the parties referred to in each case require, and the number of the verb agreeing therewith shall be construed as agreeing with the said word or pronoun so substituted. And that all rights, advantages, privileges, immunities, powers and things hereby secured to the Chargor or Chargors, Chargee or Chargees, shall be equally secured to and exercisable by his, her, their or its heirs, executors, administrators and assigns, or successors and assigns, as the case may be. The word "successor" shall also include successors and assigns of corporations including amalgamated and continuing corporations. And that all covenants, liabilities and obligations entered into or imposed hereunder upon the Chargor or Chargors, Chargee or Chargees, shall be equally binding upon his, her, their or its heirs, executors, administrators and assigns, or successors and assigns, as the case may be, and that all such covenants and liabilities and obligations shall be joint and several. And the headings beside each paragraph herein are for reference purposes only and do not form part of the covenants herein contained.

ACKNOWLEDGMENT

This Set of Standard Charge Terms is included in a Charge dated the day of
made by

as Chargor(s)

To

as Chargee(s)

as Guarantor(s)

and each Chargor and Guarantor hereby acknowledges receipt of a copy of this Set of Standard Charge Terms before signing the Charge.

_______________ _______________
Guarantor(s) *Chargor(s)*

_______________ _______________

CHAPTER 7

Liens Against Land

A **lien** is a claim against land that acts as security for the payment of a debt owed by the landowner. A lien can be enforced by selling the property and applying the sale proceeds to the unpaid debt.

lien
charge for payment of a debt that allows the land to be sold to satisfy the debt

There are many statutes that affect property owners by providing lien rights to their land. Some statutes provide lien rights to private individuals and businesses, and other statutes give lien rights to the government.

THE MUNICIPAL ACT

The *Municipal Act* requires property owners to pay realty taxes annually. The amount of tax is calculated by multiplying the tax rate by the current value assessment of the property. For example, assume that a home has an assessed value of $330,700.00. If the residential property tax rate for the year is set at 0.8889546 percent, the realty taxes on the property for that year will be $2,939.77.

Realty taxes, depending on the municipality, may be paid in quarterly installments (March, April, June, and September) or on a monthly basis by automatic withdrawal from the owner's bank account. It is also possible for owners to arrange to have their taxes paid through the bank that holds their mortgage.

The *Municipal Act* provides that unpaid realty taxes create a lien against land. The lien is automatic; the municipality does not have to register the lien against title to the land. It is a special lien on the land that takes priority over any other claim or lien of anyone except the Crown. If the owner fails to pay tax arrears, the *Municipal Act* permits the municipality to sell the property under a tax sale.

The *Municipal Act* also permits municipalities to add to a property owner's taxes any unpaid fees and charges relating to the supply of a **public utility**. A public utility is defined in the Act to include a system that provides to the public any of the following supplies or services:

public utility
system that provides to the public water, sewage, fuel (including natural gas), energy (excluding electricity), heating, cooling, or telephone supplies or services

- water;
- sewage;
- fuel, including natural gas;
- energy, excluding electricity;
- heating and cooling; and
- telephone.

These unpaid fees may be collected in the same manner as taxes.

Pursuant to the Act, proceeds received from a tax sale are applied first to pay the tax arrears. Any surplus is paid to others claiming an interest in the land, in order of their respective priorities. Any remaining balance is paid to the owner.

A purchaser of real estate should get a certificate from the municipal tax department confirming that all taxes have been paid to make sure there is no lien against the land for unpaid taxes.

THE CORPORATIONS TAX ACT

This Act permits the province to levy a tax against corporations that are incorporated outside Canada but have a "permanent establishment" (branch, factory, or workshop) in Ontario. The Act allows the government to register a lien on title to property owned by the corporation for unpaid taxes. A title search will reveal whether or not such a lien exists.

THE INCOME TAX ACT

Section 116 of the federal *Income Tax Act* imposes taxes on non-residents of Canada who sell real property located in Canada. If these taxes are not paid, the purchaser of the property will be liable to pay the tax. The purchaser must therefore ensure that the vendor is not a non-resident; or, if he or she is a non-resident, that the required taxes have been paid; or that the property is exempt from this tax. Otherwise, the purchaser should withhold sufficient funds from the purchase price to cover the potential tax liability.

The standard form of agreement of purchase and sale requires the vendor to supply the purchaser with either a sworn statement that the vendor is not a non-resident of Canada or a certificate from the Canada Revenue Agency exempting the transaction.

THE LAND TRANSFER TAX ACT

Land transfer tax is a provincial tax payable by the purchaser of real property in Ontario. It is calculated on the value of the real property only. Any chattels (movable personal property) included in the sale are subject to retail sales tax. There are some conveyances that may be exempt from the payment of land transfer tax, including

- property transferred under a will;
- property transferred between spouses; and
- property transferred by gift.

Section 15.1(1) of the *Land Transfer Act* provides for a lien against real property for any unpaid tax.

Under this Act, a purchaser is required to complete a land transfer tax affidavit and attach it to the transfer form before registration. The affidavit is used to calculate the land transfer tax, which is payable when the transfer is registered. This tax and affidavit are further discussed in chapter 21, Document Preparation, and chapter 22, Preparation for Closing.

THE EXECUTION ACT

A **judgment creditor** (someone who is owed money pursuant to a court judgment) may enforce the judgment by filing a **writ of execution** (or writ of seizure and sale) with the sheriff in the jurisdiction where the **judgment debtor** (someone who owes money pursuant to a court judgment) owns real property. The writ of execution is a lien against the land, and the sheriff can execute the writ by seizing and selling the property. A writ of execution expires after six years but can be renewed indefinitely by the judgment creditor for consecutive six-year periods.

judgment creditor
party to whom a court awards the payment of money

writ of execution
judicial order addressed to the sheriff requiring the enforcement of a judgment

judgment debtor
party against whom a court awards the payment of money

If the judgment debtor does not own any real property at the time the writ is filed with the sheriff, but subsequently acquires real property, the writ will bind that property if the following conditions are met:

- the writ has not expired;
- the debt remains unpaid; and
- the property is situated in the jurisdiction where the writ has been filed.

If a writ of execution is on file against a judgment debtor during the period that he or she owns the land, the writ can be enforced against any person who subsequently acquires an interest in the land. As a result, it is necessary for a purchaser or lender to search for executions against the current owner (and past owners in the Registry system).

THE CONSTRUCTION LIEN ACT

Tradespeople, labourers, and material suppliers whose efforts contribute to an **improvement** of real property are entitled to a **construction lien** against that land for the value of the services performed. Improvements include construction, alterations, repairs, installations, erections, and demolitions.

improvement
changes made to real property, including construction, alteration, repair, installation, erection, and demolition

construction lien
lien against land that may be claimed by a person providing labour, services, or materials to a construction project

The Construction Process

There can be many people involved in a construction project, each having a different contractual relationship with the property owner. To understand construction lien concepts, it is helpful to know who these people are and how they are connected to a construction project.

The owner of the land usually hires a general contractor to supervise and complete the entire project. The general contractor then enters into subcontracts with companies or individuals who specialize in the required trade, such as carpentry, electrical, mechanical, painting, and so on. These companies or individuals may then enter into subcontracts with workers and suppliers. In a very large construction project, there can be many different tradespeople supplying work and materials.

FIGURE 7.1 The Construction Pyramid

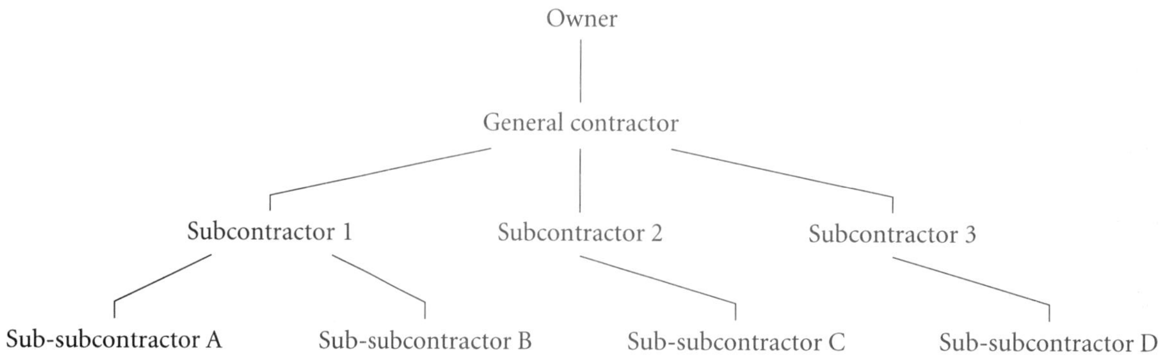

construction pyramid illustration of the contractual relationships between parties in a typical large construction project

It is possible to think of the relationships between these parties as resembling a pyramid, referred to as the **construction pyramid**, with the owner at the top followed by the general contractor and different levels of subcontractors. The construction pyramid is illustrated in figure 7.1.

Each contractor shown in the figure has a contractual relationship (privity of contract) only with the person directly above or below him or her in the construction pyramid. The general contractor is the only one who has privity of contract with the owner.

Each contractor must also look to the person directly above for payment. For example, sub-subcontractor A is paid by subcontractor 1; subcontractor 1 is paid by the general contractor; and the general contractor is paid by the owner.

The Need for Construction Lien Legislation

The *Construction Lien Act* is designed to provide financial protection for all subcontractors in the construction pyramid. Without this legislation, subcontractors could not assert a direct claim against the owner, even though they had supplied services or materials to the construction project, thereby enhancing the value of the owner's property.

For example, assume that Olive hires George, a general contractor, to supervise the renovation of her kitchen. George hires Kitchens R Us to install the kitchen. George tells Kitchens R Us to bill him, and he bills Olive for the work performed by Kitchens R Us plus a fee for himself. Assume that Olive pays George, but George does not pay Kitchens R Us. At common law, Kitchens R Us could sue only George, not Olive.

Even though Kitchens R Us has contributed to the improvement of Olive's home and has thereby enhanced its value, without construction lien legislation, Kitchens R Us would have no direct claim against either Olive or the real property. Kitchens R Us would be forced to wait in line for payment by George, together with all his other ordinary judgment creditors. Construction lien legislation allows Kitchens R Us to make a claim directly against Olive and her land, even though there is no direct contractual relationship between the parties.

The Construction Lien

To summarize, a construction lien is a lien against land that may be claimed by a person who provides labour, services, or materials to a construction project. Every subcontractor in the construction pyramid has lien rights regardless of how contractually far removed he or she is from the owner of the land. The lien attaches to the land upon which the construction takes place and is for the value of the work completed or the materials supplied by the subcontractor claiming the lien.

How To Preserve a Lien

The right to claim a construction lien arises as soon as the work starts or the materials are supplied. No further action is required to acquire the right to claim a lien. The claimant must, however, take steps to **preserve** an existing lien by registering the claim for lien against the property within 45 days of completion of work or delivery of materials.

preserve
ensure that lien rights are protected and do not expire by registering a claim for lien against title to the property on which work was performed within 45 days of completion of the work

The Expiry of Lien Rights

Even though the right to a lien arises as soon as services or materials are supplied to an improvement, most subcontractors and tradespeople will not register a lien immediately. Instead, they will wait for payment for a reasonable period of time after the work has been completed or abandoned. However, they can't wait forever: they must take steps to preserve their lien rights within 45 days of completion of the job. Otherwise, the rights will be deemed to have expired.

If a subcontractor fails to preserve a lien, the subcontractor will lose only the right to claim a lien against the owner and the owner's property. Legal remedies for breach of contract can still be pursued against the person directly above in the construction pyramid (the person with whom there is privity of contract).

The legislation provides for the expiry of unregistered claims to prevent liens from looming over title indefinitely and to allow owners and contractors to finalize construction projects.

Perfecting a Lien

Once a lien has been preserved, it must be **perfected** within a prescribed time in order to remain enforceable. To perfect the lien, the lien claimant must commence legal proceedings by issuing a statement of claim in the court office of the jurisdiction where the land is located. The lien claimant must also register a **certificate of action** against title to the property.

perfect
ensure that a preserved lien does not expire by commencing an action to enforce the lien and registering a certificate of action against title to the property

certificate of action
certificate of the court verifying that a statement of claim has been filed in a construction lien action

A preserved lien must be perfected within 45 days of the last day on which the lien could have been preserved — in other words, 90 days after the work has been completed. If it is not perfected by this time, the lien will be deemed to have expired.

A perfected lien will also expire if a lien action is not set down for trial within two years of the date the statement of claim was issued.

The Holdback

holdback
sum of money required to be deducted by the payer and held for a specified period of time from the amount owing to a payee in a construction contract

A **holdback** is money that is required to be deducted by a payer from an amount owing to a payee and held for a specified period of time. The *Construction Lien Act* requires each level of payer in the construction pyramid to retain a 10 percent holdback when the payer makes a payment to a payee at the next level below in the construction pyramid. The holdback is for the benefit of those tradespeople who are one level below the payee, and two levels below the payer, in the pyramid.

The statutory holdback amount is 10 percent of the value of the work performed or the materials supplied. The holdback is released or paid out when all potential liens have either expired or been resolved.

In the example above, assume that Olive and George have agreed upon a contract price of $10,000. When Olive pays George, she must hold back 10 percent, or $1,000, from this payment. If George does not pay Kitchens R Us, the holdback ensures that these funds will be available for Kitchens R Us to draw from. If George pays Kitchens R Us in full, and no liens are claimed, Olive will be able to release the $1,000 to George.

If an owner receives written notice of a construction lien, in addition to the 10 percent statutory holdback, the owner must hold back from future payments an amount equal to the amount being claimed under the lien.

The holdback is mandatory: parties to a construction or renovation contract cannot contract out of the holdback requirement. As long as the owner has fulfilled the statutory requirements and retained the required amount, the owner has no further liability toward the lien claimant. In other words, the owner's personal liability toward the lien claimant does not exceed the amount of the required holdback.

If the owner fails to hold back the required amount, lien claimants may enforce their lien rights by claiming the amount of the holdback. If the owner doesn't pay, the lien claimants can demand that the property be sold to satisfy their claims. In the above example, if George does not pay Kitchens R Us and Olive has failed to hold back the $1,000, Olive will be required to pay $1,000 to Kitchens R Us. If Olive doesn't pay, Kitchens R Us can force the sale of Olive's property to satisfy the debt.

Completion Date of the Contract

It is important to determine the completion date of an improvement since this date starts the clock running on the limitation periods for preserving and perfecting liens and affects the timing of the release of holdback funds.

It may be difficult to establish the completion date on a very large construction project, so the *Construction Lien Act* contains detailed procedural rules for determining the date of completion. For example, a contract will be deemed to be complete when the value of the work remaining to be finished or corrected is not more than $1,000 or 1 percent of the contract price, whichever is less.

The Act also permits release of holdback funds 45 days after substantial performance of the project. Substantial performance is defined in the Act as the time at which the improvement can be used for its intended purposes and can be completed for a specified percentage amount of the contract price.

Clearing a Lien from Title

A lien can be cleared from title by obtaining a release from the lien claimant and registering it on title. The owner can also obtain an order discharging the lien and vacating the certificate of action by paying the full amount of the lien claim plus a prescribed amount of costs into court. The money paid into court takes the place of the land as security for the lien. A **discharge of lien** can be registered or the certificate of action can be **vacated** if a perfected lien has expired because no action has been taken for two years following perfection of the lien.

discharge of lien
document registered on title that discharges a construction lien

vacated
removed from title by registration of a court order that vacates or annuls the certificate of action

IMPLICATIONS FOR TITLE SEARCHING

Purchasers of real property must ensure that no liens have been registered on title to the property on or before closing. If the search of title discloses a lien, the purchaser's lawyer should requisition its discharge. Requisitions are discussed in chapter 18, Requisitions: An Overview.

If no liens are registered on title at the time of closing, the purchaser will obtain title free from any future lien claims as long as the purchaser has not paid more than 30 percent of the purchase price before closing and title is not transferred until the home is ready for occupancy, as evidenced by a certificate of completion and possession. In that case, the purchaser will not be liable for liens that are preserved or registered after the date of closing.

REFERENCES

Construction Lien Act, RSO 1990, c. C.30.

Corporations Tax Act, RSO 1990, c. C.40.

Execution Act, RSO 1990, c. E.24.

Income Tax Act, RSC 1985, c. 1 (5th Supp.), as amended.

Land Transfer Tax Act, RSO 1990, c. L.6.

Municipal Act, SO 2001, c. 25.

REVIEW QUESTIONS

1. What is a lien?
2. How is a lien enforced?
3. What legislation governs the payment of realty taxes?
4. What happens if realty taxes are not paid?
5. What happens if a vendor of real property is a non-resident of Canada?
6. What is a writ of execution?
7. What is a construction lien, and who is entitled to claim it?

8. When does the right to claim a construction lien arise?
9. How is a construction lien preserved?
10. How is a construction lien perfected?
11. What is a holdback?
12. What happens if an owner fails to hold back the required amount?
13. How is a construction lien cleared from title?

DISCUSSION QUESTIONS

1. George files a writ of execution with the sheriff on February 2 against Sam. Sam does not own any real property. On November 15 Sam buys his first home. Does the writ bind this property?
2. Willy is a subcontractor who has not been paid for painting services he provided to a renovation. Can he sue the owner of the property? Explain.
3. Dimitre is the owner of a property. He hired Ali as a contractor to renovate his kitchen, and Ali hired Susan to install the kitchen cabinets. Susan completed the work on April 15 and sent Ali a bill for $3,000. It is now May 1 and Susan has not been paid.
    a. What are Dimitre's obligations under the *Construction Lien Act* when he pays Ali?
    b. What steps must Susan take to collect the money owing to her?

CHAPTER 8

Government Controls over the Use and Subdivision of Land

An owner of land is not free to do absolutely anything with that land because the rights of the owner are subject to governmental regulation. The government controls the way an owner uses land to protect neighbours from undesirable uses. The government controls the subdivision of land because increased development requires increased government services.

For example, if someone purchases a home on a very large lot in a quiet residential neighbourhood and decides to convert the property into a restaurant, the neighbours will likely object. Their expectations are that the neighbourhood will remain both quiet and residential. If the new owner wants to tear down the house and build three townhouses for resale, again, the neighbours will likely object because the character of the neighbourhood would change. In addition, the city might object because three homes would occupy an area that was intended for only one, creating an increased demand for the provision of city services such as water, sewage, garbage pickup, and schools.

The *Planning Act* is provincial legislation created to prevent owners from using or developing land in ways that are inconsistent with good municipal planning. The *Planning Act* was first passed after World War II when there was a sudden increase in urban growth and development. Though the Act has been amended many times, the methods of control used in the first legislation have not changed substantially.

The Act regulates undesirable uses of land through **zoning** and ensures that land is divided in an orderly way through **subdivision control**.

zoning
classification of permitted land use that includes categories such as residential, commercial, industrial, and agricultural

subdivision control
government control over the division of land into smaller parcels

ZONING

Zoning regulates undesirable land use in developed areas through the use of an **official plan** and **zoning bylaws**.

official plan
statement of planning principles prepared for a municipality by the local planning board

zoning bylaws
bylaws enacted by a municipality to regulate the use of land

Official Plan

An official plan is a statement of planning principles for a municipality. It is prepared for the municipality by the local planning board and is submitted to the municipal council for adoption, and then to the provincial government for approval.

The municipality cannot create or amend bylaws or undertake any public work that does not conform to the official plan.

Zoning Bylaws

The municipality regulates the use of land through the enactment of bylaws. These bylaws divide the municipality into zoning areas and define, in each, the use to which land and buildings can be put. For example, property in one zoning area can be used only for single-family dwellings while property in another area can be used only for commercial or industrial purposes. All parcels of land are currently in a prescribed zoning area and cannot be used for any purpose other than the one specified for that area, unless a rezoning application is successful.

Bylaws also regulate the size, shape, and location of all buildings and structures on a lot by providing specific set-back requirements, yard allowances, and lot sizes. For example, a bylaw may state that a house cannot be situated less than four feet from the side lot line.

Sometimes the use of land or the size or location of a structure does not conform to a current bylaw but was legal prior to the enactment of the bylaw. If the use has not been discontinued or the structure has not changed, then both are permitted to continue as a **legal non-conforming use**.

legal non-conforming use status of a building or use of a property that does not conform to the current municipal bylaw but is acceptable because the building or use existed before the passing of the bylaw and has not subsequently been altered or discontinued

If a property does not conform to a current bylaw and the use is not a legal non-conforming use, then the owner can seek a **consent to variance** from the municipal **committee of adjustment**. A consent will be granted if the failure to conform is minor in nature and the overall intent and purpose of the bylaw and official plan is maintained. Otherwise, it may be necessary to obtain an amendment to the bylaw for the use or structure to continue.

consent to variance committee of adjustment approval of a building or use of a property when it does not conform to a current bylaw and is not a legal non-conforming use

committee of adjustment independent body appointed by a municipality with the authority to grant consent to conveyances that result in a severance

BUILDING CONTROLS

A form of land use regulation is found in the *Building Code Act*, a provincial statute that sets the standard of construction for buildings throughout Ontario. It is enforced by municipalities, which may also have additional municipal property standard bylaws.

Municipalitics also regulate land use by requiring a **building permit** to be issued before construction or renovation of a building. A building permit is a document that grants legal permission to start construction of a "building," as defined by the *Building Code Act*. The definition of "building" is quite broad and, in addition to houses, includes additions, garages, porches, decks, and so on.

building permit document that grants legal permission to start construction of a "building"

The permit ensures that building construction meets the minimum standards set out in the *Building Code Act* and in any municipal bylaws regulating such things as height, location, floor area, external design, character, parking facilities, and use of structures. An applicant will be granted a building permit only after demonstrating that the plans comply with the *Building Code Act* and all relevant bylaws.

Some buildings are designated as historic sites under the *Ontario Heritage Act* and cannot be altered or demolished without the consent of the muncipality.

SUBDIVISION CONTROL

The purpose of subdivision control is to restrict the division of land into smaller parcels. When such a **severance** takes place, the population of the area increases, as does the need for municipal services such as roads, street lights, curbs, sewers, schools, and parks. The subdivision control provisions of the *Planning Act* ensure that these additional services are paid for by the developer and not the municipality.

severance
division of land into smaller parcels

Landowners must seek government consent to any transfers of land that result in the division of an owner's property into two or more smaller parcels. The Act controls the division of land whether one parcel is being divided into 2, 20, or 200 smaller parcels of land.

Section 50 of the Planning Act

Section 50 of the *Planning Act* is the main instrument of subdivision control in Ontario. It affects virtually every transaction that involves the creation of an interest in real property. The legislation is designed to ensure that owners cannot, without permission, deal with their land in any way that will result in a division of that land.

The Basic Prohibition

Section 50(3) of the Act essentially prohibits every "transaction" conveying an interest in land, unless the transaction falls within one of the exceptions specified in the Act. The definition of "transaction" is very broad and covers virtually all common dealings with land, including

- selling land;
- mortgaging or charging land;
- entering into an agreement of purchase and sale of land; and
- leasing land for more than 21 years.

A conveyance contrary to the *Planning Act* does not create or convey any interest in land. In other words, the transaction will be void.

Exceptions to the Basic Prohibition

There are four exceptions to the basic prohibition in section 50(3). A transaction is *permitted* as long as it falls within any one of the exceptions. The exceptions are designed to cover situations in which either land is not being divided, or, if it is, there has already been municipal or governmental consideration of planning issues. Therefore, the exceptions allow a transaction to proceed because, in the case of each exception, the purposes of subdivision control have already been served.

1. WHOLE LOT ON A PLAN OF SUBDIVISION

Section 50(3)(a) provides an exception to the basic prohibition if the property being sold is within a registered plan of subdivision. If it is a whole lot, planning and subdivision control issues would already have been considered and approved by the government prior to registration of the plan of subdivision. As a result, the underlying purpose of section 50 has been served and there is no need to prohibit the conveyance of the lot. If it is part of a lot, it must further comply with section 50(5). (See the discussion under the heading "Part Lot Control," below.)

Under section 50(4), a municipality may pass a bylaw deeming an existing plan that is at least eight years old *not* to be a registered plan of subdivision for the purposes of section 50(3)(a) of the Act. A municipality will pass this kind of bylaw to regain planning control if it believes that a previously approved plan is outdated or no longer effective because of changes in development. A lot situated on the affected plan will no longer qualify as a lot on a registered plan of subdivision and the protection of this exception will therefore be lost.

Assume that the two subdivision lots in figure 8.1 are on Plan 2345. John owns lots 1 and 2 and wants to convey Lot 1 and keep Lot 2. John can rely on the exception provided in section 50(3)(a) and convey Lot 1 without violating the *Planning Act*. If, however, Plan 2345 is deemed by a bylaw *not* to be a registered plan of subdivision, John cannot rely on this exception and must meet another exception in order to proceed.

FIGURE 8.1 Adjoining Lots on a Plan of Subdivision

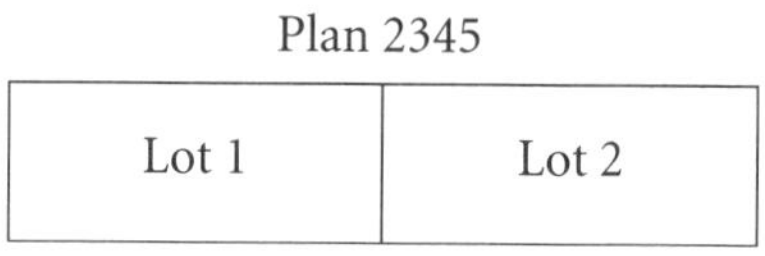

2. NO FEE IN ABUTTING LANDS

Section 50(3)(b) sets out the major exception to the basic prohibition that deals with adjoining, or abutting, land. Land is considered to be abutting, or adjoining, when it shares a common boundary. Look at the parcels in figure 8.2. Lots 1, 3, and 5 abut Lot 2 because they each share a common boundary with Lot 2. However, parcels 2 and 6 are not considered to be adjoining land.

FIGURE 8.2 Adjoining Parcels of Land

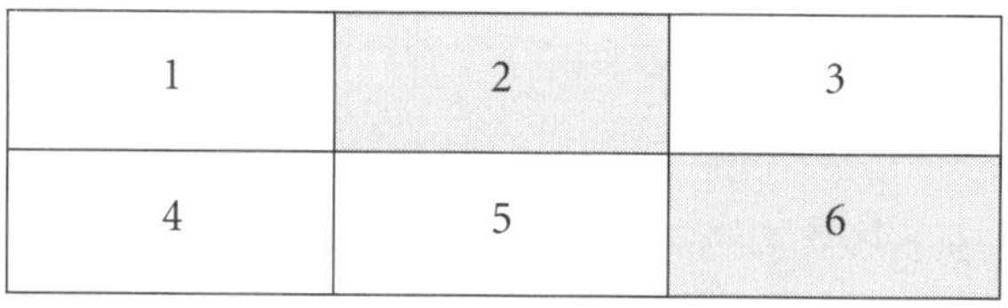

Section 50(3)(b) is easier to understand if broken down into two parts. The first part provides an exception to the basic prohibition, and the second part provides an exception to the first part.

The exception in the first part applies if the person dealing with the property does not retain the fee (ownership) or equity of redemption (a mortgagor's interest in mortgaged land) in any land abutting the land that is being dealt with. This type of transaction is permitted because there is no division of the owner's holdings into smaller parcels when the owner conveys everything that is owned. If, however, a person deals with part of the land, while retaining ownership of adjoining land, the person is effectively dividing the land into two parcels. This is exactly the type of situation the Act is designed to prevent, and the transaction is prohibited.

Under the *Planning Act*, it doesn't matter if adjoining properties were originally acquired as separate parcels of land. For example, assume that John acquired concession Lot 1 in 1990 and concession Lot 2 in 2000, illustrated in figure 8.3. He now wants to convey Lot 1. For *Planning Act* purposes, adjoining lands owned by the same person merge into one parcel. As a result, John cannot sell Lot 1 while retaining an interest in Lot 2, even though, historically, they were two separate properties.

FIGURE 8.3 Adjoining Concession Lots

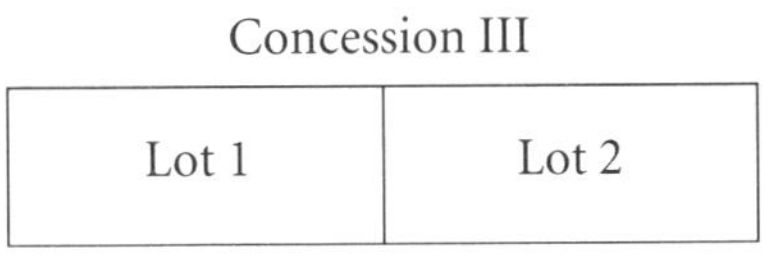

The second part of section 50(3)(b) provides an exception to the first part of the section. This exception applies if the retained land is a whole lot on a plan of subdivision. In other words, if the owner conveys land while retaining an interest in adjoining land, the transaction will not be prohibited as long as the retained land is a whole lot on a plan of subdivision.

In figure 8.1, assume this time that John owns only Lot 1. If lots 1 and 2 are whole lots on a plan of subdivision, John can convey an interest in Lot 1 and rely on the first exception. If these lots are concession lots, as illustrated in figure 8.3, John can also convey an interest in Lot 1 and rely on the first part of the second exception. Since he owns only Lot 1, he is not retaining an interest in adjoining land, and the transaction is not prohibited.

In figure 8.3, assume that John owns both lots 1 and 2 and wants to convey an interest in Lot 1, while retaining an interest in Lot 2. If these lots are concession lots, John cannot convey an interest in Lot 1 because he retains an interest in adjoining concession Lot 2. However, if Lot 2 (the parcel that John retains) is a whole lot on a plan of subdivision, the transaction will be permitted because of the second part of the second exception.

In figure 8.2, assume that John owns parcels 1, 3, and 5 and wants to convey an interest in parcel 5 while retaining an interest in parcels 1 and 3. Since parcels 1, 3, and 5 do not abut, John can convey an interest in parcel 5 and rely on the second exception.

When developers acquire land, they often use this "checkerboard" scheme to avoid future *Planning Act* issues. They register alternating parcels of land in the names of different owners to avoid *Planning Act* problems when subsequently selling off parcels of land.

In the past, developers also used **simultaneous conveyances** as a device to get around the prohibition against retaining abutting land. For example in figure 8.3, assume that John owns the two abutting concession lots. He could convey the two lots at exactly the same time to two different people and try to rely on the second exception. He would argue that at the time of the conveyance, he did not retain the

simultaneous conveyance
two abutting parcels of land conveyed at the same time to two different people

fee in abutting land. Section 50(15) was enacted to close this loophole. It provides that if two parcels of land are being conveyed at the same time to two different people, the owner is deemed to retain the ownership in abutting land for the purposes of section 50(3).

3. TRANSACTIONS INVOLVING THE GOVERNMENT

Conveyances to and from governmental authorities are permitted. Sections 50(3)(c), (d), and (e) set out the exceptions as follows:

- government acquisitions and dispositions;
- acquisitions for transmission lines (pipelines);
- acquisitions for conservation purposes.

4. GOVERNMENT CONSENT OBTAINED

If a conveyance will result in the division of a larger piece of property into smaller parcels, and the transfer does not fall into any of the previous exceptions, the owner must seek government consent to the transaction. The nature of the consent will depend on the extent of the division. If a parcel is being divided into relatively few parcels, the owner of the land can seek consent of the committee of adjustment under section 50(3)(f). If a parcel is being divided into many parcels, the owner of the land must seek government approval for a registered plan of subdivision.

Consent of the Committee of Adjustment

A committee of adjustment is an independent body appointed by a municipality. It can grant consent to conveyances that result in a severance. A consent lapses after two years if the transaction for which it was granted is not completed. Once the transaction takes place, no further consent is required to deal with that particular parcel of land. The procedure for obtaining consents is described in section 53 of the Act.

Registered Plan of Subdivision

When a large block of undeveloped land is divided into lots for sale, the developer must register a plan of subdivision. Before the province will approve the plan of subdivision, it will require the developer to enter into agreements with the municipality and public utilities to provide the extra services required by the increased population at the developer's expense. Such services might include water mains, sewers, street lights, sidewalks, curbs, schools, and parks.

Part Lot Control

As discussed above, there is an exception to the basic prohibition for transactions that deal with a whole lot on a registered plan of subdivision. The exception does not, however, apply to *part* of a subdivision lot. If an owner wants to convey only part of a subdivision lot and retain the remainder, the exception provided in section 50(3)(a) will not apply.

part lot control government control over transactions involving part of a subdivision lot

Section 50(5) deals with transactions involving part of a subdivision lot. These provisions (referred to as the **part lot control** provisions) are identical in structure to those contained in section 50(3). A person cannot deal with part of a lot on a registered plan of subdivision unless the transaction falls within one of the specified exceptions. The exceptions mirror those contained in section 50(3). In order to deal with a part of a lot, you must

- not be retaining the fee in abutting land, other than a whole lot on a plan of subdivision;
- be selling to or purchasing from the government; or
- be seeking municipal consent.

Figure 8.4 illustrates the application of the part lot control provisions. Assume that John owns lots 1 and 2 and divides the lots as shown, in order to convey the west ½ of Lot 1. He cannot do so because he retains an interest in the abutting east ½ of Lot 1. The retained land is not a whole lot on a plan of subdivision and therefore the exception does not apply.

FIGURE 8.4 Part Lots on a Plan of Subdivision

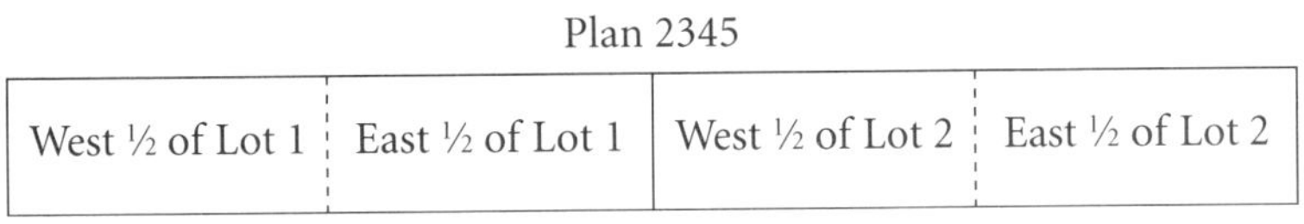

Section 50(5)(e) provides an exception if you are dealing with the remaining part of a parcel of land after the other part was acquired by a body with rights of expropriation. In figure 8.5, lots 1 and 2 are whole lots on a plan of subdivision. The owner could therefore convey either lot and not be in breach of the Act. Assume that the municipality acquires an interest by way of expropriation in the front 10 feet of these lots. Without section 50(5)(e), the owner would not be able to convey either lot because it could no longer be described as a whole lot on a plan of subdivision.

FIGURE 8.5 Expropriation of Parts of Lots on a Plan of Subdivision

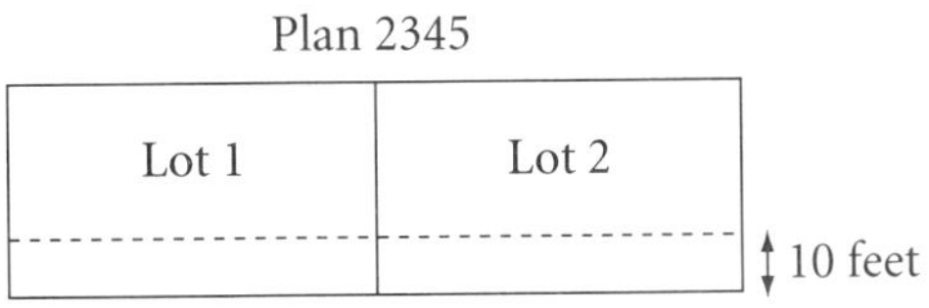

Under section 50(7), a municipality can pass a bylaw exempting land from the part lot control provisions. If such a bylaw is passed, the sale of part of a lot that would otherwise contravene the Act can proceed without consent. In some circumstances, it may be less trouble for a developer to get a municipality to pass a part lot exemption bylaw than to obtain consent for each transaction.

For example, assume that a developer has bought the land in figure 8.5 and intends to divide the two lots in half so that she can build four semi-detached homes. The developer cannot sell any of the homes because they are each located on part of a lot and she retains an interest in adjoining land. The developer can either seek consent from the committee of adjustments for each transfer or ask the municipality to pass a part lot exemption bylaw.

The provisions of the *Planning Act* are complex. See figure 8.6 for an orderly approach to determining whether the sale of property will comply with the Act.

Important Dates

Over the years, there have been many amendments to the *Planning Act*. As loopholes were discovered, new provisions were added to close them. What may not have been a contravention of the Act at one point in time may, in fact, be a contravention later. As a result, the date of a conveyance is extremely important. The following list includes some of the more significant amendments to consider when reviewing title to determine whether previous transactions have complied with the *Planning Act*:

- June 15, 1967 — Any contraventions that occurred prior to this date were forgiven. This is as far back in time as you need to search for *Planning Act* compliance.
- June 27, 1970 — Subdivision control was imposed on all land in Ontario. Prior to this date, subdivision control applied only if the particular municipality had passed a subdivision control bylaw designating land as subject to the Act's subdivision control provisions.
- March 31, 1979 — A parcel of land created by a conveyance with consent does not require further consent even though the subsequent grantor owns abutting land.
- August 1, 1983 — Consent is not required for a conveyance of a parcel of land where consent has been obtained to convey the abutting parcel.
- July 26, 1990 — Severances in wills are prohibited without consent. Prior to this date, the *Planning Act* did not affect such severances. An owner of a parcel of land could convey parts to different beneficiaries, even though such a subdivision was contrary to the intentions of the Act.

Curing Provisions

As mentioned above, the *Planning Act* was amended on June 15, 1967 to forgive all previous contraventions of the Act. This amendment is now irrelevant, as it is outside the 40-year search period.

There is an additional curing provision if boxes 13 and 14 of a transfer/deed of land form under the *Land Registration Reform Act* (see figure 5.1) have been completed. These boxes contain three statements confirming compliance with the *Planning Act*. That transfer, and all previous conveyances affecting the parcel of land, are deemed to comply with the *Planning Act*. If a contravention of the Act has previously occurred, it will, in effect, be forgiven. There are serious penalties for anyone who knowingly makes a false statement.

Implications for Title Searching

The penalty for non-compliance with the *Planning Act* is very serious: the transfer, and any transfer that flows from it, is null and void. Accordingly, a title search must include steps to ensure that the *Planning Act* has been complied with, not only by the current owner, but by past owners as well. Therefore, the search of title will

FIGURE 8.6 An Approach to Planning Act Issues

In trying to determine whether there is a *Planning Act* problem, ask yourself the following questions:

1. Is the land being conveyed the whole of a lot on a registered plan of subdivision?
   - If the answer is yes, there is no contravention of the Act and no concern about ownership of abutting lands (unless a bylaw has been registered deeming the registered plan of subdivision *not* to be a registered plan of subdivision).
   - If the answer is no, proceed to question 2.
2. Does the owner of the land being conveyed also own adjoining property?
   - If the answer is no, there is no contravention of the Act.
   - If the answer is yes, proceed to question 3.
3. Is the adjoining land that the owner is retaining a whole lot on a plan of subdivision?
   - If the answer is yes, there is no contravention of the Act.
   - If the answer is no (and the transfer is not to or from a government agency), proceed to question 4.
4. Has there been consent to the conveyance (and therefore consent to the severance into two or more parcels) by either an application to the committee of adjustment or the registration of a plan of subdivision?
   - If the answer is yes, there is no contravention of the Act.
   - If the answer is no, there is a contravention of the Act and the conveyance will be a nullity. It will not create or convey any interest in land.

---

extend to adjoining property to determine the owners of the land adjoining the land your client is purchasing.

When conducting a *Planning Act* search, you are checking to determine whether there was ever any common ownership between the subject property and the adjoining properties. If there was never any common ownership, then there could never have been an illegal division of land or violation of the Act. On the other hand, if at any point during the relevant period the same person owned both the subject property and an adjoining property, you must ensure that any transactions dealing with those properties complied with the provisions of the *Planning Act.*

Determine the answers to the following questions and follow the steps outlined.

1. Is the property you are searching a whole lot on a plan of subdivision?

   If yes, there can be no contravention of the *Planning Act* (unless a bylaw has been registered deeming the registered plan of subdivision not to be a registered plan of subdivision) and you do not have to search abutting land.

   If no, you must search the title to adjoining properties.

2. What are you searching for?

   You are checking the registration records to ascertain the names of the current and past owners of all adjoining properties. Determine whether any owners of those adjoining properties also, at the same time, owned the property being searched.

3. How far back must you search?

   If the property you are searching was previously conveyed with a transfer/deed of land containing the completed *Planning Act* statements in boxes 13 and 14, you need only search back to the date of that transfer. You do not need to search beyond that date because all previous conveyances are deemed to comply with the *Planning Act.*

   If the property has been converted from the Registry system to the Land Titles system (as a result of POLARIS), then title is guaranteed to be free of *Planning Act* contraventions as of the date of the conversion. You must still do a *Planning Act* search from the date of conversion forward.

   If there has been a conveyance or other transaction with consent, the consent cures prior contraventions. Also, sections 50(3) and (5) will not apply to subsequent dealings with the same parcel of land.

   In all other cases, you must search back as necessary (40 years if in the Registry system).

Figure 8.7 illustrates the sale of part of a lot on a plan of subdivision and the land adjoining that property. Your client is purchasing the east ½ of Lot 15, Plan 400. In addition to doing a full search of title to the east ½ of Lot 15, you must also search the title to the adjoining properties — Lot 16, Lot 2, and the west ½ of Lot 15 — to determine the identity of past owners.

FIGURE 8.7 Adjoining Land Search

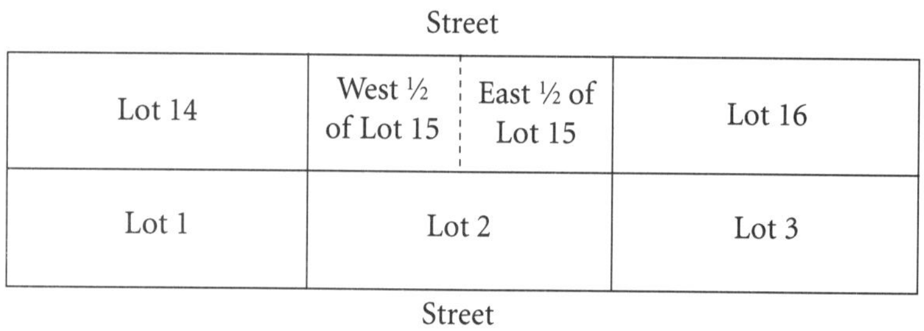

Assume that the registrar's abstract for each of the properties discloses the following ownership:

East ½ Lot 15	West ½ Lot 15	Lot 2	Lot 16
Fred Black	Fred Black	Frank Jones	Ted Long
1960–1972	1960–1985	1966–present	1965–1977
Al Green	Stan Smith		Larry Bird
1972–present	1985–present		1977–present

Note that to ascertain ownership as of June 15, 1967, you may have to go back to a conveyance registered before that date.

In this example, there is a potential *Planning Act* problem because Fred Black owned both the east ½ and the west ½ of Lot 15 from 1960 to 1972. At that time, he conveyed the east ½ (the property your client is now purchasing) to Al Green. The property Fred Black conveyed to Al Green was part of a lot, and Fred Black still retained ownership of the adjoining west ½. Unless the deed to Al Green contained a consent from the committee of adjustment, this transaction contravened the *Planning Act*, and the transfer to Al Green is a nullity. If Al Green does not have valid title to the property, your client will not receive good title on completion of this transaction.

Now assume in the above example that Al Green conveyed the property to Sara Fotia in 1986. In that transfer/deed of land, boxes 13 and 14 were properly completed. You would not have to search for *Planning Act* compliance on adjoining land before 1986 because any previous contraventions are forgiven. You would not even find out about the earlier possible contravention on the transfer from Fred Black to Al Green. Even if there was no consent to that conveyance, the contravention of the Act would be forgiven.

REFERENCES

Building Code Act, SO 1992, c. 23.

Land Registration Reform Act, RSO 1990, c. L.4.

Ontario Heritage Act, RSO 1990, c. O.18.

Planning Act, RSO 1990, c. P.13.

REVIEW QUESTIONS

1. Why was the *Planning Act* established?
2. How does the municipality regulate the use of land?
3. What is a legal non-conforming use?
4. What is the purpose of subdivision control?
5. How does the *Planning Act* ensure control over the subdivision of land?
6. What are the four main exceptions to the basic prohibition under section 50(3) of the *Planning Act*?
7. What is the penalty for non-compliance with the *Planning Act*?
8. When title searching, what steps must be taken to ensure compliance with the *Planning Act*?

CHAPTER 9

Legal Status of the Owner

The legal status of the owner of real property can have an impact on the owner's title and affects the requirements for conveying interests in the land. In this chapter we will look at the impact of each of the following matters:

- change of name
- marriage
- death
- age
- corporations
- partnerships
- trustees

CHANGE OF NAME

Owners of real property may change their names. A man or woman may apply for a formal change of name under the *Change of Name Act*, or a woman may informally change her family name upon marriage or divorce.

A change of name has an impact on title if it takes place between the time the owner acquires the property and the time the owner transfers it. Anyone reviewing the title must be satisfied that the person transferring the property is the same person who acquired the property.

If the property is registered in the Registry system, the transfer from the person must contain information to indicate that the person granting title (with the new name) is the same person as the person who took title (under the old name). The transfer should use the new name when naming the transferor and, in parentheses, state "formerly. …"

If the property is registered in the Land Titles system, the registered owner must use the exact name currently entered on the parcel register in any future dealings with that parcel of land. A change of name application must be registered on the parcel before the owner can convey the parcel using a different name.

MARRIAGE

Husbands and wives have had different property rights with respect to each other over the years. These rights can have an impact on a spouse's title to real property.

Dower

dower
entitlement of a widow to a one-third life interest in the total value of any land that her husband owned during their marriage

Before April 1978, a widow was entitled to a one-third life interest in the total value of any land that her husband owned during their marriage. This ancient right, known as **dower**, was designed to protect widows in the days when married women were not legally allowed to own property. Dower not only applied to property owned by the husband at the time of his death, but could also apply to property he had previously transferred. This would affect subsequent owners, unless the wife had barred her dower by signing the deed.

Dower rights did not attach to land

- owned by a man in joint tenancy with any other person;
- owned by a man in partnership with any other person;
- owned by a man in trust for another person;
- in a state of nature (unimproved land);
- dedicated as streets and public highways;
- in which the man had only the equity of redemption[1] during marriage and which he disposed of during his lifetime; or
- granted to the husband "to uses."[2]

In addition, a wife's dower right ended on her death or if

- the parties divorced;
- the wife committed adultery;
- the parties separated;
- the wife's whereabouts were unknown;
- the wife lived outside Ontario since the marriage; or
- the wife was confined to a mental hospital when the husband acquired the land.

To protect the purchaser against potential dower claims, a male grantor was required to disclose his marital status by swearing an affidavit contained in the deed. If the affidavit stated that he was married, the grantee would know that the grantor's wife's consent to the transfer must be obtained.

Dower was abolished on March 31, 1978 by the *Family Law Reform Act*.

Rights Under the Family Law Act

The *Family Law Reform Act*, which abolished dower, instead gave both husbands and wives special rights to their matrimonial home. These rights are continued under the current *Family Law Act*.

DEFINITION OF MATRIMONIAL HOME

A **matrimonial home** is defined under the *Family Law Act* to include every property in which a person has an interest and that is (if the parties are still married), or was (if the parties have separated) at the time of separation, occupied by the spouses as their family residence. Spouses may have more than one matrimonial home. For example, a family may have a city home and a cottage. If they are both used as a family residence, they will both be matrimonial homes.

matrimonial home defined under the *Family Law Act* to include every property in which a person has an interest and that is (if the parties are still married) or was (if the parties have separated) at the time of separation occupied by the spouses as their family residence

If spouses have more than one matrimonial home, they can *jointly* choose to designate only one of their properties as their matrimonial home. If they do this, then only the designated property is considered to be a matrimonial home, and any other property is no longer considered to be a matrimonial home. This designation must be signed by both parties and registered on the title to that property. If the designation is later cancelled, all properties that meet the definition of a matrimonial home are again considered as such.

RIGHTS OF THE SPOUSES

Under first the *Family Law Reform Act* and now the *Family Law Act*,

- both spouses have equal rights to possession of a matrimonial home; and
- neither spouse can dispose of or encumber an interest in a matrimonial home without the consent of the other spouse. If a matrimonial home is transferred without the appropriate consent, the transaction may be set aside by a court.

These rights apply even if the matrimonial home is registered in the name of one spouse only. They apply only to legally married spouses and are dependent on the continuation of the marital relationship. If the marriage ends by either death or divorce, the rights end. The rights may also be ended by a separation agreement or court order.

IMPLICATIONS FOR TITLE SEARCHING

These rights have implications for title searching. Since 1978, the marital (or spousal) status of every person, male or female, who conveys or mortgages land is relevant. Every transfer since 1978 should contain evidence of the marital status of the transferors. Before the *Land Registration Reform Act*, this evidence took the form of an **affidavit of spousal status** attached to the transfer. After the *Land Registration Reform Act* eliminated affidavits, it was provided in the certification of age and spousal status in box 8 of the transfer/deed of land.

affidavit of spousal status affidavit attached to a deed (in use after 1978 until the *Land Registration Reform Act* came into force) that provided evidence of the marital status of the grantors or transferors

If the affidavit or certification discloses that a transferor is married, the consent of the transferor's spouse is required unless

- the property is not a matrimonial home;

- some other property has been designated as the matrimonial home; or
- the spousal rights have been released by a separation agreement or court order.

Specific wording is required in the transfer to satisfy the requirements of the *Family Law Act.* The statements required are covered in chapter 21, Document Preparation, under the heading "Transfer of Title."

bona fide purchaser for value
purchaser of property who gives valuable consideration for the property and is acting in good faith

If a transfer contains an affidavit or statement in the correct form indicating that no spousal consent is necessary, a **bona fide purchaser for value** without notice to the contrary may rely upon the statement. Notice, however, means constructive notice, not actual notice. Accordingly, any evidence that would indicate that the transferor in question was, in fact, married, and the property was therefore a matrimonial home, could constitute constructive notice. Such evidence would prevent you from being able to rely on the statement.

For example, assume that your title search discloses a transfer containing a statement that the transferor is not a spouse. However, prior to that transfer, the same transferor executed and registered a charge/mortgage in which there is a statement that he is a spouse and his spouse consented. The prior document gives you notice that the property might be a matrimonial home and the current statement may therefore be false. You would have to find out what happened to the spouse and why she didn't sign the transfer.

DEATH

The death of a registered owner of real property has an effect on the title to real property.

Joint Tenancy

If land is registered in the names of two or more persons as joint tenants and one of the joint tenants dies, title automatically passes to the surviving joint tenant(s) by right of survivorship. Property owned in joint tenancy cannot be left to a beneficiary in a will by anyone other than the last surviving joint tenant.

REGISTRY SYSTEM

If jointly owned land is registered under the Registry system, when a joint tenant dies, no action is necessary to amend title until the surviving joint tenant (or tenants) wishes to deal with the land. At that time, the transfer, charge, or lease must contain recitals or statements indicating what happened to the other joint tenant. The party receiving the interest in land may require proof of death. A subsequent title searcher will want proof of the death as well. Proof of death may take the form of a death certificate attached to the document as a schedule or registered separately as a document general. Before the *Land Registration Reform Act*, proof of death could also be found as a sworn statement in one of the affidavits such as the affidavit of age and spousal status. It should be noted that a **recital** in a deed or transfer that is more than 20 years old constitutes proof of the fact recited.

recital
statement that sets out facts on which a document is based

LAND TITLES SYSTEM

Under the Land Titles system, the surviving joint tenant(s) must submit an application to the Land Titles office to delete the name of the deceased joint tenant from the register and to show the surviving joint tenant(s) as the owner(s). The application must be accompanied by an affidavit and evidence of the death of the joint tenant in the form of a death certificate or a "certificate of appointment of estate trustee" (in the past called letters of administration or letters probate).

Estate Conveyancing

If property is not held in joint tenancy, the property will be transferred in accordance with the instructions in the owner's will, if there is one. If the owner dies without a will, the property will be transferred to next of kin as provided by statute.

On the death of the owner, the property automatically passes to the estate trustee (previously called the executor if there was a will and the administrator if there was not). If there is a will, the estate trustee must deal with the property as directed by the will — either by transferring the property to a named beneficiary or by selling it to a third party.

A transfer from an estate trustee must be in a particular form containing specific recitals or statements.

Succession Duty

From January 1, 1970 until April 10, 1979, the Ontario government collected succession duties with respect to the property of deceased persons. Unpaid succession duties constituted a lien on the property of the deceased. Accordingly, if a Registry system search of title discloses that an owner of land died between January 1, 1970 and April 10, 1979, you must make sure that an Ontario succession duty release has been registered on the title to the property. A release is necessary for jointly owned property as well, unless the property was held jointly with the deceased's spouse.

Estate Tax

The federal government also collected taxes with respect to the property of deceased persons. Releases under the federal *Estate Tax Act* were required for property if the owner died between January 1, 1959 and December 31, 1971.

AGE

Generally, a contract entered into by a minor, other than a contract for necessities, is not enforceable against him or her, and is voidable at the minor's option. Transfers and charges of land made by a minor are void. All transfers contain an affidavit or statement of age confirming that the transferor is at least 18 years of age.

Land cannot be sold or transferred by a minor without the consent and approval of the **Children's Lawyer**, a government official who has the responsibility of protecting the best interests of children in the province.

Children's Lawyer
government official charged with protecting the best interests of children in the province

CORPORATIONS

A corporation is a legal entity capable of owning land.

Corporate Status

A corporation may be dissolved voluntarily by its shareholders or involuntarily by the government. If a corporation is dissolved, the ownership of any real property that the corporation has not disposed of escheats, or reverts to the Crown. As a result, it is necessary to make sure that all companies in the chain of title were in existence during the entire period they were on title.

Mortmain Licence

mortmain licence licence to own land in Ontario that a corporation was required to obtain if it was incorporated in a jurisdiction other than Ontario, Quebec, or Canada

Corporations incorporated elsewhere than in Ontario, Quebec, or Canada were once required to obtain a licence to own land in Ontario, called a **mortmain licence**. The penalty for failure to do so was forfeiture of the land. However, forfeiture could take place only while the land was owned by the corporation. Once the land was transferred, the land could no longer be forfeited. The statute in question was repealed in 1982. Accordingly, mortmain is no longer a concern, and you can ignore any affidavits found in old documents relating to mortmain.

Change of Name

Under the Registry system, a corporation that changes its name during the period of ownership of the land must register the articles of amendment by which the name was changed. The transfer must refer to the existence and registration of the articles of amendment. Under the Land Titles system, it is necessary either to apply to amend the register to change the name of the corporate owner or to give evidence of the change of name at the time the land is conveyed.

Indoor Management Rule

Outsiders dealing with a corporation can assume that the corporation acted properly and in accordance with its bylaws in selling land that it owns. Deeds by corporations registered before the *Land Registration Reform Act* came into effect must have a corporate seal and a signature. Now a transfer by a corporation must be signed under the words "I have the authority to bind the corporation."

PARTNERSHIPS

A partnership is a form of business arrangement. If land is owned as partnership property, all partners must sign the transfer and it must also contain a statement that

- the land was bought as partnership land;
- the land was held as partnership land; and
- the partners signing the transfer were at all relevant times the only partners.

TRUSTEES

If property is held by a trustee in trust for someone else, a purchaser does not have to question or investigate the trustee's authority to deal with the property.

ENDNOTES

1. A mortgage constituted a transfer of the legal estate. If a man bought land subject to a mortgage, he acquired only the equity of redemption or the right to redeem the property after repayment of the loan. If he mortgaged the property before marriage, he would own only the equity of redemption during the marriage.
2. Rather than stating that title was being granted "in fee simple," a deed would state that the title was granted "to such uses as the grantee may permit."

REFERENCES

Change of Name Act, RSO 1990, c. C.7.

Estate Tax Act (repealed).

Family Law Act, RSO 1990, c. F.3.

Family Law Reform Act (repealed).

Land Registration Reform Act, RSO 1990, c. L.4.

REVIEW QUESTIONS

1. Does the change of a property owner's name affect title?
2. What is dower?
3. What is a matrimonial home?
4. Can spouses have more than one matrimonial home?
5. What are a spouse's ownership rights in respect of a matrimonial home?
6. Do the above rights apply to common law spouses?
7. When title searching, why must you determine the transferor's spousal status?
8. If a joint tenant dies and the property is registered in the Registry system, what is required in the transfer when the surviving joint tenant sells the property?
9. If a joint tenant dies and the property is registered in the Land Titles system, what is the surviving joint tenant required to do before selling the property?

10. When a sole owner of property dies, to whom does the property pass?
11. If a search of title discloses that an owner of land died on January 13, 1974, what document must be registered on title?
12. If a corporation is dissolved, what happens to any real property that has not been disposed of?
13. Who must sign the transfer of property owned by a partnership?

DISCUSSION QUESTIONS

1. Susan Smith owns real property registered in the Registry system. Susan has recently changed her name to Susan Wong. When she sells the property, what information must the transfer contain?
2. Patty Purchaser's transfer from Victor Vendor contains the following statement: "I am a spouse. The property is not designated under section 20 of the *Family Law Act* as a matrimonial home by me and my spouse, but there is such a designation of another property as our matrimonial home, which has been registered and which has not been cancelled." Is Victor's spouse required to consent to the transfer? Explain your answer.

CHAPTER 10
Condominiums

Condominium ownership combines individual ownership of a condominium unit with shared ownership of the common elements of the condominium development. This legal structure of ownership can apply to various types of physical structures — high-rise and low-rise multiple unit building, townhouses, and free-standing homes. Condominiums may be residential or commercial. Condominium ownership in Ontario is governed by the *Condominium Act, 1998*.

THE NATURE OF A CONDOMINIUM

There are three elements of condominium ownership:

1. the *condominium unit*, which is individually owned in fee simple;
2. the *common elements*, which are owned by all of the individual unit owners as tenants in common; and
3. the *condominium corporation*, of which each unit owner is a voting member.

Condominium Unit

The **condominium unit** may be a residential suite in a multiple unit building, an office suite in a commercial building, a townhouse, or a free-standing house. The owner of each unit usually has title only to the interior of the unit.

condominium unit
unit that is part of a condominium development

Common Elements

The **common elements** are generally areas such as the lobby, grounds, parking lot, corridors, and recreational facilities, which are used by all the unit owners. The common elements also include the exterior structure of the condominium buildings and all shared mechanical equipment, such as heating, cooling, and water systems. Certain common elements may be **exclusive use common elements**, to be used only by specific unit owners. These include designated parking spots and lockers, balconies, patios, and back or front yards attached to the specific units. Note, however, that in some cases parking spots and lockers are separate units that are bought and sold apart from the main units.

common elements
areas of the condominium development owned as tenants in common by all of the individual unit owners

exclusive use common elements
areas of the condominium development owned by all unit owners but used only by designated unit owners

Condominium Corporation

condominium corporation corporation that comes into existence upon registration of the condominium plan

The role of the **condominium corporation** is to manage and administer the condominium property. The duties usually include arranging for the maintenance of the property, repairs to the common elements, insurance coverage of the property, administration of common expenses, and administration of the reserve fund.

COMMON EXPENSES

common expenses monthly fees paid by unit owners to cover the condominium corporation's obligations

As an owner of the common elements and a member of the condominium corporation, each unit owner must pay monthly fees, known as **common expenses**, to meet the corporation's obligations, such as maintenance and repair of the common elements, insurance, snow removal, gardening and landscaping, management, cleaning, and legal and accounting fees.

Common expenses are assessed for each owner on the basis of the size of his or her unit. For example, an owner whose unit occupies $\frac{1}{30}$ of the total area of all condominium units will pay common expenses equal to $\frac{1}{30}$ of the total common expenses paid by all the unit owners. If all units are the same size, the share of common expenses will be the same for all unit owners; if some units are bigger, those owners will pay a larger proportion of the common expenses.

If a unit owner does not pay the common expenses, the condominium corporation has a lien against the property for the amount outstanding. The lien expires three months after the default unless a certificate of lien is registered by the corporation within that time.

RESERVE FUND

reserve fund covers costs of major repairs to and replacement of common elements

Every condominium corporation is required to maintain a **reserve fund**, which is used to cover costs when the common elements are in need of replacement or major repair. Every new condominium corporation carries out a reserve fund study, which recommends the appropriate amount. A subsequent study is conducted every three years. Part of the monthly common expense payments is deposited into the reserve fund.

Under the *Condominium Act, 1998*, the amount in the reserve fund should be the greater of

- the amount recommended by the reserve fund study and
- 10 percent of the total annual common expenses.

In order to start a reserve fund for a new condominium, unit owners are usually required to make an initial lump sum payment equivalent to between one and three months' common expenses.

Special Assessment

If there are insufficient funds available from the common expenses or in the reserve fund to cover the regular expenses of the corporation or any unforeseen major expense, the unit owners can be required to pay a special assessment to cover the expense.

CREATION OF A CONDOMINIUM

Under the *Condominium Act, 1998* a condominium plan is created when a declaration and description are registered in the Land Titles office. At the same time, a corporation without share capital is created. The members of the corporation are the unit owners, who share the assets of the corporation in the same proportion as their proportion of ownership of the common elements.

Declaration

The **declaration** describes the units, setting out their boundaries. It sets out the percentage of the common elements associated with each unit and the percentage of common expenses each unit owner will be required to pay.

The declaration may also set out any conditions or restrictions regarding the occupation or use of the units or common elements, and it may describe the obligations of unit owners with respect to maintenance and repair of the units and the common elements.

declaration
document stating that the property is governed by the *Condominium Act, 1998* and providing the consent of all mortgagees of the property, setting out the percentage of common elements associated with each unit and the percentage of common expenses that each unit owner will be required to pay, providing the address of the condominium corporation, and designating exclusive use common elements

Description

The **description** includes a survey showing the boundaries of the units, the common elements, and the exclusive use common elements, if any. The condominium plan is given a number upon registration, and each unit is also given a number. For example, the legal description of a unit in a condominium in Aurora, which is the 647th condominium registered in York Region, might be Unit 23, York Condominium Plan 647, Town of Aurora, Regional Municipality of York. If the condominium structure is a multilevel, multiple unit building, the legal description will include a level (floor) number following the unit number.

description
document containing a plan of survey of the condominium property, architectural plans of the buildings, specification of unit boundaries, unit diagrams, and the certificates of the architect and land surveyor

OPERATION OF THE CONDOMINIUM CORPORATION

The duties and functions of the corporation are governed by the *Condominium Act, 1998*, the declaration, and the specific bylaws, rules, and regulations passed by the board of directors of the condominium corporation.

Bylaws

The **bylaws** are the rules that govern the internal operation of the condominium corporation and cover such matters as

bylaws (condominium)
rules governing the internal operation of the condominium corporation

- holding of meetings;
- notice of meetings;
- quorum requirements;
- composition of the board of directors;

- appointment of officers;
- duties and powers of the corporation; and
- banking arrangements.

The board of directors passes bylaws, after which they must be confirmed by a majority of the members of the corporation (the unit owners) at a general meeting. Bylaws may be amended by a vote of members holding 51 percent of the common elements. A certified copy of each bylaw must be registered on title for the bylaw to be effective.

Rules and Regulations

Rules and regulations govern the everyday rights and obligations of the owners regarding the use of units and common elements. For example, rules may prohibit the use of barbeques on balconies, prohibit the installation of satellite dishes, and impose restrictions on the use of recreational facilities by unit owners and their guests. In order for the rules and regulations to be effective, notice must be given to all unit owners, who have 30 days to register an objection. If at least 15 percent of unit owners object to a rule, a meeting of unit owners must be held to conduct a vote.

IMPLICATIONS FOR PURCHASERS

There are special considerations that arise on the purchase of a condominium because of the special nature of condominium ownership. These are discussed in chapter 28, Purchase of a Condominium.

REFERENCES

Condominium Act, 1998, SO 1998, c. 19.

REVIEW QUESTIONS

1. What are the three elements of condominium ownership?
2. What form may a condominium unit take?
3. What are the common elements of a condominium?
4. What are exclusive use common elements?
5. What is the role of the condominium corporation?
6. What are common expenses?
7. How are common expenses assessed?
8. What happens if a unit owner does not pay his or her common expenses?
9. What is the reserve fund?
10. What is a special assessment?
11. How is a condominium created?
12. What does the declaration do?
13. What is the description?
14. What is the purpose of the bylaws of the condominium corporation?
15. How are bylaws passed and amended, and what is required to make them effective?
16. What is the purpose of the rules and regulations of the condominium corporation, and how are they created?

CHAPTER 11

Residential Rental Properties

The residential property that a purchaser buys may be occupied by one or more tenants. The property may be a single-family dwelling that the purchaser wishes to occupy personally but is currently occupied by a tenant, or it may be a residential rental property such as a duplex, triplex, or small apartment building that the purchaser is buying as an investment. Whether the purchaser wishes to keep the tenants or have them move out, there are specific concerns that must be addressed. In addition, a purchaser who wishes to keep the tenants must be well informed about the legal and financial implications of becoming a landlord.

OVERVIEW OF RESIDENTIAL TENANCY LAW

All aspects of the residential landlord and tenant relationship are governed by the *Residential Tenancies Act, 2006* (effective January 31, 2007). The Act provides specific rules about

- the rights and obligations of the tenant and the landlord;
- the amount of rent and permissible rent increases;
- termination of tenancies by the landlord and the tenant; and
- the Landlord and Tenant Board.

The Act applies to landlords and tenants of all residential units in Ontario, regardless of the type of rental housing. In other words, the Act applies whether the tenant rents an apartment in a high-rise building, an entire single-family home, or a basement apartment. Each of these is considered a "rental unit" under the Act. The Act also applies regardless of any agreement or waiver to the contrary. If there is any conflict between the terms of a tenancy agreement and the provisions contained in the *Residential Tenancies Act*, the Act will prevail.

The Act contains special provisions for care homes, mobile home parks, land lease communities, residences in educational institutions, and government housing. These do not concern the typical purchaser of a residential complex and will not be discussed in this chapter.

The following material provides a summary of some of the aspects of the residential landlord and tenant relationship that may be of particular concern to a prospective purchaser of a residential complex.

The Landlord and Tenant Board

The Landlord and Tenant Board (LTB) is an independent administrative tribunal established by the *Residential Tenancies Act.* It hears virtually all applications dealing with the rights and obligations of residential landlords and tenants. Applications to the tribunal may be brought by either the landlord or the tenant. There are very specific rules and procedures that must be followed, and failure to comply may jeopardize a party's application.

Landlords who apply to the tribunal are usually seeking to enforce remedies for non-payment of rent or disruptive behaviour. Tenant applications usually deal with maintenance and repair issues. All landlord and tenant applications are resolved through either mediation or adjudication by a tribunal member.

The tribunal's website (www.ltb.gov.on.ca) provides free access to detailed information about all matters concerning residential tenancies. There are links to

- the *Residential Tenancies Act* and its regulations;
- the rules of practice and procedure that govern the operation of the LTB;
- the required forms; and
- information pamphlets explaining the rights and obligations of landlords and tenants, and applications and hearings before the LTB.

Creating a New Tenancy

tenancy agreement written, oral, or implied agreement between a landlord and a tenant that creates the tenancy

A residential tenancy is created when a landlord and a tenant enter into a **tenancy agreement** or lease. This agreement is usually in writing, but it can also be oral or implied. If it is in writing, the landlord must deliver a signed copy of the agreement to the tenant within 21 days. For all new tenancy agreements, the landlord must provide the tenant with written notice of its legal name and address for service. A tenant is not obligated to pay rent until the landlord provides this information. Before the tenancy begins, the landlord must also provide the tenant with information relating to the rights and responsibilities of landlords and tenants, the role of the LTB, and how to contact the LTB.

leasehold estate right to exclusive possession of property for a specified period of time in return for the payment of rent

A residential tenant has a **leasehold estate** in the property owned by the landlord. In exchange for the payment of rent, the tenant acquires the right to exclusive possession of the property for a specified period of time.

Rules About Rental Payments

When an apartment becomes vacant and a new tenancy is entered into, the landlord is free to charge any amount of rent the landlord and the new tenant agree to, without any regard to past rents or former tenants. As soon as the new tenant takes possession, however, rent control provisions in the Act regulate future rent increases.

In most cases, rent can be increased only once every 12 months and only by the statutory guideline amount. This amount is set each August by the Ontario government and applies to rent increases that start on or after January 1 of the following year. In 2008 landlords were allowed to increase rents by 1.4 percent. The guideline amount for 2009 is 1.8 percent. The tenant must be served with written notice of the rent increase on the proper form at least 90 days before the increase is to take effect.

Increases above the guideline can be obtained upon application and with the approval of the LTB or, in some cases, by agreement with the tenant. The grounds for rent increases above the guideline are

- extraordinary increase in cost of taxes or utilities (no limit on the increase);
- capital expenditures; or
- operating costs related to outside security services.

In the latter two cases, the LTB will determine whether the capital expenditures or costs related to outside security services were justified. If so, the increase cannot be more than 3 percent above the statutory guideline amount per year for a maximum of three years.

SECURITY DEPOSITS

When a new tenancy is created, a landlord can require a deposit equal to one month's rent. If there is an increase in rent during the time the landlord is holding the deposit, the landlord may require the tenant to pay an additional amount to bring the deposit up to the amount of the increased rent. The landlord must pay the tenant annual interest on this deposit in the amount of the guideline percentage increase in effect at the time the payment becomes due. The landlord cannot demand any other payment or deposit from the tenant as a condition of renting the premises. This deposit is to be applied toward rent owing for the last rental period before the termination of the tenancy.

POSTDATED CHEQUES

A tenant may, but is not required to, provide the landlord with postdated cheques.

Types of Tenancies

Tenancies are either periodic or for a fixed term. The distinction is important because the Act provides for different notice periods depending on the type of tenancy. A **fixed-term tenancy** has a specified beginning date and end date, and can be for any period of time. The usual written lease provides for a fixed term of at least one year. A **periodic tenancy** is a tenancy that renews automatically at the end of the relevant period until terminated by either the tenant or the landlord. The period is defined by the frequency of rental payments. The most common form of periodic tenancy is a **monthly tenancy** (also referred to as a month-to-month tenancy).

A fixed-term tenancy that ends and is not renewed for another fixed term automatically becomes a monthly tenancy. For example, assume that Tina Tenant enters into a one-year lease with her landlord and pays rent monthly. The tenancy is a fixed-term tenancy for one year. At the end of the year, if Tina and her landlord do not sign another one-year lease, the tenancy will become a monthly tenancy.

fixed-term tenancy
tenancy that has a specified beginning and end date and can be for any period of time, from months to years

periodic tenancy
a tenancy that renews automatically at the end of the relevant period until terminated by either the tenant or the landlord, the period being defined by the frequency of rental payments

monthly tenancy
a periodic tenancy that renews automatically at the end of each month until terminated by the landlord or the tenant

Rights of the Residential Tenant

Residential tenants are given a number of rights under the *Residential Tenancies Act.*

PRIVACY

The Act ensures that tenants have the right to privacy by limiting the landlord's ability to gain access to the unit once it has been rented. A landlord can enter without written notice only

- in the event of an emergency;
- if the tenant consents at the time of entry; or
- if the landlord is showing the premises to a prospective tenant after notice of termination has been given.

The landlord can enter with 24 hours' written notice to the tenant only for the reasons specified in section 21 of the Act. These reasons include the following:

- to carry out a repair or do work in the rental unit, or to determine whether repairs are necessary;
- to allow a potential mortgagee or insurer of the residential complex to view the rental unit;
- to allow a potential purchaser to view the rental unit; and
- any other reasonable reason for entry specified in the tenancy agreement.

The notice must specify the reason for entering, the date, and the time of day, which must fall between 8 a.m. and 8 p.m. The Act provides specific remedies to a tenant if the landlord enters the unit illegally.

MAINTENANCE AND REPAIRS

The tenant is responsible for cleaning the rental unit and for repairing any damage caused to the premises by the willful or negligent conduct of the tenant or his or her guests. The landlord is responsible for providing and maintaining the rental premises in a "good state of repair and fit for habitation" and for complying with all health, safety, and maintenance standards. The landlord must not withhold the supply of any vital services such as heat, gas, and electricity that the landlord is obligated to provide.

sublet
arrangement whereby a tenant moves out of a rental unit for a period of time and allows another person to reside in the unit until the tenant returns at a specified future date

assignment
arrangement whereby a tenant transfers tenancy to another person for the remainder of the tenancy's term

SUBLETTING AND ASSIGNING A TENANCY

There are very specific provisions dealing with **sublet** and **assignment** of a tenancy. Basically, the Act permits the tenant to sublet or assign the tenancy but only with the consent of the landlord. The landlord cannot unreasonably withhold consent to a request to sublet the rental unit but is entitled to refuse consent to an assignment, in which case the tenant is entitled to terminate the tenancy early.

SECURITY OF TENURE

A landlord can terminate a tenancy only for one of the grounds or reasons specified in the Act and, even then, cannot regain possession of the rental unit without an order from the LTB.

Rights of the Residential Landlord

The primary right of the landlord is the right to be paid rent by the tenant. The landlord is entitled to receive rental payments when due, as provided for in the tenancy agreement. Non-payment of rent and persistently late payment of rent are both grounds for early termination of the tenancy by the landlord. Unlike a commercial landlord, the residential landlord does not have the right of **distress** (the right to seize the tenant's property) for non-payment of rent.

distress
the right of a commercial landlord to seize and dispose of a tenant's property

Terminating a Tenancy

A tenancy can be terminated by

- agreement between the landlord and the tenant;
- the tenant, with proper notice to the landlord; or
- the landlord, with grounds and proper notice to the tenant.

TERMINATION BY AGREEMENT

A tenant and a landlord can agree to terminate a tenancy at any time.

TERMINATION BY THE TENANT

A tenant may terminate a fixed-term or periodic tenancy at the end of the term or period by giving proper notice to the landlord in accordance with section 47 of the Act. The tenant does not need to provide a reason or establish grounds to terminate the tenancy. The length of the notice required depends on the type (periodic or fixed) and term (yearly, monthly, or weekly) of the tenancy.

In most cases, for a monthly tenancy, notice must be given at least 60 days before the termination date, and that date must be the last day of a rental period. For example, assume that Susan has a monthly tenancy. It is August 15 and Susan has decided she wants to move out. She must give at least 60 days' notice, which takes her to October 14. However, the termination date must be the last day of the month, so the earliest termination date she can specify in her notice is October 31. A special rule allows a tenant to give less than 60 days' notice when the termination date is the last day of February or March. If a tenant is moving at the end of February or March, he or she may give notice by January 1 or February 1, respectively.

For a fixed-term tenancy, notice must be given at least 60 days before the termination date, and that date must be the last day of the fixed term. If Susan had a fixed-term tenancy ending January 31, 2008, she must give notice no later than December 2, 2007. However, even if she were to give notice on August 14, the earliest termination date would still be January 31, 2008.

There are also provisions in the Act giving tenants the right to terminate a tenancy early when a landlord breaches one of its obligations under the Act.

TERMINATION BY THE LANDLORD

fault grounds grounds for termination based on conduct or behaviour of the tenant or a guest of the tenant

termination for cause termination by the landlord on fault grounds

no-fault grounds grounds for termination unrelated to the conduct or behaviour of the tenant or a guest of the tenant

The landlord can terminate a tenancy only for the grounds or reasons specified in the Act. Some of the reasons deal specifically with the conduct or behaviour of tenants or their guests (referred to as **fault grounds** or **termination for cause**), while other reasons do not (referred to as **no-fault grounds**).

The Act provides very specific procedural rules for each of the grounds for termination, including

- the form, content, and timing of the notice of termination that must be given to the tenant;
- the earliest possible termination date the landlord can specify on the notice of termination;
- what, if anything, a tenant can do to remedy the situation and void the notice of termination; and
- what the landlord can do if the tenant does not remedy the situation or does not move out on the termination date specified in the notice.

It is important to read these provisions very carefully. While the process is quite similar for most grounds, the timing of the notice and the earliest possible termination date can be very different depending on the type of tenancy and the ground for termination. For most fault grounds, the landlord can terminate the tenancy before the end of a rental period or term. For most no-fault grounds, the landlord must wait until the end of a rental period or term.

arrears of rent unpaid rent that is owed to a landlord

One of the most common grounds for early termination by a landlord is nonpayment of rent or **arrears of rent**. Section 59 of the *Residential Tenancies Act* provides that a tenant is considered to be in arrears of rent on the day following the day on which rent is due and payable.

Assume that Tina Tenant has a monthly tenancy and her rent is due on the 1st of each month. It is August 10 and Tina has not paid August's rent. Her landlord wants to commence proceedings to terminate her tenancy as early as possible and must take the following steps:

1. The landlord must serve Tina with the proper notice of termination. For this ground, the required form is called Notice To End a Tenancy Early for Nonpayment of Rent (Form N4). This form can be downloaded from the LTB website. The termination date specified in the notice cannot be earlier than the 14th day after the notice is served on the tenant. If the landlord serves Tina on August 10, the earliest date that can be inserted in the notice of termination is August 24.

   This ground allows the tenant an opportunity to remedy the situation and void the notice of termination by paying the arrears of rent within 14 days after the notice is served. The landlord's notice must specify what the tenant must do, and by what date, in order to avoid termination of tenancy. Accordingly, if Tina pays all the rent owing any time before August 24, the notice will be void.

2. If Tina does not pay the rent owing by August 24, and does not move out by this date, the landlord must then commence an application before the LTB. The landlord will typically seek an order terminating the tenancy and evicting the tenant, and requiring the payment of the arrears of rent.

   The earliest date that the landlord can commence the application is the day after the termination date specified in the notice, or August 25. In other words, the landlord must wait for the remedy period to expire.

   The latest date that an application can be commenced is provided for in section 69 of the Act. For all grounds except non-payment of rent, an application may not be made more than 30 days after the termination date specified in the notice. For non-payment of rent, there is no limitation period as long as the rent remains unpaid.

The Act also provides for early termination by the landlord for the following additional "fault" grounds:

- the tenant or a guest has committed an illegal act in the rental unit or the residential complex;
- the tenant or a guest has willfully or negligently caused damage to the rental unit or residential complex;
- the conduct of the tenant or a guest interferes with the reasonable enjoyment of the residential complex by the landlord or another tenant;
- an act or omission of the tenant or a guest seriously impairs the safety of any person; or
- there are too many persons residing in the tenant's unit.

The Act also provides grounds for termination by the landlord at the end of a period or term. These are mostly no-fault grounds and include the following:

- the landlord requires possession of the rental unit for occupation by the landlord, the landlord's spouse or same-sex partner, or the child or parent of one of them;
- a purchaser of the rental unit requires possession of the rental unit for occupation by himself or herself or a family member, as listed above;
- the landlord requires possession to demolish, convert, or renovate the residential complex;
- the residential complex is being converted to a condominium; or
- the tenant has persistently failed to pay rent on time.

Whenever a landlord is seeking to terminate a tenancy early, the following questions should be considered:

- What is the ground or reason for wanting to terminate the tenancy early?
- Does the *Residential Tenancies Act* permit early termination for this ground or reason?

- What sections of the Act deal with this ground?
- What is the earliest termination date possible?
- Is there a remedy period available to the tenant?
- What is the earliest date the landlord can commence an application to the tribunal in the event that the tenant does not move out voluntarily?

For each ground or reason, you will probably have to look at two or three sections of the Act to determine the answers to these questions.

Proceedings at the Landlord and Tenant Board

Once an application has been commenced, there are many procedural rules that must be followed in order to obtain a hearing before a tribunal adjudicator. The landlord should be familiar with the Act, the LTB's Rules of Practice, and its Interpretation Guidelines. This information is available at the tribunal's website.

IMPLICATIONS FOR THE PURCHASE OF A RESIDENTIAL COMPLEX

As is the case with other real property, the onus is on the purchaser to ensure that good title is acquired on closing. In that sense, the purchase of a residential rental complex is no different. There are, however, additional concerns to the purchaser of real property with a rental component.

Vacant Possession

The purchaser of a residential rental building may or may not intend to reside in one of the units. A rental building is an income-producing asset and is often purchased solely for business or investment purposes. If the purchaser intends to reside in the building after closing and vacant possession of a rental unit is required, there are two options available.

1. Try to convince a tenant to enter into an agreement to terminate the tenancy early.
2. Ask the vendor/landlord to serve a notice of termination on the tenant (on behalf of the purchaser) pursuant to section 49 of the Act.

For the first option, the agreement should specify a termination date well in advance of closing, so that the landlord will have time to obtain an LTB order terminating the tenancy if the tenant does not move out as agreed.

The second option is available only if

- the residential complex does not contain more than three units;
- there is a signed agreement of purchase and sale;

- the purchaser needs vacant possession personally or for a family member as defined in the Act; and
- the termination date is at least 60 days after notice is given, and is at the end of a period or term of the tenancy.

Once a notice is served, the landlord can immediately commence an application to terminate the tenancy and evict the tenant. In other words, the landlord does not have to wait and see whether or not the tenant moves out in accordance with the notice given. If the tenant refuses to move out, the matter will proceed to a hearing. The tribunal requires a declaration that the purchaser does, in fact, require the unit for personal use. If successful, the order evicting the tenant will take effect 10 days later and can then be enforced by the sheriff's office.

This entire process may take several months. The lawyer must carefully explain the procedures and timing involved to a prospective purchaser who intends to reside in the property.

Assuming Existing Tenancies

If the purchaser does not intend to reside in the building, the only concern will be stepping into the shoes of the vendor and assuming all existing tenancies. The purchaser will want an assignment of all tenancies together with a direction to tenants telling them to make future rent cheques payable to the new owner. Finally, an estoppel certificate or statutory declaration is required to confirm the terms and conditions of all existing tenancy agreements.

In addition, there are adjustments that must be made for the current rent, the last month's rent deposits, and interest on those deposits. These amounts will be allocated between the vendor and the purchaser up to the date of closing. Adjustments are discussed in detail in chapter 21, Document Preparation. The purchaser and vendor must also negotiate how they will deal with any arrears of rent outstanding on the date of closing.

The purchaser also wants to confirm that the rental income declared by the vendor is legal and will continue. For example, if rents include the use of a swimming pool and the pool has closed, rents could decrease. The purchaser must also inquire whether there will be a reduction in realty taxes. If so, tenants may seek a reduction in rent, thereby decreasing the expected cash flow to the purchaser.

Finally, the purchaser should search LTB records to determine whether any applications relating to the residential complex are pending.

REFERENCES

Residential Tenancies Act, 2006, SO 2006, c. 17.

REVIEW QUESTIONS

1. What does the *Residential Tenancies Act, 2006* govern?
2. What is the Landlord and Tenant Board (LTB)?
3. How is a residential tenancy created?
4. How much can a landlord charge as rent?
5. Can the landlord require the tenant to pay a deposit?
6. Can a tenant be required to pay rent with postdated cheques?
7. What is the difference between a fixed-term tenancy and a periodic tenancy?
8. How does the *Residential Tenancies Act* protect tenants' right to privacy?
9. What are the responsibilities of the landlord and the tenant with respect to cleanliness, maintenance, and repairs?
10. Can a tenant sublet or assign the tenancy?
11. How can a tenancy be terminated?
12. What must a tenant do in order to terminate a tenancy by notice?
13. In what circumstances can a landlord terminate a tenancy?
14. What are the options available to a purchaser of a residential complex if the purchaser wishes to reside in the building after closing?
15. What issues need to be addressed if the purchaser wishes to assume any existing tenancies?

CHAPTER 12

Environmental Issues

Any piece of land may have suffered environmental damage as a result of the conduct of previous or neighbouring owners. For example, an industry located on the property may have used toxic chemicals, or an owner of a neighbouring property may have released toxins into the environment. There may be environmental concerns with residential property as well — for example, as a result of a leak from an old fuel oil tank. Properties that were previously rural may have been contaminated by animal waste or chemical fertilizers and pesticides.

Environmental damage is often hard to detect on a standard inspection of a property. As a result, it is important to consider how a purchaser of land may seek protection against unknowingly assuming the liability for an environmentally contaminated piece of land.

OVERVIEW OF ENVIRONMENTAL LAW

Environmental matters in Ontario are primarily governed by the *Environmental Protection Act*, a statute administered by the Ministry of the Environment. The statute generally prevents any person from discharging any contaminant into the **natural environment** — the air, water, or land.

natural environment
air, land, and water, or any combination or part thereof

In an effort to prevent or control the discharge of contaminants, the ministry is authorized under the Act to issue the following orders, as required:

- stop orders — to stop the source of contamination if danger is imminent;
- control orders — to control discharges that exist but do not pose any immediate danger;
- preventive orders — to prevent anticipated contamination; and
- cleanup orders — to clean up contamination that has actually occurred.

Under the Act, the owner of contaminated property is responsible for the cleanup and repair of environmental damage regardless of who caused the contamination.

IMPLICATIONS FOR PURCHASERS

A purchaser who does not investigate the environmental condition of property being purchased may later discover that the property is, in fact, contaminated. The purchaser may then be responsible for all costs associated with the cleanup and repair of the environmental damage. If the government is forced to step in and clean up the property, a lien can be registered against the property.

The Act does not require vendors of real property to disclose that the property has been contaminated. As a result, the purchaser may have no claim against the vendor unless

- the vendor represented that the property was *not* contaminated; or
- the vendor knew about the contamination and the purchaser did not and could not have known about it. (This would constitute a **latent defect**.)

latent defect
defect of which the vendor of a property was aware but which the purchaser did not know about and could not have discovered upon reasonable inspection of the property

A prudent purchaser should consider the environmental condition of the property in question before signing the agreement of purchase and sale. If there is any question about the condition of the property, the purchaser should include an environmental audit clause, which provides the right to obtain an environmental audit or soil test of the property. The clause should give the purchaser the right to either terminate the transaction or insist that the vendor clean up the contamination if the audit discloses the existence of contamination on the property. The purchaser could also negotiate to include clauses representing and warranting that the property is not contaminated, and agreeing to indemnify the purchaser in the event of contamination. The purchaser should be wary if the vendor is seeking to sell the property "as is, where is." Without investigating the environmental condition of the property, the purchaser may not only acquire contaminated property, but may have no recourse against the vendor for costs associated with cleanup and remediation.

The more difficult situation occurs where neither the vendor nor the purchaser is aware of the existence of contamination and the agreement of purchase and sale is silent on the issue. This is especially of concern if the property is at risk of environmental contamination, as is the case where the property has a buried oil tank or is situated near a chemical plant or gas station.

caveat emptor
Latin term meaning "let the buyer beware"

Unfortunately for the purchaser, the general principle of ***caveat emptor*** ("let the buyer beware") governs purchases of real property. The onus is clearly on the purchaser to arrange an environmental inspection of the property. If there is an environmental concern because of the nature and/or location of the property, the purchaser should

- review any existing environmental audits of the property;
- determine whether any notices or orders have been issued with respect to the property; and
- conduct a **phase I environmental assessment** of the property to determine whether contamination is likely and, if so, conduct a **phase II environmental assessment**, which includes soil and groundwater analysis.

phase I environmental assessment
assessment of property conducted to determine the likelihood that one or more contaminants have affected all or part of the property

phase II environmental assessment
assessment of property conducted to determine the location and concentration of contaminants on the property; follows completion of a phase I assessment

If serious contamination is discovered, further site assessment and site remediation are required pursuant to the provisions of the *Environmental Protection Act*.

REFERENCES

Environmental Protection Act, RSO 1990, c. E.19.

REVIEW QUESTIONS

1. What does the *Environmental Protection Act* govern?
2. What is the risk to a purchaser who does not confirm the environmental condition of the property?
3. Will the purchaser of contaminated property have any claim against the vendor?
4. What should a prudent purchaser do in order to avoid unexpected environmental problems?

CHAPTER 13

Title Searching

It is necessary to **search the title** to a particular piece of land to find out who owns the property and whether that person's ownership interest is subject to any other claims or encumbrances. Searching title involves checking the entries in the **abstract book** or parcel register for a particular piece of land and then examining the listed documents.

search the title
conduct an investigation into the status and history of title to land

abstract/abstract book
record of all registrations affecting a parcel of land

Titles are most often searched in the context of a real estate transaction. When a person agrees to buy real estate, an agreement of purchase and sale is signed. The agreement states what the purchaser is agreeing to buy, for example, a single-family dwelling located at 123 Elm Street in Oshawa. The agreement will also set out the size of the lot and describe specific encumbrances to which the title will be subject at the closing date (the date on which the purchaser pays the vendor and the vendor actually transfers title to the purchaser).

It is the role of the purchaser's lawyer to ensure that the purchaser receives the title that was promised. The lawyer does this by searching the title to the property, first, to confirm that the vendor, in fact, owns the property and then to find out what encumbrances are, in fact, outstanding. If the title search discloses any encumbrances that are not listed in the agreement of purchase and sale, the purchaser's lawyer will ask the vendor's lawyer to remove those encumbrances before the closing.

When the deal closes, the purchaser's lawyer provides an opinion to the purchaser about the state of the title and certifies that the title is free and clear of any encumbrances other than the ones agreed to in the agreement of purchase and sale. The title search provides the basis upon which the lawyer determines the state of title and provides this opinion.

WHO CONDUCTS THE TITLE SEARCH

Land registry records are public, and anyone can gain access to them. However, most title searches are conducted by law firms acting for purchasers or mortgagees in connection with real estate transactions. While lawyers can, and often do, conduct title searches, usually lawyers use in-house law clerks or freelance title searchers to carry out their searches. While it is permissible for a law clerk or title searcher to search a title, the title search must be prepared for and under the supervision of a lawyer. Only a lawyer can give an opinion about title to a client. It is the lawyer's responsibility to carefully review the results of the title search so that he or she can properly certify title to the client.

WHEN A TITLE SEARCH IS CONDUCTED

The agreement of purchase and sale will provide the purchaser with a specific amount of time in which to search title and submit any requisitions (objections to title) to the vendor. If the agreement does not specify a date, the *Vendors and Purchasers Act* provides that the purchaser has 30 days after the agreement is signed in which to complete the search and submit requisitions.

WHERE A TITLE SEARCH IS CONDUCTED

If the property is registered in the Registry system, you search the title to the property at the land registry office for the geographic area in which the property is situated. The municipal address of the property determines the region or county and, therefore, which land registry office you must go to in order to search title. For example, the city of Richmond Hill is located in York Region. If you are searching title to a property located in Richmond Hill, you go to the land registry office for York Region, which is located in Newmarket.

You can find information about the location of registry offices and the services they provide at the following website: www.ontario.ca/en/residents/index.htm. Choose the link "Land Registration" under "Popular Topics." If the property is registered in the Land Titles system and has been automated, you can conduct the title search online using the Teraview software (discussed in chapter 5, Land Registration Systems).

PRELIMINARY STEPS

Several factors determine the steps you must take to complete your search of title. Before starting your search, you must answer the following questions:

- Is the property registered in the Registry system or the Land Titles system?
- If the property is registered in the Land Titles system, was it originally located in the Land Titles system, or has it been recently converted to Land Titles as a result of POLARIS (Province of Ontario Land Registration Information System)?
- Has the property been automated, and, if so, when was it automated?

THE DIFFERENCE BETWEEN REGISTRY SYSTEM AND LAND TITLES SYSTEM TITLES

As discussed in chapter 5, Land Registration Systems, the Registry system is a notice system only. It provides notice of documents registered against title to a property; it does not guarantee the legal effectiveness of any of the documents — nor does it certify the title of the current owner. As a result, in a Registry system search, you must examine all registered documents affecting title to ensure their legal effectiveness. The Land Titles system, on the other hand, does provide a guarantee of title; title is certified. As a result, you do not have to conduct as extensive a search of title records under this system.

TITLE SEARCHES IN THE REGISTRY SYSTEM

A property that is registered in the Registry system requires the longest and most complicated search of title. The property may be automated, in which case you may be able to gain access to some of the title records online using the property's PIN (property identifier number). But even though some of the records may be available online, the property remains in the Registry system, and you must still conduct a full title search.

A Registry system title search involves examining the history of ownership of the property for the last 40 years prior to the date on which the real estate transaction is scheduled to close. If, for example, an agreement of purchase and sale sets a closing date of September 1, 2004, you must search title back to September 1, 1964. There are a number of steps in a Registry system search. A discussion of each of the steps follows.

1. Determine the Legal Description and PIN

Before you can start a search, you will need the legal description of the property and, if the property has been automated, its PIN. Often the agreement of purchase and sale will contain the information you need to start your search. If not, and you know only the municipal address of the property, you can obtain the legal description and/or PIN using cross-reference resources available at the land registry office.

If the property is not automated, you need the legal description of the property to locate the appropriate paper abstract book for the property. If the property is automated, you need the PIN to access the computerized abstract.

2. Access the Abstract Book and/or Computerized Abstract

In most cases, you will need to look in the abstract book for the property whether or not the property is automated. There is no fee to examine the abstract book, but there is a fee if you want to obtain a copy of the abstract pages. If the property is not automated (and has not been assigned a PIN), use the legal description to locate the appropriate abstract book. If the property has been automated and you have the PIN but not the legal description, you can use the PIN to get the computerized abstract first. At the top of the computerized abstract, you will find the legal description for the property.

Once you have the abstract book for the property, determine which pages deal with your property. You must find all registrations relating to your property over the last 40 years. If the property is located on a plan of subdivision that was registered at least 40 years ago, all the relevant registrations will be located in the abstract book for the plan of subdivision. If the property is located on a plan of subdivision that is less than 40 years old, you will also have to examine the abstract book for the original concession lot to complete your full 40-year search. This is referred to as **searching behind the plan**.

searching behind the plan examining the abstract book for the original concession lot of which property was a part prior to the registration of the plan of subdivision

If the property is the whole of a lot on a concession or on a plan of subdivision, the page for the lot will deal only with that property, and every instrument noted on the page will affect the property in some way. If the property is a part of a lot on a concession or on a plan of subdivision, the page for that lot will contain entries for instruments relating to all the different parts of the lot. As a result, not every instrument recorded on the page will necessarily relate to your property. You must check the description in the right-hand column of the abstract to determine which instruments affect the part of the land that you are searching.

Check the page in the abstract book to see if there is a stamp indicating that the property has been automated. If it has been automated, you will also have to obtain the computerized abstract for the property. You need the property's PIN to get the abstract. You can get the PIN using computers located at the land registry office. Search for the PIN by entering an instrument registration number, the owner's name, or the municipal address of the property. Once you have the PIN, you can view the computerized abstract by entering the PIN and following the onscreen prompts. You will have to pay a fee.

Usually the computerized abstract will list only the documents registered after the property was automated and a PIN assigned. Documents registered before this date will be listed only in the paper abstract book. This system of mixed paper and computerized registration records is called the **Parcelized Day Forward Registry (PDFR)** system. Most automated properties in the Registry system are PDFR properties. You will need to check both the computerized abstract and the paper abstract book to do a full 40-year search of a PDFR property.

Parcelized Day Forward Registry (PDFR) computerized abstract listing only the most recent transfer prior to automation and those documents registered after the property was automated

In rare cases, a property remains in the Registry system, instead of being immediately transferred to the Land Titles system, even though all documents registered in the last 40 years were transferred into the computerized system when the property was automated. These properties are known as **Automated Registry** properties. You do not need to look at the paper abstract book for Automated Registry properties.

Automated Registry computerized abstract listing all registered documents, including those registered prior to automation

Figure 13.1 is an example of a page of an abstract book for a concession lot — Lot 57, Concession 6, Township of Whitford. Figure 13.2 is an example of an abstract page for a lot on a plan of subdivision — Lot 11, Plan 1209, Township of Whitford. Note how the pages are divided into columns with the following titles:

- Registration Number — This column identifies the registration number assigned to the document at the time of registration. In older abstracts, this column may be headed "Instrument Number."
- Instrument Type — This column identifies the type of document — grant (used to identify an older deed), transfer, mortgage, discharge of mortgage, etc.
- Registration Date — This column identifies the date on which the document was registered. In older abstracts, this column may be preceded by a column entitled "Date of Instrument," which sets out the date on which the document was prepared or signed.

- Parties from — This column identifies the party or parties who gave an interest in land. In older abstracts, this column may be headed "Grantor."
- Parties to — This column identifies the party or parties to whom the interest in land was given. In older abstracts, this column may be headed "Grantee."
- Consideration — This column sets out the amount of consideration recited in the document.
- Land/Remarks — This column includes a brief legal description of the land affected by the document.

3. Obtain the Whiteprint for the Property

A **whiteprint** is a copy of a plan of survey of the plan of subdivision on which the property is situated. It is helpful to look at the plan or obtain a whiteprint because it

whiteprint
copy of the plan of survey of a plan of subdivision that shows the dimensions of individual building lots

- enables you to see the location of the property, as well as its relationship to adjoining and other properties;
- contains measurements of the lots on the plan, which can be used to confirm the size of the lot being purchased;
- shows the location of the property on the original concession lot, so that if the plan is less than 40 years old, you will know the concession and lot number you will have to look at to complete your search;
- confirms the relationship to any previous plans of subdivision at the same location; and
- reveals the location of the property in relation to main roadways or intersections and confirms that the property has access to a public road.

Mark the location of the property on the whiteprint by either outlining the property or colouring it in. Figure 13.3 is an example of a whiteprint of a plan of subdivision.

If the legal description refers to a reference plan, you should also get a copy of the reference plan.

If the property is part of a lot and the legal description includes a metes and bounds description, you will need to prepare a freehand sketch of the property by following the written instructions in the description. The sketch will illustrate how your part of the lot relates to the whole of the lot. This will help you decide which documents registered on the title to the lot in fact affect the part of the lot you are searching.

4. Trace Back to a Good Root of Title (Root Deed)

Section 112(1) of part III of the *Registry Act* provides that the title search period is 40 years. To establish the starting point of your search, you must count back 40 years from the closing date in the agreement of purchase and sale. For example, if the closing date is July 5, 2008, the starting point of your search is July 5, 1968. (In practice, most title searchers go back 40 years from the date on which they conduct the search.)

You must then look for the first conveyance of the fee simple estate (a deed or transfer) registered after the commencement date. Assume that since the commencement date in our example there have been two conveyances: the first on December 15, 1970 and the second on May 28, 1992. The deed dated 1970 is the **root of title**, or **root deed**. You do not need to search back any further.

root of title (root deed) first conveyance of the fee simple estate (a deed or transfer) registered after the commencement date of a title search

However, if there has not been a conveyance of the fee simple estate since the commencement date (July 5, 1968), you must go back beyond 40 years and find the first conveyance of the fee simple estate registered before the commencement date. If the most recent conveyance of the fee simple estate was on March 13, 1930, this deed will be the root of title, or root deed, even though it was registered far beyond the statutory 40-year search period.

This practice has been affirmed by the Supreme Court of Canada in the case of *Fire v. Longtin*. However, many real estate lawyers still prefer to start their searches with the conveyance of the fee simple estate to the person who owned the property at the commencement of the 40-year search period. Assume in our example that there is a conveyance of the fee simple estate in 1955 to Smith, and a conveyance from Smith to Tran in 1980. Smith is the person who owned the property at the commencement of the 40-year period. Some lawyers would start the search with the 1955 deed to Smith and check every document registered from then on. Based on the Supreme Court of Canada decision, however, the 1980 deed to Tran will be the root of title, and any other instruments registered on title between 1955 and 1968, such as mortgages or other liens, can be ignored (since they are outside the title search period of 40 years).

Look at the abstract pages in figures 13.1 and 13.2, and assume that the search was conducted in September 2008. Based on the Supreme Court of Canada decision, the root deed will be instrument number 44796, the August 1977 grant to Willard Marshall. Many lawyers, however, will start the search with the previous deed to Walter Fitzgerald, instrument number 42347 registered in September 1951.

If the property you are searching is a whole lot on a concession or on a plan of subdivision, then all of the documents recorded in the abstract book on the pages for that lot will be relevant to your search. However, if the property is a part of a lot on a concession or on a plan of subdivision, some of the documents recorded in the abstract book on the pages for that lot may relate to the other part or parts of the lot. As a result, you should check the description column of the abstract book to determine which entries apply to the part of the lot that you are searching.

Note that in figure 13.1, the instruments listed refer to different parts of Lot 57, Concession 6. In figure 13.2, all of the registrations refer to the whole of Lot 11, Plan 1209.

5. Prepare a Chain of Title by Name

The **chain of title** shows the names of all the registered owners during the title search period and the dates on which they acquired ownership. Its function is to

chain of title
list of all owners within the 40-year search period

- serve as a table of contents for the title search;
- provide a list of owners for the purpose of searching executions; and
- alert you to any gap in the chain of ownership.

Start by looking through the abstract book and/or computerized abstract to pick out all of the deeds and transfers registered during the title search period. (Look in the "Instrument Type" column for documents called "grant," "deed," or "transfer.") For purposes of the chain of title, the date in the "Registration Date" column is the date on which the person named in the "Parties to" or "Grantee" column became the owner of the property.

Starting with the grantee in the root deed, prepare a chain of title by listing the names of all the grantees in all of the deeds and transfers throughout the title search period up to and including the current owner. Copy the names exactly as they appear in the abstract book. Beside the name of each grantee, provide the registration date and registration number of the deed or transfer that conveyed ownership. Figure 13.4 shows the chain of title for Lot 11, Plan 1209, Township of Whitford, starting with the deed to Willard Marshall — instrument number 44796 registered in August 1977.

Starting with the first deed in the chain of title, make sure the grantee in one deed was the grantor in the next. If this is not the case, you must check the abstract book and documents for an explanation of the apparent break in the chain of title. For example, an owner may have died and left the property to the next grantor by way of will.

6. Abstract the Instruments

Abstracting involves examining and summarizing into **search notes** the contents of all the registered documents that affect title. The purpose of search notes is to provide the lawyer reviewing the notes with enough information to determine the state of the title to the property and any encumbrances that may be registered on title. Keep in mind that, in the Registry system, the land registrar does not guarantee the accuracy of information recorded in the abstract index. Therefore, the lawyer reviewing the title search must ensure that all registered documents are legally effective.

abstracting
process of examining and summarizing into search notes the contents of all registered documents that affect title

search notes
summary of the contents of all registered documents affecting title; reveals the state of the title including any encumbrances

The lawyer must be satisfied that

- the conveyance is in the proper form;
- the land is properly described;
- there is no gap in the chain of title;
- the document was properly executed and, when required, witnessed; and
- any affidavits and other statutory requirements that affect the validity of the document have been completed.

Prepare your search notes by using a separate sheet of paper for each document registered during the title search period that affects your land. Title searchers use preprinted sheets that already contain columns similar to those in the abstract book to abstract the documents and prepare their search notes.

Starting with the root deed, copy on a separate sheet of paper the entry of each instrument from the abstract book onto your abstract paper, exactly as it appears in the abstract book. (You will later compare this information with the information contained in the actual document.) Leave lots of room on the sheet for additional notes that you will need to make when you review the actual document.

7. Obtain a Copy of All Abstracted Instruments

You must obtain a copy of every registered document that you have abstracted. In Toronto, you will be viewing original documents unless they have been lost or destroyed, in which case they are on microfilm. In most other registry offices, you will be viewing microfilmed copies of the documents.

8. Review Each Instrument

Begin by comparing all the information you copied from the abstract book with the information contained in the actual document by checking the dates, names, consideration, and legal description of the property. If the information is the same in the instrument as it is on your abstract sheet, place a check mark in each column to verify that the information matches. If there are any differences, identify them by drawing a line through any information that needs correcting and then making the correction in a different colour ink. Do not whiteout or erase the information that you copied from the abstract book. This way, the lawyer reviewing the search knows that the information in the abstract book was incorrect. For instruments other than deeds, such as mortgages, claims for liens, and deposits, provide a brief summary of the contents of the instrument.

Next, you must check each instrument to see if the document contains all the necessary information to make it legally effective. Your notes must be detailed enough for the lawyer reviewing them to ensure that each instrument complies with all the legal requirements in place at the time the instrument was registered. If a document does not comply with the legal requirements, this may constitute a title defect that needs to be corrected before the transaction closes. Title search paper contains a number of abbreviations representing the legal requirements for registered documents that have been in effect over the time covered by most searches today. As you note that a particular item appears in a document, check the appropriate box.

The search notes for the property in the abstract book pages in figures 13.1 and 13.2 are found in the appendix to chapter 19, Reviewing the Search of Title. Chapter 19 contains a detailed examination of these search notes.

9. Search Adjoining Land (Planning Act Search)

You must complete a *Planning Act* search if you are searching title to property that is not a whole lot on a plan of subdivision. A *Planning Act* search involves a review of the history of ownership of **adjoining land**. You must check to see whether there was ever any common ownership between your land and adjoining lands.

adjoining land property that shares a common boundary with the property being searched

A search of adjoining land is completed to ensure compliance with the *Planning Act*— legislation that controls the division of land in Ontario. The Act generally prohibits people from selling or mortgaging land if they retain an interest in adjoining land. There are serious consequences if a transfer of land violates the provisions of the *Planning Act*. No interest in land will pass (the transfer is void) and all subsequent transfers of the same land will also not convey any interest in the land. A violation of the Act can therefore disrupt the chain of title.

A *Planning Act* or adjoining land search involves a number of steps:

- Look at the whiteprint and identify and mark all adjoining land. If the property is automated, the property mapping function can help you identify adjoining land.
- For each adjoining parcel of land, check the deeds and transfers to ascertain the owners.
- Determine whether, at any time, the property you are searching and any adjoining property were owned by the same person. If so, government consent may have been required to validate the sale of only one parcel of land by the owner of both.

You search back only as far as June 15, 1967 because contraventions prior to that date are forgiven. You do not have to go back all the way to 1967 if there is a later transfer containing completed *Planning Act* statements; you need to search back only to the date of that transfer. A *Planning Act* search is required only if the land for which you are searching title is all or part of a concession lot or part of a lot on a plan of subdivision. You do *not* have to search adjoining property if the land is a whole lot on a plan of subdivision.

The *Planning Act* is discussed in more detail in chapter 8, Government Controls over the Use and Subdivision of Land.

10. Conduct an Execution Search (Writs of Execution)

An execution is a claim against a person resulting from a court judgment that is then registered against that person's name with the sheriff of the judicial district in which the debtor owns real property. Executions create a lien against any lands already owned by the person named in the execution at the time of filing and any lands that the person acquires after the date of filing.

As a result, you must make sure that there were no executions outstanding against any owner within the 40-year search period during the time that person was the owner of the land. Make a list of all owners in the chain of title and the dates during which they were owners. You can electronically submit the names and dates to the appropriate sheriff's office for searching.

See chapter 7, Liens Against Land, for a more complete discussion of writs of execution.

11. Conduct a Corporate Search

If there are any corporate owners on title during the 40-year search period, you must check to ensure that the corporation did not dissolve at any time during the time it owned the land. The *Business Corporations Act* provides that title to property owned by a dissolved corporation escheats to or vests in the Crown.

12. Complete a Subsearch

subsearch
a brief examination of title records to update an earlier search

A **subsearch** is a brief examination of title records to update an earlier search of title. It is often performed just before registration of a transfer/deed or mortgage to ensure that no new instruments that may affect title have been registered since the date the title search was completed.

If the property has been automated, you need to look only at the computerized abstract. If the property has not been automated, you must check the last page in the abstract book. You must also check the **day book**, which lists recent registrations that have not yet been entered into the abstract book.

day book
record listing recent registrations not yet entered into the abstract book

You must also check executions again, but only against the current owner.

TITLE SEARCHES IN THE LAND TITLES SYSTEM

If the property is registered in the Land Titles system, the title search process is far simpler than it is for property registered in the Registry system. Under the Land Titles system, the state of title is guaranteed, and there is therefore no need to conduct a 40-year search. For example, if the parcel register reveals Demetre Papadepoulos as the owner, then it is guaranteed that he is the legal owner and has good title to the property, subject to any encumbrances that are noted in the register. In Land Titles, the parcel register shows only the current owner and any outstanding encumbrances. Any other entries that no longer affect title are ruled off.

Land Titles Absolute (LT Absolute)
properties originally in the Land Titles system; corporate existence and *Planning Act* compliance are not guaranteed

Land Titles Conversion Qualified (LTCQ)
properties originally in the Registry system and converted to the Land Titles system as a result of POLARIS; *Planning Act* compliance and corporate existence are guaranteed for the period prior to the date of conversion; properties remain subject to any pre-existing mature claims for adverse possession, prescription, or misdescription

In theory, a title searcher need only check the register for the parcel in question, and the register alone tells who the registered owner is and what encumbrances are outstanding. However, as stated in chapter 5, Land Registration Systems, there are some exceptions or qualifications regarding title to property in the Land Titles system. These qualifications are set out in section 44(1) of the *Land Titles Act*.

There are three different types or classifications for Land Titles properties, each of which has different title qualifications and exceptions:

1. **Land Titles Absolute (LT Absolute)** — These properties were originally in the Land Titles system.
2. **Land Titles Conversion Qualified (LTCQ)** — These properties were originally in the Registry system and have been converted to the Land Titles system as a result of POLARIS.

3. **Land Titles Plus (LT Plus)** — These properties have been upgraded from LTCQ on the application of the owner of the property.

Land Titles Plus (LT Plus) properties upgraded from LTCQ with the additional guarantee against any mature claims for adverse possession

LT Absolute properties are subject to any claim by the Crown to land owned by a corporation that ceased to exist during its ownership of the land. In addition, *Planning Act* compliance is not guaranteed.

LTCQ properties guarantee *Planning Act* compliance and corporate existence but only up to the date the title was converted to LTCQ. You must still check for *Planning Act* compliance and corporate existence after the conversion date (which will be indicated on the parcel register). You must also check LTCQ properties for any pre-existing mature claims for adverse possession, prescription, or misdescription because these claims are not eliminated in the conversion process. As discussed in chapter 3, Estates and Interests in Land, generally, it is not possible to acquire possessory title to land that is registered in the Land Titles system.

LT Plus properties have all the guarantees of LTCQ properties and also guarantee against any mature claims for adverse possession.

If the property is in Land Titles (either LT Absolute, LTCQ, or LT Plus), you can do the search from your office using the Teraview software. You must open a Teraview docket for the transaction. Be sure to name both the purchaser and the vendor when identifying the transaction, and include your instructing lawyer's name as the solicitor for the "party to." The steps for searching title are listed below.

1. Obtain a copy of the parcel register.
2. Obtain the whiteprint of the plan of subdivision or a copy of any other plan that affects the land.
3. Obtain a copy of the transfer to the current owner and any other registered interests that remain outstanding.
4. Review outstanding instruments.
5. Conduct an execution search against the current owner only. There is no need to search against prior owners.
6. Conduct a *Planning Act* search of adjoining property if the land is not a whole lot on a plan of subdivision.
7. Conduct a corporate owner search if there are any corporate owners on title.
8. Conduct a subsearch by checking the parcel register just before registration. Land Titles abstract indexes are updated immediately following the registration of a new instrument affecting the property. Therefore, there are no day books.

SUMMARY OF TITLE SEARCH VARIATIONS IN THE LAND REGISTRY AND LAND TITLES SYSTEMS

There are a number of variations in title searching practices as a result of the existence of the two systems of land registration, and because of the effects of automation and other POLARIS initiatives. It is easy to become confused. The following summary of the various possible title searches may be helpful.

Registry System Searches

- **Registry System Non-Automated**
  - The property is totally non-automated and in the Registry system.
  - Conduct a standard 40-year search using paper abstract books only.
- **Parcelized Day Forward Registry (PDFR)**
  - Registry records for the property have been computerized as of a certain automation date (and a PIN has been assigned).
  - The property has *not* been converted to Land Titles.
  - Conduct a 40-year search using both the computerized and paper records.
- **Automated Registry**
  - Records for this property have been fully automated but have not yet been converted to Land Titles. Most properties are transferred to the Land Titles system once they are automated. Only a small percentage of Registry properties are fully automated yet are not transferred into Land Titles, usually because of an unresolved title issue.
  - Conduct a full 40-year search using Teraview.

Land Titles System Searches

- **Land Titles Non-Automated**
  - Obtain copies of the relevant pages in the parcel register.
  - Instruments that no longer affect the land are ruled off.
  - Review documents that are currently shown on title.
  - Title is subject to the qualifiers listed in section 44(1) of the *Land Titles Act*.
  - Title is subject to *Planning Act* considerations.
  - Title is not subject to adverse possession claims.

- **Automated Land Titles (LT Absolute)**
  - These are original Land Titles system properties that have been automated.
  - Obtain the computerized parcel printout by using the PIN.
  - Title is subject to the qualifiers listed in section 44(1) of the *Land Titles Act*.
  - Title is subject to *Planning Act* considerations.
  - Title is not subject to adverse possession claims.
- **Land Titles Conversion Qualified (LTCQ)**
  - These are Registry system properties that have been both automated and converted from Registry to Land Titles.
  - Title remains subject to any adverse possession claims in existence when the property was converted.
  - Title is confirmed for *Planning Act* compliance as of the date of conversion, but you must check for compliance after that date.
  - Title is protected with respect to Crown claims against land as a result of the dissolution of any corporate owners prior to the conversion.
  - Any other Crown claims are also excluded as of the date the property was converted.
- **Land Titles Plus (LT Plus)**
  - These are LTCQ properties that have been upgraded to LT Plus on application by the owner.
  - Title is protected against adverse possession claims.

REFERENCES

Business Corporations Act, RSO 1990, c. B.16.

Fire v. Longtin, [1995] 4 SCR 3, (1995), 128 DLR (4th) 767.

Land Titles Act, RSO 1990, c. L.5.

Planning Act, RSO 1990, c. P.13.

Registry Act, RSO 1990, c. R.20.

Vendors and Purchasers Act, RSO 1990, c. V.2.

REVIEW QUESTIONS

1. Why is it necessary to search the title to property?
2. Who conducts a title search?
3. When is a title search conducted?
4. Where is a title search conducted?
5. What is the major difference between a Registry system search and a Land Titles system search?
6. What are the steps in a Registry system search?
7. What are the three different types or classifications of Land Titles properties, and what are the title qualifications and exceptions for each?
8. What are the steps in a search under the Land Titles system?

FIGURE 13.1 Abstract Index for Lot 57, Concession 6, Township of Whitford

Abstract Index
Répertoire par lot

Township of Whitford Lot 57 Plan/Concession 6 Page 3

Ontario

Registration Number / Numéro d'enregistrement	Instrument Type / Type d'acte	Registration Date / Date d'enregistrement YY/MM/DD (AA/MM/JJ)	Parties from / Parties	Parties to / Parties	Consideration / Contrepartie	Land/Remarks / Bien-fonds/Observations
42347	Grant	51/Sept./15	Herbert George Smith	Walter Fitzgerald	$6,000.00	Pt., commencing at S.E. <
44796	Grant	77/Aug./14	Walter Fitzgerald	Willard Marshall	$9,500.00	as in 42347
~~44797~~	~~Mort.~~	~~77/Aug./14~~	~~Willard Marshall~~	~~Royal Bank of Canada~~	~~$5,000.00~~	~~as in 44796~~ R 83/04/11
75581	Transfer	85/Apr./2	MARSHALL, Willard	GUNTHER, Fritz	$6,000.00	Pt. on N'ly boundary (150 ft. x 150 ft.)
76384	Transfer	85/May/28	MARSHALL, Willard	MARSHALL, Alexander MARSHALL, Wanda, jt.	$12,000.00	As in 44796, s.+e. land in 75581
~~76385~~	~~Charge~~	~~85/May/28~~	~~MARSHALL, Alexander MARSHALL, Wanda~~	~~MARSHALL, Willard~~	~~$10,000.00~~	~~as in 76384~~ R 85/12/12
84336	Transfer	85/Nov./23	MARSHALL, Alexander MARSHALL, Wanda	Stavros Subdivisions Ltd.	$300,000.00	Pt. commencing at S.E. < 500 ft. x 2000 ft.
		86/Dec/2	PLAN 1209			
99744	Transfer	90/Mar. 29	MARSHALL, Alexander MARSHALL, Wanda	BILLINGS, Harvey	$60,000.00	Pt. as in 76384, s.+e. land in 84336

10321 (88) FORM 1 Continued on/Suite à la page

Note: The search notes for the property in the abstract book page shown here are found in the appendix to chapter 19, Reviewing the Search of Title, and are examined in detail in the text of chapter 19.

FIGURE 13.2 Abstract Index for Lot 11, Plan 1209, Township of Whitford

Abstract Index
Répertoire par lot

Township of Whitford Lot 11 Plan/Concession 1209 Page 1

Ontario

Registration Number / Numéro d'enregistrement	Instrument Type / Type d'acte	Registration Date / Date d'enregistrement YY/MM/DD AA/MM/JJ	Parties from / Parties	Parties to / Parties	Consideration / Contrepartie	Land/Remarks / Bien-fonds/Observations
84922	Bylaw	88/Feb./2	Re: Part Lot control			
90248	Notice of Agreement	89/Jan./15	Stavros Subdivisions Ltd.	The Corp. of the Twp. of Whitford	$2.00	All and O.L.
91764	Transfer	89/Feb/19	Stavros Subdivisions Ltd.	McTAVISH, Duncan McTAVISH, Marla	$35,000.00	All
~~91765~~	~~Charge~~	~~89/Feb/19~~	~~McTAVISH, Duncan McTAVISH, Marla~~	~~TORONTO-DOMINION BANK~~	~~$25,000.00~~	~~All~~ 92/06/15
	See DEPOSIT NO. 148902					
153117	Transfer	92/May/2	McTAVISH, Marla	BOND, Frederick COULTER, Suzanne	$110,000.00	All
~~153118~~	~~Charge~~	~~92/May/2~~	~~BOND, Frederick COULTER, Suzanne~~	~~TORONTO-DOMINION BANK~~	~~$85,000.00~~	~~All~~ 97/05/04
~~153119~~	~~Charge~~	~~92/May/2~~	~~BOND, Frederick COULTER, Suzanne~~	~~BOND, Allister~~	~~$10,000.00~~	~~All~~ 97/05/04
	See DEPOSIT NO. 170003					
170004	Transfer	97/03/15	BOND, Frederick COULTER, Suzanne	BAKER, Murphy R. BAKER, Leslie T., j.t.	$170,000.00	All
170005	Charge	97/03/15	BAKER, Murphy R. BAKER, Leslie T.	BANK OF NOVA SCOTIA	$65,000.00	All
191436	Transfer	02/09/02	BAKER, Murphy BAKER, Leslie	MERCIER, Francois LAFRAMBOISE, Huguette Marie, j.t.	$219,000.00	All

10321 (88) FORM 1 Continued on/Suite à la page

Note: The search notes for the property in the abstract book page shown here are found in the appendix to chapter 19, Reviewing the Search of Title, and are examined in detail in the text of chapter 19.

FIGURE 13.2 Concluded

Ontario

Abstract Index
Répertoire par lot

Township of Whitford Lot 11 Plan/Concession 1209 Page 2

Registration Number / Numéro d'enregistrement	Instrument Type / Type d'acte	Registration Date / Date d'enregistrement YY/AA MM/MM DD/JJ	Parties from / Parties	Parties to / Parties	Consideration / Contrepartie	Land/Remarks / Bien-fonds/Observations
191437	Charge	02/09/02	MERCIER, Francois LAFRAMBOISE, Huguette Marie	TORONTO-DOMINION BANK	$40,000.00	All
192600	Charge	02/11/02	MERCIER, Francois MERCIER, Huguette Marie	ABC COMPANY LTD.	$15,060.00	All

10321 (88) FORM 1

Continued on/Suite à la page

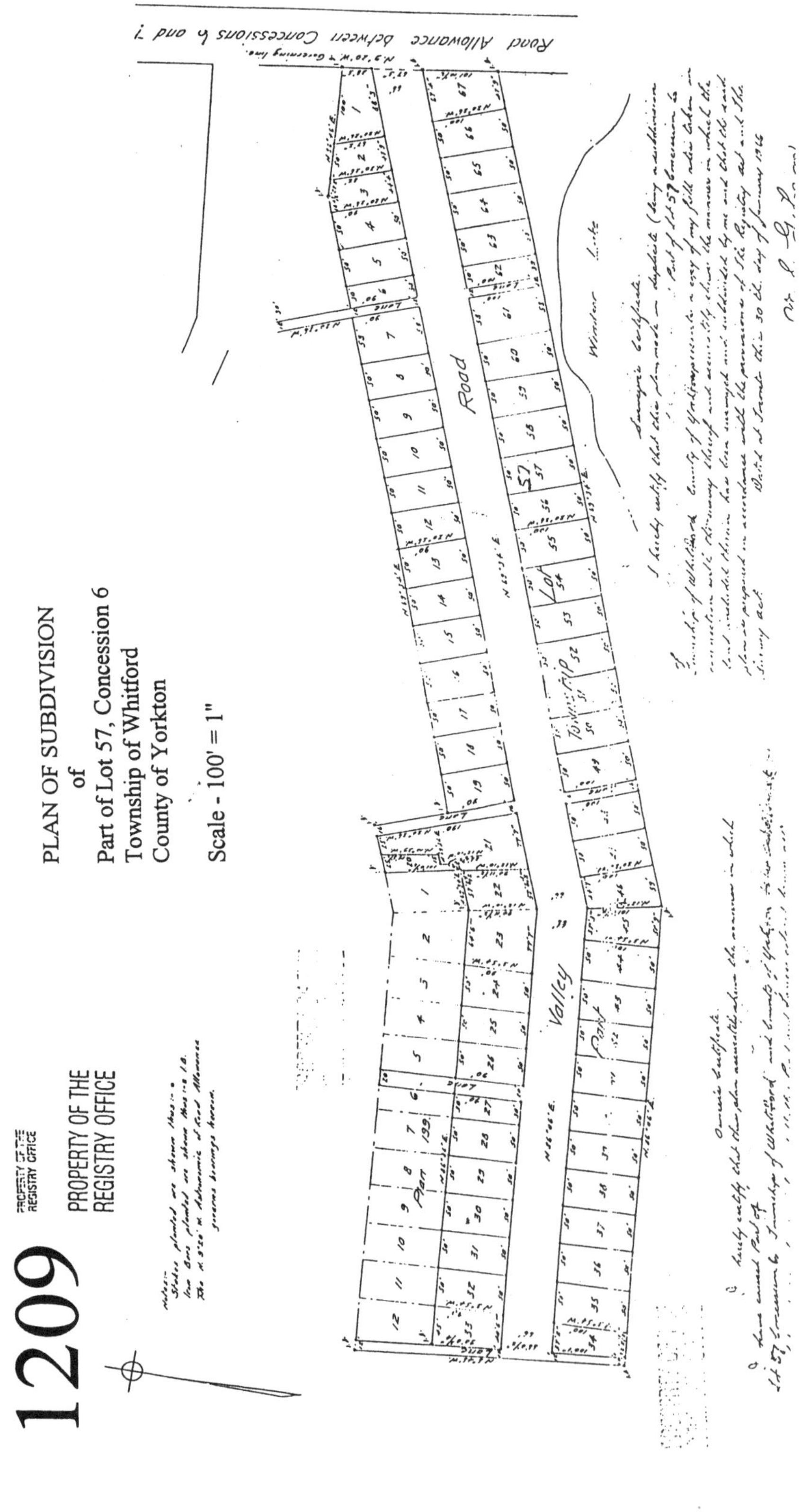

FIGURE 13.3 Whiteprint of Plan 1209, Township of Whitford

FIGURE 13.4 Chain of Title for Lot 11, Plan 1209, Township of Whitford

Willard Marshall (August 14, 1977)

↓

Alexander Marshall and Wanda Marshall (j.t.) (May 28, 1985)

↓

Stavros Subdivisions Ltd. (November 23, 1985)

↓

~~Duncan McTavish~~ and Marla McTavish (j.t.) (February 19, 1989)

↓

Frederick Bond and Suzanne Coulter (May 2, 1992)

↓

Murphy R. Baker and Leslie T. Baker (j.t.) (March 15, 1997)

↓

François Mercier and Huguette Marie Laframboise (j.t.) (September 2, 2002)

Note: The diagonal line through Duncan McTavish's name signifies that he died, leaving Marla McTavish as the surviving joint tenant.

PART III

The Standard Residential Real Estate Transaction

CHAPTER 14

Opening and Organizing a Real Estate File

When opening a real estate file, you should focus on organizing the file and recording deadlines. The general principles and concerns discussed in this chapter apply in all law firms, although the specific procedures will vary from office to office.

FILE OPENING

Whenever a lawyer or law firm is retained to act on a matter, a file is **opened**, or started. A single client may retain a law firm to act on several different matters. There should be a separate file opened for each matter. As a law clerk, you will probably open the file.

open a file
start a file

There are a number of steps involved in opening a file. At the end, there will be a physical file in existence for keeping the relevant documents and correspondence relating to the matter. The existence of the file will be noted in various law firm records.

You must assign a name to the file. Although the procedure will vary from office to office, usually the name of the file is made up of the client's name — family name first — with a "Re:" line stating the matter to which the file relates. For example, if Harold Smith is purchasing a property at 123 Elm Street, Toronto, his file might be named: Smith, Harold, Re: Purchase of 123 Elm Street, Toronto.

You must make a record of the file in the law firm's general index of files. This may be accomplished manually or by computer. Usually a number is assigned to the file as well. Each lawyer or law firm has a system for assigning file numbers. Make sure there is a record of the file in the law firm's accounting system so that fees, disbursements, and moneys received with respect to the file will be accounted for.

Use a file folder to hold the documents and correspondence relating to the matter. Some law firms use specially designed real estate file folders that have checklists printed on them. Other firms use different coloured file folders for different types of files. Place a label on the folder setting out the file name and number. Note the names, addresses, and telephone numbers of the client, the other lawyer, and other relevant parties on the file folder where the information will be easy to find. Some firms have labels or other printed forms they use for recording this information.

DIARIZING

diarize
record on a calendar the dates by which work must be completed

In every real estate file, there will be a number of deadlines that you must not miss, including the requisition date and the closing date. These dates must be diarized. **Diarizing** is a way of reminding you and the lawyer of the dates by which work must be completed. Diarizing is done well before the deadline, so that when the date in question approaches, you can ensure that the work will be performed by that date.

There are various methods of diarizing. The simplest method uses a standard desk or pocket diary. Let's say that you are reviewing a file on January 2 and note that an important document must be prepared and delivered by February 1. You will, on January 2, turn to the page for February 1 in your diary and make an entry on that page, such as "To Do — prepare and deliver Smith transfer." When you arrive at your office on February 1 and open your diary, you will be reminded of that deadline. Another, more common method uses a calendar program installed on your personal computer.

Whatever diarizing method you use, the method will work only for those dates and tasks you enter into the diarizing system. Give top priority to determining the relevant deadlines in any file and to entering those dates into the system. Failure to meet requisite deadlines may result in professional negligence claims being made against the law firm, and failure to diarize the relevant dates may result in a denial of coverage under the law firm's errors and omissions insurance policy.

Accordingly, as soon as you open the file, you should review the agreement of purchase and sale for relevant deadlines and enter those deadlines into the law firm's diarizing system. You should also maintain your own system as a backup. Dates to be diarized include

- *any condition dates* these are dates until which the agreement of purchase and sale is conditional, and by which steps may have to be taken to firm up the agreement of purchase and sale;
- *the requisition date* this is the date by which any requisitions on title must be submitted to the vendor's lawyer; and
- *the closing date* this is the date on which the transaction is to be completed.

In addition to diarizing the deadline itself, you should make an entry some time before the deadline to allow yourself time to start the work in advance of the actual deadline.

As the file progresses, you should also diarize a date to check on responses to your inquiry letters. To avoid cluttering your diary, make one entry for all of the letters relating to a file. For example, on January 2 you write to the tax office, the building department, the gas company, the water department, and hydro. You can reasonably expect responses within three weeks. You should make an entry in your diarizing system for January 23, such as "Smith file — awaiting letter responses." When you check your diary on January 23, you will be reminded that you should have received responses to your letters. You will then check the Smith file and call or write to the offices that have not responded to your letters.

Do not forget to check your diary daily.

FILE ORGANIZATION

There are many different kinds of documents in a real estate file. There are letters to and from your law firm (correspondence), title searches, and various other documents. You should organize the file in such a way that the different types of documents are kept separately and can be easily identified and located.

Keep correspondence separately, either on a brad, clipped together, or in a separate subfile. Unless the instructing lawyer specifically requires otherwise, file both incoming and outgoing correspondence together in reverse-chronological order — that is, the oldest correspondence is at the bottom and the newest at the top. Make a copy of every letter that is sent by the law firm, and place the copies in the file together with the original response letters.

Make notes of any telephone or other conversations, and keep these notes in the file. Some lawyers maintain a separate subfile for notes; others file notes in chronological order along with the correspondence.

Set up and label separate subfiles to hold

- all title search documents;
- closing documentation; and
- any mortgage documentation.

Finally, insert the agreement of purchase and sale in the file in an easily accessible location. Many lawyers attach the agreement to the inside back cover of the file folder.

CHECKLISTS

Use a checklist in every real estate file. This is a list of the various things that must be prepared, requested, or received in a real estate file and serves as a quick way of ascertaining what is outstanding on the file at any given time. Whenever you perform a task or receive a document, make a notation on the checklist. When you want to confirm whether a document has been received, you simply look at the checklist — you will not have to search through the entire file.

If there is no checklist on the file folder itself, you should use the one in general use in the law firm, or prepare one and attach it to the inside front cover of the file. There are a lot of documents and steps to keep track of in a real estate transaction. If you do not use a checklist, you may neglect something until it is too late. Figure 14.1 is an example of a checklist for use in a purchase transaction.

FIGURE 14.1 Purchase Checklist

- ❑ Letter to client & checklist: Fee $ _______ Fee mrtg. $ _______ LTT ________
- ❑ Letter to vendor's lawyer
- ❑ Order search from ____________________ Date ordered: ________________
- ❑ Receive & review search
  - ❑ Executions OK _______________ Declaration? ______________________
  - ❑ Acknowledgement & direction for registration of transfer/deed — OR — LTT affidavit
- ❑ Letters to bldg./planning dept re: work orders, zoning, occupancy permits, set-backs, dev/subd. agt/heritage (if not ttl ins.)
- ❑ Receive & review complete (if e-reg) draft transfer
- ❑ Order tax certificate — ask re: local improvements, weed removal, drainage act, etc.
  - ❑ Survey: Send to client ❑ Check for encroachments, access, etc.
- ❑ Requisition letter Req. date: _______________________________
  - ❑ Title direction
  - ❑ Undertaking/warranty/bill of sale: insert extra warranties as in offer
  - ❑ Statutory declaration: refer to restrictions and/or compliance with agreements registered on title, etc.
- ❑ LSUC form of e-reg agreement: sign & send to vendor's lawyer
- ❑ Title insurance acknowledgement: add in reference to title matters, e.g., easements, noise controls, restrictive covenants, etc.
- ❑ Review statement of adjustments: check accuracy of figures
- ❑ REALTY TAXES: get copy of current tax bill — check if instalments paid
- ❑ If property less than 2 years old, get holdback for supplemental tax assessment
- ❑ Utilities: Water arrears o/s _______ Hydro arrears (if not privatized) o/s _____
  - ❑ Estimated account prepared & sent Funds reqd. $ ______________________
  - ❑ Discharge statement ❑ Redirection re: funds
  - ❑ Undertaking to discharge signed by lawyer
- ❑ Closing letter to lawyer enclosing $ and documents ❑ KEYS: to be held or delivered
- ❑ Closing memo to agent ❑ LTT & reg'n transferred to spec. trust acct or sent to agent
- ❑ Tax department advised of change of ownership
- ❑ Complete & send title insurance

MORTGAGE Mortgagee ________________________________

- ❑ Request agent to prepare mortgage
- ❑ Acknowledgement & direction for registration of mortgage
- ❑ Interim report to mortgage & request for funds ___________________________ NET ADVANCE $
- ❑ Acknowledgement standard charge terms [attach copy of SCT]
- ❑ Acknowledgement I act for all parties
- ❑ Insurance binder: check names, address, amount, mortgagee's name & address & if full insurable value
- ❑ Direction to pay funds (if required)
- ❑ Declaration (if required) re: principal residence, no secondary financing
- ❑ ID: get photocopy
- ❑ PAC form & VOID cheque (if required)
- ❑ Final report & cover letter
  - ❑ Report to client & statement of account

UNDERTAKINGS completed [list on file cover]

- ❑ Discharge of 1st mortgage ____
- ❑ Proof of payment of ____

REVIEW QUESTIONS

1. What are the steps involved in opening a file?
2. What is the purpose of diarizing?
3. List and describe three dates to be diarized on the opening of a real estate purchase file.
4. Briefly describe how a real estate file should be organized.
5. What is the purpose of a checklist, and how is it used?

CHAPTER 15

Reviewing the Agreement of Purchase and Sale

The agreement of purchase and sale is the document on which the entire real estate transaction is based. This chapter reviews the agreement of purchase and sale from your perspective as a law clerk who has received a fully executed agreement. It contains a clause-by-clause examination of the standard form of agreement and sale, and discusses particular items of importance, together with the steps you should take as you go through the agreement.

Most resale property transactions in Ontario are prepared on the Ontario Real Estate Association (OREA) form of agreement of purchase and sale. A copy of this form is reproduced as figure 15.1 at the end of the chapter. (A different version of the form, used for condominium resale transactions, is reproduced as figure 28.1.) Once you become familiar with the standard form of agreement and sale, you will review each executed agreement only for changes to the printed form and for terms set out in Schedule A.

THE PARTIES

The parties to the agreement of purchase and sale are the **seller** and the **buyer**. Most lawyers still refer to the seller as the vendor and the buyer as the purchaser. However, since the OREA form refers to buyer and seller, for this chapter only, we will use those terms.

seller
vendor of the property

buyer
purchaser of the property

Different steps are required depending on which party your firm represents.

The Seller

When you receive the completed search of title for review, you should make sure that the person named as the seller in the agreement of purchase and sale is, in fact, the registered owner of the property. If the seller is not the registered owner, there could be complications in the transaction. For example, if the person named as the seller in the agreement of purchase and sale is a different person from the registered owner shown in the search of title, you must get a transfer on closing from the registered owner (rather than the seller) to the buyer. If a transfer is offered from the seller, it may be necessary to first register on title a transfer from the registered owner to the seller. This situation might arise in the case of a new subdivision, where the land is still registered in the name of the subdivider rather than the builder, or in the case of a **flip**, where the property is purchased by a party and resold before the closing of the original purchase.

flip
resale of property before the closing of the original purchase

If the seller is a corporation, you must check its corporate status. Also, you will require supporting corporate documentation on or before closing to ensure that the corporation has the proper authority to sell the property and that an authorized person has signed the agreement.

If the seller is a partnership, you must find out the names of all partners because if the sale is outside the normal course of business, all partners must sign the transfer.

If the seller is an estate, there are very particular conveyancing requirements to be met.

The Buyer

Note the way the buyer is named in the agreement of purchase and sale. If the buyer wishes to take title in any other way, you must give the seller's lawyer a direction to that effect before the seller will give you a transfer made out in that way. For example, a direction will be necessary if only the wife signed the agreement but wishes to take title with her husband as joint tenants. If your law firm is acting for the buyer, you will have to prepare the direction. If your law firm is acting for the seller, you will have to make sure that you get a direction from the buyer on closing.

DESCRIPTION OF THE PROPERTY

Usually the property description line of the agreement of purchase and sale contains a municipal address, followed by the dimensions of the lot and a brief description.

For search of title and registration purposes, it is necessary to convert the municipal address to a lot and plan or concession number. You can get this information from the seller's solicitor, from a private title service, from the assessment or tax office, or, with a little bit of effort, from the land registry office.

If the property is subject to any easements (for example, a mutual driveway or an easement for repair and access), overhanging eaves, or other encroachments, they should be set out in the agreement. If any easements are specified, the buyer must accept title subject to them. If none are specified here, the buyer is not required to accept title subject to any easement subsequently disclosed on a search of title (other than minor easements for utilities and sewers). If an easement that is not mentioned in the agreement turns up on the title search, the lawyer will have to contact the client to determine whether title will be accepted subject to the easement. If the easement in question is minor, the client will often choose to close the transaction, but instructions from the client must be obtained.

If the property is part of a lot, compare the lot size as set out in the agreement of purchase and sale with the description in the last transfer of land to the property. If the property is a whole lot, compare it to the dimensions shown on the whiteprint of the plan of subdivision. Also, compare the lot size as set out in the agreement with the size of the lot as set out on any plan of survey.

With respect to plans of survey, the standard form agreement of purchase and sale requires an existing survey to be provided only if it is in the seller's possession. As soon as you receive the agreement, if there is no plan of survey attached to it, you should contact the seller's solicitor to obtain the lot and plan number of the property and a copy of any survey. If the seller has no survey, or the only survey available is not up to date, the lawyer should contact the buyer to get instructions about obtaining an up-to-date survey at the buyer's expense. If a new mortgage with an institutional lender is being placed on the property, the lender may insist that an up-to-date survey be obtained.

If the survey, the deed, or the whiteprint discloses any variation in size that is significantly different from that set out in the agreement of purchase and sale, you must immediately point this out so that the lawyer handling the file can contact the client for instructions.

PURCHASE PRICE

The amount of money shown in this part of the agreement of purchase and sale is not the amount that will actually have to be paid by the buyer on closing. The final amount is calculated in the statement of adjustments, but the purchase price is the starting point for that calculation. Mortgages assumed are deducted from the purchase price, as is any deposit paid. Other items are adjusted as well. It is the adjusted amount that the buyer must actually pay on closing.

The purchase price set out in the agreement is the amount on which land transfer tax is calculated.

DEPOSIT

The deposit may be paid by the buyer on presentation of the offer or upon acceptance of the offer. It is generally paid to the seller's real estate broker (the listing broker) to be held in trust pending completion of the agreement. It is then applied to the broker's commission on the transaction following closing.

Many agreements contain an added term that requires interest to be paid on the deposit. The usual provision requires the seller's broker to place the deposit into an interest-bearing account with interest being paid or credited to the buyer on or after closing. If there is such a provision in the agreement, make a note to ensure that the buyer receives the interest on or after closing.

This paragraph ends with a statement that the buyer agrees to pay the balance of the purchase price as set out in Schedule A attached to the agreement. This clause usually provides that the buyer will pay the balance, subject to adjustments, on completion, by certified cheque or bank draft.

SPECIAL TERMS

Following the above provision, there is a line indicating that a schedule or schedules may be attached, by which "customized" terms may be inserted into the agreement. Examples of such terms include:

- *Mortgages to be assumed* Particulars of the mortgage will be set out. When you get the search of title, check to make sure that it shows a mortgage that complies with those particulars. All other mortgages must be discharged on or before closing.
- *Conditions* The agreement of purchase and sale may be conditional until a specified date on the happening of various events such as financing, inspections, or municipal approval. Any condition date should be diarized because, depending on the condition, some action may have to be taken. If the agreement is conditional, the client may not wish to incur the expense of a title search until the agreement becomes binding. This may cause a problem if there is an early requisition or closing date. In this case, the lawyer should get specific written instructions from the client.
- *Rights of inspection* Some agreements provide the buyer with the right to inspect the condition of the property or obtain measurements on one or more occasions before closing.
- *Survey* The seller may have agreed to provide an up-to-date survey.
- *Tenancies* If the buyer is assuming any tenancies, the details will be provided here, and you will require supporting documentation on closing.
- *Warranties* If the seller is making a specific warranty such as the state of a well or septic system on a rural property, it should be set out here. Similarly, there may be warranties regarding the working order of any chattels and fixtures.

IRREVOCABILITY (PARAGRAPH 1)

This paragraph sets out the length of time the offer is open for acceptance by the offeree. Once the offer is accepted, this paragraph has no relevance.

COMPLETION DATE (PARAGRAPH 2)

The completion date is the day fixed for closing. You should make sure that the date is not a Saturday, Sunday, or statutory holiday. If it is, you must make arrangements with the other side to change the closing date. Any change to the closing date must be *confirmed in writing*.

Diarize the closing date. It is also a good idea to diarize a date approximately one week in advance of closing as a reminder to have the file ready for that date.

This paragraph states that the agreement is to be completed by no later than 6 p.m. and also states that, unless the agreement provides otherwise, **vacant possession** of the property is to be given to the buyer on closing. Vacant possession will not be provided if the property is a rental property and the premises are tenant-occupied. In this case, you will have to prepare additional documents to deal with the tenancies on closing.

vacant possession
free or empty of all people and chattels

NOTICES (PARAGRAPH 3)

This paragraph deals with delivery of any notices under the agreement. The seller appoints the listing broker as agent for the purpose of giving and receiving notices. The buyer appoints the cooperating broker if the cooperating broker is, in fact, representing the interests of the buyer. Also, notice is deemed to be properly given if delivered to the address for service that the parties provide in the acknowledgement section of the agreement or faxed to the fax number provided by the parties.

CHATTELS INCLUDED (PARAGRAPH 4)

If **chattels** (movable possessions such as appliances and draperies) are included in the purchase price, they will be specified in this paragraph. Where chattels are listed, the buyer will have to allocate a value to them for the purpose of **land transfer tax** and **retail sales tax** calculations. In addition, the lawyer handling the file may wish to obtain a *Personal Property Security Act* (PPSA) search and may require a bill of sale on closing.

chattels
movable possessions not attached to the real property

land transfer tax
provincial (and possibly municipal) tax on the purchase of land

retail sales tax
provincial tax on the purchase of chattels

FIXTURES EXCLUDED (PARAGRAPH 5)

Fixtures, such as broadloom and interior doors, are automatically included in the sale of a house. However, sometimes a seller will want the right to take certain fixtures out of the house (for example, a dining room chandelier). In order for the seller to do so, those fixtures must be listed in this paragraph.

fixtures
immovable possessions attached to the real property

RENTAL ITEMS (PARAGRAPH 6)

In order to avoid any confusion, equipment that is rented (for example, a hot water heater), and therefore not included in the purchase, is set out in this paragraph.

GST (PARAGRAPH 7)

This paragraph states whether goods and services tax (GST) is included in the purchase price or to be paid in addition to the purchase price. If the transaction is not subject to GST, the seller agrees to certify that fact.

TITLE SEARCH (PARAGRAPH 8)

title requisition request made to the vendor (seller) to clear up a problem found during the search of title

requisition date deadline by which the purchaser (buyer) must submit any title requisitions to the vendor (seller)

This paragraph sets out the date by which the buyer must complete the title search and submit any **title requisitions** to the seller. Requisitions are requests to clear up problems found with the title during the title search. This deadline is called the **requisition date**, and most title requisitions must be received by the seller by that date. If a requisition is received by the seller on or before the requisition date and the seller cannot properly answer it, the buyer may be able to negotiate a reduction in the purchase price or back out of the contract. If a requisition is received by the seller after the requisition date, the buyer may not have the right to insist on its satisfaction or resolution before closing.

There are different types of title requisitions. Some may be submitted until closing, while others must be submitted by the requisition date. Requisitions relating to matters of contract, matters of conveyance, and matters going to the root of title may be submitted until closing. Requisitions on matters of title not going to the root of title must be submitted by the requisition date. The distinctions between the various types of requisitions are far from clear. The most prudent course is therefore to have all of your title requisitions delivered by this date. For a further discussion of title requisitions, see chapter 18, Requisitions: An Overview, and chapter 20, The Requisition Letter.

The buyer is given a longer period of time to submit requisitions with respect to work orders, zoning, and the insurability of the principal building. This is because there is usually a long wait to receive an answer to zoning and work order inquiries from municipal building departments. The agreement also gives the seller's consent to the release of this information.

When you receive the agreement of purchase and sale, check the requisition date. If it is too soon after a condition date, the lawyer for the buyer may wish to have the requisition date extended to have more time to complete the search of title. Any extension of the requisition date must be agreed to by the seller and *confirmed in writing.*

Diarize the requisition date. Also make a diary entry for approximately one week before to ensure that the requisitions will be ready on time. Requisitions must be *received* by the seller on or before the requisition date, so it is not a good idea to mail the requisition letter. It is common practice to transmit the requisition letter by facsimile or to have it delivered by courier. If the requisition date is a weekend or holiday, the requisitions must be in the hands of the seller's lawyer *before* that date. The time period is not extended to the next business day.

FUTURE USE (PARAGRAPH 9)

The previous paragraph also contains a promise that the current use of the property may be lawfully continued. This paragraph makes it clear that there is no promise that any other intended use of the property is lawful, unless the agreement specifically states that it is. If the buyer wishes to purchase the property only if it can be put to a specific use, the agreement should be stated to be conditional on that use being lawful.

TITLE (PARAGRAPH 10)

In this paragraph, the seller agrees that title is free from all encumbrances, registered restrictions, charges, and liens except:

- *As specified in the agreement of purchase and sale* This exception would include such things as mortgages to be assumed, easements, encroachments, and so on that are specifically dealt with elsewhere in the agreement.
- *Registered restrictions that run with the land provided that such are complied with* If any registered restrictions (also called restrictive covenants) are found during the search of title, the buyer cannot insist that they be removed from title, *provided that they have been complied with*. Accordingly, if the search discloses such restrictions, you will have to requisition proof that the restrictions have been complied with. Usually this proof takes the form of a statutory declaration or undertaking.
- *Any registered municipal agreements and registered agreements with publicly regulated utilities, provided that such have been complied with or security has been posted to ensure compliance and completion, as evidenced by a letter from the relevant municipality or regulated utility* This paragraph refers to subdivision agreements. The buyer cannot insist that any of these agreements be discharged, but can only require proof of compliance or posting of security.
- *Minor easements for the supply of domestic utility or telephone services to the property or adjacent properties* The buyer cannot object to the existence of easements that include telephone and electrical lines and sewers servicing the property and adjoining properties. This exception covers minor easements only — not hydro towers or trunk sewer lines.
- *Any easements for drainage, storm, or sanitary sewers, public utility lines, telephone lines, cable television lines, or other services that do not materially affect the present use of the property* This exception prevents the buyer from demanding the removal of any easement for the provision of services that does not have a major impact on the present use of the property.

The paragraph goes on to describe what happens if the buyer raises an objection to the title that the seller cannot or will not correct. If the buyer makes a valid objection to the title within the requisition period that the seller cannot or will not remove, and the buyer will not waive, the agreement ends. The buyer is entitled to receive the return of the deposit but no **damages** (compensation) in addition.

damages
financial compensation for losses arising out of a breach of contract

The paragraph concludes by stating the effect of failing to submit a title requisition on time: unless the defect is a matter going to the root of title, the buyer is deemed to have accepted title subject to the defect. In other words, the buyer must accept title subject to any defects (other than matters going to the root of title) that were not objected to in time.

CLOSING ARRANGEMENTS (PARAGRAPH 11)

This paragraph describes how the closing of the transaction will take place if it is to be done electronically. With electronic registration, the actual exchange of documents, keys, and money does not take place at the same time as the registration of the transfer. The parties agree that their lawyers will enter into a document registration agreement (DRA) in a form recommended by the Law Society of Upper Canada. This agreement sets out the terms of the closing.

If closing is not to be done electronically, it will take place at the appropriate land registry office.

DOCUMENTS AND DISCHARGE (PARAGRAPH 12)

This paragraph provides that the seller is not required to produce any title documents, including a survey, unless they are within the seller's possession or control. Any survey in the seller's possession must be delivered, if requested by the buyer, as soon as possible and before the requisition date.

institutional lender
a lender other than an individual, including a bank, trust company, credit union, or insurance company

This paragraph also deals with mortgages that are supposed to be discharged on closing. If the mortgagee is an **institutional lender** (a chartered bank, trust company, credit union, or insurance company), the buyer cannot insist that a discharge of the mortgage be registered on or before closing. If the discharge is not available in time for closing, the buyer agrees to accept the seller's solicitor's *personal* undertaking to obtain a discharge out of the closing funds and register the discharge within a reasonable time after closing, provided that the seller also gives the buyer

- a mortgage statement prepared by the mortgagee setting out the amount that is required to pay off the mortgage and get the discharge; and
- a direction to pay out of the closing funds the required amount directly to the mortgagee if the lawyers are not using a real-time electronic funds transfer system.

This provision is necessary because in most cases the seller will not be able to obtain a discharge of mortgage from an institutional lender in time for the closing. An institutional lender will not usually prepare a discharge of mortgage until it has actually received the discharge funds. Without this provision in the agreement of purchase and sale, the buyer does not have to accept an undertaking from the seller to discharge the mortgage, and the seller would have to have a discharge of mortgage available on closing.

If a seller is seeking to rely on the provisions of this paragraph, the seller's lawyer must, on closing, give the buyer's lawyer a direction with regard to funds, a mortgage statement, and a solicitor's personal undertaking.

This provision applies only to institutional mortgages. It does not apply to a mortgage with a private lender. Accordingly, if there is a private mortgage on title that is not being assumed by the buyer, the seller must have a discharge of that mortgage available on closing. This can put the seller in a very difficult position because the seller must discharge the mortgage in order to complete the sale but needs the money from the sale to discharge the mortgage. If your law firm is acting for a seller, and you find that there is a private mortgage on title that is not being assumed by the buyer, you will have to take special steps to make sure that the seller is in a position to provide proper title on closing.

You must contact the mortgagee to obtain a discharge in time for closing. The mortgagee might be willing to prepare a discharge before the closing and give it to the seller's solicitor to be held **in escrow** pending receipt of the discharge funds from the closing proceeds. In that case, the seller's solicitor would act as the mortgagee's agent on closing and receive the discharge funds and register the discharge on the mortgagee's behalf. Instead, the mortgagee may agree to prepare the discharge in advance and arrange for the mortgagee's own lawyer to attend at the closing to receive the money and hand over the discharge.

in escrow
holding of funds or documents by a third party to be released only on certain specified conditions

There will be some mortgagees, however, who will refuse to prepare a discharge until they actually have the discharge funds. In such a case, if the seller wishes to be in a position to close the transaction, he or she will have to borrow the funds required to discharge the mortgage and repay the loan out of the proceeds of sale.

INSPECTION (PARAGRAPH 13)

In the first part of this paragraph, the buyer acknowledges having had the opportunity to inspect the property before submitting the offer, and that acceptance by the seller constitutes a binding agreement of purchase and sale. The buyer may believe that he or she was misled and may allege non-disclosure or misrepresentation, but the success of such an allegation will depend on the extent to which the buyer relied on the non-disclosure or misrepresentation. Where the matter could have been easily discovered on an inspection, this clause serves as evidence that the buyer, in fact, had the chance to inspect the property. This clause is also relied upon by the seller in a situation where the property is smaller than stated in the agreement, but the lot is fully fenced and the boundaries are apparent on examination of the property.

In the latter part of this paragraph, the buyer acknowledges having had the opportunity to include a requirement for a building inspector to examine the property, and acknowledges having waived that right (unless there is an added clause in a schedule allowing for an inspection).

INSURANCE (PARAGRAPH 14)

This paragraph states that the buildings remain at the risk of the seller until closing. This means that any loss prior to the closing date would be the seller's, not the buyer's. It is up to the seller to maintain any insurance on the property. If the buildings are substantially damaged before closing, the seller holds any insurance proceeds in trust for the buyer. The buyer has a choice: to terminate the agreement and receive a refund of the deposit, or to take the insurance proceeds and close the transaction.

This paragraph also states that the seller's insurance will not be transferred to the buyer on closing. It is up to the buyer to obtain a new insurance policy. If the buyer is assuming a mortgage or if the seller is taking back a mortgage, the buyer must give the seller proof that there is enough insurance to cover the mortgage. Even if there is no mortgage, the buyer's lawyer should always advise the buyer to arrange insurance on the premises to take effect as of the closing date. Send a letter to the buyer confirming this advice.

PLANNING ACT (PARAGRAPH 15)

This paragraph provides that the agreement creates an interest in the property only if the *Planning Act* is complied with. The agreement is void if there was a contravention of the *Planning Act*. The seller also agrees to proceed diligently and pay any expenses involved in obtaining any necessary *Planning Act* consent by the closing date.

DOCUMENT PREPARATION (PARAGRAPH 16)

The seller is responsible for the preparation of the transfer, with the exception of the land transfer tax affidavit, which must be prepared and signed by the buyer. The buyer is responsible for the preparation of any mortgage back. If the buyer requests it, the seller must complete the *Planning Act* statements contained in the transfer.

RESIDENCY (PARAGRAPH 17)

capital gains tax
federal tax levied on the profit realized when capital property, other than a principal residence, is sold

When non-residents of Canada sell real property, the government requires them to make immediate arrangements to pay any **capital gains tax** as a result of the sale. If the seller does not pay any capital gains tax owing, the buyer will be liable for it. The buyer will have no tax liability if

- the seller is, in the language of the *Income Tax Act*, "not a non-resident" of Canada; or
- the seller is a non-resident but either owes no tax or has made satisfactory arrangements to pay any tax owing.

A buyer will therefore want either proof that the seller is not a non-resident of Canada or a certificate from the government stating that the non-resident seller either owes no tax or has made satisfactory arrangements for payment.

This paragraph protects the buyer by allowing the buyer a credit against the purchase price in the amount that must be paid to the Canada Revenue Agency to satisfy the non-resident seller's tax liability. In other words, the buyer may hold back sufficient funds on closing to cover the tax liability (up to 25 percent of the purchase price). The buyer will not claim this credit if the seller provides the buyer with the government certificate or provides a declaration that the seller is not a non-resident of Canada as of the date of closing.

ADJUSTMENTS (PARAGRAPH 18)

When completing the statement of adjustments, the expenses listed in this paragraph are to be apportioned between the seller and the buyer to the date of closing. The buyer assumes responsibility as of the date of closing. Accordingly, if the closing is on the 265th day of the year, the seller's share is for 264 days and the buyer's share is for the balance of the year.

TIME LIMITS (PARAGRAPH 19)

This paragraph states that time is in all respects of the essence of the agreement. Time can be extended or abridged by agreement in writing signed by the seller and the buyer or their respective solicitors.

If a contract does not contain this kind of provision, time is not of the essence. This means that performance of the contract is not required to take place on the date specified in the agreement, but may take place any time before the contract is terminated by the other party.

With this provision, any missed deadlines are non-negotiable unless they have been waived in writing. For example, if the requisition date is missed, nothing can be done. If the closing date is missed, the deal is at an end, and the defaulting party will be liable for that result.

As a result of this provision, if the closing date, requisition date, or any other date is changed, you must confirm the change in writing. The confirming letter should always state that time is to continue to be of the essence.

TENDER (PARAGRAPH 20)

Either party may **tender** (present) money or documents to the other party, or to his or her lawyer, on the closing date. Money may be tendered by bank draft or by certified cheque.

What is the significance of tender? If one party tries to back out of the deal, the other party may want to continue to rely on the agreement of purchase and sale, and sue for **specific performance** (a court order that the transaction be completed). To be successful in such an action, the plaintiff must prove that he or she was ready, willing, and able to complete his or her part of the bargain — in other words, ready to close on the closing date. A party proves this by presenting to the other party executed copies of all necessary closing documents or funds.

tender
presentation of executed copies of all closing documents or funds to the other party in a real estate transaction

specific performance
court order requiring a transaction to be completed; a type of remedy for breach of contract

FAMILY LAW ACT (PARAGRAPH 21)

By the terms of this paragraph, the seller warrants that no **spousal consent** under the *Family Law Act* is required to complete the transaction. The seller's spouse is usually required to consent to the sale of a matrimonial home, even if the seller is the sole registered owner. Unless the spouse has signed the agreement of purchase

spousal consent
consent of the spouse of the owner on title to the transfer or mortgage of a matrimonial home, required under the *Family Law Act*

and sale, he or she cannot be forced to consent to the ultimate transfer of title. Without the required consent, the transfer may be set aside. If spousal consent is necessary but a spouse has not signed the agreement and refuses to consent to the transfer, the buyer's only recourse is to sue the seller for breach of warranty.

Before the enactment of the *Land Registration Reform Act*, deeds and transfers contained an affidavit of age and spousal status indicating whether spousal consent was required to complete the transfer. Now there is simply an unsworn statement in the transfer. Some law firms require supporting **statutory declarations** from the seller.

statutory declaration
sworn statement given by a person that attests to a given set of facts

UFFI (PARAGRAPH 22)

UFFI
ureaformaldehyde foam insulation

UFFI is the acronym for ureaformaldehyde foam insulation. A number of homes were insulated with UFFI in the 1970s. It was later discovered that UFFI caused health problems, and homes that were insulated with UFFI suffered a loss in resale value.

In this paragraph, the seller warrants that, during the time the seller has owned the property, the seller has not caused the property to be insulated with UFFI, and that, to the best of the seller's knowledge, no building on the property has ever been insulated with UFFI. This warranty is stated to survive and not merge (end) on closing. Accordingly, the buyer will require the seller to deliver a warranty to this effect on closing.

CONSUMER REPORTS (PARAGRAPH 23)

This paragraph warns the buyer that the seller may obtain a consumer credit report on the buyer. The seller may wish to do this if there will be a vendor take back mortgage from the buyer.

AGREEMENT IN WRITING (PARAGRAPH 24)

This paragraph states that there is no other agreement except as set out in the agreement of purchase and sale and that there are no collateral warranties or representations. It also states that, where there is a conflict between the printed form and any clauses inserted in the agreement, including those in schedules, the inserted clauses govern.

This paragraph also explains that "buyer" and "seller" mean purchaser and vendor, respectively.

SUCCESSORS AND ASSIGNS (PARAGRAPH 25)

This paragraph states that the agreement is binding on the parties' heirs, executors, successors, and assigns. For example, if the buyer died prior to closing, the estate trustee would be bound to close the transaction, regardless of the heirs' wishes.

SIGNATURES OF THE PARTIES

The buyer signs the form as offeror. The seller signs the form to signify acceptance of the offer, subject to any sign-backs.

By signing the agreement, the seller is also instructing the lawyer to pay to the listing broker the unpaid balance of the real estate commission out of the proceeds of sale. Keep this responsibility in mind when your law firm is acting for the seller.

SPOUSAL CONSENT

Below the signatures of the parties, there is a place for the seller's spouse to sign the agreement. By signing, the spouse consents to the transaction pursuant to the *Family Law Act* and agrees to sign any other necessary documents.

INFORMATION ON BROKERAGE(S)

This section applies in transactions where there are two real estate agents or brokers involved and confirms which one is representing each party. Usually the seller will list the property for sale with one broker (the listing broker) and the buyer will shop for a house with a different broker (the cooperating broker). The parties deal with individual agents working for that broker. In most cases, the listing broker represents the interests of the seller, and the cooperating broker represents the interests of the buyer. Sometimes both brokers act for the seller or one broker acts for both seller and buyer, and these representations must be clearly outlined.

Make a note of the identity of the individual real estate agent who listed the property. The agent can be helpful in a number of situations:

- If there were several sign-backs, you may find it difficult to read the agreement, but the agent can provide assistance.
- If the agreement is conditional, the agent will provide any amending agreements waiving the condition.
- If the agreement provides for the right to inspect the property, you will make arrangements for the inspection through the agent.
- If the deal becomes jeopardized in any way, the real estate agent (whose commission is then jeopardized as well) may be able to assist in negotiating a resolution.

ACKNOWLEDGEMENT

Both parties sign here to acknowledge receipt of a signed agreement and identify the names and addresses of the law firms that will be representing them.

REFERENCES

Family Law Act, RSO 1990, c. F.3.

Income Tax Act, RSC 1985, c. 1 (5th Supp.), as amended.

Land Registration Reform Act, RSO 1990, c. L.4.

Personal Property Security Act, RSO 1990, c. P.10, as amended.

Planning Act, RSO 1990, c. P.13.

REVIEW QUESTIONS

1. What must you do if the person named as the seller in the agreement of purchase and sale is a different person from the registered owner shown in the search of title?
2. What must you do if the seller is a corporation?
3. What must you do if the seller is a partnership?
4. What must you do if the buyer wishes to take title differently than the way he or she is named in the agreement of purchase and sale?
5. What should be done if the title search reveals an easement that is not mentioned in the agreement of purchase and sale?
6. What should you do if the agreement of purchase and sale states that interest is to be paid on the deposit?
7. What should you do if the agreement of purchase and sale is conditional until a specified date?
8. What steps may be necessary if chattels are included in the agreement of purchase and sale?
9. What steps must you take with respect to the completion date?
10. What is the requisition date, and why is it important?
11. What does the standard agreement of purchase and sale provide with respect to mortgages that are supposed to be discharged on closing? Why is this provision necessary?
12. When preparing the statement of adjustments, who is responsible for the various expenses on the date of closing?
13. What is a tender, and what is its significance?
14. Why does the agreement of purchase and sale contain a seller's warranty with respect to spousal consent under the *Family Law Act*?
15. What is UFFI? What does the agreement of purchase and sale say about it, and why?
16. Why is it a good idea to make a note of the individual agent who listed the property?

FIGURE 15.1 Ontario Real Estate Association (OREA) Agreement of Purchase and Sale

OREA Ontario Real Estate Association

Agreement of Purchase and Sale

Form 100
for use in the Province of Ontario

This Agreement of Purchase and Sale dated this 21ST day of September 20 08

BUYER, Henry Albert Grant and Wilma Heather Grant, agrees to purchase from
(Full legal names of all Buyers)

SELLER, Francois Mercier and Huguette Marie Mercier, the following
(Full legal names of all Sellers)

REAL PROPERTY:
Address 166 Valley Road fronting on the east side of Valley Road in the Township of Whitford, County of Yorkton and having a frontage of 50 feet more or less by a depth of 100 feet more or less and legally described as Lot 11, Plan 1209, Township of Whitford, County of Yorkton (the "property").
(Legal description of land including easements not described elsewhere)

PURCHASE PRICE: Dollars (CDN$) 258,000.00
Two hundred fifty-eight thousand Dollars

DEPOSIT: Buyer submits upon acceptance
(Herewith/Upon Acceptance/as otherwise described in this Agreement)

Ten thousand Dollars (CDN$) 10,000.00

by negotiable cheque payable to Home Life Winners Ltd. "Deposit Holder" to be held in trust pending completion or other termination of this Agreement and to be credited toward the Purchase Price on completion. For the purposes of this Agreement, "Upon Acceptance" shall mean that the Buyer is required to deliver the deposit to the Deposit Holder within 24 hours of the acceptance of this Agreement. The parties to this Agreement hereby acknowledge that, unless otherwise provided for in this Agreement, the Deposit Holder shall place the deposit in trust in the Deposit Holder's non-interest bearing Real Estate Trust Account and no interest shall be earned, received or paid on the deposit.

Buyer agrees to pay the balance as more particularly set out in Schedule A attached.

SCHEDULE(S) A **attached hereto form(s) part of this Agreement.**

1. **IRREVOCABILITY:** This Offer shall be irrevocable by Buyer (Seller/Buyer) until 8:00 ~~a.m.~~/p.m. on the 22ND day of September 20 08, after which time, if not accepted, this Offer shall be null and void and the deposit shall be returned to the Buyer in full without interest.
2. **COMPLETION DATE:** This Agreement shall be completed by no later than 6:00 p.m. on the 28th day of November, 20 08. Upon completion, vacant possession of the property shall be given to the Buyer unless otherwise provided for in this Agreement.
3. **NOTICES:** Seller hereby appoints the Listing Brokerage as Agent for the purpose of giving and receiving notices pursuant to this Agreement. **Only if the Co-operating Brokerage represents the interests of the Buyer in this transaction,** the Buyer hereby appoints the Co-operating Brokerage as Agent for the purpose of giving and receiving notices pursuant to this Agreement. Any notice relating hereto or provided for herein shall be in writing. This offer, any counter offer, notice of acceptance thereof, or any notice shall be deemed given and received, when hand delivered to the address for service provided in the Acknowledgement below, or where a facsimile number is provided herein, when transmitted electronically to that facsimile number.

FAX No. 416-555-6923 (For delivery of notices to Seller) FAX No. 416-555-8721 (For delivery of notices to Buyer)

INITIALS OF BUYER(S): HG WG **INITIALS OF SELLER(S):** [illegible]

 Form 100 2007 **Page 1 of 5**

FIGURE 15.1 Continued

4. **CHATTELS INCLUDED:** White stove, Kenmore model #1250 white refrigerator, Kenmore model #1360

5. **FIXTURES EXCLUDED:** Dining-room chandelier

6. **RENTAL ITEMS:** The following equipment is rented and **not** included in the Purchase Price. The Buyer agrees to assume the rental contract(s), if assumable: hot water tank

7. **GST:** If this transaction is subject to Goods and Services Tax (G.S.T.), then such tax shall be included in (included in/in addition to) the Purchase Price. If this transaction is not subject to G.S.T., Seller agrees to certify on or before closing, that the transaction is not subject to G.S.T.

8. **TITLE SEARCH:** Buyer shall be allowed until 6:00 p.m. on the 17th day of October, 2008, (Requisition Date) to examine the title to the Property at Buyer's own expense and until the earlier of: (i) thirty days from the later of the Requisition Date or the date on which the conditions in this Agreement are fulfilled or otherwise waived or; (ii) five days prior to completion, to satisfy Buyer that there are no outstanding work orders or deficiency notices affecting the Property, and that its present use (single family residential) may be lawfully continued and that the principal building may be insured against risk of fire. Seller hereby consents to the municipality or other governmental agencies releasing to Buyer details of all outstanding work orders affecting the property, and Seller agrees to execute and deliver such further authorizations in this regard as Buyer may reasonably require.

9. **FUTURE USE:** Seller and Buyer agree that there is no representation or warranty of any kind that the future intended use of the property by Buyer is or will be lawful except as may be specifically provided for in this Agreement.

10. **TITLE:** Provided that the title to the property is good and free from all registered restrictions, charges, liens, and encumbrances except as otherwise specifically provided in this Agreement and save and except for (a) any registered restrictions or covenants that run with the land providing that such are complied with; (b) any registered municipal agreements and registered agreements with publicly regulated utilities providing such have been complied with, or security has been posted to ensure compliance and completion, as evidenced by a letter from the relevant municipality or regulated utility; (c) any minor easements for the supply of domestic utility or telephone services to the property or adjacent properties; and (d) any easements for drainage, storm or sanitary sewers, public utility lines, telephone lines, cable television lines or other services which do not materially affect the present use of the property. If within the specified times referred to in paragraph 8 any valid objection to title or to any outstanding work order or deficiency notice, or to the fact the said present use may not lawfully be continued, or that the principal building may not be insured against risk of fire is made in writing to Seller and which Seller is unable or unwilling to remove, remedy or satisfy or obtain insurance save and except against risk of fire in favour of the Buyer and any mortgagee, (with all related costs at the expense of the Seller), and which Buyer will not waive, this Agreement notwithstanding any intermediate acts or negotiations in respect of such objections, shall be at an end and all monies paid shall be returned without interest or deduction and Seller, Listing Brokerage and Co-operating Brokerage shall not be liable for any costs or damages. Save as to any valid objection so made by such day and except for any objection going to the root of the title, Buyer shall be conclusively deemed to have accepted Seller's title to the property.

11. **CLOSING ARRANGEMENTS:** Where each of the Seller and Buyer retain a lawyer to complete the Agreement of Purchase and Sale of the Property, and where the transaction will be completed by electronic registration pursuant to Part III of the Land Registration Reform Act, R.S.O. 1990, Chapter L4 and the Electronic Registration Act, S.O. 1991, Chapter 44, and any amendments thereto, the Seller and Buyer acknowledge and agree that the exchange of closing funds, non-registrable documents and other items (the "Requisite Deliveries") and the release thereof to the Seller and Buyer will (a) not occur at the same time as the registration of the transfer/deed (and any other documents intended to be registered in connection with the completion of this transaction) and (b) be subject to conditions whereby the lawyer(s) receiving any of the Requisite Deliveries will be required to hold same in trust and not release same except in accordance with the terms of a document registration agreement between the said lawyers. The Seller and Buyer irrevocably instruct the said lawyers to be bound by the document registration agreement which is recommended from time to time by the Law Society of Upper Canada. Unless otherwise agreed to by the lawyers, such exchange of the Requisite Deliveries will occur in the applicable Land Titles Office or such other location agreeable to both lawyers.

INITIALS OF BUYER(S): HB WB **INITIALS OF SELLER(S):**

FIGURE 15.1 Continued

12. **DOCUMENTS AND DISCHARGE:** Buyer shall not call for the production of any title deed, abstract, survey or other evidence of title to the property except such as are in the possession or control of Seller. If requested by Buyer, Seller will deliver any sketch or survey of the property within Seller's control to Buyer as soon as possible and prior to the Requisition Date. If a discharge of any Charge/Mortgage held by a corporation incorporated pursuant to the Trust And Loan Companies Act (Canada), Chartered Bank, Trust Company, Credit Union, Caisse Populaire or Insurance Company and which is not to be assumed by Buyer on completion, is not available in registrable form on completion, Buyer agrees to accept Seller's lawyer's personal undertaking to obtain, out of the closing funds, a discharge in registrable form and to register same, or cause same to be registered, on title within a reasonable period of time after completion, provided that on or before completion Seller shall provide to Buyer a mortgage statement prepared by the mortgagee setting out the balance required to obtain the discharge, and, where a real-time electronic cleared funds transfer system is not being used, a direction executed by Seller directing payment to the mortgagee of the amount required to obtain the discharge out of the balance due on completion.
13. **INSPECTION:** Buyer acknowledges having had the opportunity to inspect the property and understands that upon acceptance of this Offer there shall be a binding agreement of purchase and sale between Buyer and Seller. **The Buyer acknowledges having the opportunity to include a requirement for a property inspection report in this Agreement and agrees that except as may be specifically provided for in this Agreement, the Buyer will not be obtaining a property inspection or property inspection report regarding the property.**
14. **INSURANCE:** All buildings on the property and all other things being purchased shall be and remain until completion at the risk of Seller. Pending completion, Seller shall hold all insurance policies, if any, and the proceeds thereof in trust for the parties as their interests may appear and in the event of substantial damage, Buyer may either terminate this Agreement and have all monies paid returned without interest or deduction or else take the proceeds of any insurance and complete the purchase. No insurance shall be transferred on completion. If Seller is taking back a Charge/Mortgage, or Buyer is assuming a Charge/Mortgage, Buyer shall supply Seller with reasonable evidence of adequate insurance to protect Seller's or other mortgagee's interest on completion.
15. **PLANNING ACT:** This Agreement shall be effective to create an interest in the property only if Seller complies with the subdivision control provisions of the Planning Act by completion and Seller covenants to proceed diligently at his expense to obtain any necessary consent by completion.
16. **DOCUMENT PREPARATION:** The Transfer/Deed shall, save for the Land Transfer Tax Affidavit, be prepared in registrable form at the expense of Seller, and any Charge/Mortgage to be given back by the Buyer to Seller at the expense of the Buyer. If requested by Buyer, Seller covenants that the Transfer/Deed to be delivered on completion shall contain the statements contemplated by Section 50(22) of the Planning Act, R.S.O.1990.
17. **RESIDENCY:** Buyer shall be credited towards the Purchase Price with the amount, if any, necessary for Buyer to pay to the Minister of National Revenue to satisfy Buyer's liability in respect of tax payable by Seller under the non-residency provisions of the Income Tax Act by reason of this sale. Buyer shall not claim such credit if Seller delivers on completion the prescribed certificate or a statutory declaration that Seller is not then a non-resident of Canada.
18. **ADJUSTMENTS:** Any rents, mortgage interest, realty taxes including local improvement rates and unmetered public or private utility charges and unmetered cost of fuel, as applicable, shall be apportioned and allowed to the day of completion, the day of completion itself to be apportioned to Buyer.
19. **TIME LIMITS:** Time shall in all respects be of the essence hereof provided that the time for doing or completing of any matter provided for herein may be extended or abridged by an agreement in writing signed by Seller and Buyer or by their respective lawyers who may be specifically authorized in that regard.
20. **TENDER:** Any tender of documents or money hereunder may be made upon Seller or Buyer or their respective lawyers on the day set for completion. Money may be tendered by bank draft or cheque certified by a Chartered Bank, Trust Company, Province of Ontario Savings Office, Credit Union or Caisse Populaire.
21. **FAMILY LAW ACT:** Seller warrants that spousal consent is not necessary to this transaction under the provisions of the Family Law Act, R.S.O.1990 unless Seller's spouse has executed the consent hereinafter provided.
22. **UFFI:** Seller represents and warrants to Buyer that during the time Seller has owned the property, Seller has not caused any building on the property to be insulated with insulation containing ureaformaldehyde, and that to the best of Seller's knowledge no building on the property contains or has ever contained insulation that contains ureaformaldehyde. This warranty shall survive and not merge on the completion of this transaction, and if the building is part of a multiple unit building, this warranty shall only apply to that part of the building which is the subject of this transaction.
23. **CONSUMER REPORTS: The Buyer is hereby notified that a consumer report containing credit and/or personal information may be referred to in connection with this transaction.**
24. **AGREEMENT IN WRITING:** If there is conflict or discrepancy between any provision added to this Agreement (including any Schedule attached hereto) and any provision in the standard pre-set portion hereof, the added provision shall supersede the standard pre-set provision to the extent of such conflict or discrepancy. This Agreement including any Schedule attached hereto, shall constitute the entire Agreement between Buyer and Seller. There is no representation, warranty, collateral agreement or condition, which affects this Agreement other than as expressed herein. For the purposes of this Agreement, Seller means vendor and Buyer means purchaser. This Agreement shall be read with all changes of gender or number required by the context.

INITIALS OF BUYER(S): (HG UG) **INITIALS OF SELLER(S):** (HH HH)

 Form 100 2007 **Page 3 of 5**

FIGURE 15.1 Continued

25. **SUCCESSORS AND ASSIGNS:** The heirs, executors, administrators, successors and assigns of the undersigned are bound by the terms herein.

SIGNED, SEALED AND DELIVERED in the presence of: IN WITNESS whereof I have hereunto set my hand and seal:

(Witness) .... (Buyer) H. Grant .... (Seal) DATE Sept. 20/08

(Witness) .... (Buyer) W. Grant .... (Seal) DATE Sept. 20/08

I, the Undersigned Seller, agree to the above Offer. I hereby irrevocably instruct my lawyer to pay directly to the Listing Brokerage the unpaid balance of the commission together with applicable Goods and Services Tax (and any other taxes as may hereafter be applicable), from the proceeds of the sale prior to any payment to the undersigned on completion, as advised by the Listing Brokerage to my lawyer.

SIGNED, SEALED AND DELIVERED in the presence of: IN WITNESS whereof I have hereunto set my hand and seal:

(Witness) .... (Seller) F. .... (Seal) DATE Sept 21/08

(Witness) .... (Seller) H. Mercier .... (Seal) DATE Sept. 21/08

SPOUSAL CONSENT: The Undersigned Spouse of the Seller hereby consents to the disposition evidenced herein pursuant to the provisions of the Family Law Act, R.S.O.1990, and hereby agrees with the Buyer that he/she will execute all necessary or incidental documents to give full force and effect to the sale evidenced herein.

(Witness) .... (Spouse) .... (Seal) DATE ....

CONFIRMATION OF ACCEPTANCE: Notwithstanding anything contained herein to the contrary, I confirm this Agreement with all changes both typed and written was finally accepted by all parties at 2:30 a.m./p.m. this 21st day of September, 2008.

.... (Signature of Seller or Buyer)

INFORMATION ON BROKERAGE(S)

Listing Brokerage HomeLife Winners Ltd. Tel.No.(416) 555-6922

Co-op/Buyer Brokerage Century 21 Sales 'R Us Ltd. Tel.No.(416) 555-8720

ACKNOWLEDGEMENT

I acknowledge receipt of my signed copy of this accepted Agreement of Purchase and Sale and I authorize the Agent to forward a copy to my lawyer.

(Seller) F. .... DATE Sept.21/08

(Seller) H. Mercier .... DATE Sept.21/08

Address for Service 166 Valley Road Whitford, Ont. Tel.No.(416) 555-3041

Seller's Lawyer Brooks + Dunn

Address 16 Main St., Whitford, Ont. L6J 3S7

(416) 555-6789 Tel.No. (416) 555-6790 FAX No.

I acknowledge receipt of my signed copy of this accepted Agreement of Purchase and Sale and I authorize the Agent to forward a copy to my lawyer.

(Buyer) H. Grant .... DATE Sept.21/08

(Buyer) W. Grant .... DATE Sept.21/08

Address for Service 621 Augustus St. Seneca, Ont. K1K 0T4 Tel.No.(555) 555-7511

Buyer's Lawyer Kurtz, Emmans + Blatt

Address 321 Any St., Seneca, Ont. K1K 6L2

(416) 555-3872 Tel.No. (416) 555-3873 FAX No.

FOR OFFICE USE ONLY

COMMISSION TRUST AGREEMENT

To: Co-operating Brokerage shown on the foregoing Agreement of Purchase and Sale:
In consideration for the Co-operating Brokerage procuring the foregoing Agreement of Purchase and Sale, I hereby declare that all moneys received or receivable by me in connection with the Transaction as contemplated in the MLS® Rules and Regulations of my Real Estate Board shall be receivable and held in trust. This agreement shall constitute a Commission Trust Agreement as defined in the MLS® Rules and shall be subject to and governed by the MLS® Rules pertaining to Commission Trust.

DATED as of the date and time of the acceptance of the foregoing Agreement of Purchase and Sale. Acknowledged by:

.... (Authorized to bind the Listing Brokerage) .... (Authorized to bind the Co-operating Brokerage)

FIGURE 15.1 Concluded

OREA Ontario Real Estate Association

Schedule A
Agreement of Purchase and Sale

Form 100
for use in the Province of Ontario

This Schedule is attached to and forms part of the Agreement of Purchase and Sale between:

BUYER, Henry Albert Grant and Wilma Heather Grant, and

SELLER, Francois Mercier and Huguette Marie Mercier

for the purchase and sale of 166 Valley Road, Whitford, Ontario

dated the 21st day of September, 2008.

Buyer agrees to pay the balance as follows:

The Buyer agrees to pay the balance of the purchase price, subject to adjustments, by bank draft or certified cheque, to the Seller on the completion of this transaction.

The buyer agrees to assume an existing second mortgage held by the Toronto-Dominion Bank for approximately thirty-one thousand six hundred forty-four dollars and ninety-seven cents ($31,644.97), bearing interest at the rate of 6.5% per annum, calculated semi-annually not in advance, and repayable in blended monthly payments of two hundred ninety-six dollars and zero cents ($296.00), including both principal and interest, and due on September 1st, 2009.

This offer is conditional upon the inspection of the subject property by a home inspector at the Buyer's expense, and the obtaining of a report satisfactory to the Buyer in the Buyer's sole and absolute discretion. Unless the buver gives notice in writing delivered to the Seller not later than 8:00 p.m. on Sept. 29, 2008 that this condition is fulfilled, this Offer shall be null and void, and the deposit returned to the Buyer in full without deduction. The Seller agrees to co-operate in providing access to the property for the purpose of this inspection. This condition is included for the benefit of the Buyer and may be waived at the Buyer's sole option by notice in writing to the Seller within the time period stated herein.

This form must be initialed by all parties to the Agreement of Purchase and Sale..

INITIALS OF BUYER(S): INITIALS OF SELLER(S):

 Form 100 2007 Page 5 of 5

CHAPTER 16

Title Insurance

Purchasers of real property want to be sure that they are getting good title to the property. Until recently, a purchaser's only option in that regard was to rely on the legal opinion of the lawyer handling the purchase transaction as to whether the purchaser was getting good and marketable title to the property. Now, however, purchasers can choose how to protect their interests: they can either (1) rely on the lawyer's **title opinion** or certification of title, or (2) take out a title insurance policy.

title opinion
lawyer's statement as to whether or not the purchaser has good title to the property

When title insurance was first offered, it appealed particularly to buyers who did not have an up-to-date survey of their property. The insurance companies insured against any problems that an up-to-date survey might have revealed, and the title insurance premium was considerably cheaper than the cost of a new survey. In recent years, title insurance has become an increasingly popular option for purchasers and for the lawyers representing them.

CERTIFICATION OF TITLE VERSUS TITLE INSURANCE

If a purchaser chooses to rely on the lawyer's title opinion, it is the lawyer's responsibility to perform all the necessary searches, make all the required inquiries, and take all the appropriate steps to ensure that the purchaser receives good and marketable title to the property. If it turns out later that there is a problem with the title, the purchaser contacts the lawyer to correct it. If the lawyer is not able to correct the problem, the purchaser can sue the lawyer for negligence, and the lawyer may make a claim under the law firm's mandatory errors and omissions insurance. The purchaser will have to prove that the lawyer acted negligently to be able to receive compensation for the loss. If the lawyer acted reasonably or had no way of discovering the problem — for example, in the case of fraud — then there may not be a valid cause of action, in which case the purchaser will not be compensated. In addition, a purchaser cannot make a claim against the lawyer for a problem that arises after the purchase transaction is completed, such as a transfer, lien, or charge fraudulently registered once the purchaser is the owner.

If the purchaser chooses to take out a title insurance policy, the policy protects the purchaser against most title problems whether they arise before or after the purchase transaction is completed. If a problem arises with title, the purchaser contacts the insurance company to correct it. There is no need to sue the lawyer and establish negligence on the lawyer's part. The purchaser need only prove that a problem exists that is covered by the policy purchased, and the purchaser is then covered for damages or the cost of clearing title.

Under the Law Society of Upper Canada's *Rules of Professional Conduct*, lawyers are obligated to advise their purchaser-clients of the choices available for assuring title. The provisions of the rules are discussed more fully under the heading "The Role of the Lawyer When Title Insurance Is Purchased," below.

WHAT IS TITLE INSURANCE?

Title insurance is insurance that shares many of the features of home insurance or car insurance. With home insurance or car insurance, you pay a premium to protect you in the event that you suffer loss or damage to your home or your car. With title insurance, you pay a premium to protect you against loss or damage suffered as a result of problems with title to your property.

All other insurers — life, home, automobile — assess the degree of risk involved in a particular insurance policy before issuing the policy. Title insurers are no different. Before agreeing to provide coverage for a particular title, they assess the degree of risk with respect to the specific property to decide on which risks they are willing to assume and the premium they will charge to do so. A title insurer reviews the state of the title to the property before issuing a policy just as a home insurer might physically inspect the property. A title insurer may exclude certain risks that it is not prepared to cover, just as a home insurer might exclude coverage against the risk of flood to a house located on a flood plain. However, the premium for title insurance is paid only once, with no annual renewals, unlike other types of insurance in which insurance premiums are paid on a schedule, usually annually. A title insurance policy is usually obtained at the time the property is purchased, but may be purchased by existing homeowners as well.

WHOM DOES TITLE INSURANCE PROTECT AND FOR HOW LONG?

Title insurance policies can be issued in favour of both purchasers of real property and lenders of money secured by real property. In fact, some lenders require that title insurance be taken out as a condition of granting a loan.

A policy issued in favour of a purchaser, called an owner's policy, remains in effect as long as the insured has title to the property. Some policies also continue to protect those who have received title because of the owner's death or as a result of a transfer to them by way of gift or for nominal consideration — for example, a spouse or child of the owner.

A lender's policy covers the principal amount of the mortgage and may be required only for the duration of the loan — in other words, for the time that the mortgage remains on title. The lender is covered in the event that it acquires the property as a result of default, by realizing on the security, and suffers loss with respect to a risk covered under the policy.

WHAT TYPES OF LOSSES ARE COVERED UNDER A TITLE INSURANCE POLICY?

Each title insurance policy lists the risks or losses that the policy will cover and those that it will not cover (exclusions). Generally, the owner of a title insurance policy is insured against title problems that were in existence at the time the policy was purchased, both "on title" and "off title." "On-title" matters are those that are reflected in the registered title to the property and include

- conflicting ownership interests in the property;
- any charge, lien, or encumbrance on or other defect in the title;
- unmarketability of title; and
- lack of a right of access to and from the property, if title to the insured property turns out to be different from that shown in the policy for whatever reason, including past fraud or forgery.

"Off-title" matters are those that are not reflected in the registered title to the property and include

- work orders;
- zoning issues;
- defects that would have been revealed by an up-to-date survey, including encroachments; and
- realty tax arrears.

Title insurance policies may also offer protection for defects that arise after the policy is purchased, including fraud, encroachments, and certain construction liens (if they arose before closing but are registered after closing).

Standard exclusions from coverage include

- problems that the purchaser agreed to accept (in the agreement of purchase and sale);
- certain government rights in the land;
- certain expropriations;
- environmental and conservation authority issues; and
- native land issues.

HOW MUCH DOES TITLE INSURANCE COST?

The cost of title insurance is determined by the purchase price of the property. The one-time premium is approximately $225 to $300 for a resale home costing less than $500,000. The premium goes up by approximately $1 for each $1,000 in price over $500,000.

In addition to the cost of the policy, the purchaser will also have to pay the lawyer's legal fees and disbursements for the searches and inquiries required by the title insurance company.

Depending on the searches required by the insurance company before issuing the policy, the overall cost of the insurance premium plus lawyer's fees and disbursements may be less than the legal fees and disbursements involved in obtaining a lawyer's opinion on title. (For a more complete discussion, see "The Role of the Lawyer When Title Insurance Is Purchased," below.)

TITLE INSURANCE COMPANIES AND THEIR POLICIES

There are a number of insurance companies offering title insurance in Ontario — several private title insurance companies and TitlePLUS, which is administered by the Lawyers' Professional Indemnity Company (LAWPRO). The main private title insurers in Ontario are First Canadian Title, Stewart Title, and Chicago Title.

There is no standard policy currently in use in Ontario, but there are similarities among all the policies in use. The body of the policy outlines what is included in the policy coverage. The policy will contain a number of schedules. Usually, the first schedule, Schedule A, describes the property covered and the amount of insurance. It also provides the name of the insured (either the owner or the lender, depending on the type of policy), a description of the estate or interest in land covered under the policy (usually fee simple if it's an owner's policy), and the name of the title holder of the fee simple estate or other interest in land. The second schedule, Schedule B, usually lists exceptions — both standard, preprinted exceptions and property-specific exceptions to the policy. The preprinted policy form may also contain exclusions from coverage. Any risk that is excluded from coverage by either the standard exclusions in the preprinted policy or by the exceptions in Schedule B will not be covered by the insurance policy.

THE ROLE OF THE LAWYER WHEN TITLE INSURANCE IS PURCHASED

A lawyer must still be involved in a real estate purchase transaction involving title insurance. In fact, only a lawyer can arrange title insurance on behalf of a purchaser.

The lawyer will carry out most of the same steps involved in a purchase without title insurance. He or she will

- open and organize a file;
- review the agreement of purchase and sale;
- advise the client on how to take title to the property;
- prepare or review all the necessary documents;
- prepare for the closing, including the execution of documents by the client;

- close the transaction and register the documents;
- notify utilities and government offices of the change in ownership; and
- provide the client with a **reporting letter**.

reporting letter
letter signed by the lawyer, outlining what was done in the transaction

It is also the role of the lawyer to advise the client on the alternative methods of assuring good title — the lawyer's certification of title or title opinion.

When the client chooses to purchase a title insurance policy, the lawyer applies for it on the purchaser's behalf. The lawyer must still search title to the property because the insurance company will require a title opinion from the lawyer before issuing a policy. However, generally, the lawyer will not have to conduct as thorough a title search as would be required if he or she were certifying title to the purchaser, because all insurers are willing to waive certain off-title searches and inquiries that would otherwise be required.

All title insurers in Ontario waive the following searches or inquiries:

- execution searches against prior owners;
- corporate status certificates for prior owners;
- proof of subdivision agreement compliance; and
- an up-to-date survey of the property.

Depending on which insurer provides the policy, some or all of the following searches or inquiries will also be waived:

- hydro, water, and gas certificates;
- tax certificates;
- evidence of building and zoning compliance;
- unregistered hydro easement inquiries;
- conservation authority clearance; and
- proof of restrictive covenant status.

By waiving these searches, the insurer is agreeing to accept the risk of or "insure over" these potential problems. If the lawyer discovers a title defect in the course of the searches required by the insurer, the lawyer can ask the insurer to insure over the known defect or problem in whole or in part for the purchaser and/or the lender. This will ensure that the problem does not become an exception to the coverage provided under the policy.

The choice of insurer may affect the way in which various steps in the application process are completed. Some conveyancing software — for example, Conveyancer — provides access to certain insurers, allowing the lawyer to complete the policy. If a lawyer prefers to use TitlePLUS, he or she must complete a questionnaire and submit it to the insurer. The insurer will then issue a policy.

The lawyer also has an important role to play in advising the client with respect to the insurance policy itself. For example, the lawyer may advise the client about which insurer to choose, the amount of insurance to be purchased, and the premium to be paid. The lawyer may also review the initial report from the insurer to determine what coverage is excluded from the policy and to make sure that the client is properly named in the policy as the insured, the property is properly described in the policy, and there are no title problems that should be resolved instead of being insured over. When the final policy is issued, the lawyer may review it to ensure that it complies with the commitment.

The role of the lawyer with respect to title insurance in real estate conveyancing is dealt with in the *Rules of Professional Conduct*. Subrules 2.02(10) to (13) state:

> 2.02(10) A lawyer shall assess all reasonable options to assure title when advising a client about a real estate conveyance and shall advise the client that title insurance is not mandatory and is not the only option available to protect the client's interests in a real estate transaction.
>
> **Commentary**
>
> A lawyer should advise the client of the options available to protect the client's interests and minimize the client's risks in a real estate transaction. The lawyer should be cognizant of when title insurance may be an appropriate option. Although title insurance is intended to protect the client against title risks, it is not a substitute for a lawyer's services in a real estate transaction.
>
> The lawyer should be knowledgeable about title insurance and discuss with the client the advantages, conditions, and limitations of the various options and coverages generally available to the client through title insurance. Before recommending a specific title insurance product, the lawyer should be knowledgeable about the product and take such training as may be necessary in order to acquire the knowledge.
>
> 2.02(11) A lawyer shall not receive any compensation, whether directly or indirectly, from a title insurer, agent or intermediary for recommending a specific title insurance product to his or her client.
>
> 2.02(12) A lawyer shall disclose to the client that no commission or fee is being furnished by any insurer, agent, or intermediary to the lawyer with respect to any title insurance coverage.
>
> **Commentary**
>
> The fiduciary relationship between lawyer and client requires full disclosure in all financial dealings between them and prohibits the acceptance of any hidden fees by the lawyer, including the lawyer's law firm, any employee or associate of the firm, or any related entity.
>
> 2.02(13) If discussing TitlePLUS insurance with the client, a lawyer shall fully disclose the relationship between the legal profession, the Society, and the Lawyers' Professional Indemnity Company (LawPRO).

Under subrule 5.01(5) of the *Rules of Professional Conduct*, these matters must be dealt with by the lawyer, and cannot be delegated to a law clerk. According to the subrule, a lawyer may not permit a non-lawyer to

- provide advice to a client with respect to any insurance, including title insurance, without supervision;
- present insurance options or information regarding premiums to a client without supervision;

- recommend one insurance product over another without supervision; or
- give legal opinions regarding the insurance coverage obtained.

FRAUD AND TITLE INSURANCE

In recent years there has been a dramatic increase in real estate title fraud in Ontario. The following examples illustrate ways in which title fraud can be perpetrated:

1. A fraud artist obtains title to a property by registering a fraudulent transfer or deed of land transferring title to himself or herself. The fraudster then arranges a mortgage on the property with a bank and registers the mortgage against title. The fraudster makes no mortgage payments. The owner first becomes aware of the scheme when the bank serves a notice of sale as a result of the default.
2. A married woman arranges a mortgage on property owned by her and her husband, without notice to the husband. She has an accomplice pose as her husband when the mortgage documents are signed, and then receives the proceeds from the mortgage. Her husband does not find out about the mortgage until they are going through a divorce, and the property is sold.
3. A lawyer breaches his undertaking to use proceeds from closing to pay off and discharge an outstanding mortgage. The lawyer instead disappears with the money, and title to the property remains subject to the prior mortgage.

In cases similar to these, innocent homeowners have either lost their homes or been left with properties subject to hefty mortgages.

The case law dealing with title fraud left homeowners in a vulnerable position when the Ontario Court of Appeal ruled in *Household Realty Corp. v. Liu* that a fraudulently signed mortgage (signed by way of a forged power of attorney) was valid, because the plaintiff was a bona fide mortgagee for value. The innocent homeowner was left with a mortgage of which he had no knowledge.

Title insurance was the only way an innocent homeowner could protect against title fraud. Without title insurance, if a homeowner lost his or her home to a fraudster, the only recourse was to apply to the Land Titles Assurance Fund. It was a time-consuming, and often costly, procedure that only provided the homeowner with money to compensate for the lost property; it did not restore title to the homeowner.

After much media coverage on the subject of title fraud, the Ontario government enacted the *Ministry of Governmental Services Consumer Protection and Service Modernization Act, 2006*, which amended the *Land Registration Reform Act* and the *Land Titles Act*. Ownership of property can no longer be lost as a result of a falsified mortgage, fraudulent sale, or a counterfeit power of attorney. There is a streamlined and expedited Land Titles Assurance Fund process for victims of fraud. For most cases of fraud, title will be returned to the owner who was on title immediately before the fraud and a decision on compensation will be made within 90 days. As well, fines for real estate fraud have been increased from a maximum of $1,000 to a maximum of $50,000.

Shortly after passage of this legislation, the Court of Appeal reversed itself on *Household* in the case of *Lawrence v. Maple Trust Company* and ruled that a mortgage that had been obtained on the basis of a fraudulent transfer of title was not valid.

Given these recent developments in the law regarding title fraud, it will become essential for purchasers to obtain title insurance when purchasing property. Although the legislation protects current homeowners from any subsequent title fraud against their property, it does not do the same for purchasers. A lawyer acting for a purchaser of land in the Land Titles system can no longer rely on the title index as an accurate reflection of the state of the title. There may have been a fraudulent transaction in the past that is not evident on the title index. When the fraud is discovered, title will be restored to the owner who was registered immediately before the fraud. Thus, lawyers will be unable to certify title to their clients and will have to rely on title insurance policies to insure against the possibility of a prior undiscovered fraud.

Title insurers will no longer be able to make claims against the Land Titles Assurance Fund after they have made payouts to their policy holders. If a homeowner or mortgage lender has title insurance and suffers a loss due to fraud, he or she will have to make a claim against his or her insurance policy (rather than the Land Titles Assurance Fund) to recover compensation. This situation will likely result in an increase in title insurance premiums.

REFERENCES

Household Realty Corp. v. Liu (2005), OJ No. 5001.

Land Titles Act, RSO 1990, c. L.5.

Land Registration Reform Act, RSO 1990, c. L.4.

Lawrence v. Maple Trust Company, 2007 ONCA 74 (CanLII).

REVIEW QUESTIONS

1. How is the purchaser protected against potential title problems in a transaction where title insurance is not purchased?
2. How is the purchaser protected against potential title problems in a transaction where title insurance has been purchased?
3. How does title insurance affect the work that has to be done on a file?
4. How frequently does a person have to pay a premium for title insurance?
5. How long does a title insurance policy stay in effect in the case of an owner's policy?
6. What types of losses are covered under a title insurance policy?
7. Under the *Rules of Professional Conduct*, can a lawyer receive a fee from a title insurance company for using its policy?
8. How does title insurance protect against fraudulent transactions?
9. Under what circumstances might a lawyer not be able to rely on a Land Titles title index as an accurate reflection of the state of the title?

CHAPTER 17

Preliminary Matters

Once you have opened the file, reviewed the agreement of purchase and sale, and diarized the relevant dates, you must perform a number of tasks designed to obtain the information you need before the transaction can close. The specific tasks involved will depend on whether the client decides to purchase title insurance. The lawyer handling the file must advise the client of the options available, and the client must decide early on which to choose. Many of the letters discussed in this chapter will not be necessary if the client purchases title insurance. Any letters in this chapter may be signed by a law clerk or a lawyer.

PRELIMINARY LETTER TO THE PURCHASER

You must send a preliminary letter to the purchaser confirming that your firm is representing him or her in the purchase of the property, advising the purchaser of various aspects of the transaction, and requesting whatever information you need. Questions may include the following:

- If there are two purchasers, do they want to take title as joint tenants or as tenants in common?
- Are the names shown on the agreement of purchase and sale the purchaser's full given names?
- What is the purchaser's birthdate?
- Is the purchaser financing the purchase by way of a mortgage? If so, who is the mortgagee, and what are the terms of the mortgage?

You must get answers to these questions before you can proceed with any document preparation. Figure 17.1 is an example of a preliminary letter to the purchaser.

SEARCH OF TITLE

The next matter that you must deal with is the title search. Start by using the property identifier number (PIN) to find out whether it is registered in the Registry or Land Titles system. If the property is registered in the Registry system, a full 40-year search will be required, and you will likely have to make arrangements to have the title searched by an experienced title searcher. If the property is in Land Titles (either Land Titles Absolute, Land Titles Conversion Qualified, or Land Titles Plus), you can do the search from your office using the Teraview software. See chapter 13, Title Searching, for a more complete discussion.

If you are not doing the title search yourself, you must give instructions to the title searcher. You can do this orally or in writing. If you give the title searcher oral instructions, make a note in the file setting out the name of the title searcher, the date you made the request for the title search, and any instructions you provided.

You must give the title searcher sufficient information on which to act, including

- the date by which you require the search;
- the requisition date;
- a description of the land — if possible, the lot and plan or concession number; if not, the municipal address and the land registry office in which the land is registered;
- the dimensions of the property;
- the names of the current registered owners;
- the kind of search you require — if the land is registered in the Registry system, you should request a full 40-year search, unless your law firm has previously certified title to the property;
- whether abutting lands should be searched for *Planning Act* compliance — this will be necessary if the land in question is part of a lot;
- what instruments, if any, should be copied; and
- which names should be searched for executions — in a 40-year search, you will have to search against all owners in the chain of title; if a mortgage is being taken back by the vendor, you will have to search against the purchaser as well.

Figure 17.2 is an example of a title search request.

INDEPENDENT CONVEYANCER FOR CLOSING

If the property records have not been automated, someone will have to attend at the land registry office for the closing. If your law firm uses independent conveyancers, you should book one to ensure that the conveyancer will be available on the date of closing.

ELECTRONIC CLOSING

If the property records have been automated, there will be no attendance at the Registry Office on closing. Instead, the lawyers will enter into a document registration agreement (DRA), which sets out their respective obligations on closing. Figure 17.3 is an example of a DRA.

PERSONAL PROPERTY SECURITY ACT (PPSA) SEARCH

If any chattels are included in the agreement of purchase and sale, you will need to search against the vendor under the PPSA. The purpose of the search is to make sure that these chattels are free of encumbrances.

PRELIMINARY LETTER TO THE VENDOR'S SOLICITOR

Find out the name of the vendor's solicitor by checking the acknowledgement section of the agreement of purchase and sale, or by telephoning the real estate agent. It is customary to write to the vendor's solicitor to confirm that your firm is acting for the purchaser and to request a survey and a statement of adjustments, and to advise how the client is taking title. If you don't yet know how the client wants to take title, ask for the draft transfer to be endorsed in blank. The law firm acting for the vendor will often send a similar preliminary letter to your law firm to confirm that they are acting for the vendor. Figure 17.4 is an example of a preliminary letter to the vendor's solicitor.

MUNICIPAL TAX CERTIFICATE

You must obtain a tax certificate from the municipality in which the property is located to confirm the current amount of the realty taxes and whether there are any arrears. Make sure that there are no unpaid taxes because these arrears constitute a lien on the land. You will also need this information to review the statement of adjustments when you receive it from the vendor's solicitor. Figure 17.5 is an example of a letter requesting a municipal tax certificate.

WATER DEPARTMENT, SEWERS, AND DRAINS

You must write to the water department of the municipality in which the property is located to find out the status of the water account, to advise of the impending change of name on the account, and, if the water service is metered, to arrange to have a final meter reading on the day before closing. You need this information because water account arrears can be added to the tax account and then become a lien against the land. You also need this information to check the statement of adjustments if the water account is billed on a flat-rate basis.

You also want to find out

1. whether the property is serviced by water and storm and sanitary sewers, and, if so, whether the sewer and water connections are completed and fully paid for; and

2. whether there are any easements or rights of way for drains, sewers, and water pipes.

The first item is particularly important for new houses, although there are older houses as well, even within urban areas, that are not connected to the municipal sewers. If there are any easements, the purchaser's lawyer will have to determine whether they fall within the scope of the utility easements provided for in the agreement of purchase and sale.

Figure 17.6 is an example of a letter to the water department.

SEPTIC TANKS

If the property is not connected to the municipal sewer system, you must write to the health department of the relevant municipality to ensure that the septic tank has been approved by them. Figure 17.7 is an example of a letter to the health department.

HYDRO AND GAS ACCOUNTS

Gas account arrears do not constitute a lien on the property, nor do hydro account arrears, unless hydro is provided by the municipality. However, most lawyers will write to the utility companies servicing the property to arrange for a final meter reading the day before closing and to advise the utility companies of the impending change of name on the account. Figure 17.8 is an example of a letter to the local hydro company, and figure 17.9 is an example of a letter to the local gas company.

BUILDING DEPARTMENT

You must also write a letter to the building department of the municipality in which the property is located to find out

1. whether the size of the building and its location on the lot comply with applicable zoning bylaws;
2. what the permitted use of the property is; and
3. whether or not there are any outstanding work orders against the property.

You will have to provide a copy of an up-to-date survey of the property to get the first item of information. If a building has been constructed contrary to the relevant zoning bylaws, a demolition order could conceivably be issued against the building. If the intended use of the property is contrary to the relevant zoning bylaws, the municipality may be able to get a court order to prohibit the intended use. Finally, if there are outstanding work orders against the property, the new owner will be required to make the mandated repairs to the property at the new owner's expense.

Depending on the municipality, you will receive different types of answers to this letter. Many municipalities are declining to provide an opinion as to compliance with the relevant bylaws. Instead, they simply give the number of the relevant bylaw and leave it to the purchaser's lawyer to review it and decide whether the property complies. If you receive that kind of letter, you must get a copy of the relevant bylaw and give it to the lawyer handling the file.

Very often a building was erected or a property was used in a particular way before the passage of the current bylaw. Zoning bylaws are rarely retroactive, and the existing size and location of the buildings and use of the property may be allowed to continue as a legal non-conforming use. To qualify as such, the use of the property or the size and location of the buildings, as the case may be,

- must not have changed since the bylaw was enacted; and
- must have complied with the bylaw in effect when the building was constructed or the use started.

Few, if any, municipalities will provide an opinion that the property qualifies as a legal non-conforming use. The law firm acting for the purchaser will be required to provide it. In order to give that opinion, you will have to

- find out the date of the enactment of the existing bylaw;
- find out the date of the construction of the building or commencement of its present use, as the case may be;
- obtain a copy of the bylaw in effect at the time the construction or use, as the case may be, started; and
- obtain evidence that the construction or use, as the case may be, has not changed since the bylaw came into effect.

In order to obtain the last item, you may have to requisition a statutory declaration from the vendor. In addition, you can check the municipal building department files to find out whether any building permits have been issued for the property.

Figure 17.10 is an example of a letter to the building department.

UNREGISTERED HYDRO EASEMENTS

Under the *Electricity Act, 1998*, hydro easements may be created that are not registered on title. These easements occur most often in rural or cottage areas, but it is possible for one to exist on an urban property that has not been subdivided. To find out whether there are any unregistered hydro easements affecting the property, you must write to Hydro One at the appropriate regional office or inquire online at http://unregeasement.hydroone.com/lvr.

Figure 17.11 is an example of a letter to Hydro One.

ONTARIO HERITAGE ACT

If a property has been "designated" under the *Ontario Heritage Act*, the owner's right to make alterations or improvements to the property is limited. Clearly, the application of this Act is not a concern in most transactions. However, if there is any doubt, write an inquiry letter to the clerk of the relevant municipality.

CONSERVATION AUTHORITY

If a property is designated as being within a fill line or flood plain, no building on the property or change in the grading pattern of the property is permitted without a permit from the appropriate conservation authority. Again, this designation is not a concern in all transactions. If there is any question, write to the local conservation authority to determine whether the property has been specially designated. This may well be of concern even if the property is located within an urban area. If the property is near a ravine, contains a stream, or is in a low-lying area, it may be a designated property.

NEW HOMES

If the property includes a newly constructed home, it is important to make sure that the builder is enrolled with the Tarion Warranty Corporation, which administers the *Ontario New Home Warranties Plan Act*. This inquiry can be made online at www.tarion.com; click on the "Find a Builder" link. The procedures involved in the purchase of a new home are discussed in chapter 27.

SPECIALIZED INQUIRIES

In some transactions, additional inquiries may be required to

- the Ministry of the Environment about a pollutant;
- the Ministry of Transportation about limitations on construction if the property is within 800 metres of a Queen's highway;
- the fire marshal's office about work orders; and
- the health department about work orders.

ADDRESSES AND FEES

Before you can write any of the letters described in this chapter, you must find out the address of the appropriate department or company, and confirm the fee (if any) charged for the information provided. There are a number of ways to obtain this information:

- Your law firm may maintain a master file containing this information.
- Your law firm may have a solicitor's desk book that you can check.
- You can telephone the relevant municipality.

If a fee is payable, remember to enclose a cheque with your letter.

REFERENCES

Electricity Act, 1998, SO 1998, c. 15, sched. A.

Ontario Heritage Act, RSO 1990, c. O.18.

Ontario New Home Warranties Plan Act, RSO 1990, c. O.31.

Personal Property Security Act, RSO 1990, c. P.10, as amended.

REVIEW QUESTIONS

1. Why do you send a preliminary letter to the client?
2. What information should you give to a title searcher?
3. What is a PPSA search, and when do you need one?
4. Why should you write a preliminary letter to the vendor's solicitor?
5. Why should you obtain a municipal tax certificate?
6. Why should you write to the water department?
7. Why do most lawyers write to the utility companies servicing the property?
8. Why must you write a letter to the building department of the municipality in which the property is located?
9. To qualify as a legal non-conforming use, what conditions must be met for the existing size and location of the buildings or use of the property?
10. What information will the law firm acting for the purchaser require in order to provide an opinion about a legal non-conforming use?

FIGURE 17.1 Preliminary Letter to the Purchaser

Date

Purchaser's name
Purchaser's address

Dear (*Purchaser's name*):

Re: *Name of transaction*
Address and municipality of property

We acknowledge receipt of a copy of your agreement of purchase and sale for the above property, which is closing on (*closing date*), and wish to thank you for requesting us to act on your behalf.

If you are financing the purchase by means of a mortgage, and wish us to do the legal work on your mortgage, please send us a copy of your **mortgage commitment**. As well, we will need **mortgage instructions** from your bank or lending institution ("mortgagee"), in order to prepare the necessary documents before closing. You should know that if we do the mortgage work for you, we will also be representing the mortgagee's interests, and any information we receive about the transaction from either party cannot be kept confidential from the other party. If a conflict of interest should occur between you and the mortgagee, we may be obliged to stop acting for both of you. Such a conflict of interest is rare.

If there is a mortgage, we will need a copy of your **fire insurance policy**, showing loss payable to the mortgagee(s). The amount of the insurance coverage must not be less than the combined totals of all the mortgages. If your insurance agent is unable to provide a copy of the policy in time for closing, we must have from him/her a **binder letter** indicating the name of the insuring company, the effective date, the expiry date, the amount of coverage, and the names of the mortgagees, with a certified copy of the policy to follow.

It is possible to purchase **title insurance** for your property. It may provide cost savings due to reduced search expenses, and it would provide coverage against certain deficiencies and fraud that a lawyer's opinion of title normally would not. Please contact us to discuss the pros and cons of title insurance in your case.

If you have a copy of a **plan of survey** of the property, please forward it to us. It will show the boundaries of the property, as well as the location of all buildings and fences, easements, and encroachments (parts of either a neighbour's fence or building on your land, or your fence or building on a neighbour's land). It is important that the survey be up-to-date. If it is not, and you do not purchase title insurance, it may be necessary to have a new survey prepared, depending on your mortgagee's requirements. Please call us to discuss your survey if you are unsure of its accuracy.

Depending on whether or not you purchase title insurance, we may be writing to the tax department to make sure that realty taxes are paid up to the date of closing, and to the building department to confirm that there are no outstanding zoning violations or work orders against the property. We will be writing to companies providing utilities to the property, to request meter readings just before closing, and to advise them that you will be the new owners, and that you can be reached at the property.

Please advise us whom you wish to be named on the deed as owner(s). We will require their **full names** and **dates of birth**. If more than one person is to be named on the deed, you must decide whether they should be shown as joint tenants or tenants-in-common. Usually, married couples take title as joint tenants, so that if one of them should die, the

FIGURE 17.1 Concluded

other automatically becomes the sole owner. If you are not sure how you wish to take title, please call to discuss it with us.

If there is a **second living unit** in the residence, please advise us. If you plan to use it as a separate apartment, you should contact the Fire Department and Hydro One to confirm that it complies with the Fire Code (Ontario Regulation 388/97, as amended by O. Reg. 315/01, of the *Fire Protection and Prevention Act*). It may be necessary to obtain inspections and clearance certificates to ensure that the unit is legal.

Before the closing date, you will need to attend at our offices to sign documents and to provide us with a **certified cheque** to cover the following:

(a) the amount to be paid to the seller;
(b) land transfer tax and registration costs;
(c) cost of title insurance, if applicable; and
(d) our account, including fees and disbursements.

In order to help you estimate these costs, here are a few hints. The amount to be paid to the seller is the purchase price, minus your deposit, plus adjustments. Before closing, the seller's lawyer will send us a statement of adjustments in which certain items such as property taxes, fuel oil (if applicable), and unmetered utilities may be adjusted. You should allow for possible adjustments of several hundred dollars.

Provincial land transfer tax can be calculated by using the following formula (as of the time of writing):

Purchase price	*Calculation*
purchase price ("p.p.") up to $55,000:	p.p. × 0.005
p.p. between $55,000.01 and $250,000:	p.p. × 0.01 – $275
p.p. over $250,000	p.p. × 0.015 – $1,525
p.p. over $400,000 *and* containing 1 or 2 single-family residences	p.p. × 0.02 – $3,525

If this is your first home, you would be entitled to a rebate of the provincial land transfer tax of up to $2,000.

If the property you are buying is located in the City of Toronto, **municipal land transfer tax** is also payable. It can be calculated using the following formula (as of the time of writing):

Purchase price	*Calculation*
Up to $55,000	p.p. × 0.005
p.p. between $55,000.01 and $400,000	p.p. × 0.01 – $275
p.p. over $400,000	p.p. × 0.02 – $4,275

If this is your first home, you will be exempt from the municipal land transfer tax for up to $400,000 of the purchase price.

The cost of a title insurance policy is approximately (*insert amount*). Our fees and disbursements for the purchase (*and the mortgage, if applicable*) will usually total approximately (*insert amount*).

We will advise you several days before the closing date what the exact amount of your certified cheque should be. We will also set up an appointment for you to come in and sign the necessary documents, and to deliver your cheque.

If you have any questions, please feel free to contact us.

Yours very truly,

FIGURE 17.2 Title Search Request

FILE NAME FILE NO.
REQUESTED BY
DATE OF REQUEST DATE REQUIRED
DATE OF CLOSING REQUISITION DATE
DESCRIPTION OF LAND MUNICIPALITY
MUNICIPAL ADDRESS
DIMENSIONS OF PROPERTY
REGISTERED OWNERS
PIN

Instructions

( ) Full 40-year search (Registry)
Attached: ( ) Agreement of purchase and sale
( ) Survey
( ) Full search (Land Titles)
( ) Search abutting lands
( ) Subsearch only
From date
From instrument no.
Purpose of subsearch
( ) Attached previous search

Obtain copies of the following instruments:
( ) Registered agreements
( ) Outstanding mortgages
( )
( )
( )
( )
( ) Check executions against
( ) all owners
( ) purchaser(s)
( )
( )

( ) Register the following documents:

Special Instructions

FIGURE 17.3 Document Registration Agreement

DOCUMENT REGISTRATION AGREEMENT

BETWEEN:

____

(hereinafter referred to as the "**Purchaser's Solicitor**")

AND:

____

(hereinafter referred to as the "**Vendor's Solicitor**")

RE: ____________________ (the "**Purchaser**") purchase from____________ (the "**Vendor**") of ____________________ (the "**Property**") pursuant to an agreement of purchase and sale dated________________, as amended from time to time (the "**Purchase Agreement**"), scheduled to be completed on ____________________ (the "**Closing Date**")

FOR GOOD AND VALUABLE CONSIDERATION (the receipt and sufficiency of which is hereby expressly acknowledged), the parties hereto hereby undertake and agree as follows:

Holding Deliveries In Escrow

1. The Vendor's Solicitor and the Purchaser's Solicitor shall hold all funds, keys and closing documentation exchanged between them (the "Requisite Deliveries") in escrow, and *shall* not release or otherwise deal with same except in accordance with the terms of this Agreement. Both the Vendor's Solicitor and the Purchaser's Solicitor have been authorized by their respective clients to enter into this Agreement. Once the Requisite Deliveries can be released in accordance with the terms of this Agreement, any monies representing payout funds for mortgages to be discharged shall be forwarded promptly to the appropriate mortgage lender.

Advising of Concerns with Deliveries

2. Each of the parties hereto shall notify the other as soon as reasonably possible following their respective receipt of the Requisite Deliveries (as applicable) of any defect(s) with respect to same.

Selecting Solicitor Responsible for Registration

3. The Purchaser's Solicitor shall be responsible for the registration of the Electronic Documents (as hereinafter defined) unless the box set out below indicating that the Vendor's Solicitor will be responsible for such registration has been checked. For the purposes of this Agreement, the solicitor responsible for such registration shall be referred to as the "Registering Solicitor" and the other solicitor shall be referred to as the "Non-Registering Solicitor":

Vendor's Solicitor will be registering the Electronic Documents ☐

Responsibility of Non-Registering Solicitor

and

Release of Requisite Deliveries by Non-Registering Solicitor

4. The Non-Registering Solicitor shall, upon his/her receipt and approval of the Requisite Deliveries (as applicable), electronically release for registration the Electronic Documents and shall thereafter be entitled to release the Requisite Deliveries from escrow forthwith following the earlier of:

a) the registration of the Electronic Documents;

b) the closing time specified in the Purchase Agreement unless a specific time has been inserted as follows [________ a.m./p.m. on the Closing Date] (the "**Release Deadline**"), and provided that notice under paragraph 7 below has not been received; or

c) receipt of notification from the Registering Solicitor of the registration of the Electronic Documents.

If the Purchase Agreement does not specify a closing time and a Release Deadline has not been specifically inserted the Release Deadline shall be 6.00 p.m. on the Closing Date.

FIGURE 17.3 Concluded

Responsibility of Registering Solicitor	5. The Registering Solicitor shall, subject to paragraph 7 below, on the Closing Date, following his/her receipt and approval of the Requisite Deliveries (as applicable), register the documents listed in Schedule "A" annexed hereto (referred to in this agreement as the "**Electronic Documents**") in the stated order of priority therein set out, as soon as reasonably possible once same have been released for registration by the Non- Registering Solicitor, and immediately thereafter notify the Non-Registering Solicitor of the registration particulars thereof by telephone or telefax (or other method as agreed between the parties).
Release of Requisite Deliveries by Registering Solicitor	6. Upon registration of the Electronic Documents and notification of the Non-Registering solicitor in accordance with paragraph 5 above, the Registering Solicitor shall be entitled to forthwith release the Requisite Deliveries from escrow.
Returning Deliveries where Non-registration	7. Any of the parties hereto may notify the other party that he/she does not wish to proceed with the registration of the Electronic Documents, and provided that such notice is received by the other party before the release of the Requisite Deliveries pursuant to this Agreement and before the registration of the Electronic Documents, then each of the parties hereto shall forthwith return to the other party their respective Requisite Deliveries.
Counterparts & Gender	8. This Agreement may be signed in counterparts, and shall be read with all changes of gender and/or number as may be required by the context.
Purchase Agreement Prevails if Conflict or Inconsistency	9. Nothing contained in this Agreement shall be read or construed as altering the respective rights and obligations of the Purchaser and the Vendor as more particularly set out in the Purchase Agreement, and in the event of any conflict or inconsistency between the provisions of this Agreement and the Purchase Agreement, then the latter shall prevail.
Telefaxing Deliveries & Providing Originals if Requested	10. This Agreement (or any counterpart hereof), and any of the closing documents hereinbefore contemplated, may be exchanged by telefax or similar system reproducing the original, provided that all such documents have been properly executed by the appropriate parties. The party transmitting any such document(s) shall also provide the original executed version(s) of same to the recipient within 2 business days after the Closing Date, unless the recipient has indicated that he/she does not require such original copies.

Dated this ________ day of ___________, 20_____.

Name/Firm Name of Vendor's Solicitor	Name/Firm Name of Purchaser's Solicitor
______________________________	______________________________
______________________________	______________________________
______________________________	______________________________
Name of Person Signing	Name of Person Signing
______________________________	______________________________
(Signature)	(Signature)

Note: *This version of the Document Registration Agreement was adopted by the Joint LSUC-CBAO Committee on Electronic Registration of Title Documents on March 29, 2004 and posted to the web site on April 8, 2004.*

FIGURE 17.4 Preliminary Letter to the Vendor's Solicitor

Date

Law firm name
Address

Dear Sir or Madam:

Re: *Name of transaction*
Address and municipality of property

We are the solicitors for ____________________ , the purchaser(s) in the above transaction, and we understand that you are acting on behalf of the vendor(s).

Please forward a statement of adjustments and a survey of the property. Our client(s) will be taking title as follows:

[*Insert purchaser(s)' name(s) and birthdate(s) or "in blank."*]

Your prompt attention to this matter is appreciated.

Yours very truly,

FIGURE 17.5 Letter Requesting a Municipal Tax Certificate

Date

Tax Department
Name of municipality
Address

Dear Sir or Madam:

Re: *Name of transaction*
Address and municipality of property

We are the solicitors for ____________________, the purchaser(s) in the above transaction, which is scheduled to close on (*date*).

Would you please provide us with a tax certificate showing:

- the arrears of taxes, if any;
- a statement showing current taxes;
- any charges for work orders, snow shovelling, demolition, water, or other public utilities;
- any other statutory charges, liens, or levies including local improvement rates that may be collectable by you.

Enclosed is our cheque payable to __________________ in the amount of $ __________, in payment of your fee, together with a stamped self-addressed envelope.

Thank you for your attention to this matter.

Yours very truly,

FIGURE 17.6 Letter to the Water Department

Date

Water Department
Name of municipality
Address

Dear Sir or Madam:

Re: *Name of transaction*
Address and municipality of property

We are the solicitors for ______________________, the purchaser(s) in the above transaction, which is scheduled to close on (*date*).

Would you please advise us whether or not there are any arrears of water payments owing with respect to the subject property.

We would also ask that you ensure that a meter reading is made one day before the date of closing, and that a final bill is forwarded to the vendor in care of (*his/her*) solicitor, (*vendor's law firm name*) at (*vendor's law firm address*). Our client(s) should then be shown on your records as the new owner(s), and future bills should be forwarded to (*him/her/them*) at the address of the property.

Would you also please advise us whether or not this property is serviced by water and storm and sanitary sewers, and, if so, whether or not all drains, sewers, and water connections servicing this property are completed and paid for in full.

We would also like to know whether or not you have any claim for easements or rights of way for drains, sewers, and water pipes that would affect this property.

Enclosed is our cheque payable to ________________ in the amount of $ ________, in payment of your fee, together with a stamped self-addressed envelope.

Thank you for your attention to this matter.

Yours very truly,

FIGURE 17.7 Letter to the Health Department

Date

Health Department
Name of municipality
Address

Dear Sir or Madam:

Re: *Name of transaction*
Address and municipality of property

We are the solicitors for ____________________, the purchaser(s) in the above transaction, which is scheduled to close on (*date*).

Would you please advise us whether or not the septic tank located on the property has been approved by the local health unit. In order to facilitate future servicing, would you also please provide us with a copy of the diagram showing the location of the septic tank and tile bed.

If jurisdiction over the property lies with the Ministry of the Environment, please advise us by telephone.

Enclosed is our cheque payable to ____________________ in the amount of $ ________, in payment of your fee, together with a stamped self-addressed envelope.

Thank you for your assistance in this matter.

Yours very truly,

FIGURE 17.8 Letter to the Local Hydro Company

Date

Name of hydro company
Address

Dear Sir or Madam:

Re: *Name of transaction*
Address and municipality of property

We are the solicitors for ________________________, the purchaser(s) in the above transaction, which is scheduled to close on (*date*).

Kindly arrange for a meter reading one day before the date of closing, and forward a final bill to the vendor in care of (*his/her*) solicitor, (*vendor's law firm name*) at (*vendor's law firm address*). Our client(s) should then be shown on your records as the new owner(s), and future bills should be forwarded to (*him/her/them*) at the address of the subject property.

Thank you for your cooperation.

Yours very truly,

FIGURE 17.9 Letter to the Local Gas Company

Date

Name of gas company
Address

Dear Sir or Madam:

Re: *Name of transaction*
Address and municipality of property

We are the solicitors for ________________________, the purchaser(s) in the above transaction, which is scheduled to close on (*date*).

Kindly arrange for a meter reading one day before the date of closing, and forward a final bill to the vendor in care of (*his/her*) solicitor, (*vendor's law firm name*) at (*vendor's law firm address*). Our client(s) should then be shown on your records as the new owner(s), and future bills should be forwarded to (*him/her/them*) at the address of the subject property.

Thank you for your cooperation.

Yours very truly,

FIGURE 17.10 Letter to the Building Department

Date

Building Department
Name of municipality
Address

Dear Sir or Madam:

Re: *Name of transaction*
Address and municipality of property

We are the solicitors for ________________________, the purchaser(s) in the above transaction, which is scheduled to close on (*date*).

Would you please provide us with the following information with respect to the subject property:

- zoning, zoning bylaw number, and date of the zoning bylaw;
- the number and date of any part lot control bylaw with respect to the property;
- whether the land complies with the lot area, lot frontage, and lot depth requirements;
- whether the building complies with the height, floor area density, and set-back requirements;
- whether there are any prohibitions or limitations with respect to the use of the land and building;
- whether all other relevant bylaws and ordinances have been complied with; and
- whether there are any outstanding work orders or stop work orders or notices of violation with respect to the property. Would you please advise us of the amount of money advanced, if any, and the unpaid amount outstanding for development charges in respect of any past work orders or notices of violation.

We enclose our cheque payable to ___________________ in the amount of $ ________, in payment of your fee, together with a copy of the survey with respect to the property.

Thank you for your assistance in this matter.

Yours very truly,

FIGURE 17.11 Letter to Hydro One

Date

Hydro One
Address

Dear Sir or Madam:

Re: *Name of transaction*
Address and municipality of property

We are the solicitors for the purchaser(s) in the above transaction, which is scheduled to close on (*date*).

Would you please advise us whether or not Hydro One claims any easements under the *Electricity Act, 1998* with respect to the subject property.

We enclose a copy of the survey with respect to the property and our cheque payable to Hydro One in the amount of $ __________ , in payment of your fee.

Thank you for your assistance in this matter.

Yours very truly,

CHAPTER 18

Requisitions: An Overview

This chapter deals with the steps you must take arising from the matters discussed in chapter 17, Preliminary Matters — the search of title and the responses to your inquiry letters.

You and the lawyer handling the file must decide whether the searches and answers to your inquiry letters disclose a satisfactory state of affairs. If not, you must take steps to resolve the disclosed problems by way of a request made to the vendor to do so. These requests are known as **requisitions**.

requisition
request made to the vendor to clear up problems revealed by the title search and other inquiries

This chapter deals with requisitions in general and reviews those matters that give rise to requisitions. The drafting of requisitions will be dealt with in chapter 20, The Requisition Letter.

The word "requisition," in its widest sense, means anything the purchaser formally requires of the vendor in a real estate transaction — the correction of a title defect, the production of a document, or any other thing to which the purchaser is entitled. The purpose of making a requisition may be simply to remind the other party of a contractual obligation, or it may be to preserve the purchaser's rights under the contract with respect to an alleged title defect. All requisitions are based on the provisions in the agreement of purchase and sale. It is therefore always essential to read the agreement of purchase and sale before preparing requisitions.

The making of a requisition may give rise to the purchaser's right to terminate the agreement of purchase and sale under paragraph 10 of the agreement. For this to occur, the requisition must deal with one of the matters referred to in paragraph 10, the vendor (acting in good faith) must be unwilling or unable to remove the defect, and the purchaser must be unwilling to waive the requisition.

CATEGORIES OF REQUISITIONS

There are different categories of requisitions. The distinction between these categories is important primarily for determining whether or not the time limit in the agreement of purchase and sale set for the making of requisitions applies to a particular requisition.

Requisitions on Title

Requisitions on title raise objections to the title, based on the title search, and set out specific corrective actions that the purchaser requires. Requisitions on title are either **requisitions going to the root of title** or other **requisitions on title**.

requisition going to the root of title requisition based on a defect that calls into question the legal enforceability/validity of the title

requisition on title query of directives made by the purchaser that asks the vendor to remedy problems with title

Requisitions going to the root of title are those that call into question the vendor's title to the property, or that raise very serious defects in the vendor's title — so serious that, if required to accept title, the purchaser would be receiving something substantially different from what was bargained for.

Other requisitions on title include all requisitions flowing from the search of title that are not requisitions going to the root of title and that do not fall under the category of requisitions on conveyance or requisitions on contract.

Requisitions on Conveyance

requisition on conveyance requisition that requires the vendor to produce an effective conveyance, assuming that the vendor has the ability to do so

Requisitions on conveyance require the vendor to produce an effective conveyance of the property, assuming that the vendor has the ability to do so. If the vendor is unable to do so, the requisition is not one on conveyance but a requisition on title.

Requisitions on Matters of Contract

requisition on matters of contract requisition for specific things that the purchaser is entitled to receive under the contract

Requisitions on matters of contract are for specific things that the purchaser is entitled to receive under the contract. It may not be necessary to requisition those matters because the obligation already exists under the contract. However, it is good practice to remind the vendor's lawyer of the specific things that the purchaser expects under the terms of the agreement of purchase and sale.

Requisitions on Matters of Zoning and Building Bylaws

These matters have been held to be matters of land use and not matters of title. However, the wording of the particular agreement of purchase and sale may also cause some of these matters to be matters of contract.

PROCEDURE FOR REQUISITIONS

To be valid, a title requisition must set out a specific objection to or problem with the particular title and must then require a specific solution (or propose one or more alternative solutions).

Before you can determine what requisitions to make, you must, *under the supervision of the lawyer handling the file*, read the agreement of purchase and sale, obtain and review a proper search of title, send out and receive responses to the various preliminary letters, and review an up-to-date survey of the property. Only then can you determine what, if any, problems exist and what requisitions should be made. In general, both parties to a real estate transaction want the deal to close, so there will usually be a great deal of cooperation between the parties. There is therefore no need to be adversarial when drafting the requisitions. However, the requisitions must be sufficiently particular for the purchaser's lawyer to be able to rely on them if problems arise.

RESULTS OF PRELIMINARY LETTERS AS A SOURCE OF REQUISITIONS

When you receive responses to your preliminary letters, be sure to read them to see if they disclose any matters that might give rise to a requisition.

Municipal Tax Certificate

If the municipal tax certificate discloses that taxes have been paid up to or beyond the closing date, no requisition will be necessary, and the taxes will simply be adjusted on the statement of adjustments.

If the tax certificate discloses arrears of taxes — and particularly if the arrears are substantial — the matter should be dealt with in the requisition letter. The requisition will set out the particulars of the state of the tax account and require proof on closing of payment of the taxes. Taxes will be adjusted in the statement of adjustments on the basis that they have been paid up until closing (because, as of closing, they will have been). Often payment of the tax arrears will be made out of the closing funds. In such a case, the vendor will provide a direction to the purchaser that the appropriate portion of the closing funds be made payable to the municipality and delivered to the vendor's solicitor. The vendor's solicitor will then provide a personal undertaking to the purchaser to deliver the cheque to the municipality and to bear any responsibility for further penalties.

Water Department, Sewers, and Drains

If water charges are calculated on a flat-rate basis, they may be dealt with in the same way as municipal realty taxes. If the water charges are metered, however, the final balance will not be ascertainable until after closing. However, you should make sure that all bills delivered before closing have been paid. Request that evidence of that payment be provided on closing. If necessary, arrangements can be made for payment of any outstanding bills out of the closing proceeds, following the procedure applicable to tax certificates above.

The final bill will be delivered to the vendor after closing. To ensure that the vendor will pay the final water bill, you must require delivery of an undertaking signed by the vendor to that effect. However, if the bills have historically been large, you can call the water department to get an estimate of the final bill and request that the vendor's lawyer provide an undertaking to hold back sufficient money from the closing proceeds to pay it.

If the letter from the water department discloses the existence of an easement more significant than that required to be assumed by the terms of the agreement of purchase and sale, you must ask the vendor to obtain a release of the easement from the municipality. There is virtually no possibility that the vendor will be able to obtain such a release, but by making the requisition, the purchaser's rights under the agreement of purchase and sale are preserved.

If a significant easement is disclosed by the response from the water department, it will be necessary to obtain the purchaser's written instructions on how to proceed. Even though the purchaser is not required to accept title subject to this easement, the purchaser may choose to close regardless.

On a practical note, do not notify the client as each problem arises. Rather, it is a good practice to review the state of the title with the client once the search, the survey, and the replies to the preliminary letters have been reviewed.

Building Department

As discussed in chapter 17, Preliminary Matters, the first step following receipt of the letter from the building department is to fill in the details necessary to analyze the response.

You must review the cited zoning bylaws to determine the existing permitted use. If it is not as specified in the agreement of purchase and sale, you must requisition an amendment to the bylaw, a variance to allow the use, or satisfactory evidence that the use constitutes a legal non-conforming use. Advise the client of the potential problem.

If the location of the building does not comply with existing zoning provisions, again, you must requisition an amendment to the bylaw, a variance to allow the use, or satisfactory evidence that the use constitutes a legal non-conforming use. Again, you must advise the client.

If it appears that the location of the building or use of the premises may constitute a legal non-conforming use, you cannot simply rely on the vendor to provide the necessary evidence. You must also try to collect evidence that may resolve the question. For example, there may be declarations of possession registered on title that establish a continuous use or that the physical state of the buildings has not changed since before the date the current bylaw was enacted.

A survey predating the bylaw can help to establish a legal non-conforming use as to building location if the purchaser can confirm that there have been no changes to the structure since the date of the survey. If there have been changes made to the structure, ask the municipality whether building permits were issued and, if so, whether they seem to cover the work done. If building permits were issued, it is possible that there will not be a problem with zoning. Ordinarily, a building permit is issued only if the work complies with the existing zoning requirements or if a variance has been obtained.

In addition to getting independent evidence, you should require the vendor to provide as much evidence as possible — in particular, a declaration of possession that addresses the issue of use or location of the structures. Even if the vendor's ownership does not extend back beyond the passage of the current bylaw, the vendor may possess statutory declarations from previous owners that can, when added together, establish continuity of use or physical state of the buildings.

If there are outstanding work orders, you must requisition their rectification and removal. If the vendor is unwilling to do this, you should obtain written instructions from the client about whether to accept title subject to the outstanding work orders. Occasionally, a purchaser will agree to assume responsibility for the work orders in return for a reduction in the purchase price in an amount equal to the amount required for the repairs. In such a case, the client should be advised that the work may well end up costing more than estimated.

Unregistered Hydro Easements

If the response from Hydro One states that there is an unregistered easement, you must decide whether it is one that falls within the category of easements that the purchaser is required to accept. If it does not, you must request that the vendor obtain a discharge of the easement from Hydro One. It is most unlikely that such a discharge can be obtained, but by making the requisition, you protect the purchaser's rights under the agreement of purchase and sale. You must also get the client's written instructions.

THE SURVEY AS A SOURCE OF REQUISITIONS

An up-to-date plan of survey of the property can disclose one or more of the following problems:

- the property being purchased is the wrong property — not the property the purchaser had in mind;
- the property being purchased is the wrong size;
- buildings on the property being purchased encroach on someone else's property;
- buildings on someone else's property encroach on the property being purchased; or
- there is a right of way over the property being purchased that is not in accordance with the agreement of purchase and sale.

The Wrong Property

This is a concern that almost never arises in urban transactions. In the unlikely event that such a problem does arise, you must get the client's written instructions as soon as possible.

The Wrong Size

If the property shown on the survey is smaller than described in the legal description, or smaller than the size indicated by the dimensions in the agreement of purchase and sale, the purchaser's rights will depend on a number of circumstances, including the extent of the discrepancy and whether the size of the property was apparent on examination of the property. If the extent of the discrepancy is large enough, the purchaser may either seek an abatement (reduction) in the purchase price or terminate the transaction. The client must give specific, written instructions.

If you discover a discrepancy in size, in order to preserve the purchaser's rights under the agreement of purchase and sale, you must requisition resolution of the matter. The requisition should point out the deficiency, referring to the survey (and the most recent transfer if it discloses the problem as well), and should require a correcting transfer.

Encroachments on Other Property

The survey may show that buildings or structures encroach on adjoining property. For example, the fence may be located partly on the neighbouring property, the eaves of the house may hang over the neighbouring property, or the front steps may be located on municipal property.

An encroachment by a building or structure on adjoining property is not a problem if the owner of the other property consents or if the encroachment has existed long enough to establish possessory title. If the survey discloses an encroachment, you must submit a requisition on the matter. The requisition should set out the particulars of the encroachment and seek proof of consent of the other owner or satisfactory evidence of possessory title.

Encroachments on Property Being Purchased

If the survey discloses that adjoining buildings or structures are encroaching on the property being purchased, the purchaser's rights will depend on the nature and extent of the encroachment. If the encroachment is minor, the purchaser may be obliged to accept title notwithstanding the encroachment. If the encroachment is major, however, the purchaser may be entitled to terminate the transaction or seek an abatement in the purchase price. You must get the client's written instructions.

If you find this kind of encroachment, you must submit a requisition on the matter. The requisition should set out the particulars of the encroachment and require its removal. Although the vendor will generally not be able to have the encroachment removed (there may, in fact, be possessory title), the requisition is made to protect the purchaser's rights under the agreement of purchase and sale.

Rights of Way

If the survey discloses the existence of a right of way over the property that has not been provided for in the agreement of purchase and sale, you must submit a requisition on the matter. The requisition should set out the particulars of the right of way and require its removal. Although the vendor may not be in a position to have the right of way removed, you must make the requisition to protect the purchaser's rights under the agreement of purchase and sale. The client may be entitled to seek an abatement or to terminate the transaction. You will need specific written instructions from the client.

THE TITLE SEARCH AS A SOURCE OF REQUISITIONS

When the search notes are received from the title searcher, you must review them to determine the answers to a number of questions:

- Is the parcel the size expected?
- Does the search start with a good root of title?

- Is the chain of title connected?
- Have all mortgages been discharged?
- Are there any other outstanding matters?
- Are there any mortgages to be assumed?
- Are there any outstanding executions?
- Are there any special concerns?
- Do the instruments conform with all formal requirements?
- Are there any inconsistencies in affidavits?
- Have adjoining properties been searched?

Size of the Parcel

Compare the metes and bounds description in the most recent transfer or the measurements shown on the whiteprint of the plan of subdivision with the dimensions in the agreement of purchase and sale. They should be the same. It may be necessary to convert from metric to imperial measurement. If so, there are calculators available with that function.

Good Root of Title

A good root of title will be the first conveyance after the commencement date of the search (40 years before the date of closing), or a certificate of title, or a Crown patent. If the property is a lot or part of a lot on a plan of subdivision that is less than 40 years old, you will see that the title searcher has to "search behind the plan." In other words, the searcher has to locate the abstract in which instruments that pertain to the property were registered before the registration of the plan. Then, the searcher has to check all the documents in that book, starting from the root of title, up to the date that the plan of subdivision was registered; the search must then be continued in the abstract book containing the lot and plan up to the present date.

Chain of Title

Starting with the earliest grant in the chain of title, all grants to date should be listed. In any conveyance, the grantor should be the same person as the grantee in the previous conveyance. The last person in the chain should be the same person as the vendor.

Discharge of Mortgages

All mortgages, other than mortgages to be assumed, should have been discharged. Review the search to make sure that all these mortgages have been discharged or **ruled off.** Make a list of all mortgages that are still outstanding, and requisition a discharge of each.

ruled off
the land registrar's drawing of a line through the entry in the abstract book of a mortgage that has been discharged

The search should contain sufficient particulars of any outstanding mortgage (including the date and time of registration, the registration number, and the parties) to enable the person closing the deal to be sure that the discharge produced on or before closing is proper. The search should also contain sufficient information (the mortgage terms, the name and address of the mortgagee, and the mortgage number) to allow the purchaser's law firm to follow up on the discharge and ensure that one will be available.

Other Outstanding Matters

Review the search of title again for any other liens, charges, agreements such as subdivision agreements, restrictive covenants, bylaws, or other matters that have not been adequately dealt with. Make a note of any outstanding item, and determine what, if any, action is required — for example, a discharge, evidence of compliance, etc. Requisition the required action, and then take any necessary followup steps with third parties. The search should contain sufficient particulars to allow you to do this.

SUBDIVISION AGREEMENTS

The search of title may disclose an outstanding subdivision agreement. Paragraph 10 of the agreement of purchase and sale requires the purchaser to accept title subject to such agreements, provided they have been complied with. You must requisition proof of compliance or posting of security to secure compliance. It is not enough, however, to rely on the vendor to look after this matter. In addition, you should write a letter to the relevant municipality to ascertain whether a discharge is available and, if not, whether the agreement has been complied with or adequate security posted. Figure 18.1 is an example of this kind of letter.

RESTRICTIVE COVENANTS

The search of title may disclose outstanding restrictive covenants (registered restrictions running with the land). Under the agreement of purchase and sale, the purchaser must accept title subject to these restrictions, provided they have been complied with. Accordingly, you must requisition evidence that the restrictions have been complied with. Again, in addition to making the requisition, you should contact any third party involved to try to obtain evidence of compliance.

Mortgages to Be Assumed

If the agreement of purchase and sale states that the purchaser is to assume an existing mortgage, make sure that you instruct the title searcher to obtain a photocopy of the mortgage for review. When you review the search, look at the mortgage to confirm that the terms of the mortgage registered on title comply with the terms of the mortgage as described in the agreement of purchase and sale.

If the mortgage on title matches the description of the mortgage to be assumed in the agreement of purchase and sale, you must requisition confirmation that the mortgage on title is the mortgage to be assumed. You will also requisition the production of a mortgage statement on closing that confirms the balance outstanding on the mortgage and states that the mortgage is in good standing. You should also write to the mortgagee, asking for a mortgage statement. Figure 18.2 is an example of this letter.

If the mortgage on title differs from the description of the mortgage to be assumed in the agreement of purchase and sale, you must requisition either production and registration of an amending agreement that amends the mortgage to conform with the terms of the agreement, or a discharge of the existing mortgage and replacement with a mortgage containing the appropriate terms. Rather than an amending agreement or a new mortgage, the vendor may provide a mortgage statement, signed by the mortgagee, confirming that the terms of the mortgage, in fact, comply with the terms in the agreement. In most circumstances, production of this kind of a mortgage statement will be satisfactory.

You must also review any mortgage to be assumed to make sure that there are no restrictions on assumability. If the mortgage is not assumable by a purchaser, it will be necessary to requisition an amendment to the mortgage or a discharge of the existing mortgage and a replacement with a mortgage that complies with the agreement. If the mortgage requires the approval by the mortgagee of any subsequent purchaser, it is necessary to requisition the approval. Review the agreement of purchase and sale to determine who is responsible for obtaining this approval. In any event, ask the mortgagee what steps must be taken by the purchaser to be approved, and advise the purchaser accordingly.

Executions

If the client has chosen not to obtain title insurance, it is standard procedure, when conducting a 40-year Registry system search, to search executions against all owners during the 40-year period. The search notes should therefore include a sheriff's certificate containing a list of names and indicating whether there are any executions against the persons named.

If there are outstanding executions against any person in the chain of title, you must requisition a discharge of the execution. If the execution disclosed on the certificate is, in fact, outstanding against the vendor or a prior owner, the vendor will be required to have the execution lifted before closing, usually by paying the amount of the judgment.

Often, however, the execution disclosed on the certificate turns out to be not against the vendor or a prior owner, but rather against someone with a similar name. In that case, you will requisition production of sufficient evidence to ensure that the person named in the execution is not the same person as the person in the chain of title. In the Land Titles system, if the amount of the execution is greater than $50,000, you will need a letter from the execution creditor or from the execution creditor's lawyer that the owner or former owner of the property is not the same person as the execution debtor. If the amount is less than $50,000, an affidavit from the owner is sufficient.

In addition to requiring production of the appropriate evidence from the vendor, you should take steps to obtain the evidence as well. If the outstanding execution is against a name similar to that of the vendor, you can contact the execution creditor or the lawyer acting for the creditor to obtain information confirming the debtor's age, occupation, address, etc. This information can help satisfy the lawyer handling the file that the vendor's affidavit is acceptable. However, if the outstanding execution is against a prior owner, the vendor's lawyer is in no better position to obtain the necessary information than you are.

Special Concerns

The search of title may disclose matters that require special attention.

DEEDS UNDER POWER OF SALE

If the search of title discloses a deed under power of sale, you must review the mortgage to get particulars of the power of sale, including the default period and notice period. If there is no power of sale contained in the mortgage, part II of the *Mortgages Act* governs the notice and default periods.

Check that there is a declaration deposited on title stating that the required default has taken place (default for the period in the mortgage or the Act) and that service of the notice has been effected on the required parties (see part III of the *Mortgages Act* regarding parties). There must be a statement by the mortgagee or by the lawyer representing the mortgagee that the sale complies with part III (and, where there is no power of sale in the mortgage, with part II) of the *Mortgages Act.*

Section 34 of the *Mortgages Act* provides that a statutory declaration is conclusive evidence of compliance with the power of sale provisions and is sufficient to give good title. However, the statutory declaration must make sense on the surface. In other words, if it is clear that there was no proper default, notice period, or service on all parties, the purchaser cannot rely on the statutory declaration.

FINAL ORDERS OF FORECLOSURE

Where the search reveals a final order of foreclosure, check the order to make sure that it contains the proper legal description and that all persons with an interest on title subsequent to the mortgage, as well as the spouse of the mortgagor (where the order is after March 31, 1978), are identified as being foreclosed.

CONSTRUCTION LIENS AND CERTIFICATES OF ACTION

Where the search of title discloses a construction lien on title, review the search to ensure that the lien has been properly discharged. The lien itself may be discharged by either registration of a discharge of lien or a court order. If a certificate of action has been registered as well, a court order is required for it to be properly vacated or removed. The court order must state that the certificate of action is vacated and, where applicable, the lien is discharged.

If either the lien or the certificate of action is outstanding, you must requisition that the lien be discharged or the certificate of action be vacated.

CORPORATIONS

In reviewing the search of title, make a note of all corporate owners on title and the dates during which they owned the property. You must arrange for a corporate search of each corporation to confirm that it was in existence during the time the property was owned. If the corporate existence lapsed at any time during its ownership of the property, the land escheats, or reverts to the Crown.

Although there is software that enables online corporate searches, most residential real estate law firms get their corporate searches done by a service provider such as Dye & Durham, Cyberbahn, or Oncorp.

TRANSFERS BY AN ESTATE

If the search is in the Registry system, and it discloses a transfer by an estate or if the vendor is an estate, a special form of transfer containing a number of specific recitals will be required. A notarial copy of the certificate of appointment of estate trustee, with or without a will, must also be registered on title. In addition, if the deceased died between 1970 and 1979, an Ontario succession duty release must be registered on title.

If the property is in Land Titles, and the vendor is an estate, the estate trustee must first register a transmission application, registering the estate trustee as the owner of the deceased's property. The application must contain a compliance with law statement by the lawyer for the estate, stating that debts have been paid in full, and setting out the particulars of the appointment of the estate trustee, which must still be in full force and effect.

RIGHTS OF WAY

If the agreement of purchase and sale states that the property includes a right of way over another property, it is necessary to search the title to the servient tenement to ensure that the right of way is registered against that property.

Formal Requirements

Many statutes affecting the registration requirements of various instruments have come into and gone out of effect during the period of time covered by a 40-year Registry system search. Accordingly, the formalities required of each instrument will differ for different dates in the search period.

You can find lists of these different requirements and their relevant dates in various title searching manuals. These lists set out, for example, the effective dates for certain affidavits, as well as other technical requirements in force from time to time. A list of dates that were important for searches prior to electronic conversion is reproduced in figure 18.3.

For each instrument abstracted, the title searcher should have checked off boxes to indicate various items that appear in the instruments. When reviewing the search notes, you must check the notes for each instrument and compare them with the various items on one of the lists to ensure that the instrument complies with the technical requirements in effect at the relevant time.

Inconsistencies in Affidavits

Review the contents of affidavits of marital status and spousal status to make sure there is no inconsistency from one transaction to the next. If a deed contains a statement or affidavit that the property is not a matrimonial home, but there is a previous affidavit on title with respect to the same parties that contradicts it, you cannot rely on the latter statement or affidavit. You will have to requisition evidence that explains the contradiction.

Adjoining Property

If the property being purchased is part of a lot, it may be necessary to search adjoining properties back to 1967 to ensure compliance with the *Planning Act*. This is not required if a part lot exemption bylaw is registered on title, if a consent to the severance has been registered in the past, or if a transfer containing the completed *Planning Act* statements in boxes 13 and 14 of the transfer/deed of land has been registered on title. It is not necessary to search adjoining properties if the property being purchased is a whole lot, unless there is registered on title a bylaw that states that the plan of subdivision no longer constitutes a plan of subdivision.

If any contravention of the *Planning Act* is disclosed, you must requisition the obtaining and registration of a consent to the severance.

FOLLOW UP ON ALL REQUISITIONS

If problems are disclosed when reviewing the title search, survey, and responses to preliminary letters, it is not sufficient to simply requisition a correction of the matter — you cannot rely on the vendor to rectify matters. You should take steps to do so as well. For example, you should

- contact municipalities for occupancy permits, releases, or confirmation of compliance with subdivision agreements;
- contact third-party lawyers with regard to executions, affidavits, or technical deficiencies; and
- contact mortgagees for statements or discharges.

REFERENCES

Mortgages Act, RSO 1990, c. M.40.

Planning Act, RSO 1990, c. P.13.

REVIEW QUESTIONS

1. What is a requisition?
2. What are the implications of making a requisition?
3. Why is it important to distinguish between the different categories of requisitions?
4. What are requisitions on title?
5. What are requisitions on conveyance?
6. What are requisitions on matters of contract?
7. What is required for a requisition to be valid?
8. How can a tax certificate give rise to a requisition?
9. How can the response from the water department give rise to a requisition?
10. What requisitions may arise from the building department letter?
11. What requisitions may arise from the response from Hydro One?
12. What requisition is made if the survey discloses that the property is smaller than the description in the agreement of purchase and sale?
13. What requisition is made if the survey discloses that buildings or structures encroach on adjoining property?
14. What requisition is made if the survey discloses that adjoining buildings or structures encroach on the property being purchased?
15. What requisition is made if the survey discloses the existence of a right of way over the property that is not provided for in the agreement of purchase and sale?
16. What requisition is made if there are mortgages on title other than any mortgages to be assumed?
17. What requisition is made if the search of title discloses an outstanding subdivision agreement?
18. What requisition is made if the search of title discloses outstanding restrictive covenants?
19. What requisition is made if there is a mortgage to be assumed?
20. What requisition is made if there are outstanding executions against any person in the chain of title?
21. What requisition is made if a construction lien has been registered on title?

FIGURE 18.1 Subdivision Agreement Letter

Date

Building Department
Name of municipality
Address

Dear Sir or Madam:

Re: *Name of transaction*
Address of property

We are the solicitors for ______________________, the purchaser(s) in the above transaction, which is scheduled to close on (*date*).

Our search of title has disclosed the following agreements registered on title:

- Instrument number ___________________, dated (*date*) and registered on (*date*) between (*subdivider*) and (*municipality*)
- Instrument number ___________________, dated (*date*) and registered on (*date*) between (*subdivider*) and (*municipality*)

With respect to each of the above agreements, would you please advise us

- whether all the terms and provisions of the agreement have been complied with, or whether there are any outstanding items still to be completed;
- if the agreement has been complied with, whether a release is available;
- if there are still outstanding items, whether you hold adequate security to guarantee completion of all outstanding matters;
- whether there are any outstanding levies or other charges; and
- whether any occupancy provisions of the agreement have been complied with.

We enclose a stamped, self-addressed envelope for your convenience, together with our cheque payable to _________________ in the amount of $ ___________ , in payment of your fee.

Thank you for your assistance in this matter.

Yours very truly,

FIGURE 18.2 Letter Requesting Mortgage Statement for Assumption Purposes

Date

Mortgagee's name
Mortgagee's address

Dear Sir or Madam:

Re: Your mortgage with (*vendor's name*)
Address of property
Mortgage number

We act for ______________________, the purchaser(s) in the above transaction, which is scheduled to close on (*date*). Pursuant to the agreement of purchase and sale, our clients are assuming the mortgage that you hold.

Please forward a mortgage statement to us setting out the amount of principal and interest outstanding as of the closing date and the terms of the said mortgage including the interest rate, the payment date and period, the balance due date, and the amount and frequency of each payment.

As well, please confirm that the said mortgage may be assumed by our clients, and that it is in good standing.

Thank you for your assistance in this matter.

Yours very truly,

FIGURE 18.3 Important Dates Affecting Registration Requirements

Date		Requirement
June 1	1921	Land transfer tax affidavit
June 1	1929	Affidavit of celibacy
January 1	1937	All documents perforated with the word "registered"
June 25	1939	Affidavit of age and marital status required by men in deed or mortgage where wife has joined to bar her dower
April 30	1954	Affidavit of mortmain for corporations (revoked June 23, 1965)
April 1	1957	Affidavit of age required by men and women
		Affidavit of marital status by men in deed or mortgage if no one joins in as wife
January 1	1959	Dominion estate tax consents required (revoked January 1, 1972)
May 8	1964	Retail sales tax clearance (repealed April 1, 1976)
July 1	1964	Affidavit of age required in power of attorney, lease, assignment of lease and mortgage
		Affidavit of marital status may be sworn by either spouse
		Instruments must contain the surname and at least one given name of grantee other than a corporation
June 23	1965	No affidavit of mortmain required for Ontario companies
January 1	1967	Affidavit of age required on discharge of mortgage
May 3	1967	Power of consent under *Planning Act* transferred from Planning Board to committees of adjustment or Ministry of Municipal Affairs
June 15	1967	Prior violations of subdivision and part lot control requirements of *Planning Act* are forgiven
May 3	1968	*Planning Act* 10-acre consent rule cancelled
May 13	1969	Affidavit of marital status required any time wife joins in a document
June 27	1969	Conveyance of land as gift made subject to subdivision and part lot control under *Planning Act*
January 1	1970	Succession duty consent required (repealed April 10, 1979)
June 27	1970	*Planning Act* subdivision and part lot control applies throughout Ontario
April 28	1971	Simultaneous conveyances prohibited under *Planning Act*
September 1	1971	Age of majority changed to 18 years from 21 years
January 1	1972	Dominion estate tax consent requirement cancelled
		Affidavit of residence—section 116 of the *Income Tax Act*
January 1	1973	All new subdivisions must be registered in Land Titles system

FIGURE 18.3 Concluded

Date		Requirement
April 1	1973	Retail sales tax on chattels paid at registry office
July 1	1973	All tax sales registered before July 1, 1973 pursuant to *Municipal Affairs Act* and *Assessment Act* confirmed under *Tax Sales Confirmation Act*
August 1	1973	Registration of notice of agreement of purchase and sale, option to purchase or assignment good for one year under *Registry Act*
December 17	1973	Partial discharge of mortgage subject to subdivision and part lot control under *Planning Act*
April 10	1974	Affidavit of residency by purchaser to be included in deed, *Land Speculation Tax Act* affidavit or lien clearance to be inserted in deed (repealed October 24, 1978)
April 1	1976	Retail sales tax clearance cancelled
March 31	1978	*Family Law Reform Act* abolishes dower unless previously vested; creates statutory right of possession by spouse to matrimonial home; affidavits required
October 24	1978	*Land Speculation Tax Act* repealed
December 15	1978	*Planning Act* contravention of consent requirements forgiven except where judgment or court order provides otherwise
March 31	1979	Once *Planning Act* consent is given to convey a parcel, further consent not required for subsequent sale
April 10	1979	Succession duty consent cancelled
November 30	1979	Corporation tax lien must be registered against property to be effective
July 1	1980	Requirement to register estate tax consent cancelled
June 26	1981	*Planning Act* consent required for partition orders
June 15	1982	*Mortmain and Charitable Uses Act* repealed
April 2	1983	*Construction Lien Act* in force
August 1	1983	*Planning Act, 1983* in force
November 1	1984	*Land Registration Reform Act* in force in County of Oxford, *Planning Act* statements available; *Planning Act* affidavits not required
January 1	1985	*Municipal Tax Sales Act* in force
April 1	1985	*Land Registration Reform Act* in force in all of Ontario
March 1	1986	*Family Law Act* in force; new statements regarding matrimonial home
March 31	1988	Vested dower rights extinguished unless notice of claim registered

CHAPTER 19

Reviewing the Search of Title

This chapter reviews the search notes for the 40-year Registry system search of Lot 11, Plan 1209, Township of Whitford, following the steps set out in chapter 13, Title Searching. In the next chapter, these search notes will serve as the basis for the drafting of requisitions on title. At the end of the chapter, we show what the Teraview printout looks like if the property is a Parcelized Day Forward Registry (PDFR) property or, alternatively, if the property is a Land Titles Conversion Qualified (LTCQ) property.

The search notes are reproduced as an appendix at the end of the chapter. The search was conducted using the abstract index for Lot 57, Concession 6, Township of Whitford, reproduced as figure 13.1, and the abstract index for Lot 11, Plan 1209, Township of Whitford, reproduced as figure 13.2.

IS THE PARCEL THE RIGHT SIZE?

This property is a whole lot, so you must review the whiteprint of the plan of subdivision to make sure that the dimensions of the lot are the same as the dimensions specified in the agreement of purchase and sale. A copy of the whiteprint is reproduced as figure 13.3. Assume that the dimensions shown on the whiteprint are satisfactory.

DOES THE SEARCH START WITH A GOOD ROOT OF TITLE?

Assuming that the search was conducted in September 2008, our root of title is the deed to Willard Marshall registered on August 14, 1977 as instrument number 44796. This is the oldest deed that is within the 40-year search period.

However, as stated in chapter 13, Title Searching, many real estate lawyers still prefer to start their searches with the conveyance of the fee simple estate to the person who owned the property at the commencement of the 40-year search period. By that standard, our root of title is the deed to Walter Fitzgerald registered on September 15, 1951 as instrument number 42347. This is the first deed that is at least 40 years old.

IS THE CHAIN OF TITLE CONNECTED?

The chain of title as disclosed in the search notes is reproduced in figure 13.4. The diagonal line through Duncan McTavish's name signifies that he died, leaving Marla McTavish as the surviving joint tenant. There appears to be no break in the chain of title.

HAVE ALL MORTGAGES BEEN DISCHARGED?

The cover page of the search notes discloses three outstanding mortgages: instrument number 170005 from Baker and Baker to the Bank of Nova Scotia, instrument number 191437 from Mercier and Laframboise to the Toronto-Dominion Bank, and instrument number 192600 from Mercier and Mercier to ABC Company Ltd. You must review the agreement of purchase and sale to determine whether or not these mortgages are to be discharged.

ARE THERE ANY OTHER OUTSTANDING MATTERS?

The search discloses a number of matters that must be examined.

Instrument Number 75581

Instrument number 75581 (page 2 of the search notes) is a deed from Willard Marshall to Fritz Gunther that the searcher has noted is "NOL" (not our land). It is a good idea to check the description, if provided, to verify that the property is not, in fact, part of the subject property. Since Marshall conveyed this property, and it was only a part of the property he owned, there could be a contravention of the *Planning Act*. However, he obtained Land Division Committee consent. Thus, no requisition is necessary.

Instrument Number 99744

Instrument number 99744 (figure 13.1) is a deed from Alexander Marshall and Wanda Marshall, but it does not affect our land in any way because our land is on Plan 1209. Anything registered on the concession lot after registration of the plan is of no interest to us.

Instrument Number 84922

Instrument number 84922 (page 5 of the search notes) is a bylaw dealing with part lot control. This bylaw does not affect our property because the property is the whole of Lot 11.

Instrument Number 90248

Instrument number 90248 (page 6 of the search notes) is a notice of agreement relating to a subdivision agreement between Stavros Subdivisions Ltd. and The Corporation of the Township of Whitford. Paragraph 10 of the agreement of purchase and sale requires the purchaser to accept title subject to any municipal agreements, as long as they have been complied with. You should requisition proof of compliance with this agreement in the form of a letter from the township. As well, you should write to the Township of Whitford yourself, to make sure that the terms of the subdivision agreement have been complied with.

Instrument Number 153117

Instrument number 153117 (page 9 of the search notes) is a deed from Marla MacTavish alone, containing **recitals** regarding the death of Duncan McTavish and Marla's right to convey as surviving joint tenant. The *Vendors and Purchasers Act* provides that recitals more than 20 years old are sufficient evidence of the truth of the facts recited, unless there is evidence to contradict those facts. Since these recitals are not more than 20 years old, they cannot be accepted as proof of what is stated. There is also a death certificate for Duncan McTavish (deposited as instrument number 148902, noted on page 8), which provides proof of his death. Thus, there is sufficient evidence that Marla McTavish had the right to convey the property on her own.

recitals
statements that set out the facts on which the document is based

Another concern with this document is a spelling discrepancy between Marla *Mc*Tavish in instrument number 91764 (page 7 of the notes) and Marla *Mac*Tavish in instrument number 153117. This, however, is explained in deposit number 170003 (page 10 of the notes), which is a statutory declaration by Marla McTavish, explaining that she is one and the same person as Marla McTavish in instrument number 91764 and Marla MacTavish in instrument number 153117. Therefore, no requisitions are necessary with respect to these documents.

HAVE ALL FORMAL REQUIREMENTS BEEN MET?

You must check each instrument against the important dates listed in figure 18.3 to ensure that it complies with the various registration requirements in effect at the relevant time.

When reviewing a deed, you should make sure that the parties are properly named. Compare each grantor's name with the name appearing as grantee in the deed by which title was obtained. In addition, in deeds predating the *Land Registration Reform Act*, check for the granting clause, the ***habendum* clause**, the four usual covenants, and the release clause. Also, check the legal description to verify that the parcel is properly described. You must also make sure that the deed was executed and, where the deed predates the *Land Registration Reform Act*, that there are affidavits of witness and of age and marital status (age and spousal status after March 31, 1978).

***habendum* clause**
clause in a deed (old form) that indicates that ownership is subject to reservations, limitations, provisos, and conditions expressed in the original Crown grant

With respect to affidavits of age and marital status, while dower rights were abolished by the *Family Law Reform Act* on March 31, 1978, there was an exception for dower rights that had vested. This is no longer of concern because the 10-year limitation period for any dower claims has passed (as of March 31, 1988).

ARE THERE OUTSTANDING EXECUTIONS?

The search notes provided by the title searcher should include a sheriff's certificate that lists the names against which executions were searched and the results of the search. Figure 19.1 is a sheriff's certificate. In this case, executions have been searched against all names disclosed in the chain of title, and they are clear.

POTENTIAL SOLUTIONS TO PROBLEMS

When reviewing a search of title, keep in mind the following basic principles because they may provide an answer to potential title problems.

The first possible solution is "the 40-year rule." The combined effect of the various sections of part III of the *Registry Act* is that title is not affected by any question more than 40 years old if there have been conveyances during that 40-year search period. If there have been no conveyances during that period, you must search back to the last recorded conveyance.

In fact, on the basis of the case of *Fire v. Longtin*, there is no need to check any instrument registered more than 40 years before the date of closing, unless there is no conveyance within the 40-year period (in which case you would then check for a conveyance before the 40-year period). In other words, it is not necessary to look for a root deed outside the 40-year period provided there is a conveyance some time within the 40-year period. Notwithstanding this decision, some lawyers will look for a conveyance at least 40 years old as the root deed, while relying on the 40-year rule to answer any questions with regard to intervening registrations between the root deed and the closing date of the current transaction.

Another potential solution is addressed by the *Vendors and Purchasers Act* provision with respect to recitals as discussed above, regarding instrument number 153117.

PARCELIZED DAY FORWARD REGISTRY SEARCH

If this property is automated, in addition to the paper abstract book, there will also be a computerized abstract for the property. Usually the computerized abstract will list only the documents registered after the property was automated. Documents registered before that date will be listed only in the paper abstract book. A complete title search for a PDFR property will include a check of both the computerized abstract and the paper abstract book going back 40 years.

The Teraview computerized abstract for Lot 11, Plan 1209, Township of Whitford is reproduced in figure 19.2. There have been no documents registered since the property was automated, so there are no concerns additional to or different from those raised in the previous discussion of the 40-year search.

LAND TITLES CONVERSION QUALIFIED SEARCH

LTCQ properties were originally in the Registry system and have been converted to the Land Titles system as a result of POLARIS (Province of Ontario Land Registration Information System). Unlike the Registry system, which simply provides a record of documents affecting title, the Land Titles system provides a statement of title as a fact; the government guarantees the accuracy of title to land registered in the Land Titles system. The parcel register always reflects the current state of title. There are, however, a number of exceptions to the government's certification of title. Title to LTCQ properties remains subject to any adverse possession claims in existence when the property was converted. Title is confirmed for *Planning Act* compliance as of the date of conversion, but you must check for compliance after that date. Title is protected from Crown claims against land as a result of the dissolution of any prior corporate owners. Crown claims are excluded as of the date the property was converted.

Figure 19.3 shows the Teraview printout for Lot 11, Plan 1209, Township of Whitford once the property has been converted.

Because of the differences between the Registry and Land Titles systems, not all of the issues raised with respect to the 40-year Registry system search apply. Those concerns are re-examined below:

1. Is the parcel the right size? This is a concern for an LTCQ property. A whiteprint of the plan of subdivision is available for LTCQ properties and should be reviewed.
2. Does the search start with a good root of title? This is not a concern for an LTCQ property.
3. Is the chain of title connected? This is not a concern for an LTCQ property.
4. Have all mortgages been discharged? This is a concern for an LTCQ property. The LTCQ printout shows the three outstanding mortgages.
5. Are there any other outstanding matters? This is a concern for an LTCQ property. However, the number of outstanding instruments will be greatly reduced. In this case, the only other outstanding instrument is instrument number 90248 — the notice of subdivision agreement.
6. Have the formal requirements of outstanding documents been met? This is not a concern for an LTCQ property because all Land Titles documents are reviewed before they are accepted for registration.
7. Are there executions outstanding? It is necessary to search executions against the current owners only.

REFERENCES

Family Law Reform Act, RSO 1990, c. F.3.

Fire v. Longtin, [1995] 4 SCR 3, (1995), 128 DLR (4th) 767.

Land Registration Reform Act, RSO 1990, c. L.4.

Planning Act, RSO 1990, c. P.13.

Registry Act, RSO 1990, c. R.20.

Vendors and Purchasers Act, RSO 1990, c. V.2.

APPENDIX Search Notes to Lot 11, Plan 1209, Township of Whitford

Title Search : Lot 11, Plan 1209, Township of Whitford.

Present owners : Francois Mercier
Huguette Marie Laframboise, (j.t.)

Outstanding mortgages : #170005 Bank of Nova Scotia $65,000.
#191437 Toronto-Dominion Bank $40,000
#192600 ABC Company Ltd. $15,000.

Easements : None
Subdivision Agreements : # 90248

Notes: ① Present owner by deed #191436 : Huguette Marie Laframboise
mortgagor in #192600 : Huguette Marie Mercier

② #170004 : Murphy T. Baker + Leslie R. Baker
#191436 : Murphy Baker + Leslie Baker

PIN : 12345-6789 (R)

Executions : None

Whiteprint of Plan 1209 enclosed

APPENDIX Continued

CCNS
66 Gerrard St. East
Toronto, Ont. M5B 1G3
Form 156

☑ REGISTRY ☐ LAND TITLES ☑ DATE OF SEARCH: September/08 ☐ SEARCHER: PAGE 1 OF 15 PAGES

LOT: 57 CON: 6 PLAN: MUNICIPALITY: Whitford REGION/COUNTY:

INSTRUMENT NUMBER	INSTRUMENT	DATE OF INSTRUMENT	DATE OF REGISTRY	TRANSFEROR/CHARGOR	TRANSFEREE/CHARGEE	CONSIDERATION	DESCRIPTION (P.I.N.)
44796	Deed	Aug.10/77	Aug.14/77	Walter Fitzgerald	Willard Marshall		Pt. Lot 57, commencing at S.E.< of Lot 57;
				—bar of dower by Rosa Fitzgerald			thence N'ly along E'ly boundary to N.E.<;
							thence W'ly along N'ly boundary, 2,150' to a pt.;
							thence S'ly // to E'ly boundary to a pt. in S'ly boundary;
							thence E'ly along S'ly boundary, 2150' to pt. of commencement.

☑ SFCA
☐ DEA/EAA
☐ SFMA
☑ GRANT
☑ FEE SIMPLE
☐ JOINT TEN.
☐ TEN. IN COM.
☐ TO USES
☐ AND APPOINT
☑ HAB (~~as JT~~)
☑ UC (4) (1)
☑ REL
☑ B OF DWR (31/3/78)
☐ SPOUSAL CONSENT & REL
☑ S & S BY
☐ CS OF
☐ ONT SUC DUTY (10/1/70) – (10/4/79)
☐ FED ESTATE TAX (1/1/59) – (1/1/72)
☐ A OF MM (30/4/54) ONT. CO. (23/6/65) OTHER (15/6/82)
☑ A OF LTT (V & C) (1/6/21)

☑ A OF SUB. WIT.
☐ COM. ADJUST. CONSENT (1/6/67) DATE: ______ SIGNED CH. & SEC.
☐ AF PL. ACT
☐ STATE RE PL. ACT (1) (2) (3)
☑ A OF AGE (3/4/57) (26/5/68) – CHARGOR (1/1/61) – GUARANTOR
☐ STATE OF AGE (1/4/85)
☑ A OF MS (25/6/39) – (31/3/78)
☐ A OF SP. STATUS (31/3/78)
☐ STATE OF SP. STATUS (1/4/85)
☐ SP/NOT A SP/SP OF EA OTHR
☐ NOT A MAT. HOME
☐ REL UNDR SEP. AGRMNT
☐ DT OF BRTH – TRANSFEREE(S) 1. ______ 2. ______
☐ AF OF PARTNER PROP PUR AS PP HELD AS PP ONLY PARTNERS
☐ DOCUMENT GENERAL
☐ SCHEDULE

☐ PHOTOCOPY ATTACHED ☐ SKETCH ATTACHED

SOLICITOR FOR 1ST PARTY(IES)	SOLICITOR FOR 2ND PARTY(IES)
Smith + Jones	Smith + Jones
202 Main St.	
Whitford	
MUNICIPAL ADDRESS 1ST PARTY(IES)	MUNICIPAL ADDRESS 2ND PARTY(IES)

APPENDIX Continued

CCNS
66 Gerrard St. East
Toronto, Ont. M5B 1G3
Form 156

☐ REGISTRY ☐ LAND TITLES ☐ DATE OF SEARCH: ☐ SEARCHER: PAGE 2 OF 15 PAGES

LOT: 57 CON: 6 PLAN: MUNICIPALITY: REGION/COUNTY:

INSTRUMENT NUMBER	INSTRUMENT	DATE OF INSTRUMENT	DATE OF REGISTRY	TRANSFEROR/CHARGOR	TRANSFEREE/CHARGEE	CONSID-ERATION	DESCRIPTION (P.I.N.)
75581	Deed	Mar.20/85	Apr.2/85	MARSHALL, Willard	GUNTHER, Fritz		Pt. of Lot 57, commencing at a pt. on the N'ly boundary, a distance of 2,000' from the N.E.<; thence W'ly along the N'ly boundary, a distance of 150'; thence S'ly // to the E'ly boundary, 150' to a pt.; thence E'ly // to the N'ly boundary, 150' to a pt.; thence N'ly to the pt. of commencement.
				NOL			
				Land Division consent	Committee		

☐ SFCA
☐ DEA/EAA
☐ SFMA
☐ GRANT
☐ FEE SIMPLE
☐ JOINT TEN.
☐ TEN. IN COM.
☐ TO USES
☐ AND APPOINT
☐ HAB (as JT)
☐ UC (4) (1)
☐ REL
☐ B OF DWR (31/3/78)
☐ SPOUSAL CONSENT & REL
☐ S & S BY
☐ CS OF
☐ ONT SUC DUTY (10/1/70) – (10/4/79)
☐ FED ESTATE TAX (1/1/59) – (1/1/72)
☐ A OF MM (30/4/54) ONT. CO. (23/6/65) OTHER (15/6/82)
☐ A OF LTT (V & C) (1/6/21)

☐ A OF SUB. WIT.
☑ COM. ADJUST. CONSENT (1/6/67) DATE: Mar. 2/85 SIGNED CH. & SEC.
☐ AF PL. ACT
☐ STATE RE PL. ACT (1) (2) (3)
☐ A OF AGE (3/4/57) (26/5/68) – CHARGOR (1/1/61) – GUARANTOR
☑ STATE OF AGE (1/4/85)
☐ A OF MS (25/6/39) – (31/3/78)
☐ A OF SP. STATUS (31/3/78)
☑ STATE OF SP. STATUS (1/4/85)
☑ SP/NOT A SP/SP OF EA OTHR
☐ NOT A MAT. HOME
☐ REL UNDR SEP. AGRMNT
☐ DT OF BRTH – TRANSFEREE(S) 1. 2.
☐ AF OF PARTNER PROP PUR AS PP HELD AS PP ONLY PARTNERS
☐ DOCUMENT GENERAL
☐ SCHEDULE

☐ PHOTOCOPY ATTACHED ☐ SKETCH ATTACHED

SOLICITOR FOR 1ST PARTY(IES)	SOLICITOR FOR 2ND PARTY(IES)
MUNICIPAL ADDRESS 1ST PARTY(IES)	MUNICIPAL ADDRESS 2ND PARTY(IES)

APPENDIX Continued

CCNS
66 Gerrard St. East
Toronto, Ont. M5B 1G3
Form 156

☐ REGISTRY ☐ LAND TITLES ☐ DATE OF SEARCH: ☐ SEARCHER: PAGE 3 OF 15 PAGES

LOT: 57 CON: 6 PLAN: MUNICIPALITY: REGION/COUNTY:

INSTRUMENT NUMBER	INSTRUMENT	DATE OF INSTRUMENT	DATE OF REGISTRY	TRANSFEROR/CHARGOR	TRANSFEREE/CHARGEE	CONSIDERATION	DESCRIPTION (P.I.N.)
76384	Deed	May 24/85	May 28/85	MARSHALL, Willard	MARSHALL, Alexander MARSHALL, Wanda (j.t.)		Pt. Lot 57, commencing @ S.E. ∠; thence N'ly along E'ly boundary to N.E. ∠; thence W'ly along N'ly boundary, 2000' to a pt.; thence S'ly ∥ to E'ly boundary, 150' to a pt.; thence W'ly ∥ to N'ly boundary, 150' to a pt; thence S'ly ∥ to E'ly boundary, to a pt. in the S'ly boundary; thence E'ly along, 2150' to the pt. of commencement.

☐ SFCA
☐ DEA/EAA
☐ SFMA
☐ GRANT
☐ FEE SIMPLE
☐ JOINT TEN.
☐ TEN. IN COM.
☐ TO USES
☐ AND APPOINT
☐ HAB (as JT)
☐ UC (4) (1)
☐ REL
☐ B OF DWR (31/3/78)
☐ SPOUSAL CONSENT & REL
☐ S & S BY
☐ CS OF
☐ ONT SUC DUTY (10/1/70) – (10/4/79)
☐ FED ESTATE TAX (1/1/59) – (1/1/72)
☐ A OF MM (30/4/54)
ONT. CO. (23/6/65)
OTHER (15/6/82)
☐ A OF LTT (V & C) (1/6/21)

☐ A OF SUB. WIT.
☐ COM. ADJUST. CONSENT (1/6/67)
DATE: ______
SIGNED CH. & SEC.
☐ AF PL. ACT
☑ STATE RE PL. ACT (1) (2) (3) [(1) (2) (3) circled]
☐ A OF AGE (3/4/57)
(26/5/68) – CHARGOR
(1/1/61) – GUARANTOR
☑ STATE OF AGE (1/4/85)
☐ A OF MS (25/6/39) – (31/3/78)
☐ A OF SP. STATUS (31/3/78)
☑ STATE OF SP. STATUS (1/4/85)
☑ SP/~~NOT A SP~~/SP OF EA OTHR
☐ NOT A MAT. HOME
☐ REL UNDR SEP. AGRMNT
☑ DT OF BRTH – TRANSFEREE(S)
1. 1949/06/02
2. 1957/03/21
☐ AF OF PARTNER PROP
PUR AS PP
HELD AS PP
ONLY PARTNERS
☐ DOCUMENT GENERAL
☐ SCHEDULE

☐ PHOTOCOPY ATTACHED ☐ SKETCH ATTACHED

SOLICITOR FOR 1ST PARTY(IES)	SOLICITOR FOR 2ND PARTY(IES)
Smith + Jones	Martin + Martin
202 Main St.	165 Main St.
Whitford	Whitford
MUNICIPAL ADDRESS 1ST PARTY(IES)	MUNICIPAL ADDRESS 2ND PARTY(IES)

APPENDIX Continued

66 Gerrard St. East
Toronto, Ont. M5B 1G3
Form 156

☐ REGISTRY ☐ LAND TITLES ☐ DATE OF SEARCH: ☐ SEARCHER: PAGE 4 OF 15 PAGES

LOT: 57 CON: 6 PLAN: MUNICIPALITY: REGION/COUNTY:

INSTRUMENT NUMBER	INSTRUMENT	DATE OF INSTRUMENT	DATE OF REGISTRY	TRANSFEROR/CHARGOR	TRANSFEREE/CHARGEE	CONSIDERATION	DESCRIPTION (P.I.N.)
84336	Deed	Nov. 21/85	Nov. 23/85	MARSHALL, Alexander MARSHALL, Wanda (j.t.)	Stavros Subdivisions Ltd.		Pt. Lot 57, commencing @ S.E. <; thence N'ly along the E'ly boundary, 500' to a pt.; thence W'ly // to N'ly boundary, 2,000' to a pt.; thence S'ly // to E'ly boundary, 500' to a pt.; thence E'ly along S'ly boundary, 2,000' to pt. of commencement.
				Land Division Committee consent			

☐ SFCA
☐ DEA/EAA
☐ SFMA
☐ GRANT
☐ FEE SIMPLE
☐ JOINT TEN.
☐ TEN. IN COM.
☐ TO USES
☐ AND APPOINT
☐ HAB (as JT)
☐ UC (4) (1)
☐ REL
☐ B OF DWR (31/3/78)
☐ SPOUSAL CONSENT & REL
☐ S & S BY
☐ CS OF
☐ ONT SUC DUTY (10/1/70) – (10/4/79)
☐ FED ESTATE TAX (1/1/59) – (1/1/72)
☐ A OF MM (30/4/54) ONT. CO. (23/6/65) OTHER (15/6/82)
☐ A OF LTT (V & C) (1/6/21)

☐ A OF SUB. WIT.
☑ COM. ADJUST. CONSENT (1/6/67) DATE: Nov. 1/85 SIGNED CH. & SEC.
☐ AF PL. ACT
☐ STATE RE PL. ACT (1) (2) (3)
☐ A OF AGE (3/4/57) (26/5/68) – CHARGOR (1/1/61) – GUARANTOR
☑ STATE OF AGE (1/4/85)
☐ A OF MS (25/6/39) – (31/3/78)
☐ A OF SP. STATUS (31/3/78)
☑ STATE OF SP. STATUS (1/4/85)
☑ SP/NOT A SP/SP OF EA OTHR
☐ NOT A MAT. HOME
☐ REL UNDR SEP. AGRMNT
☐ DT OF BRTH – TRANSFEREE(S) 1. ___ 2. ___
☐ AF OF PARTNER PROP PUR AS PP HELD AS PP ONLY PARTNERS
☐ DOCUMENT GENERAL
☐ SCHEDULE

☐ PHOTOCOPY ATTACHED ☐ SKETCH ATTACHED

SOLICITOR FOR 1ST PARTY(IES)	SOLICITOR FOR 2ND PARTY(IES)
Martin + Martin	Smith + Jones
165 Main St.	202 Main St.
Whitford	Whitford
MUNICIPAL ADDRESS 1ST PARTY(IES)	MUNICIPAL ADDRESS 2ND PARTY(IES)

APPENDIX Continued

66 Gerrard St. East
Toronto, Ont. M5B 1G3
Form 156

☐ REGISTRY ☐ LAND TITLES ☐ DATE OF SEARCH: ☐ SEARCHER: PAGE 5 OF 15 PAGES

LOT: 11 CON: PLAN: 1209 MUNICIPALITY: REGION/COUNTY:

NSTRUMENT NUMBER	INSTRUMENT	DATE OF INSTRUMENT	DATE OF REGISTRY	TRANSFEROR/CHARGOR	TRANSFEREE/CHARGEE	CONSID-ERATION	DESCRIPTION (P.I.N.)
84922	Bylaw	Jan.21/88	Feb.2/88	Re: part lot control			All of Twp. of Whitford

❏ SFCA
❏ DEA/EAA
❏ SFMA
❏ GRANT
☐ FEE SIMPLE
☐ JOINT TEN.
☐ TEN. IN COM.
☐ TO USES
☐ AND APPOINT
❏ HAB (as JT)
❏ UC (4) (1)
❏ REL
❏ B OF DWR (31/3/78)
❏ SPOUSAL CONSENT & REL
❏ S & S BY
❏ CS OF
❏ ONT SUC DUTY
(10/1/70) – (10/4/79)
☐ FED ESTATE TAX
(1/1/59) – (1/1/72)
☐ A OF MM (30/4/54)
ONT. CO. (23/6/65)
OTHER (15/6/82)
☐ A OF LTT (V & C) (1/6/21)

☐ A OF SUB. WIT.
☐ COM. ADJUST. CONSENT
(1/6/67)
DATE: ________
SIGNED CH. & SEC.
☐ AF PL. ACT
☐ STATE RE PL. ACT (1) (2) (3)
☐ A OF AGE (3/4/57)
(26/5/68) – CHARGOR
(1/1/61) – GUARANTOR
☐ STATE OF AGE (1/4/85)
☐ A OF MS (25/6/39) – (31/3/78)
☐ A OF SP. STATUS (31/3/78)
☐ STATE OF SP. STATUS (1/4/85)
☐ SP/NOT A SP/SP OF EA OTHR
☐ NOT A MAT. HOME
☐ REL UNDR SEP. AGRMNT
☐ DT OF BRTH – TRANSFEREE(S)
1. ________
2. ________
☐ AF OF PARTNER PROP
PUR AS PP
HELD AS PP
ONLY PARTNERS
☐ DOCUMENT GENERAL
☐ SCHEDULE

☐ PHOTOCOPY ATTACHED ☐ SKETCH ATTACHED

SOLICITOR FOR 1ST PARTY(IES)	SOLICITOR FOR 2ND PARTY(IES)
MUNICIPAL ADDRESS 1ST PARTY(IES)	MUNICIPAL ADDRESS 2ND PARTY(IES)

APPENDIX Continued

56 Gerrard St. East
Toronto, Ont. M5B 1G3
Form 156

☐ REGISTRY ☐ LAND TITLES ☐ DATE OF SEARCH: ☐ SEARCHER: PAGE 6 OF 15 PAGES

LOT: 11 CON: PLAN: 1209 MUNICIPALITY: REGION/COUNTY:

INSTRUMENT NUMBER	INSTRUMENT	DATE OF INSTRUMENT	DATE OF REGISTRY	TRANSFEROR/CHARGOR	TRANSFEREE/CHARGEE	CONSID-ERATION	DESCRIPTION (P.I.N.)
90248	Notice of Agmt.	Jan. 8/89	Jan. 15/89	Stavros Subdivisions Ltd.	The Corporation of the Township of Whitford		
				- subdivision agreement			
				- deals mainly with roads, hydro and parkland.			

☐ SFCA
☐ DEA/EAA
☐ SFMA
☐ GRANT
☐ FEE SIMPLE
☐ JOINT TEN.
☐ TEN. IN COM.
☐ TO USES
☐ AND APPOINT
☐ HAB (as JT)
☐ UC (4) (1)
☐ REL
☐ B OF DWR (31/3/78)
☐ SPOUSAL CONSENT & REL
☐ S & S BY
☐ CS OF
☐ ONT SUC DUTY (10/1/70) - (10/4/79)
☐ FED ESTATE TAX (1/1/59) - (1/1/72)
☐ A OF MM (30/4/54) ONT. CO. (23/6/65) OTHER (15/6/82)
☐ A OF LTT (V & C) (1/6/21)

☐ A OF SUB. WIT.
☐ COM. ADJUST. CONSENT (1/6/67)
DATE: ____
SIGNED CH. & SEC.
☐ AF PL. ACT
☐ STATE RE PL. ACT (1) (2) (3)
☐ A OF AGE (3/4/57) (26/5/68) - CHARGOR (1/1/61) - GUARANTOR
☐ STATE OF AGE (1/4/85)
☐ A OF MS (25/6/39) - (31/3/78)
☐ A OF SP. STATUS (31/3/78)
☐ STATE OF SP. STATUS (1/4/85)
☐ SP/NOT A SP/SP OF EA OTHR
☐ NOT A MAT. HOME
☐ REL UNDR SEP. AGRMNT
☐ DT OF BRTH - TRANSFEREE(S)
1. ____
2. ____
☐ AF OF PARTNER PROP
PUR AS PP
HELD AS PP
ONLY PARTNERS
☐ DOCUMENT GENERAL
☐ SCHEDULE

☐ PHOTOCOPY ATTACHED ☐ SKETCH ATTACHED

SOLICITOR FOR 1ST PARTY(IES)	SOLICITOR FOR 2ND PARTY(IES)
MUNICIPAL ADDRESS 1ST PARTY(IES)	MUNICIPAL ADDRESS 2ND PARTY(IES)

APPENDIX Continued

60 Gerrard St. East
Toronto, Ont. M5B 1G3
Form 156

☐ REGISTRY ☐ LAND TITLES ☐ DATE OF SEARCH: ☐ SEARCHER: PAGE 7 OF 15 PAGES

LOT: 11 CON: PLAN: 1209 MUNICIPALITY: REGION/COUNTY:

INSTRUMENT NUMBER	INSTRUMENT	DATE OF INSTRUMENT	DATE OF REGISTRY	TRANSFEROR/CHARGOR	TRANSFEREE/CHARGEE	CONSID-ERATION	DESCRIPTION (P.I.N.)
91764	Deed	Feb.17/89	Feb.19/89	Stavros Subdivisions Ltd.	McTAVISH, Duncan McTAVISH, Marla (j.t.)		All lot 11.

☐ SFCA
☐ DEA/EAA
☐ SFMA
☐ GRANT
☐ FEE SIMPLE
☐ JOINT TEN.
☐ TEN. IN COM.
☐ TO USES
☐ AND APPOINT
☐ HAB (as JT)
☐ UC (4) (1)
☐ REL
☐ B OF DWR (31/3/78)
☐ SPOUSAL CONSENT & REL
☐ S & S BY
☐ CS OF
☐ ONT SUC DUTY (10/1/70) – (10/4/79)
☐ FED ESTATE TAX (1/1/59) – (1/1/72)
☐ A OF MM (30/4/54) ONT. CO. (23/6/65) OTHER (15/6/82)
☐ A OF LTT (V & C) (1/6/21)

☐ A OF SUB. WIT.
☐ COM. ADJUST. CONSENT (1/6/67)
DATE: ____
SIGNED CH. & SEC.
☐ AF PL. ACT
☑ STATE RE PL. ACT (1) (2) (3)
☐ A OF AGE (3/4/57) (26/5/68) – CHARGOR (1/1/61) – GUARANTOR
☐ STATE OF AGE (1/4/85)
☐ A OF MS (25/6/39) – (31/3/78)
☐ A OF SP. STATUS (31/3/78)
☐ STATE OF SP. STATUS (1/4/85)
☐ SP/NOT A SP/SP OF EA OTHR
☐ NOT A MAT. HOME
☐ REL UNDR SEP. AGRMNT
☑ DT OF BRTH – TRANSFEREE(S)
1. Dec. 1/48
2. Jan. 18/55
☐ AF OF PARTNER PROP
PUR AS PP
HELD AS PP
ONLY PARTNERS
☐ DOCUMENT GENERAL
☐ SCHEDULE

☐ PHOTOCOPY ATTACHED ☐ SKETCH ATTACHED

SOLICITOR FOR 1ST PARTY(IES)	SOLICITOR FOR 2ND PARTY(IES)
Smith + Jones 202 Main St. Whitford	Frank Milhouse 25 Wilson St. Bakersville
MUNICIPAL ADDRESS 1ST PARTY(IES)	MUNICIPAL ADDRESS 2ND PARTY(IES)

APPENDIX Continued

60 Gerrard St. East
Toronto, Ont. M5B 1G3
Form 156

☐ REGISTRY ☐ LAND TITLES ☐ DATE OF SEARCH: ☐ SEARCHER: PAGE 8 OF 15 PAGES

LOT: 11 CON: PLAN: 1209 MUNICIPALITY: REGION/COUNTY:

INSTRUMENT NUMBER	INSTRUMENT	DATE OF INSTRUMENT	DATE OF REGISTRY	TRANSFEROR/CHARGOR	TRANSFEREE/CHARGEE	CONSIDERATION	DESCRIPTION (P.I.N.)
148902	Deposit		Feb.11/92	Death Certificate of Duncan McTavish			
				-died Nov. 22/91			

☐ SFCA
☐ DEA/EAA
☐ SFMA
☐ GRANT
☐ FEE SIMPLE
☐ JOINT TEN.
☐ TEN. IN COM.
☐ TO USES
☐ AND APPOINT
☐ HAB (as JT)
☐ UC (4) (1)
☐ REL
☐ B OF DWR (31/3/78)
☐ SPOUSAL CONSENT & REL
☐ S & S BY
☐ CS OF
☐ ONT SUC DUTY (10/1/70) – (10/4/79)
☐ FED ESTATE TAX (1/1/59) – (1/1/72)
☐ A OF MM (30/4/54)
ONT. CO. (23/6/65)
OTHER (15/6/82)
☐ A OF LTT (V & C) (1/6/21)

☐ A OF SUB. WIT.
☐ COM. ADJUST. CONSENT (1/6/67)
DATE: ____
SIGNED CH. & SEC.
☐ AF PL. ACT
☐ STATE RE PL. ACT (1) (2) (3)
☐ A OF AGE (3/4/57)
(26/5/68) – CHARGOR
(1/1/61) – GUARANTOR
☐ STATE OF AGE (1/4/85)
☐ A OF MS (25/6/39) – (31/3/78)
☐ A OF SP. STATUS (31/3/78)
☐ STATE OF SP. STATUS (1/4/85)
☐ SP/NOT A SP/SP OF EA OTHR
☐ NOT A MAT. HOME
☐ REL UNDR SEP. AGRMNT
☐ DT OF BRTH – TRANSFEREE(S)
1. ____
2. ____
☐ AF OF PARTNER PROP
PUR AS PP
HELD AS PP
ONLY PARTNERS
☐ DOCUMENT GENERAL
☐ SCHEDULE

☐ PHOTOCOPY ATTACHED ☐ SKETCH ATTACHED

SOLICITOR FOR 1ST PARTY(IES)	SOLICITOR FOR 2ND PARTY(IES)
Frank Milhouse	
25 Wilson St.	
Bakersville	
MUNICIPAL ADDRESS 1ST PARTY(IES)	MUNICIPAL ADDRESS 2ND PARTY(IES)

APPENDIX Continued

Toronto, Ont. M5B 1G3
Form 156

☐ REGISTRY ☐ LAND TITLES ☐ DATE OF SEARCH: ☐ SEARCHER: PAGE 9 OF 15 PAGES

LOT: 11 CON: PLAN: 1209 MUNICIPALITY: REGION/COUNTY:

INSTRUMENT NUMBER	INSTRUMENT	DATE OF INSTRUMENT	DATE OF REGISTRY	TRANSFEROR/CHARGOR	TRANSFEREE/CHARGEE	CONSIDERATION	DESCRIPTION (P.I.N.)
153117	Deed	Apr. 29/92	May 2/92	Marla MacTavish	BOND, Frederick		All
					COULTER, Suzanne		

☐ SFCA
☐ DEA/EAA
☐ SFMA
☐ GRANT
☐ FEE SIMPLE
☐ JOINT TEN.
☐ TEN. IN COM.
☐ TO USES
☐ AND APPOINT
☐ HAB (as JT)
☐ UC (4) (1)
☐ REL
☐ B OF DWR (31/3/78)
☐ SPOUSAL CONSENT & REL
☐ S & S BY
☐ CS OF
☐ ONT SUC DUTY (10/1/70) – (10/4/79)
☐ FED ESTATE TAX (1/1/59) – (1/1/72)
☐ A OF MM (30/4/54) ONT. CO. (23/6/65) OTHER (15/6/82)
☐ A OF LTT (V & C) (1/6/21)

☐ A OF SUB. WIT.
☐ COM. ADJUST. CONSENT (1/6/67) DATE: ______ SIGNED CH. & SEC.
☐ AF PL. ACT
☑ STATE RE PL. ACT (1) (2) (3)
☐ A OF AGE (3/4/57) (26/5/68) – CHARGOR (1/1/61) – GUARANTOR
☑ STATE OF AGE (1/4/85)
☐ A OF MS (25/6/39) – (31/3/78)
☐ A OF SP. STATUS (31/3/78)
☑ STATE OF SP. STATUS (1/4/85)
☑ SP/NOT A SP/SP OF EA OTHR
☐ NOT A MAT. HOME
☐ REL UNDR SEP. AGRMNT
☐ DT OF BRTH – TRANSFEREE(S) 1. Mar. 20/60 2. May 29/63
☐ AF OF PARTNER PROP PUR AS PP HELD AS PP ONLY PARTNERS
☐ DOCUMENT GENERAL
☐ SCHEDULE

* surname is MacTavish (took title as McTavish)

O.K. see # 170003

☐ PHOTOCOPY ATTACHED ☐ SKETCH ATTACHED

SOLICITOR FOR 1ST PARTY(IES)	SOLICITOR FOR 2ND PARTY(IES)
Frank Milhouse	Farb + Farb
25 Wilson St.	62 Drake Ave
Bakersville	Whitford
MUNICIPAL ADDRESS 1ST PARTY(IES)	MUNICIPAL ADDRESS 2ND PARTY(IES)

APPENDIX Continued

Gerrard St. East
Toronto, Ont. M5B 1G3
Form 156

☐ REGISTRY ☐ LAND TITLES ☐ DATE OF SEARCH: ☐ SEARCHER: PAGE 10 OF 15 PAGES

LOT: 11 CON: PLAN: 1209 MUNICIPALITY: REGION/COUNTY:

INSTRUMENT NUMBER	INSTRUMENT	DATE OF INSTRUMENT	DATE OF REGISTRY	TRANSFEROR/CHARGOR	TRANSFEREE/CHARGEE	CONSIDERATION	DESCRIPTION (P.I.N.)
170003	Deposit	Mar. 1/97	Mar. 15/97	Stat. decl. by	Marla McTavish		
				– one + same	as Marla MacTavish		
				in Inst. #	153117 and		
				Marla Mc	Tavish in Inst. # 91764		

☐ SFCA
☐ DEA/EAA
☐ SFMA
☐ GRANT
☐ FEE SIMPLE
☐ JOINT TEN.
☐ TEN. IN COM.
☐ TO USES
☐ AND APPOINT
☐ HAB (as JT)
☐ UC (4) (1)
☐ REL
☐ B OF DWR (31/3/78)
☐ SPOUSAL CONSENT & REL
☐ S & S BY
☐ CS OF
☐ ONT SUC DUTY (10/1/70) – (10/4/79)
☐ FED ESTATE TAX (1/1/59) – (1/1/72)
☐ A OF MM (30/4/54) ONT. CO. (23/6/65) OTHER (15/6/82)
☐ A OF LTT (V & C) (1/6/21)

☐ A OF SUB. WIT.
☐ COM. ADJUST. CONSENT (1/6/67) DATE: SIGNED CH. & SEC.
☐ AF PL. ACT
☐ STATE RE PL. ACT (1) (2) (3)
☐ A OF AGE (3/4/57) (26/5/68) – CHARGOR (1/1/61) – GUARANTOR
☐ STATE OF AGE (1/4/85)
☐ A OF MS (25/6/39) – (31/3/78)
☐ A OF SP. STATUS (31/3/78)
☐ STATE OF SP. STATUS (1/4/85)
☐ SP/NOT A SP/SP OF EA OTHR
☐ NOT A MAT. HOME
☐ REL UNDR SEP. AGRMNT
☐ DT OF BRTH – TRANSFEREE(S) 1. 2.
☐ AF OF PARTNER PROP PUR AS PP HELD AS PP ONLY PARTNERS
☐ DOCUMENT GENERAL
☐ SCHEDULE

☐ PHOTOCOPY ATTACHED ☐ SKETCH ATTACHED

SOLICITOR FOR 1ST PARTY(IES)	SOLICITOR FOR 2ND PARTY(IES)
Frank Milhouse	
25 Wilson St.	
Bakersville	
MUNICIPAL ADDRESS 1ST PARTY(IES)	MUNICIPAL ADDRESS 2ND PARTY(IES)

APPENDIX Continued

66 Gerrard St. East
Toronto, Ont. M5B 1G3
Form 156

☐ REGISTRY ☐ LAND TITLES ☐ DATE OF SEARCH: ☐ SEARCHER: PAGE 11 OF 15 PAGES

LOT: 11 CON: PLAN: 1209 MUNICIPALITY: REGION/COUNTY:

INSTRUMENT NUMBER	INSTRUMENT	DATE OF INSTRUMENT	DATE OF REGISTRY	TRANSFEROR/CHARGOR	TRANSFEREE/CHARGEE	CONSIDERATION	DESCRIPTION (P.I.N.)
170004	Deed	Mar. 12/97	Mar. 15/97	BOND, Frederick	BAKER, Murphy R.		All
				COULTER, Suzanne	BAKER, Leslie T.		
					(j.t.)		

☐ SFCA
☐ DEA/EAA
☐ SFMA
☐ GRANT
☐ FEE SIMPLE
☐ JOINT TEN.
☐ TEN. IN COM.
☐ TO USES
☐ AND APPOINT
☐ HAB (as JT)
☐ UC (4) (1)
☐ REL
☐ B OF DWR (31/3/78)
☐ SPOUSAL CONSENT & REL
☐ S & S BY
☐ CS OF
☐ ONT SUC DUTY (10/1/70) – (10/4/79)
☐ FED ESTATE TAX (1/1/59) – (1/1/72)
☐ A OF MM (30/4/54) ONT. CO. (23/6/65) OTHER (15/6/82)
☐ A OF LTT (V & C) (1/6/21)

☐ A OF SUB. WIT.
☐ COM. ADJUST. CONSENT (1/6/67) DATE: ______ SIGNED CH. & SEC.
☐ AF PL. ACT
☑ STATE RE PL. ACT (1) (2) (3)
☐ A OF AGE (3/4/57) (26/5/68) – CHARGOR (1/1/61) – GUARANTOR
☑ STATE OF AGE (1/4/85)
☐ A OF MS (25/6/39) – (31/3/78)
☐ A OF SP. STATUS (31/3/78)
☑ STATE OF SP. STATUS (1/4/85)
☑ SP/NOT A SP/SP OF EA OTHR
☐ NOT A MAT. HOME
☐ REL UNDR SEP. AGRMNT
☑ DT OF BRTH – TRANSFEREE(S) 1. June 4/62 2. Apr. 28/63
☐ AF OF PARTNER PROP PUR AS PP HELD AS PP ONLY PARTNERS
☐ DOCUMENT GENERAL
☐ SCHEDULE

☐ PHOTOCOPY ATTACHED ☐ SKETCH ATTACHED

SOLICITOR FOR 1ST PARTY(IES)	SOLICITOR FOR 2ND PARTY(IES)
Farb & Farb	Smith, Jones, Avery
62 Drake Ave	202 Main St.
Whitford	Whitford
MUNICIPAL ADDRESS 1ST PARTY(IES)	MUNICIPAL ADDRESS 2ND PARTY(IES)

APPENDIX Continued

[address illegible] Toronto, Ont. M5B 1G3
Form 156

☐ REGISTRY ☐ LAND TITLES ☐ DATE OF SEARCH: ☐ SEARCHER: PAGE 12 OF 15 PAGES

LOT: 11 CON: PLAN: 1209 MUNICIPALITY: REGION/COUNTY:

INSTRUMENT NUMBER	INSTRUMENT	DATE OF INSTRUMENT	DATE OF REGISTRY	TRANSFEROR/CHARGOR	TRANSFEREE/CHARGEE	CONSIDERATION	DESCRIPTION (P.I.N.)
170005	Mort.	Mar. 14/97	Mar. 15/97	BAKER, Murphy R.	Bank of Nova Scotia		All
				BAKER, Leslie T.			
				(j.t.)			
				$65,000 @ 7% due Mar. 15/02			
				Payable 1st monthly $500.00			
				O/S			

☐ SFCA
☐ DEA/EAA
☐ SFMA
☐ GRANT
☐ FEE SIMPLE
☐ JOINT TEN.
☐ TEN. IN COM.
☐ TO USES
☐ AND APPOINT
☐ HAB (as JT)
☐ UC (4) (1)
☐ REL
☐ B OF DWR (31/3/78)
☐ SPOUSAL CONSENT & REL
☐ S & S BY
☐ CS OF
☐ ONT SUC DUTY (10/1/70) – (10/4/79)
☐ FED ESTATE TAX (1/1/59) – (1/1/72)
☐ A OF MM (30/4/54) ONT. CO. (23/6/65) OTHER (15/6/82)
☐ A OF LTT (V & C) (1/6/21)

☐ A OF SUB. WIT.
☐ COM. ADJUST. CONSENT (1/6/67)
DATE: ______
SIGNED CH. & SEC.
☐ AF PL. ACT
☐ STATE RE PL. ACT (1) (2) (3)
☐ A OF AGE (3/4/57) (26/5/68) – CHARGOR (1/1/61) – GUARANTOR
☑ STATE OF AGE (1/4/85)
☐ A OF MS (25/6/39) – (31/3/78)
☐ A OF SP. STATUS (31/3/78)
☑ STATE OF SP. STATUS (1/4/85)
☑ SP/NOT A SP/SP OF EA OTHR
☐ NOT A MAT. HOME
☐ REL UNDR SEP. AGRMNT
☐ DT OF BRTH – TRANSFEREE(S) 1. ______ 2. ______
☐ AF OF PARTNER PROP PUR AS PP HELD AS PP ONLY PARTNERS
☐ DOCUMENT GENERAL
☐ SCHEDULE

☐ PHOTOCOPY ATTACHED ☐ SKETCH ATTACHED

SOLICITOR FOR 1ST PARTY(IES)	SOLICITOR FOR 2ND PARTY(IES)
Smith, Jones, Avery	
202 Main St.	
Whitford	
MUNICIPAL ADDRESS 1ST PARTY(IES)	MUNICIPAL ADDRESS 2ND PARTY(IES)

APPENDIX Continued

66 Gerrard St. East
Toronto, Ont. M5B 1G3
Form 156

☐ REGISTRY ☐ LAND TITLES ☐ DATE OF SEARCH: ☐ SEARCHER: PAGE 13 OF 15 PAGES

LOT: 11 CON: PLAN: 1209 MUNICIPALITY: REGION/COUNTY:

INSTRUMENT NUMBER	INSTRUMENT	DATE OF INSTRUMENT	DATE OF REGISTRY	TRANSFEROR/CHARGOR	TRANSFEREE/CHARGEE	CONSIDERATION	DESCRIPTION (P.I.N.)
191436	Deed	Sept. 2/02	Sept. 2/02	BAKER, Murphy BAKER, Leslie (j.t.)	MERCIER, Francois LAFRAMBOISE, Huguette Marie (j.t.)		All

Note: Transferors took title as Murphy (R.) Baker and Leslie (T.) Baker

☐ SFCA
☐ DEA/EAA
☐ SFMA
☐ GRANT
☐ FEE SIMPLE
☐ JOINT TEN.
☐ TEN. IN COM.
☐ TO USES
☐ AND APPOINT
☐ HAB (as JT)
☐ UC (4) (1)
☐ REL
☐ B OF DWR (31/3/78)
☐ SPOUSAL CONSENT & REL
☐ S & S BY
☐ CS OF
☐ ONT SUC DUTY (10/1/70) – (10/4/79)
☐ FED ESTATE TAX (1/1/59) – (1/1/72)
☐ A OF MM (30/4/54)
ONT. CO. (23/6/65)
OTHER (15/6/82)
☐ A OF LTT (V & C) (1/6/21)

☐ A OF SUB. WIT.
☐ COM. ADJUST. CONSENT (1/6/67)
DATE: ______
SIGNED CH. & SEC.
☐ AF PL. ACT
☑ STATE RE PL. ACT (1) (2) (3)
☐ A OF AGE (3/4/57)
(26/5/68) – CHARGOR
(1/1/61) – GUARANTOR
☑ STATE OF AGE (1/4/85)
☐ A OF MS (25/6/39) – (31/3/78)
☐ A OF SP. STATUS (31/3/78)
☑ STATE OF SP. STATUS (1/4/85)
☑ SP/NOT A SP/SP OF EA OTHR
☐ NOT A MAT. HOME
☐ REL UNDR SEP. AGRMNT
☑ DT OF BRTH – TRANSFEREE(S)
1. Mar. 11/71
2. Nov. 2/75
☐ AF OF PARTNER PROP
PUR AS PP
HELD AS PP
ONLY PARTNERS
☐ DOCUMENT GENERAL
☐ SCHEDULE

☐ PHOTOCOPY ATTACHED ☐ SKETCH ATTACHED

SOLICITOR FOR 1ST PARTY(IES)	SOLICITOR FOR 2ND PARTY(IES)
Smith, Jones, Avery	Barbara White
202 Main St.	45 Miller Dr.
Whitford	Whitford
MUNICIPAL ADDRESS 1ST PARTY(IES)	MUNICIPAL ADDRESS 2ND PARTY(IES)

APPENDIX Continued

66 Gerrard St. East
Toronto, Ont. M5B 1G3
Form 156

☐ REGISTRY ☐ LAND TITLES ☐ DATE OF SEARCH: ☐ SEARCHER: PAGE 14 OF 15 PAGES

LOT: 11 CON: PLAN: 1209 MUNICIPALITY: REGION/COUNTY:

INSTRUMENT NUMBER	INSTRUMENT	DATE OF INSTRUMENT	DATE OF REGISTRY	TRANSFEROR/CHARGOR	TRANSFEREE/CHARGEE	CONSIDERATION	DESCRIPTION (P.I.N.)
191437	Mort.	Sept. 1/02	Sept. 2/02	MERCIER, Francois	Toronto-Dominion		All
				LAFRAMBOISE,	Bank		
				Huguette Marie			
				(j.t.)			
				$40,000 @ 5% due	Sept. 1/07		
				Payable 1ST	monthly		
				$262.00			
				0/S			

☐ SFCA
☐ DEA/EAA
☐ SFMA
☐ GRANT
☐ FEE SIMPLE
☐ JOINT TEN.
☐ TEN. IN COM.
☐ TO USES
☐ AND APPOINT
☐ HAB (as JT)
☐ UC (4) (1)
☐ REL
☐ B OF DWR (31/3/78)
☐ SPOUSAL CONSENT & REL
☐ S & S BY
☐ CS OF
☐ ONT SUC DUTY (10/1/70) – (10/4/79)
☐ FED ESTATE TAX (1/1/59) – (1/1/72)
☐ A OF MM (30/4/54) ONT. CO. (23/6/65) OTHER (15/6/82)
☐ A OF LTT (V & C) (1/6/21)

☐ A OF SUB. WIT.
☐ COM. ADJUST. CONSENT (1/6/67)
DATE: ______
SIGNED CH. & SEC.
☐ AF PL. ACT
☐ STATE RE PL. ACT (1) (2) (3)
☐ A OF AGE (3/4/57) (26/5/68) – CHARGOR (1/1/61) – GUARANTOR
☑ STATE OF AGE (1/4/85)
☐ A OF MS (25/6/39) – (31/3/78)
☐ A OF SP. STATUS (31/3/78)
☑ STATE OF SP. STATUS (1/4/85)
☑ SP/NOT A SP/SP OF EA OTHR
☐ NOT A MAT. HOME
☐ REL UNDR SEP. AGRMNT
☐ DT OF BRTH – TRANSFEREE(S)
1. ______
2. ______
☐ AF OF PARTNER PROP
PUR AS PP
HELD AS PP
ONLY PARTNERS
☐ DOCUMENT GENERAL
☐ SCHEDULE

☐ PHOTOCOPY ATTACHED ☐ SKETCH ATTACHED

SOLICITOR FOR 1ST PARTY(IES)	SOLICITOR FOR 2ND PARTY(IES)
Barbara White	
45 Miller Dr.	
Whitford	
MUNICIPAL ADDRESS 1ST PARTY(IES)	MUNICIPAL ADDRESS 2ND PARTY(IES)

APPENDIX Concluded

Toronto, Ont. M5B 1G3
Form 156

☐ REGISTRY ☐ LAND TITLES ☐ DATE OF SEARCH: ☐ SEARCHER: PAGE 15 OF 15 PAGES

LOT: 11 CON: PLAN: 1209 MUNICIPALITY: REGION/COUNTY:

INSTRUMENT NUMBER	INSTRUMENT	DATE OF INSTRUMENT	DATE OF REGISTRY	TRANSFEROR/CHARGOR	TRANSFEREE/CHARGEE	CONSIDERATION	DESCRIPTION (P.I.N.)
192600	Mort.	Oct. 30/02	Nov. 2/02	MERCIER, Francois	ABC Company Ltd.		All
				MERCIER, Huguette Marie			
				$15,000 @ 11.5% due Nov. 1/05			
				Payable 1ST monthly $175.00			
				O/S			
				Note: 2ND chargor's name is MERCIER (took title as LAFRAMBOISE)			

☐ SFCA
☐ DEA/EAA
☐ SFMA
☐ GRANT
☐ FEE SIMPLE
☐ JOINT TEN.
☐ TEN. IN COM.
☐ TO USES
☐ AND APPOINT
☐ HAB (as JT)
☐ UC (4) (1)
☐ REL
☐ B OF DWR (31/3/78)
☐ SPOUSAL CONSENT & REL
☐ S & S BY
☐ CS OF
☐ ONT SUC DUTY (10/1/70) – (10/4/79)
☐ FED ESTATE TAX (1/1/59) – (1/1/72)
☐ A OF MM (30/4/54) ONT. CO. (23/6/65) OTHER (15/6/82)
☐ A OF LTT (V & C) (1/6/21)

☐ A OF SUB. WIT.
☐ COM. ADJUST. CONSENT (1/6/67)
DATE: ______
SIGNED CH. & SEC.
☐ AF PL. ACT
☐ STATE RE PL. ACT (1) (2) (3)
☐ A OF AGE (3/4/57) (26/5/68) – CHARGOR (1/1/61) – GUARANTOR
☑ STATE OF AGE (1/4/85)
☐ A OF MS (25/6/39) – (31/3/78)
☐ A OF SP. STATUS (31/3/78)
☑ STATE OF SP. STATUS (1/4/85)
☑ SP/NOT A SP/SP OF EA OTHR
☐ NOT A MAT. HOME
☐ REL UNDR SEP. AGRMNT
☐ DT OF BRTH – TRANSFEREE(S)
1. ______
2. ______
☐ AF OF PARTNER PROP
PUR AS PP
HELD AS PP
ONLY PARTNERS
☐ DOCUMENT GENERAL
☐ SCHEDULE

☐ PHOTOCOPY ATTACHED ☐ SKETCH ATTACHED

SOLICITOR FOR 1ST PARTY(IES) | SOLICITOR FOR 2ND PARTY(IES)

MUNICIPAL ADDRESS 1ST PARTY(IES) | MUNICIPAL ADDRESS 2ND PARTY(IES)

FIGURE 19.1 Sheriff's Certificate

```
*****************          CERTIFICATE #:
* CLEAR / LIBRE *          NO DE CERTIFICAT:
*****************          00204679-3215459B
```

C E R T I F I C A T E / C E R T I F I C A T

SHERIFF AT / SHERIF A: LRO#00 YORKTON
DATE OF CERTIFICATE / DATE DU CERTIFICAT : 2004-05-22

THIS CERTIFIES THAT THERE ARE NO WRITS OF EXECUTION, EXTENT OR CERTIFICATES OF LIEN IN MY HANDS AT THE TIME OF SEARCHING AGAINST THE REAL AND PERSONAL PROPERTY OF:

JE CERTIFIE, PAR LES PRESENTES, NE PAS AVOIR DE BREF D'EXECUTION OU DE SAISIE, NI DE CERTIFICAT DE PRIVILEGE EN MA POSSESSION AU MOMENT DE LA RECHERCHE VISANT LES BIENS MEUBLES OU IMMEUBLES DE:

	SURNAME / NOM	GIVEN NAMES / PRENOM(S)
(PERSON/PERSONNE)	MARSHALL,	WILLARD
	MARSHALL,	ALEXANDER
	MARSHALL,	WANDA
	STAVROS SUBDIVISIONS LTD.	
	McTAVISH,	DUNCAN
	MCTAVISH,	MARLA
	MACTAVISH,	MARLA
	BOND,	FREDERICK
	COULTER,	SUZANNE
	BAKER,	MURPHY
	BAKER,	LESLIE
	MERCIER,	FRANCOIS
	LAFRAMBOISE,	HUGUETTE MARIE
	MERCIER,	HUGUETTE MARIE

CAUTION TO PARTY REQUESTING SEARCH:
ENSURE THAT THE ABOVE INDICATED NAME IS THE SAME AS THE NAME SEARCHED THIS NAME WILL REMAIN CLEAR UNTIL THE CLOSE OF BUSINESS THIS DATE.

AVERTISSEMENT A LA PARTIE QUI DEMANDE LA RECHERCHE:
ASSUREZ-VOUS QUE LE NOM INDIQUE CI-DESSUS EST LE MEME QUE CELUI QUI EST RECHERCHE. CET ETAT DEMEURE VALIDE JUSQU'A LA FIN DE LA JOURNEE DE TRAVAIL.

CHARGE FOR THIS CERTIFICATE / FRAIS POUR CE CERTIFICAT: $ 154.00
SEARCHER REFERENCE / REFERENCE CONCERNANT L'AUTEUR DE LA DEMANDE:
L11P209

FIGURE 19.2 Parcelized Day Forward Registry Abstract

Ontario — MINISTRY OF CONSUMER AND COMMERCIAL RELATIONS

LAND REGISTRY OFFICE #00

ABSTRACT INDEX (ABBREVIATED) FOR PROPERTY IDENTIFIER **12345-6789 (R)**

PAGE 1 OF 1
PREPARED FOR: SUE SEARCHER
ON 1998/05/22 AT 10:51

PROPERTY DESCRIPTION: LOT 11, PLAN 1209 ; TOWNSHIP OF WHITFORD

PROPERTY REMARKS: THIS PARCEL WAS CREATED BASED ON INFORMATION CONTAINED IN DOCUMENT 191436, WHICH IS RECORDED FOR PIN IDENTIFICATION ONLY

ESTATE/QUALIFIER	RECENTLY	BLOCK IMPLEMENTATION DATE
	PARCELIZED FROM BOOK	1997/09/22

REG. NUM.	DATE	INSTRUMENT TYPE	AMOUNT	PARTIES FROM	PARTIES TO	CERT/ CHKD	FILM	FUTURE OFFICE USE
** PRINTOUT INCLUDES ALL DOCUMENT TYPES AND DELETED INSTRUMENTS SINCE 1997/09/19 **								
** THIS ABSTRACT INCLUDES ALL INSTRUMENTS AND DOCUMENTS FROM: 1997/09/22 **								
** FOR THE PREVIOUS ABSTRACT SEE ABSTRACT BOOK **								
170004	97/03/15	TRANSFER	$ 170,000.00	BOND, Frederick COULTER, Suzanne	BAKER, Murphy R. BAKER, Leslie T., as j. t.	C		
191436	02/09/02	TRANSFER	$ 219,000.00	BAKER, Murphy BAKER, Leslie	MERCIER, Francois LAFRAMBOISE, Huguette Marie, as j.t.			
191437	02/09/02	CHARGE	$ 40,000.00	MERCIER, Francois LAFRAMBOISE, Huguette Marie	TORONTO-DOMINION BANK			
192600	02/11/02	CHARGE	$ 15,000.00	MERCIER, Francois MERCIER, Huguette Marie	ABC COMPANY LTD.			

NOTE: ADJOINING PROPERTIES SHOULD BE INVESTIGATED TO ASCERTAIN DESCRIPTIVE INCONSISTENCIES, IF ANY, WITH DESCRIPTION REPRESENTED FOR THIS PROPERTY.
NOTE: ENSURE THAT YOUR PRINTOUT STATES THE TOTAL NUMBER OF PAGES AND THAT YOU HAVE PICKED THEM ALL UP.

FIGURE 19.3 Land Titles Conversion Qualified Abstract

Ontario
MINISTRY OF CONSUMER AND COMMERCIAL RELATIONS

LAND REGISTRY OFFICE #00

PARCEL REGISTER (ABBREVIATED) FOR PROPERTY IDENTIFIER **12345-6789 (LT)**

PAGE 1 OF 1
PREPARED FOR: SUE SEARCHER
ON 2004/09/30 AT 4:45

PROPERTY DESCRIPTION: LOT 11, PLAN 1209; WHITFORD

PROPERTY REMARKS: THIS PARCEL WAS CREATED BASED ON INFORMATION CONTAINED IN DOCUMENT 191436, WHICH IS RECORDED FOR PIN IDENTIFICATION ONLY.

ESTATE/QUALIFIER	RECENTLY	PIN CREATION DATE
FEE SIMPLE LT CONVERSION QUALIFIED	FIRST CREATION FROM BOOK	1997/09/22

OWNERS' NAMES	CAPACITY
MERCIER, FRANCOIS	JOINT TENANT
LAFRAMBOISE, HUGUETTE MARIE	JOINT TENANT

REG. NUM.	DATE	INSTRUMENT TYPE	AMOUNT	PARTIES FROM	PARTIES TO	CERT/CHKD
EFFECTIVE 2000/07/29 THE NOTATION OF THE "BLOCK IMPLEMENTATION DATE" OF 1997/09/02 ON THIS PIN						
**WAS REPLACED WITH THE "PIN CREATION DATE" OF 1997/09/02 **						
** PRINTOUT INCLUDES ALL DOCUMENT TYPES (DELETED INSTRUMENTS NOT INCLUDED) **						
**SUBJECT, ON FIRST REGISTRATION UNDER THE LAND TITLES ACT, TO:						
** SUBSECTION 44(1) OF THE LAND TITLES ACT, EXCEPT PARAGRAPH 11, PARAGRAPH 14, PROVINCIAL SUCCESSION DUTIES *						
** AND ESCHEATS OR FORFEITURE TO THE CROWN.						
** THE RIGHTS OF ANY PERSON WHO WOULD, BUT FOR THE LAND TITLES ACT, BE ENTITLED TO THE LAND OR ANY PART OF						
** IT THROUGH LENGTH OF ADVERSE POSSESSION, PRESCRIPTION, MISDESCRIPTION OR BOUNDARIES SETTLED BY						
** CONVENTION.						
** ANY LEASE TO WHICH THE SUBSECTION 70(2) OF THE REGISTRY ACT APPLIES.						
**DATE OF CONVERSION TO LAND TITLES: 1997/09/02 **						
90248	1969/01/08	NOTICE OF AGREEMENT		STAVROS SUBDIVISIONS LTD.	THE CORPORATION OF THE TOWNSHIP OF WHITFORD	C C
170005	1997/03/15	MORTGAGE	$65,000.00		BANK OF NOVA SCOTIA	C
191436	2002/09/02	TRANSFER	$219,000.00		MERCIER, FRANCOIS LAFRAMBOISE, HUGUETTE MARIE AS JOINT TENANTS	C
191437	2002/09/02	MORTGAGE	$40,000.00		TORONTO-DOMINION BANK	C
192600	2002/11/03	MORTGAGE	$15,000.00		ABC COMPANY LTD.	C

NOTE: ADJOINING PROPERTIES SHOULD BE INVESTIGATED TO ASCERTAIN DESCRIPTIVE INCONSISTENCIES, IF ANY, WITH DESCRIPTION REPRESENTED FOR THIS PROPERTY.
NOTE: ENSURE THAT YOUR PRINTOUT STATES THE TOTAL NUMBER OF PAGES AND THAT YOU HAVE PICKED THEM ALL UP.

CHAPTER 20

The Requisition Letter

This chapter examines the standard form of requisition letter and provides examples of specific requisitions based on the search notes for Lot 11, Plan 1209, Township of Whitford (see the appendix to chapter 19, Reviewing the Search of Title).

To be valid, a title requisition must identify a specific objection to a particular title, a specific solution, and possibly one or more alternative solutions. Thus, the letter should not contain generalized, unnecessary requisitions. However, in order to protect the client's rights, you should requisition what the purchaser is entitled to on closing according to the terms of the agreement of purchase and sale.

REVIEW OF THE STANDARD REQUISITION LETTER

Figure 20.1, at the end of the chapter, is a sample requisition letter, which must be signed by a lawyer.

Preamble

Note that the second sentence of the opening paragraph states that the requisitions are made without prejudice. The wording in the paragraph parallels some of the wording of paragraph 10 of the agreement of purchase and sale, which gives the purchaser the right to negotiate or waive requisitions once made. If the purchaser raises an objection to the title that the vendor is unable or unwilling to remove, remedy, or satisfy, the purchaser may waive the requisition so that the vendor cannot use this failure as a reason for terminating the deal. However, if the purchaser chooses not to waive it, the purchaser then has the right to refuse to close the deal.

Standard Requisitions

There are a number of requisitions that will be made in almost every transaction. They cover standard conveyancing requirements (for example, declarations of possession) and basic contract rights (for example, keys and vacant possession on closing). Samples of these requisitions are found in paragraphs 1 through 7 of figure 20.1.

Documents to Be Executed

In most transactions, the purchaser will require the delivery of certain documents on closing in addition to the transfer. It is the usual practice for the purchaser's lawyer to prepare documents such as declarations of possession, general undertakings, and warranties, to ensure that they are in a form satisfactory to the purchaser.

When documents are prepared by the purchaser's lawyer for execution by the vendor, it is usual to enclose the documents in the requisition letter, as indicated in paragraph 8, so that they may be executed by the vendor and delivered on closing.

Specific Requisitions on Title

The next portion of the requisition letter, starting at paragraph 9, sets out the specific requisitions relating to particular issues of title. As discussed in chapter 18, Requisitions: An Overview, the sources of these requisitions will be

- the preliminary letters;
- the plan of survey; and
- the title search.

Closing

The second-last paragraph of the requisition letter confirms the purchaser's willingness to provide a land transfer tax affidavit for inclusion in the transfer. The last paragraph requests advance notice of the person to whom the closing funds are to be payable.

Signature

The requisition letter must be prepared for signature by the lawyer handling the file and must be signed by the lawyer. Law clerks cannot sign the requisition letter.

DRAFTING SPECIFIC REQUISITIONS ARISING FROM THE SEARCH

This section examines examples of specific requisitions that might arise from a review of the search of title. The purpose of this review is twofold: (1) to provide a sense of the difference between a good and a bad requisition, and (2) to provide examples of how to draft a requisition.

The requisitions below were drafted in September 2008 and are based on the search notes for Lot 11, Plan 1209, Township of Whitford in the appendix to chapter 19.

Instrument Number 44796

Most lawyers will consider this document to be the root of title — a conveyance by Walter Fitzgerald to Willard Marshall — because it is the first deed to our property within the 40-year search period. Note that because Plan 1209 was registered on December 2, 1986, in order to complete the 40-year search, it was necessary to search behind the plan on the original concession lot.

Instrument Number 90248

This instrument is a notice of agreement that contains a subdivision agreement with the Township of Whitford. Because paragraph 10 of the agreement of purchase and sale states that the purchaser must accept title subject to any registered agreements with municipalities as long as they have been complied with, the purchaser cannot demand its removal. However, you must requisition proof from the municipality that the subdivision agreement has been complied with. You must also write to the Township of Whitford for evidence of compliance. (See page 6 of the search notes, appendix, chapter 19.)

The requisition would read as follows:

> 1. Instrument number 90248 is a notice of agreement containing a subdivision agreement between Stavros Subdivisions Ltd. and The Corporation of the Township of Whitford registered January 15, 1989.
>
> REQUIRED: Satisfactory evidence from the Township of Whitford that the terms of the said agreement have been complied with or that adequate security has been posted.

Whenever you make a requisition, you must ask yourself the following questions:

1. What is the likely answer to this requisition?
2. What answer would I like to receive?
3. What can I do myself to answer the requisition?
4. What will I do if the requisition cannot be answered to my satisfaction?

With respect to this requisition, those questions would be answered as follows:

1. The likely answer will be "Please satisfy yourself." As mentioned earlier, you should write to the Township of Whitford yourself, to make sure there has been compliance with the subdivision agreement. You may ask why you need to make a requisition if you know that the answer will be "Please satisfy yourself." You must do so to protect the rights of the purchaser under the agreement of purchase and sale, in case the evidence obtained shows non-compliance with the subdivision agreement.
2. You would like to receive proof of compliance by way of letter from the municipality. Because you can obtain the letter yourself, without assistance from the vendor, "Please satisfy yourself" is an acceptable answer.
3. Write to the municipality directly for an answer.
4. If the answer from the municipality discloses non-compliance with the subdivision agreement, the purchaser will have to decide whether to complete the transaction.

Instrument Number 170005

This instrument is a mortgage in favour of the Bank of Nova Scotia. Let's assume that this mortgage is not one that the purchaser has agreed to assume. Since the mortgagee is a chartered bank, according to the terms of the agreement of purchase and sale, if a discharge is not available on closing (as is most likely the case), the purchaser is obliged to accept the vendor's lawyer's personal undertaking to obtain and register a discharge of the mortgage. The vendor's lawyer will also have to provide a mortgage statement from the bank and a direction regarding funds from the vendor, directing that the amount required to discharge the mortgage be paid directly to the bank out of closing funds.

The requisition would read as follows:

> 1. Instrument number 170005 is a mortgage from Murphy R. Baker and Leslie T. Baker in favour of the Bank of Nova Scotia, registered March 15, 1997, securing the principal sum of $65,000.00. Pursuant to the terms of the agreement of purchase and sale, this mortgage is to be discharged.
>
> REQUIRED: On or before closing, registration of a good and valid discharge of the said mortgage or, in the alternative, on or before closing, production of the vendor's lawyer's personal undertaking to obtain, out of the closing funds, a discharge in registrable form and to register same on title within a reasonable time after completion, and production of a mortgage statement prepared by the mortgagee setting out the balance required to obtain the discharge, together with a direction executed by the vendor directing payment to the mortgagee of the amount required to obtain the discharge out of the balance due on completion.

The only acceptable answer to this requisition is an agreement by the vendor's lawyer to register a discharge, either on closing (unlikely) or within a reasonable time after closing, provided all the above requirements are met.

Instrument Number 191436

This document is a deed from Murphy Baker and Leslie Baker to Francois Mercier and Huguette Marie Laframboise. The deed in which the grantors received title showed them as Murphy *R.* Baker and Leslie *T.* Baker. You may wish to requisition evidence that they are one and the same persons. The requisition would read as follows:

> 1. Instrument number 191436 is a deed from Murphy Baker and Leslie Baker to Francois Mercier and Huguette Marie Laframboise, registered September 2, 2002. By earlier grant registered March 15, 1997 as instrument number 170004, title was conveyed to Murphy R. Baker and Leslie T. Baker.
>
> REQUIRED: On or before closing, satisfactory evidence that Murphy Baker and Murphy R. Baker are one and the same person, and that Leslie Baker and Leslie T. Baker are one and the same person.

You again ask yourself the four questions posed above. The questions would be answered as follows:

1. The likely answer to your requisition will be "Please satisfy yourself."
2. The answer you would like to receive is that a statutory declaration to that effect will be provided on closing.
3. You can contact the solicitor who acted on the conveyance to obtain a statutory declaration or other evidence.

4. If the requisition cannot be answered, it is not a serious problem. In all likelihood, the parties are one and the same because there is nothing on title to indicate otherwise.

Instrument Number 191437

This instrument is a mortgage in favour of the Toronto-Dominion Bank. If this mortgage is being assumed by the purchaser, you must carefully check the search notes to compare the terms of the registered mortgage with the terms set out in the agreement of purchase and sale. You will probably find that the amount of principal outstanding pursuant to the agreement of purchase and sale is less than the amount of principal indicated on the mortgage. The reason for this difference is that 12 years have elapsed since the date of registration, and part of the principal has been repaid during that time. It is also possible that the mortgage has been renegotiated. Therefore, it is reasonable to presume that this is the mortgage being assumed.

The requisition would read as follows:

> 1. Instrument number 191437 is a mortgage from Francois Mercier and Huguette Marie Laframboise in favour of the Toronto-Dominion Bank, registered on September 2, 2002, securing the principal sum of $40,000.00. We presume that this is the mortgage to be assumed, pursuant to the agreement of purchase and sale.
>
> REQUIRED: On or before closing, production of a mortgage statement for assumption purposes confirming that the mortgage is in good standing, that the terms and conditions referred to in the mortgage are identical to those set out in the agreement of purchase and sale, and that the principal amount outstanding is not less than $31,644.97.
>
> If this is not the mortgage to be assumed, we shall require, on or before closing, production and registration of a discharge of the said mortgage and registration of a charge/mortgage of land containing terms and conditions identical to those set out in the agreement of purchase and sale.

Assume that the registered mortgage differs from the mortgage described in the agreement of purchase and sale, in that the interest rate in the registered mortgage is 5 percent instead of 6.5 percent, and the monthly payments are $296.00 instead of $262.00. In this case, the requisition would read as follows:

> 1. Instrument number 191437 is a mortgage from Francois Mercier and Huguette Marie Laframboise in favour of the Toronto-Dominion Bank, registered on September 2, 2002, securing the principal sum of $40,000.00, with interest at the rate of 5 percent per annum, and repayable in monthly installments of $262.00. Pursuant to the agreement of purchase and sale, the purchaser is to assume a mortgage bearing interest at the rate of 6.5 percent per annum, and repayable in monthly instalments of $296.00.
>
> REQUIRED: On or before closing, production and registration of a discharge of the said mortgage and registration of a charge/mortgage of land containing terms and conditions identical to those set out in the agreement of purchase and sale. In the alternative, we will require production and registration of an amending agreement that amends the provisions of the said mortgage to provisions identical to those referred to in the agreement of purchase and sale.
>
> If this is the mortgage to be assumed, we shall require, on or before closing, production of a mortgage statement for assumption purposes confirming that the

> mortgage is in good standing, that the terms and conditions in the mortgage are identical to those set out in the agreement of purchase and sale, and that the principal amount outstanding is not less than $31,644.97.

Instrument Number 192600

This instrument is a mortgage in favour of ABC Company Ltd. If this is a mortgage that the purchaser has not agreed to assume, it will give rise to two requisitions.

First, because it is not an "institutional" mortgage as defined in paragraph 10 of the agreement of purchase and sale, you must requisition that a discharge be registered on or before closing. You will not accept an undertaking to obtain and register a discharge. This requisition should read as follows:

> 1. Instrument number 192600 is a mortgage registered on November 2, 2002 from Francois Mercier and Huguette Marie Mercier in favour of ABC Company Ltd., securing the principal sum of $15,000.00. By the terms of the agreement of purchase and sale, the said mortgage is to be discharged.
>
> REQUIRED: On or before closing, registration of a good and valid discharge of the said mortgage. Please note that we will not accept an undertaking in this regard.

Second, the name of one of the mortgagors is shown as Huguette Marie Mercier, but on the deed in which she obtained title, her name was Huguette Marie Laframboise. Probably, the agreement of purchase and sale also identifies her as Mercier. You will want proof that she is the same person. The requisition would read as follows:

> 2. Instrument number 191436 is a deed registered September 2, 2002 in favour of Francois Mercier and Huguette Marie Laframboise. Instrument number 192600 is a mortgage from Francois Mercier and Huguette Marie Mercier. Also, the agreement of purchase and sale shows the vendors as Francois Mercier and Huguette Marie Mercier.
>
> REQUIRED: 1. That the transfer to our clients contain recitals explaining why the transferor's name, Huguette Marie Mercier, is different from the transferee's name, Huguette Marie Laframboise, in instrument number 191436.
>
> 2. A statutory declaration from Huguette Marie Mercier stating that she is one and the same person as Huguette Marie Laframboise, one of the transferees in instrument number 191436.

DRAFTING SPECIFIC REQUISITIONS ARISING FROM RESPONSES TO PRELIMINARY LETTERS

This section examines examples of specific requisitions that might arise from responses to the preliminary letters dealt with in chapter 17, Preliminary Matters.

Municipal Tax Certificate

Suppose the municipal tax certificate discloses arrears of 2007 taxes (prior year's taxes) in the amount of $1,200.00 plus penalties of $65.00 and arrears of current taxes in the amount of $1,850.00 plus penalties of $90.00. The requisition would read as follows:

1. Township of Whitford tax certificate dated September 15, 2008 discloses arrears of 2007 taxes in the amount of $1,200.00 plus penalties of $65.00 and arrears of 2008 taxes in the amount of $1,850.00 plus penalties of $90.00.

REQUIRED: On or before closing, satisfactory evidence that the said arrears and penalties have been paid in full.

Water Accounts

Suppose the response from the water department discloses arrears of $300.00. The requisition would read as follows:

1. By letter from the Township of Whitford Water Department, dated September 12, 2008, we were advised that the water account on the subject property is in arrears in the amount of $300.00.

REQUIRED: On or before closing, satisfactory evidence that the said arrears together with any penalties for late payment have been paid in full.

Sewers and Drains

Suppose the response from the water department discloses the existence of a storm sewer easement. Paragraph 10 of the agreement of purchase and sale requires the purchaser to accept title subject to easements for storm sewers, provided they do not materially affect the present use of the property. You would have to discuss this easement with the purchaser. If he or she confirms that it does not materially affect the present use of the property, you will not make a requisition.

Unregistered Hydro Easements

If the response from Hydro One discloses an unregistered hydro easement that materially affects the present use of the property (and is therefore not an easement that the purchaser is required to accept, according to paragraph 10 of the agreement), the requisition would read as follows:

1. By letter from Hydro One dated September 15, 2008, a copy of which is attached, we were advised that the property is subject to an unregistered easement pursuant to the *Electricity Act, 1998*. The said easement materially affects the present use of the property.

REQUIRED: On or before closing, production of a release of the said easement.

Building Department

Suppose that the response from the building department discloses a contravention of the bylaw governing side yard set-backs and the existence of two outstanding work orders. The requisition would read as follows:

1. By letter dated September 19, 2008, we were advised by the building department of the Township of Whitford that the location of the buildings on the property contravenes the provisions of bylaw number ______________ in that the side yard setbacks of the buildings are insufficient.

REQUIRED: On or before closing, amendment of the said bylaw, specifically exempting the subject property from the application of the said bylaw in this regard; or, in the alternative, a minor variance to the bylaw, approved by the committee of adjustments, permitting the said side yard set-backs; or, in the further alternative, satisfactory evidence that the existing side yard set-backs qualify as a legal non-conforming use if, in fact, they do.

2. By letter dated September 19, 2008, a copy of which is attached, we were advised by the building department of the Township of Whitford that there are outstanding work orders against the subject property.

REQUIRED: On or before closing, satisfactory evidence that all work required pursuant to the said work orders has been completed to the satisfaction of the building department and that the said work orders have been released.

Effect of Title Insurance

If the purchaser in this transaction had purchased title insurance, you may not have sent many of the preliminary inquiry letters, and there would therefore be no corresponding requisitions.

FOLLOWING UP ON REQUISITIONS

As previously discussed in chapter 18, Requisitions: An Overview, if there is a title problem, it is not sufficient to simply submit a requisition. If the purchaser wants to close the transaction, you must take all reasonable steps to solve the problem by contacting the lawyers who prepared earlier documents and anyone else who may have the information that you need.

REQUISITIONS FROM THE VENDOR'S PERSPECTIVE

It is the vendor's lawyer's responsibility to answer all valid requisitions. If the law firm acted for the vendor in the purchase of the property, valid requisitions should have been submitted at that time, and the answers will likely be in the firm's purchase file for the property. If the firm acted in the purchase and failed to submit a valid requisition at that time, the firm may find itself subject to a claim for professional negligence arising out of its work on the purchase transaction.

If the vendor's law firm did not act for the vendor in the original purchase of the property, the law firm that did act should be contacted with respect to any requisitions that the vendor's lawyer cannot answer. The previous lawyer may have an answer in the original file. If not, that lawyer may be sued for professional negligence by the vendor if the problem existed at the time of the vendor's purchase. The vendor's lawyer may also have to contact a third party (or that party's lawyer) who can provide a solution to the problem.

REFERENCES

Electricity Act, 1998, SO 1998, c. 15, sched. A.

Income Tax Act, RSC 1985, c. 1 (5th Supp.), as amended.

Land Transfer Tax Act, RSO 1990, c. L.6.

Personal Property Security Act, RSO 1990, c. P.10, as amended.

Planning Act, RSO 1990, c. P.13.

REVIEW QUESTIONS

1. What four questions should you ask yourself when making a requisition?
2. What must the vendor's lawyer do when requisitions are received from the purchaser's lawyer?
3. The search of title discloses a charge registered on October 15, 2000 as instrument number 12345 from Jennifer Annistone to Bradley Pitts in the principal amount of $100,000.00. According to the agreement of purchase and sale, this mortgage is to be discharged. Draft the appropriate requisition.

FIGURE 20.1 Requisition Letter

Date

Vendor's lawyer
Address

Dear Sirs or Madams:

Re: *Name of transaction*
Address of property

We have now completed our search of title to the above-mentioned property. Without prejudice to our client's rights under the agreement of purchase and sale herein, and reserving the right to submit such further and other requisitions as we may from time to time consider advisable, or to waive these or any other requisitions submitted by us from time to time, we wish to submit the following requisitions:

1. REQUIRED: Before closing, a statement of adjustments in duplicate.
2. REQUIRED: Before closing, transfer messaged to (*lawyer's/law clerk's name*), engrossed as follows:
3. REQUIRED: On or before closing, an affidavit executed by the vendor that the vendor is not and will not at the time of closing be a non-resident of Canada within the meaning of section 116 of the *Income Tax Act*.
4. REQUIRED: On or before closing, a statutory declaration executed by the vendor that the transaction is exempt from GST.
5. REQUIRED: Completion by the vendor and the vendor's solicitor of the statements contemplated by subsection 50(22) of the *Planning Act*, as amended, contained in boxes 13 and 14 of the transfer.
6. REQUIRED: On or before closing, satisfactory evidence of the following:
   (a) that there are no executions against the vendor or any of the vendor's predecessors on title, such as would constitute a lien against the property, in the hands of the Sheriff of ____________________;
   (b) that there are no unregistered liens, rights of way, restrictive covenants, easements, restrictions, or encumbrances of any kind against the subject property, and that possession of the subject property has been consistent with the registered title. In this regard, we enclose a statutory declaration of possession for execution in duplicate and return to us on closing;
   (c) that the subject property is not presently under any active building permit, and that there are no outstanding work orders or orders to repair against the property;
   (d) that, at the date of closing of this transaction, no part of the property has been taken or expropriated by any competent authority;
   (e) that there are no arrears of municipal realty taxes or penalties with respect to such arrears and/or charges for water with respect to the subject property;
   (f) that there are no outstanding local improvement charges, rates, or levies against the property and no such charges, rates, or levies are in the process of being assessed or contemplated;
   (g) that the fixtures installed upon the property or any of the fixtures or chattels included in the purchase price, as specified in the agreement of purchase and sale, have been fully paid for and are not subject to any security interest or interest within the meaning of the *Personal Property Security Act*. In this regard, we enclose a bill of sale for execution in duplicate by the vendor and return to us on closing;
   (h) that the property is zoned ____________________, and the construction of

the buildings thereon and the intended use of the property by the purchaser comply with all zoning and building requirements of (*municipality*).

To this end, we will be performing our usual searches.

7. REQUIRED: An up-to-date survey of the property showing all buildings and other improvements to be situate wholly within the lot lines.
8. REQUIRED: On or before closing, execution by the vendor in duplicate and return of the following documents, which are enclosed herewith:
9. Instrument No. ___ (*This will be the start of your specific requisitions.*)
10. Instrument No. ___ (*etc.*)

In the event that the balance due on closing is to be made payable to anyone other than the vendor, please advise us in advance and provide us with an executed direction in this regard on closing.

Yours very truly,
(*Purchaser's lawyer*)

CHAPTER 21

Document Preparation

Once all of your requisitions have been satisfactorily answered, you must begin to think about the closing of the transaction and the documents that will be required for the closing. Some of the documents are prepared by the purchaser's lawyer and others are prepared by the vendor's lawyer.

The purchaser's lawyer usually prepares

- a direction regarding title;
- an undertaking to readjust;
- the land transfer tax affidavit;
- any mortgage documents;
- undertakings regarding the discharge of mortgages;
- a bill of sale;
- a statutory declaration regarding writs of execution;
- a statutory declaration of possession;
- an *Income Tax Act* declaration;
- a UFFI (ureaformaldehyde foam insulation) warranty;
- a general undertaking; and
- a statutory declaration regarding goods and services tax (GST).

The vendor's lawyer usually prepares

- a statement of adjustments;
- a direction regarding funds; and
- the transfer.

Both lawyers prepare an acknowledgment and direction for their respective clients.

DOCUMENTS PREPARED BY THE PURCHASER'S LAWYER

There are very few documents that the purchaser must give to the vendor. The purchaser's primary obligation on closing is to give money to the vendor. All title obligations are those of the vendor.

Direction Regarding Title

The direction regarding title is a document given to the vendor by the party who signed the agreement of purchase and sale as purchaser. It authorizes the vendor to deliver a transfer of land naming someone else as the transferee. This direction is technically necessary only if title is being taken in a name different from that of the purchaser in the agreement of purchase and sale. For example, a direction is required if the purchaser named in the agreement is John Smith and John Smith wants the transfer to be in favour of any of the following: John James Smith; John Smith and Jane Smith as joint tenants; or Fred Jones. If John Smith wants the transfer/deed to simply name John Smith as transferee, no direction is necessary.

Although a direction regarding title is not necessary if the name of the transferee is exactly the same as the name of the purchaser in the agreement of purchase and sale, it is usual to give a direction regarding title anyway to confirm the birthdate to be inserted in the transfer.

From the perspective of the vendor, remember that, in the absence of a direction signed by the purchaser named in the agreement of purchase and sale, the vendor must deliver a transfer to that purchaser as named in the agreement and to no one else.

Figure 21.1 is an example of a direction regarding title.

Undertaking to Readjust

When calculating the balance due on closing, various costs and expenses are allocated between the vendor and the purchaser to the time of closing. This allocation is calculated in the statement of adjustments (discussed later in this chapter). The purchaser often gives an undertaking to readjust in case it turns out that any items on the statement of adjustments were incorrectly adjusted in the purchaser's favour. To readjust means to pay back any amount improperly or incorrectly credited to the purchaser. (The vendor also undertakes to readjust in the vendor's general undertaking, discussed later in this chapter.)

Figure 21.2 is a sample purchaser's undertaking to readjust.

Land Transfer Tax Affidavit (Non-Automated Properties)

If the property has not been automated, a land transfer tax affidavit (previously called an affidavit of residence and of value of the consideration) must be sworn by the purchaser and inserted in the transfer of land before registration. It provides the government with the information necessary to calculate the land transfer tax and retail sales tax payable by the purchaser as a result of the transfer. The standard form of agreement of purchase and sale provides that the affidavit is to be prepared by the purchaser. This approach is consistent with the form of the affidavit itself, which may be completed only by the transferee or his or her agent.

The following discussion deals with the completion of the affidavit, a copy of which is reproduced as figure 21.3. The actual calculation of the taxes is dealt with in chapter 22, Preparation for Closing.

THE PREAMBLE

Complete the preamble by inserting the PIN (property identifier number), lot and plan number, city and municipality, transferor(s), and transferee(s).

PARAGRAPH 1

Check the box that appropriately describes the deponent. The transferee usually swears the affidavit, and therefore box (a) and box (d) (if the transferees are spouses of one another) are most commonly checked. The affidavit is rarely sworn by the solicitor for the transferee.

PARAGRAPH 2

This paragraph sets out the allocation of the total consideration and is the most complicated paragraph to complete. The calculation of land transfer tax and retail sales tax will be based on these figures.

Land transfer tax is essentially a provincial sales tax payable on the sale of land, just as retail sales tax is a sales tax payable on the sale of goods. In most real estate transactions, some chattels (movable items) are included in the purchase price. Accordingly, part of the purchase price is allocated to the chattels and part to the land. Retail sales tax should be paid on the value of the chattels and land transfer tax on the value of the land. The affidavit requires this allocation of the purchase price between land and chattels.

When you complete this paragraph, you should fill in the total line (i) first. The amount to be inserted is the purchase price found at the top of the agreement of purchase and sale and *not* the adjusted amount found in the statement of adjustments.

Next, complete line (g) by inserting the value of all chattels. When completing this line, remember that the rate of retail sales tax is significantly higher than the rate of land transfer tax. Accordingly, most purchasers wish to allocate little, if any, value to the chattels. Get the client's instructions on the allocation. When doing this, review with the client the chattels included in the purchase price and advise the client that generally there must be some value placed on the chattels. The chattels included in the purchase price are listed in paragraph 4 of the agreement of purchase and sale. Keep in mind that real estate agents often insert items that are really fixtures (immovable items), such as broadloom, storm windows, and screens. When reviewing this paragraph with the client, you must determine which of the listed items are, in fact, chattels. Insert the value that the client allocates to the chattels in line (g). Keep notes of your discussions with the client. If you have any concern about this valuation issue, ask the lawyer handling the file to deal with it.

Next, deduct the amount of the value of the chattels from the total consideration. Insert the result in line (f), which is stated to be the value of the land, building, fixtures, and goodwill subject to land transfer tax.

Next, complete line (b), mortgages. Only two types of mortgages are relevant to this line: (1) mortgages being assumed (mortgages already registered on title and being credited against the purchase price) and (2) mortgages being taken back by the vendor. Do not include any new mortgages being arranged by the purchaser with a third party.

With respect to mortgages being assumed, insert the amount shown on the statement of adjustments (if you have received one) as the principal and interest outstanding as of the closing date. If the vendor has not yet given you a statement of adjustments, you can get this information from a mortgage statement for assumption purposes obtained from the mortgagee.

For mortgages being taken back by the vendor, insert the principal amount of the mortgage.

Paragraphs (c), (d), and (e) deal with other types of consideration that are rarely encountered in residential real estate transactions. Complete them only if they apply to the transaction.

Once these paragraphs have been completed, total the amounts from line (b)(i) to (e). (It's best to do this calculation on a separate sheet of paper.) Take your calculated total and deduct it from the amount set out in line (f). The resulting amount is the total of the moneys to be paid in cash. Insert this amount in line (a). Because adjustments are not dealt with in this affidavit, the amount inserted in line (a) is rarely the same as the balance due on closing.

PARAGRAPH 3

Complete this paragraph only if the consideration exceeds \$400,000.00 and state whether the property is a single-family residence. This statement is required because the rate of tax changes in cases where the consideration exceeds \$400,000.00 if the property is a single family residence.

When completing this paragraph, you must review with the client the definition of "single family residence" in section 1(1) of the *Land Transfer Tax Act* because the affidavit states that the client has reviewed the definition. You should get a copy of the statute and allow the client to read the appropriate section. If the client has any question on the meaning of the section (certainly if the question is one you can't answer with total confidence), you must refer the client to the lawyer handling the file.

PARAGRAPH 4

Where the consideration is nominal, you must complete this paragraph to state whether the property is subject to any encumbrances. This information is necessary because, where a transfer is made for "natural love and affection," land transfer tax is still payable on the amount of any assumed encumbrances except when the transfer is between spouses.

PARAGRAPH 5

If the consideration is nominal, you must describe the relationship between the transferor and the transferee, and state the purpose of the conveyance. This paragraph is not usually completed when fair market value is paid for the property. It is required in the case of transfers for "natural love and affection" or where former spouses convey property in divorce or *Family Law Act* settlements.

If you have to complete this paragraph, contact the land transfer tax office to find out the specific wording you should use in the particular situation.

ATTESTATION

Complete the attestation to set out the date and place the affidavit is sworn.

PROPERTY INFORMATION RECORD

At the bottom of the affidavit is a property information record that is self-explanatory.

SCHOOL TAX SUPPORT

Completion of this section is voluntary and, if the client wishes, may be completed by the client at the time of execution.

Land Transfer Tax Statements (Automated Properties)

If the property has been automated, the purchaser's lawyer prepares a land transfer tax statement. It contains similar information to that in the affidavit. Figure 21.4 is an example of the land transfer tax statements.

Mortgage Documents

If the purchaser is financing the transaction by way of a mortgage from a third-party mortgagee (such as a financial institution or a relative) or a vendor take back mortgage, the purchaser's lawyer usually prepares the mortgage documents. A detailed discussion of these documents is found in chapter 23, Acting for the Mortgagee.

DOCUMENTS PREPARED BY THE PURCHASER'S LAWYER FOR EXECUTION BY THE VENDOR OR THE VENDOR'S LAWYER

The purchaser's lawyer will require a number of documents from the vendor's lawyer to make sure that the vendor complies with the agreement of purchase and sale.

Undertakings Regarding the Discharge of Mortgages

If there is a mortgage registered on title that the purchaser has not agreed to assume under the terms of the agreement of purchase and sale, the mortgage must ordinarily be discharged on closing. However, if the mortgage is from an institutional lender, the purchaser is required to accept the personal undertaking of the vendor's lawyer to obtain the discharge and register it at a later date.

If the purchaser has agreed to accept an undertaking to discharge a mortgage, you must make sure that the form of undertaking given is satisfactory. It is essential that the undertaking be the personal undertaking of the vendor's lawyer and not an undertaking given by the lawyer on behalf of the vendor only. The undertaking must bind the vendor's lawyer and not merely the vendor. The undertaking to obtain and register a discharge of the mortgage must be stated unconditionally. It is not enough for the undertaking to require the lawyer to use his or her best efforts. To comply with the requirements of the agreement of purchase and sale, there should be a statement that the discharge will be obtained and registered within a reasonable period of time.

When an undertaking is being accepted on the closing of the transaction, you will also have to get the appropriate mortgage statement and direction regarding payment of the funds.

Some banks will prepare *and* register discharges, and then advise the vendor's lawyer of the registration particulars. The vendor's lawyer will, in turn, advise the purchaser's lawyer. Notwithstanding this possibility, the wording of the undertaking should obligate the vendor's lawyer to register the discharge.

Figure 21.5 is an example of an acceptable form of undertaking.

Bill of Sale

When chattels are included in the agreement of purchase and sale, the purchaser's lawyer may require the delivery of a bill of sale that lists all the chattels. Figure 21.6 is an example of a bill of sale.

Statutory Declaration Regarding Writs of Execution

If the property being purchased is registered under the Land Titles system, a statutory declaration will be required to clear up any executions outstanding against names similar to that of the vendor. Figure 21.7 is an example of the declaration.

Statutory Declaration of Possession

This document is a declaration sworn by the vendor setting out certain facts concerning the vendor's possession of the land. Often the declaration is expanded to include sworn statements to support the statement as to age and spousal status contained in the transfer, other recitals in the transfer, or matters such as the residency of the vendor. A declaration of possession can clear up title defects if the land is registered in the Registry system, and it has become the practice for the purchaser's lawyer to request one whether or not it is actually required.

There are many variations of the standard form of declaration of possession. Some purchaser's lawyers are content to have the vendor's lawyer prepare the declaration of possession. Others may want to prepare the declaration themselves and forward it to the vendor's lawyer for signing to make sure that it addresses the matters necessary to clear up any title questions. When you prepare a declaration of possession, you must customize the standard form to coincide with the facts of the particular title and transaction.

In addition to requiring the vendor to execute the declaration of possession prepared, the purchaser's lawyer will ask the vendor's lawyer to deliver any declarations of possession from previous owners that may be in the vendor's possession. A series of declarations of possession may establish continuity of possession over a period of 10 or 20 years sufficient to defeat a claim made against the title.

Figure 21.8 is an example of a statutory declaration of possession. The various paragraphs deal with the following matters:

- The first six paragraphs establish continuity of possession and could address possible adverse possession claims that might be advanced against the property.
- Paragraph 7 could help to establish that an old survey is still up to date and may be relied upon.
- Paragraphs 8 through 12 deal with possible liens, executions, work orders, etc., but the purchaser's law firm must still rely on its own searches with respect to these matters.
- Paragraph 13 states that there are no unregistered leases or occupancy agreements.
- Paragraph 14 states that the chattels included in the agreement of purchase and sale are owned by the vendor and unencumbered, but the purchaser's lawyer should still conduct a PPSA (*Personal Property Security Act*) search.
- Paragraph 15 deals with compliance with the *Planning Act* and is not required.
- Paragraph 16 is a sworn statement to support the statement as to age and spousal status contained in the transfer and should be drafted in the same language as the statement in the transfer.
- Paragraph 17 is a statement as to residency within the meaning of the *Income Tax Act.*

Income Tax Act Declaration

The purchaser's lawyer must obtain a sworn declaration as to the vendor's residency within the meaning of section 116 of the *Income Tax Act.* If the vendor is a non-resident, additional income tax may be payable on the sale, and if it is not paid by the vendor, the purchaser may be responsible. If the declaration discloses that the vendor is a non-resident, the purchaser will require evidence that the tax has been paid or that satisfactory arrangements for payment have been made with the government.

A separate declaration is not required if appropriate wording is included in the statutory declaration of possession. The appropriate wording states that the vendor is, or is not, a non-resident. This language parallels the language used in the *Income Tax Act.* See paragraph 17 of figure 21.8 for an example of appropriate wording in a statutory declaration of possession.

Realty Tax Declaration

If your client is purchasing title insurance and you did not write a letter to the tax department to obtain a tax certificate, you will require proof from the vendor that the realty taxes are not in arrears. This can be done by way of a statutory declaration by the vendor, together with a receipted tax bill. Figure 21.9 is an example of a realty tax declaration.

UFFI Warranty

The standard form of agreement of purchase and sale contains a warranty that the vendor has not insulated the property with UFFI (ureaformaldehyde foam insulation) and that, to the best of the vendor's knowledge, the property has never been insulated with UFFI. Figure 21.10 is an example of a UFFI warranty.

General Undertaking

The purchaser's lawyer usually requires the vendor to execute a general undertaking designed to protect and extend beyond closing a number of the purchaser's rights under the contract.

Figure 21.11 is an example of a general undertaking. In it, the vendor undertakes:

- To deliver vacant possession on closing (assuming that is a term of the agreement of purchase and sale).
- To pay all utility charges to closing — These charges are generally metered, so a final bill cannot be prepared until after the final reading, which takes place on the day before closing. This undertaking covers payment of that final bill. Although arrears no longer form a lien against the property, the purchaser may prefer to know that the charges have been paid. As discussed earlier, the purchaser's lawyer should have previously written letters to the water department. If the reply disclosed any arrears, the vendor should be required to provide evidence on closing that those arrears have been paid. If the account for the property tends to be large, as would be the case for a rental or commercial property, or if there is a history of poor payment by the vendor, the purchaser should not simply rely on the vendor's undertaking. Instead, the last bill should be estimated and the vendor's lawyer should be required to keep a sufficient sum out of the closing proceeds to pay the account. If this kind of arrangement is made, this paragraph will be deleted and, instead, the vendor's lawyer will personally undertake to pay the account out of the portion of the closing funds paid to him or her for that purpose.
- To pay all arrears of taxes and to readjust — If there are arrears of realty taxes disclosed in the tax certificate, this undertaking is not adequate to protect the purchaser. Instead, the vendor's lawyer should be required to hold back a sufficient portion of the closing funds and to personally undertake to pay the arrears out of those funds. The undertaking to readjust covers the situation where the taxes have not been assessed and are

estimated on the statement of adjustments or where there is an error in the adjustment on the statement of adjustments, as a result of either incorrect information provided by the municipality or a miscalculation. If there is an error, the vendor agrees to pay to the purchaser any amount incorrectly credited to the vendor.

- To leave on the premises any chattels and fixtures specified in the agreement, free of encumbrances.
- To readjust any items on the statement of adjustments as necessary.
- To supply fuel oil in accordance with the statement of adjustments (where applicable) — If the house is heated by oil, the vendor fills up the fuel tank on the day before closing and, on the statement of adjustments, charges the purchaser for a full tank of oil at the current cost per litre multiplied by the number of litres in the tank. If the vendor does not leave a full tank of oil on the premises, the purchaser may sue on this undertaking.
- To make all payments on any mortgage being assumed by the purchaser that fall due on or before closing and to readjust if necessary — The purchaser should not rely on this undertaking with respect to the payment of the mortgage. At the time of closing, the vendor should provide evidence that all payments have, in fact, been made. If any mortgage payment has not been made, a sufficient portion of the funds should be paid to the vendor's lawyer and the purchaser should obtain the lawyer's personal undertaking to pay any outstanding amount.

GST Declaration

GST is not generally payable on the resale of a residential property. If GST is payable on a transaction, it is the obligation of the vendor to collect the tax and remit it to the government. However, if GST was payable on the transaction and the vendor failed to obtain it from the purchaser and submit it, the government has the power to assess the tax against either the vendor or the purchaser. The purchaser should be protected against this risk by obtaining an exemption certificate from the vendor. Paragraph 7 of the agreement of purchase and sale requires the vendor to certify that the agreement is not subject to GST if such is the case.

Most law firms acting for the purchaser will require the vendor to swear a statutory declaration with regard to GST. Figure 21.12 is an example of this declaration.

DOCUMENTS PREPARED BY THE VENDOR

The Statement of Adjustments

The statement of adjustments is the document that identifies the exact amount the purchaser has to pay for the property. The document is prepared by the vendor's lawyer and shows the calculations to determine the balance due on closing. A law clerk doing real estate work must know how to do this calculation — to be able to prepare a statement of adjustments if you are working for the vendor's lawyer and to be able to review a statement of adjustments if you are working for the purchaser's lawyer.

ITEMS TO BE ADJUSTED

You calculate the balance due on closing by starting with the purchase price in the agreement of purchase and sale and then apportioning various prepaid expenses between the vendor and the purchaser to the date of closing. Items to be adjusted include such expenses as mortgages being assumed, fuel costs, unmetered utilities, realty taxes, and rents.

FORMAT OF THE STATEMENT OF ADJUSTMENTS

The document is titled "Statement of Adjustments" and identifies the transaction, including the name of the purchaser, the name of the vendor, and the address of the property. It also states the date as of which adjustments are made. This date will usually be the day of closing.

The statement of adjustments is divided into three columns. The first column contains a description of the item being adjusted and may include some calculations. The second column is headed "Credit Purchaser" and the third column is headed "Credit Vendor."

Figure 21.13 is an example of a statement of adjustments.

ADJUSTMENT FOR THE DAY OF CLOSING

The standard form of agreement of purchase and sale states that the day of closing is to be apportioned to the purchaser. This means that the purchaser assumes responsibility for the particular expense — and starts paying it — as of the day of closing.

CALCULATIONS AND CREDITS

Before you can apportion the various items between the vendor and the purchaser, you must determine what number day of the year the closing is taking place — is it the 5th day (January 5), the 25th day (January 25), or the 325th day (November 21)? You can find this information in many desk diaries, which show the place of each date in the numerical sequence for the year and also, on any particular day, how many days are left in the year. If you are working in the real estate field, make sure you purchase a diary that contains this information.

per diem
per day; for each day; daily

Once you know the day of the year, convert the relevant expense to a **per diem** (daily) amount and then allocate it between the parties. For an expense paid on a yearly basis, the per diem amount is obtained by dividing the amount of the yearly payment by 365. For an expense paid on a monthly basis, the per diem amount is obtained by dividing the amount of the monthly payment by 30 or 31. Once you know the per diem amount, you must multiply that amount by the correct number of days to take you to the day of closing. Remember that the vendor is responsible for expenses up to and including the day *before* closing. Any amount that the vendor is entitled to receive is added to the purchase price and is considered a credit to the vendor. Any amount that the purchaser is entitled to receive is deducted from the purchase price and is considered a credit to the purchaser.

AN EXAMPLE

The following is a step-by-step explanation of the various items in a statement of adjustments based on the example in figure 21.13.

Sale Price

The sale price is always the first item in the statement of adjustments. Use the total sale price found in the agreement of purchase and sale. The amount is placed in the "Credit Vendor" column because it is an amount the vendor is entitled to receive.

SALE PRICE	180,000.00

Deposit

This item is always next and is also found in the agreement of purchase and sale. Since this amount has already been paid by the purchaser, it is deducted from the sale price and credited to the purchaser.

DEPOSIT	
Paid to broker	10,000.00

Mortgage Assumed

When a purchaser agrees to assume an existing mortgage, the purchaser is agreeing to take over the vendor's debt on closing. This assumed debt is part of the purchase price and is deducted from the amount the purchaser has to pay on closing. Accordingly, the outstanding principal amount of the mortgage after the date of the last mortgage payment constitutes a credit to the purchaser.

FIRST MORTGAGE ASSUMED	
Principal outstanding as of	
January 15, (*year*)	42,563.00

In addition to crediting the purchaser with the amount of the outstanding principal of the mortgage, there will almost always be a credit in favour of the purchaser for interest payable on the mortgage. This credit is given because, some time after closing, the purchaser will have to make a mortgage payment, and that payment will include principal and interest. Because mortgage interest is payable "not in advance," the mortgage payment will include interest for the period of time since the last payment. For example, if mortgage payments are due on the 1st of each month, the payment made on February 1 will include interest for the period January 1–31. If the closing date is January 15, the purchaser should not have to pay the interest from January 1 to January 14. Since the February 1 payment that the purchaser will make will include interest for all of January, the purchaser is entitled to a credit for the interest paid on the vendor's behalf from January 1 to January 14.

To calculate the interest, you must calculate the per diem amount of interest on the principal amount of the mortgage. For example, if the interest rate is 10 percent per annum on the principal amount shown above, the per diem amount is calculated as follows:

$$\frac{\$42{,}563.00 \times 0.10}{365} = \$11.661$$

Then multiply the per diem amount of interest by the number of days to be credited to the purchaser. In this case, it would be 14 days (from January 1 to January 14):

$11.661 × 14 = $163.26

The full entry for the assumed mortgage would therefore look like this:

FIRST MORTGAGE ASSUMED

Principal outstanding as of January 15, (*year*)	42,563.00
Interest at 10% from January 1–14, (*year*)	163.26

The vendor's lawyer gets this mortgage information by asking the mortgagee for a mortgage statement for assumption purposes. You should get a copy of the mortgage statement from the vendor on closing to verify the figures in the statement of adjustments. Some purchaser's lawyers will not wait until closing to get a copy of the mortgage statement from the vendor's lawyer but will contact the mortgagee directly for a mortgage statement. That way the lawyer can verify the adjustments before the closing or prepare the statement of adjustments if the vendor's lawyer doesn't.

The example above shows the principal balance and then a separate calculation of the interest to the date of closing. Many mortgage statements provide a combined amount of principal and interest to a date specified in the mortgage statement (usually the closing date, as requested by the vendor). If the mortgage statement shows a combined amount, place that figure in the statement of adjustments. It is not necessary to break the figure down between principal and interest. Instead, the statement of adjustments would simply state:

Principal and interest outstanding as of January 14, (*year*)	42,726.26

Second Mortgage Back

If the vendor agrees to take a mortgage back from the purchaser, the purchaser is given a credit for the principal amount of that mortgage. The credit is given because the purchaser does not have to pay that portion of the closing price in cash. The vendor is accepting the mortgage instead of cash. Since the statement of adjustments calculates the amount payable on closing, this amount is deducted from the purchase price and is therefore credited to the purchaser.

SECOND MORTGAGE

Back to vendor	25,000.00

No adjustment is necessary for interest, because interest only starts to accrue as of the date of closing.

Realty Taxes

An adjustment is usually made for realty taxes because the vendor will rarely have paid the exact amount of tax owing to the date of closing. If the vendor has paid more than that amount, the vendor is entitled to a credit for the overpayment. If the vendor has paid less than that amount, the purchaser is entitled to a credit in the amount of the vendor's underpayment.

To adjust for realty taxes, you must first find out the total amount of tax payable for the year and how much of the tax the vendor has actually paid. You obtain this information by writing to the tax department of the municipality.

If your request for tax information is made very early in the year, the municipality may not yet have set its taxes. In that case, the adjustment is made on the basis of the previous year's taxes. Since the current year's taxes will almost certainly be higher, the past year's taxes are increased by a stated percentage for the purposes of the adjustment.

REALTY TAXES

(*Current year*) taxes estimated at $3,180.00
(based on (*previous year*) taxes of $3,000.00 plus 6 percent)

This is the kind of situation where undertakings to readjust are necessary because the adjustment is based on an estimate.

If your request for tax information is made a little later in the year, you may find that the municipality has set interim taxes for the first six months of the year, but not the final taxes for the whole year. In that case, the adjustment is made on the basis of the interim levy on the assumption that the final taxes will be twice the interim levy.

REALTY TAXES

(*Current year*) taxes estimated at $3,100.00
(based on (*previous year*) taxes of $3,009.71 plus 3 percent)

If you are able to obtain the final tax amount for the year, the adjustment will reflect that.

REALTY TAXES

(*Current year*) taxes — $3,100.00

Once you find out the total amount of the taxes, you must calculate how much of those taxes should have been paid by the vendor. First, you must calculate the per diem amount of taxes. Divide the amount of the taxes (actual or estimated) by 365. Then multiply the per diem amount by the number of days from the beginning of the year until the day before the closing date. (Remember that taxes for the closing date are the purchaser's responsibility.) This amount is the vendor's share and is set out in the statement of adjustments. Assuming a six-month interim levy of $1,550.00 and a closing date of January 15, the information would appear as follows:

REALTY TAXES

Based on (*current year*) six-month interim levy
of $1,550.00 — $3,100.00
Vendor's share 14 days — $118.90

Next, you must set out the amount that the vendor has actually paid. If the vendor has paid less than the vendor's share of the taxes, the purchaser should be credited with the difference. If the vendor has paid more than the vendor's share of the taxes, the vendor is credited with the overpayment. The following is an example of an adjustment for an underpayment:

REALTY TAXES

Based on (*current year*) six-month interim levy
of $1,550.00 — $3,100.00
Vendor's share 14 days — $118.90
Vendor has paid $0
Credit purchaser 118.90

The following is an example of an adjustment for an overpayment:

REALTY TAXES

Based on (*current year*) six-month interim levy
of $1,550.00 — $3,100.00
Vendor's share 14 days — $118.90
Vendor has paid $350.00
Credit vendor 231.10

Fuel Oil

If the house being purchased is heated by oil, the vendor is required to fill the oil tank on the day before closing (the vendor's lawyer should remind the vendor to do so), and the purchaser must pay the vendor for the full tank of oil. This charge is shown as a credit to the vendor on the statement of adjustments. The vendor's lawyer will find out from the vendor the capacity of the oil tank in litres (the standard tank holds 900 litres). Then you must find out the current cost per litre of home fuel oil. You can obtain this information by calling any supplier of home fuel oil. The adjustment will set out the capacity of the tank and the price of the oil. For example:

FUEL OIL

900 litres @ $0.4971/litre (including GST)
Credit vendor 447.39

Utilities

Gas, electricity, and water are usually metered. In that case, no adjustment is necessary, and the statement of adjustments would contain the following entry:

HYDRO, GAS, WATER

Metered, no adjustment

Sometimes water charges will not be metered but will be billed on a flat-rate basis. In that case, there must be an adjustment for the water charges. There are three steps involved in the calculation:

1. Find out the amount payable for the current billing period. Get this information from the municipal water department.
2. Find out how much the vendor has paid. Again, this information comes from the water department.

3. Calculate how much should have been paid by the vendor. Take the billed amount and divide it by the number of days *in the billing period* to get a per diem amount. For example, a quarterly bill for the second quarter (April, May, June) would be divided by 91 days. Multiply the per diem amount by the number of days that have elapsed since the *start of the billing period* (this will not necessarily be the beginning of the year).

For example, assume a closing date of May 15, that water is billed quarterly at the rate of $100.00 per quarter, and that the first and second quarters' bills have been paid. For the purposes of the statement of adjustments, the first quarter is not relevant. Divide the second quarter bill of $100.00 by the number of days in the quarter (91). This gives you a per diem amount of $1.0989. Multiply this amount by 44, which is the number of days from the start of the second quarter (April 1) until the day of closing. This gives you a total of $48.35, which is the vendor's share. Since the vendor has paid $100.00, the vendor is entitled to a credit of $51.65.

Insurance

Under the standard form of agreement of purchase and sale, insurance policies are not assumed by the purchaser and there will be no adjustment for insurance.

Other Possible Adjustments

There may be adjustments for rent, common expenses, and, on newly constructed homes, various inspection and installation fees. Approach the calculations for these adjustments in the same way as you would those discussed above.

Balance Due on Closing

Once all of the adjustments have been calculated, you must calculate the balance due on closing. First, total the "Credit Vendor" column. From that total deduct all of the items in the "Credit Purchaser" column. The difference is the balance due on closing. Insert this amount on the line above the total of the "Credit Purchaser" column. To double-check your calculations, add up the figures in the "Credit Purchaser" column — the total should be the same as the total for the "Credit Vendor" column. For example:

BALANCE DUE ON CLOSING	102,952.23	
	180,678.49	180,678.49

THE STATEMENT OF ADJUSTMENTS FROM THE PURCHASER'S PERSPECTIVE

As previously stated, the statement of adjustments is a document that is supposed to be prepared by the vendor's law firm. When you work for the purchaser's law firm, you must know how to check the calculations in the statement of adjustments and how to verify the information on which the calculations are based. Sometimes, however, the purchaser's law firm receives adjustments over the telephone at the last minute, or not at all. The purchaser's lawyer will then have to calculate the adjustments.

When you receive the statement of adjustments, first confirm the accuracy of the amounts used in the calculations by checking them against the information you obtained from your own sources.

- Look at the agreement of purchase and sale to confirm the purchase price, the deposit, and the principal amount of any mortgage back to the vendor.
- Write to the appropriate municipal offices to confirm the realty tax and utilities figures.
- Write to the mortgagee for a mortgage statement to confirm the principal of and interest on any mortgages the purchaser is assuming.

After you have verified the figures, check the vendor's calculations to make sure they are correct.

If any mortgages are being assumed, you must also check that the principal outstanding is close to the principal amount that was set out in the agreement of purchase and sale. It is possible that the vendor forgot about payments made on the mortgage. In that case, the principal balance will be lower than expected, and so the credit to the purchaser will also be lower. The purchaser will then require more funds than expected to close. If there is a major difference, the purchaser may not be able to come up with enough funds to close and may choose to end the transaction. Even if the purchaser chooses to proceed with the transaction, the purchaser will need enough time to arrange for the additional funds required to close. Therefore, advise the purchaser of any difference as soon as possible.

Direction Regarding Funds

The purchaser must make the balance due on closing payable to the person named as the vendor in the agreement of purchase and sale unless the vendor gives the purchaser a written direction to make the balance payable to someone else. The vendor will usually want at least some of the closing balance to be payable elsewhere. If there is a mortgage to be discharged on closing, the vendor will direct that an amount equal to the outstanding balance of the mortgage be made payable directly to the mortgagee. If there are water or tax arrears, the vendor may direct that an amount equal to the arrears be made payable to the municipality. Finally, the vendor's lawyer will usually insist that the balance of closing funds be made payable to the law firm to make sure that the law firm will have enough money to fulfill any undertakings it has given and to deduct its own legal fees.

The vendor's lawyer will usually have the vendor sign a direction stating that the closing funds are to be payable to the law firm or "as they may in writing direct." The vendor's lawyer will usually not know the exact amounts that will have to be paid to third parties until just before closing. This kind of direction allows the law firm the flexibility to redirect the closing funds as required once the lawyer has the final information on amounts owing, such as mortgages to be discharged and tax arrears. The vendor will not have to come in again to sign another direction.

Figure 21.14 is an example of a direction regarding funds.

Figure 21.15 is an example of redirection regarding funds.

A WORD ABOUT UNDERTAKINGS

Undertakings may be given and signed by a client or the client's lawyer. If the undertaking is given and signed by the client, it is binding on the client only, and the lawyer has no responsibility to ensure that it is fulfilled. Depending on the way it is worded, if the undertaking is given and signed by the lawyer, it may bind only the client or it may bind the lawyer.

Undertakings on Behalf of the Client

Undertakings on behalf of the client, although executed by the lawyer, bind only the client. These undertakings are rare and are usually given at the last minute, when the lawyer cannot arrange for the client to give one. The lawyer gets verbal approval from the client, and signs on behalf of the client. For the lawyer to escape personal liability, the undertaking must clearly state, "I/We hereby undertake on behalf of the vendor/purchaser, and without personal liability, as follows: ..." For example, if a vendor improperly removed a fixture, the lawyer could undertake on behalf of the client to return it.

Personal Undertakings

These are undertakings that are binding on the lawyer. An undertaking signed by a lawyer will bind the lawyer unless it is clearly stated to be without personal liability.

Lawyers give this kind of undertaking only if it is absolutely necessary and only with respect to items totally within the lawyer's control — for example, an undertaking to discharge an institutional mortgage where the lawyer has received a mortgage statement from the mortgagee and is receiving funds sufficient to discharge the mortgage.

Most undertakings are anticipated and are therefore prepared before closing. However, sometimes unforeseen matters arise. If you attend at the closing, you may be requested to give or accept additional undertakings on closing. You should never give or accept an undertaking without first obtaining instructions from the lawyer handling the file.

TRANSFER OF TITLE

A document that actually transfers title from the vendor to the purchaser is required in every real estate transaction. The form of the document depends on whether or not the property is automated.

Non-Automated Properties

If the property you are dealing with has not been automated, the vendor's lawyer must prepare a paper transfer/deed of land as reproduced in figure 21.16. On closing, the vendor will deliver a fully executed copy for registration by the purchaser. The purchaser's lawyer will ask for a draft of the transfer to review before the closing. When you receive it, you must review it to make sure that it has been properly completed. When reviewing the transfer, be sure to check the following:

- All transferors should be named as they were in the transfer by which they took title. The names should be set out with the family name first (in upper case letters) followed by the first given name in full, followed by any other given names in full. Initials are not permitted.
- All transferees should be named in accordance with the instructions of the purchaser's lawyer to the vendor's lawyer. Make sure that the correct birthdates are set out.
- The legal description should agree with the legal description in the last instrument registered on title.
- The statement of age and spousal status in box 8 of the Transfer/Deed of Land must be completed in the language required by the most recent registrar's bulletin on the subject and must indicate compliance with the provisions of the *Family Law Act*. Transferors must certify that they are at least 18 years old and include one of the following statements:
    - I am not a spouse.
    - We are spouses of one another. (This statement is used in cases where both spouses are registered owners and are therefore both parties to the transfer as transferors.)
    - I am a spouse.
- In the first case, because there is no spouse with an interest under the *Family Law Act*, no further statement is required. In the second case, both spouses are parties to the conveyance and therefore explicitly consent to the conveyance, and, again, no further statement is required. In the third case, however, where the statement indicates the existence of a spouse who is not a party to the conveyance as an owner, the transfer must also contain one of the following statements to demonstrate compliance with the provisions of the *Family Law Act*:
    - The person consenting below is my spouse. (In this case, the non-titled spouse must complete and execute box 9.)
    - The property transferred is not ordinarily occupied by me and my spouse, who is not separated from me, as our family residence.
    - I am separated from my spouse and the property transferred was not ordinarily occupied by us at the time of our separation as our family residence.
    - The property is not designated under section 20 of the *Family Law Act* as a matrimonial home by me and my spouse, but there is such a designation of another property as our matrimonial home, which has been registered and which has not been cancelled.
    - My spouse has released all rights under part II of the *Family Law Act* by a separation agreement.

- ◇ The transaction is authorized by court order under section 23 of the *Family Law Act*, registered as instrument number ______ , which has not been stayed.
- ◇ The property transferred is released from the application of part II of the *Family Law Act* by court order registered as instrument number ______ , which has not been stayed.
- ◇ The consent of the non-titled spouse is required only in the first case.

- In addition to indicating compliance with the *Family Law Act*, the statement must disclose facts that are consistent with the knowledge of the purchaser's lawyer. Do not accept a statement setting out facts that are inconsistent with other evidence on the title — for example, a statement that the transferor is not a spouse when a previous mortgage indicates that there is a spouse.
- Make sure that the *Planning Act* statements in boxes 13 and 14 have been completed if the purchaser's lawyer has asked the vendor to complete them. These boxes contain statements indicating compliance with the provisions of the *Planning Act*. Completion of these boxes is not required for the purpose of registration. However, the standard form of agreement of purchase and sale states that these boxes must be completed by the vendor if required by the purchaser.

Automated Properties

As discussed in earlier chapters, many of the titles to property in the province of Ontario have been automated under the Teranet system. If the property you are dealing with has been automated, you will be able to use electronic registration, or e-reg, which is a paperless system in which documents are created and registered electronically.

In order to use e-reg, your firm must have a licence to use the Teraview software. There are three levels of licence issued by Teranet. The first level allows access to the system by specific computers within an office. The second level permits specific users to access the system. (Law clerks would have access by means of this type of licence.) The third level of access is restricted to lawyers, who are the only ones authorized to make compliance with law statements on a document within the system.

Each user is given a user name and must select a unique "personal pass phrase." These are stored on a disk, which must be inserted every time the user wishes to access the system. Most lawyers will give their law clerks "blanket authority" to access any of the e-reg documents that are connected to their clients' files. This authorization will allow the law clerk to create and eventually register the documents.

To create a transfer, Teraview will use the PIN for the property to locate whatever information is available from the most recent transfer and enter it into the appropriate fields of the new transfer. For example, the transferor's name (transferee on the previous transfer), the legal description, and the roll number will all be inserted automatically in the new transfer. This function is called pre-population. You can then add the amount of consideration, the transferor's spousal status, the purchaser's name, birthdate, and address for service.

The purchaser's lawyer should advise you who in the purchaser's lawyer's office will have access to the transfer through e-reg. The purchaser's lawyer will then review the transfer and make any additions or changes. Figure 21.17 is a sample of an electronic transfer document.

DOCUMENT PREPARED BY BOTH LAWYERS

acknowledgement and direction document signed by parties to a real estate transaction authorizing their respective lawyers to sign and release the documents electronically on their behalf

Both lawyers must also prepare an **acknowledgement and direction** for their clients to sign. This acknowledges the client's understanding of the electronic documents and authorizes the purchaser's lawyer to complete the transaction on behalf of the client by way of electronic registration. It also directs the lawyer to enter into any necessary escrow closing agreement with the other's lawyer. Furthermore, it provides a warranty as to the client's identity. This document is essential when using the e-reg system because the documents submitted for registration are not physically signed by the client. Figure 21.18 is an example of an acknowledgement and direction.

REFERENCES

Family Law Act, RSO 1990, c. F.3.

Income Tax Act, RSC 1985, c. 1 (5th Supp.), as amended.

Land Transfer Tax Act, RSO 1990, c. L.6.

Personal Property Security Act, RSO 1990, c. P.10, as amended.

REVIEW QUESTIONS

1. Which documents does the purchaser's lawyer usually prepare?
2. Which documents does the vendor's lawyer usually prepare?
3. What is a direction regarding title, and why is one necessary?
4. What is an undertaking to readjust, and why is one necessary?
5. What is the land transfer tax affidavit, and why is one necessary?
6. When is the purchaser required to accept an undertaking to discharge a mortgage? What should such an undertaking state?
7. What is a statutory declaration regarding writs of execution, and when is one necessary?
8. What is a statutory declaration of possession, and why is one necessary?
9. What is the *Income Tax Act* declaration, and why is one necessary?
10. What is a general undertaking, and why is one necessary?
11. What is the statement of adjustments, and why is one necessary?
12. Is an adjustment made for insurance in the statement of adjustments?

13. After all the adjustments are made, how is the balance due on closing calculated in the statement of adjustments?
14. What is the direction regarding funds, and why is one necessary?
15. What is a GST declaration, and when is one necessary?
16. What is a client undertaking?
17. What is a personal undertaking?
18. What type of document is required to transfer title of a property that has not been automated, and who prepares it?
19. What must your law firm have in order to use e-reg?
20. What are the three levels of licence issued by Teranet?
21. What is the acknowledgement and direction in an e-reg transaction, and why is one necessary?
22. The current annual property taxes for the property being purchased are \$3,650, of which the vendor has paid \$1,000. The transaction is scheduled to close on March 31. Calculate the adjustment.

FIGURE 21.1 Direction Regarding Title

DIRECTION

To: (*Vendor*)
And to: (*Vendor's lawyer*)
Re: (*Transaction*)

I/We hereby authorize and direct you to endorse the transfer in the above-noted transaction as follows:

Name	**Birthdate**
(*SURNAME, first name*)	(*year/month/day*)

and for so doing this shall be your good and sufficient authority.

DATED at ____________________ this __________ day of ________________, (*year*)

____
(*Purchaser*)

FIGURE 21.2 Purchaser's Undertaking to Readjust

UNDERTAKING

To: (*Vendor*)
And to: (*Vendor's lawyer*)
Re: (*Transaction*)

IN CONSIDERATION OF and notwithstanding the closing of the above-noted transaction, I/we hereby undertake to readjust any items on the statement of adjustments that may require such readjustment.

DATED at ____________________ this _________ day of ______________, (*year*)

____
(*Purchaser*)

FIGURE 21.3 Land Transfer Tax Affidavit

DYE & DURHAM CO. INC. Form No. 600

Printed July 2004

Ontario — Ministry of Finance
Motor Fuels and Tobacco Tax Branch
PO Box 625
33 King St West
Oshawa ON L1H 8H9

Property Identifier(s) No. ____

Land Transfer Tax Affidavit

Land Transfer Tax Act

Refer to all instructions on reverse side.

In the Matter of the Conveyance of *(insert brief description of land)* ____

BY *(print names of all transferors in full)* ____

TO *(print names of all transferees in full)* ____

I ____

have personal knowledge of the facts herein deposed to and Make Oath and Say that:

1. I am *(place a clear mark within the square opposite the following paragraph(s) that describe(s) the capacity of the deponents)*:
   - ☐ (a) the transferee named in the above-described conveyance;
   - ☐ (b) the authorized agent or solicitor acting in this transaction for the transferee(s);
   - ☐ (c) The President, Vice-President, Secretary, Treasurer, Director or Manager authorized to act for ____ (the transferee(s)).
   - ☐ (d) a transferee and am making this affidavit on my own behalf and on behalf of *(insert name of spouse or same-sex partner)* ____ who is my spouse or same-sex partner.
   - ☐ (e) the transferor or an officer authorized to act on behalf of the transferor company and ☐ I am tendering this document for registration and ☐ no tax is payable on registration of this document.

2. **THE TOTAL CONSIDERATION FOR THIS TRANSACTION IS ALLOCATED AS FOLLOWS:**

(a) Monies paid or to be paid in cash	$ ____	***All Blanks must be filled in. Insert Nil where applicable.***
(b) Mortgages (i) Assumed ***(principal and interest)***	$ ____	
(ii) Given back to vendor	$ ____	
(c) Property transferred in exchange ***(detail below in para. 5)***	$ ____	
(d) Other consideration subject to tax ***(detail below)***	$ ____	
(e) Fair market value of the lands ***(see instruction 2)***	$ ____	
(f) Value of land, building, fixtures and goodwill subject to Land Transfer Tax ***(Total of (a) to (e))***	$ ____	$ ____
(g) Value of all chattels - items of tangible personal property which are taxable under the provisions of the *Retail Sales Tax Act*		$ ____
(h) Other consideration for transaction not included in (f) or (g) above		$ ____
(i) Total Consideration		$ ____

3. To be completed where the value of the consideration for the conveyance exceeds $400,000.00
   I have read and considered the definition of "single family residence" set out in subsection 1(1) of the Act. The land conveyed in the above-described conveyance:
   - ☐ does not contain a single family residence or contains more than two single family residences;
   - ☐ contains at least one and not more than two single family residences; or
   - ☐ contains at least one and not more than two single family residences and the lands are used for other than just residential purposes. The transferee has accordingly apportioned the value of consideration on the basis that the consideration for the single family residence is $ ____ and the remainder of the lands are used for ____ purposes.

> ***Note:*** *Subsection 2(1)(b) imposes an additional tax at the rate of one-half of one percent upon the value of consideration in excess of $400,000.00 where the conveyance contains at least one and not more than two single family residences and 2(2) allows an apportionment of the consideration where the lands are used for other than just residential purposes.*

4. If consideration is nominal, is the land subject to any encumbrance? ☐ Yes ☐ No
5. Other remarks and explanations, if necessary. ____

Sworn/affirmed before me in the

this day of , (year) .

A Commissioner for taking Affidavits, etc.

____ *Signature(s)*

Property Information Record

A. Describe nature of instrument: ____

B. (i) Address of property being conveyed ***(if available)*** ____
   (ii) Assessment Roll No. ***(if available)*** ____

C. Mailing address(es) for future Notices of Assessment under the *Assessment Act* for property being conveyed ____

D. (i) Registration number for last conveyance of property being conveyed ***(if available)*** ____
   (ii) Legal description of property conveyed: Same as in D (i) above. ☐ Yes ☐ No ☐ Not known

E. Name(s) and address(es) of each transferee's solicitor ____

For Land Registry Office Use Only
Registration No.
Registration Date (Year/Month/Day)
Land Registry Office No.

School Support (Voluntary Election) (See reverse for explanation)

	Yes	No
(a) Are all individual transferees Roman Catholic ?	☐	☐
(b) If Yes, do all individual transferees wish to be Roman Catholic Separate School Supporters ?	☐	☐
(c) Do all individual transferees have French Language Education Rights ?	☐	☐
(d) If Yes, do all individual transferees wish to support the French Language School Board (where established)?	☐	☐

NOTE: As to (c) and (d) the land being transferred will receive French Public School Board election unless otherwise directed in (a) and (b). 0449K - (2004-04)

FIGURE 21.4 Electronic Land Transfer Tax Statements

LAND TRANSFER TAX STATEMENTS

In the matter of the conveyance of:

BY:

TO: Beneficial Owner %(all PINs)

1.

I am

☐ (a) A person in trust for whom the land conveyed in the above-described conveyance is being conveyed;

☐ (b) A trustee named in the above-described conveyance to whom the land is being conveyed;

☐ (c) A transferee named in the above-described conveyance;

☐ (d) The authorized agent or solicitor acting in this transaction for ____ described in paragraph(s) (_) above.

☐ (e) The President, Vice-President, Manager, Secretary, Director, or Treasurer authorized to act for ____ described in paragraph(s) (_) above.

☐ (f) A transferee described in paragraph ( ) and am making these statements on my own behalf and on behalf of _____ who is my spouse described in paragraph (_) and as such, I have personal knowledge of the facts herein deposed to.

☐ (g) A transferee described in paragraph ( ) and am making these statements on my own behalf and on behalf of _____ who is my same-sex partner described above in paragraph(s) (_).

3. **The total consideration for this transaction is allocated as follows:**

(a) Monies paid or to be paid in cash	0.00
(b) Mortgages (i) assumed (show principal and interest to be credited against purchase price)	0.00
(ii) Given Back to Vendor	0.00
(c) Property transferred in exchange (detail below)	0.00
(d) Fair market value of the land(s)	0.00
(e) Liens, legacies, annuities and maintenance charges to which transfer is subject	0.00
(f) Other valuable consideration subject to land transfer tax (detail below)	0.00
(g) Value of land, building, fixtures and goodwill subject to land transfer tax (total of (a) to (f))	0.00
(h) VALUE OF ALL CHATTELS - items of tangible personal property	0.00
(i) Other considerations for transaction not included in (g) or (h) above	0.00
(j) Total consideration	0.00

PROPERTY Information Record

A. Nature of Instrument: Transfer
LRO Registration No. Date:

B. Property(s): PIN Address Assessment Roll No 2402090 - 91507900

C. Address for Service:

D. (i) Last Conveyance(s): PIN Registration No.
(ii) Legal Description for Property Conveyed : Same as in last conveyance? Yes ☐ No ☐ Not known ☐

FIGURE 21.5 Undertaking Regarding Discharge of Mortgage

UNDERTAKING

To: (*Purchaser*)
And to: (*Purchaser's lawyer*)
Re: (*Transaction*)

IN CONSIDERATION OF and notwithstanding the closing of the above-noted transaction, we hereby undertake to obtain and register a Discharge of Charge/Mortgage of the Charge/Mortgage of Land registered as Instrument number ________________ in favour of ____________________, within a reasonable period of time after the date of closing, and to forthwith provide you with the particulars of registration of same.

DATED at ____________________ this __________ day of _______________, (*year*)

____
(*Vendor's lawyer*)

FIGURE 21.6 Bill of Sale

BILL OF SALE

To: (*Purchaser*)
Re: (*Transaction*)

IN CONSIDERATION OF the sum of One Dollar ($1.00) and other good and valuable consideration paid to me/us, the receipt whereof is hereby acknowledged, I/we hereby assign, transfer, and set over unto (*purchaser*), his/her/their heirs, executors administrators, and assigns, free and clear of any chattel mortgages, liens or other encumbrances, the following chattels:

(*list chattels shown in agreement of purchase and sale*)

which are presently situated on the premises known municipally as (*address of property*), in accordance with the terms and conditions contained in the agreement of purchase and sale dated the _________ day of __________________ , __________.

DATED at ____________________ this _________ day of _______________ , (*year*)

____
(*Vendor*)

FIGURE 21.7 Statutory Declaration Regarding Executions

LAND TITLES ACT

IN THE MATTER OF Parcel ________________ in the Register for Section ________________

AND IN THE MATTER of certain writs of execution in the hands of the Sheriff of ________________ copies of which have been filed in the Land Registry Office for the Land Titles Division of ________________ as numbers ________________

I/WE ________________ of the ________________ in the ________________

DO SOLEMNLY DECLARE that:

1. I am/We are the registered owner(s) of the land entered as Parcel ________________ Section ________________.
2. I am/We are not the same person(s) as ________________, the judgment debtor(s) named in writ(s) of execution number ________________ wherein ________________ as plaintiff was awarded $ ________________ plus $ ________________ costs.

(SEVERALLY) DECLARED BEFORE ME at the	)	
	)	
in the	)	
this day	)	________________
of , (*year*).	)	
________________	)	
A Commissioner, etc.	)	

FIGURE 21.8 Statutory Declaration of Possession

(use legal size paper)

CANADA	)	IN THE MATTER OF the title to
	)	
PROVINCE OF ONTARIO	)	
	)	known municipally as
(judicial district)	)	
	)	
	)	AND IN THE MATTER OF the sale thereof FROM
	)	
	)	TO
	)	
TO WIT:	)	

I, ____________________ of the ____________________ in the ___________________ ,
DO SOLEMNLY DECLARE THAT:

1. I am the absolute registered owner of the above-described land, which was conveyed to me by transfer/deed dated____________________, and registered in the Registry Division of __________________, on __________________, as Instrument Number ____________________. I have been in actual, peaceable, continuous, exclusive, open, undisturbed, and undisputed possession and occupation thereof, and of the houses and other buildings used in connection therewith since on or about the date of registration of the said transfer/deed.
2. The property is subject to a mortgage in favour of___________________, registered as Instrument Number ___________________, which mortgage is to be discharged from the proceeds of disposition herein.
3. Save and except the above-mentioned mortgage(s) and any taxes and local improvement rates charged thereon, there are no encumbrances, easements, rights of way, or restrictive covenants whatsoever affecting the said lands except as disclosed by the records of the registry office.
4. Since the date of registration of my transfer/deed as aforesaid, no one has made entry onto the said lands or any part thereof or made any claim under or in respect of any claim adverse to my title and I have never heard of any claim adverse to my title.
5. My possession and occupation of the above-mentioned lands has been undisturbed throughout by any action, suit, or other proceeding or adverse possession or otherwise on the part of any person, and during such possession and occupation no payment has ever been made or acknowledgement of title given by me, or by any person in respect of any right, title, interest, or claim upon the said lands.
6. To the best of my knowledge and belief, the buildings on the subject premises are situate within the limits of the lands above described. There is no dispute as to the boundaries of the said lands and the said lands from the time which I have been the owner thereof have been partially fenced. I have never heard of any claim of easement affecting the lands, either for light, drainage, or rights of way or otherwise except as disclosed by the records of the registry office.
7. Attached hereto as schedule "A" to this declaration is a copy of the plan of survey of the said lands dated ____________________, and prepared by ____________ ________, Ontario Land Surveyors. There have been no changes to the said plan or the said lands or the premises on the lands that would affect the validity of the said plan of survey. The said plan of survey accurately depicts the location of all improvements on the lands.

FIGURE 21.8 Concluded

8. There are no construction liens registered against the said lands nor any claims for which such liens could be registered. In particular, there has been no work done on the premises or materials supplied for which full payment has not been made.
9. There are no executions in the sheriff's hands affecting the said lands.
10. All taxes on the said lands have been paid up to____________________, and there are no outstanding local improvement charges.
11. The deeds, evidences of title, and other papers that have been produced to me are all the title deeds, evidences of title, leases, and papers relating to the title to the said lands that are in my possession or my control, and to the best of my knowledge and belief, the said title deeds and papers produced and this declaration and the registered title fully and fairly disclose all facts material to the title claimed by me and all contracts and dealings that affect the same or any part thereof so far as I have any knowledge thereof.
12. I have not, to date, received any order or written request from any municipal or other governmental authority, including the fire marshall, pursuant to which any work, repairs, or replacements were required to be performed in respect of or installed in the above-mentioned lands, nor have I received any request or notification in this regard.
13. There are no unregistered leases, tenancy agreements, licences, rights of occupation, or agreements therefor with respect to the above-noted property, and nothing is affixed to the property that is the subject of a conditional sales contract, chattel mortgage, lease, security agreement, or otherwise encumbered.
14. None of the chattels covered by the agreement of purchase and sale in the above-noted matter is the subject of a conditional sales contract, chattel mortgage, lease, security agreement, or is otherwise encumbered.
15. I do not retain the fee or the equity of redemption in, or a power or right to grant, assign, or exercise a power of appointment with respect to any land abutting the subject property.
16. I am over the age of 18 years and (*insert appropriate statement of spousal status under the Family Law Act*).
17. I am not and will not be at the time of closing of the above-noted transaction a non-resident of Canada within the meaning of section 116 of the *Income Tax Act* of Canada.
18. I declare that the representations and affirmations made herein are intended to survive the closing of this transaction.

AND I MAKE this solemn declaration conscientiously believing it to be true and knowing that it is of the same force and effect as if made under oath.

DECLARED BEFORE ME at the)
)
in the)
this day) ____________________
of , (*year*).)
____________________)
A Commissioner, etc.)

FIGURE 21.9 **Realty Tax Declaration**

STATUTORY DECLARATION

CANADA	)	IN THE MATTER OF
	)	
PROVINCE OF ONTARIO	)	
	)	
	)	AND IN THE MATTER OF the sale
	)	thereof from
		to

I/WE,

DO SOLEMNLY DECLARE, that

1. I am/We are the registered owners of the above mentioned property and as such have knowledge of the matters hereinafter deposed to.
2. The (*year*) realty taxes are in the amount of $ ____________________.
3. All (*year*) interim realty tax installments have been paid in accordance with the Statement of Adjustments. There are no arrears of realty taxes in connection with the property.
4. There are no outstanding hydro, water, and gas accounts and all utility accounts will be paid up to the date of closing.

AND I/WE make this solemn Declaration conscientiously believing it to be true, and knowing that it is of the same force and effect as if made under oath.

(SEVERALLY) DECLARED BEFORE ME at the	)	
	)	
in the	)	
this day	)	____________________
of , (*year*).	)	
____________________	)	
A Commissioner, etc.	)	

FIGURE 21.10 UFFI Warranty

WARRANTY

To: (*Purchaser*)
And to: (*Purchaser's lawyer*)
Re: (*Transaction*)

IN CONSIDERATION of and notwithstanding the completion of the above transaction, I/we hereby warrant that during the time I/we have owned the property being purchased I/we have not caused any building on the property to be insulated with insulation containing ureaformaldehyde, and that to the best of my/our knowledge no building on the property contains or has ever contained insulation that contains ureaformaldehyde. It is acknowledged that this warranty shall survive the closing of the above transaction.

DATED at ____________________ this __________ day of ________________, (*year*)

____
(*Vendor*)

FIGURE 21.11 Vendor's General Undertaking

UNDERTAKING

To: (*Purchaser*)
And to: (*Purchaser's lawyer*)
Re: (*Transaction*)

In consideration of and notwithstanding the closing of the above-noted transaction, I/we hereby undertake as follows:

1. To deliver up vacant possession of the premises on closing and all keys to the premises.
2. To pay all hydroelectric, water, and gas charges, if any, to the date of closing.
3. To pay all arrears of taxes and penalties, including local improvement rates, and to readjust realty taxes and local improvement rates for the current year, if necessary.
4. To leave on the premises the chattels and fixtures specified in the agreement of purchase and sale herein, free of encumbrances, liens, charges, or claims of any kind whatsoever.
5. To readjust any of the items shown on the statement of adjustments, if necessary.
6. To have the oil tank filled in accordance with the statement of adjustments at my/our expense on the day before closing.
7. To make all payments under the existing mortgages(s) being assumed by the purchaser(s) which fall due on or before the closing date, and to readjust the amounts credited to the purchaser(s) with respect to the principal balance and interest owing and tax account status of the existing mortgage(s) being assumed by the purchaser(s) if necessary.

DATED at ____________________ this ____________ day of ________________ , (*year*)

____
(*Vendor*)

FIGURE 21.12 Statutory Declaration Regarding Goods and Services Tax

CANADA	)	IN THE MATTER OF Goods and Services Tax
	)	(GST) under part IX of the *Excise Tax Act*
PROVINCE OF	)	(Canada), RSC 1985, c. E-15, as amended
ONTARIO	)	
	)	AND IN THE MATTER OF the sale of
(*judicial district*)	)	Lot , Plan ,
	)	City of , municipally known
	)	as , by
	)	to
	)	
	)	AND IN THE MATTER OF the exemption of
	)	the said sale from GST

TO WIT:

I/WE ____________________ , of the ____________________ in the ____________________ DO SOLEMNLY DECLARE that

1. I/We am/are the owner(s) of the above property, which comprises a single-family residential dwelling unit.
2. I/We use the dwelling primarily as my/our place of residence. I/We did not acquire the property in the course of a business or as an adventure or concern in the nature of trade. No part of the property is capital property (as defined in the *Excise Tax Act*) used primarily in a business.
3. This sale is not being made in the course of my/our business nor in the course of my/our adventure or concern in the nature of trade in respect of which I/we have filed an election under the *Excise Tax Act* (Canada).
4. I/We have not carried on any construction or renovation on the property in the course of a business or an adventure or concern in the nature of trade.
5. I/We have never claimed an input tax credit under the *Excise Tax Act* (Canada) in respect of the acquisition of the property or any improvement to it.

AND I/we make this declaration conscientiously believing it to be true, and knowing that it is of the same force and effect as if made under oath and by virtue of the *Canada Evidence Act.*

(SEVERALLY) DECLARED BEFORE ME at the	)	
	)	
in the	)	
this day	)	____________________
of , (*year*).	)	
____________________	)	
A Commissioner, etc.	)	

FIGURE 21.13 Statement of Adjustments

STATEMENT OF ADJUSTMENTS

VENDOR: Victor Vendor
PURCHASER: Peter Purchaser
PROPERTY: 123 Elm Street, Toronto, Ontario

Adjusted as of January 15, (*year*)

	Credit Purchaser	*Credit Vendor*
SALE PRICE	—	180,000.00
DEPOSIT	—	—
Paid to broker	10,000.00	—
FIRST MORTGAGE ASSUMED		
Principal outstanding as of January 15, (*year*)	42,563.00	—
Interest at 10% from January 1–14, (*year*)	163.26	—
SECOND MORTGAGE		
Back to vendor	25,000.00	—
REALTY TAXES		
(*Current year*) taxes estimated at $3,100.00 (based on (*previous year*) taxes of $3,009.71 plus 3 percent)		
Vendor's share 14 days — $118.90		
Vendor has paid $350.00		
Credit vendor	—	231.10
FUEL OIL		
900 litres @ $0.4971/ litre (including GST)		
Credit vendor	—	447.39
HYDRO, GAS, WATER	—	—
Metered, no adjustment	—	—
BALANCE DUE ON CLOSING	102,952.23	—
	180,678.49	180,678.49

FIGURE 21.14 Direction Regarding Funds

DIRECTION

To: (*Purchaser*)
And to: (*Purchaser's lawyer*)
Re: (*Transaction*)

You are hereby authorized and directed to make the balance due on closing payable to my/our solicitor(s), (*vendor's lawyer*), in trust, or as he/she/they may in writing direct and for so doing this shall be your good, sufficient, and irrevocable authority.

Dated this ____________________ day of ____________________, (*year*).

____
(*Vendor*)

FIGURE 21.15 Redirection Regarding Funds

DIRECTION

To: *(Purchaser)*
And to: *(Purchaser's lawyer)*
Re: *(Transaction)*

You are hereby authorized and directed to make the balance due on closing payable as follows:

1. To: $
2. To:
3. To:
4. To: ____________________

   $

and for so doing this shall be your good and sufficient authority.

DATED at ____________________ this __________ day of ______________, *(year)*

____
(Vendor's law firm)

Per: ____________________

FIGURE 21.16 Transfer/Deed of Land

Province of Ontario

DYE & DURHAM CO. INC.—Form No. 970
Amended NOV. 1992

Transfer/Deed of Land

Form 1 — Land Registration Reform Act

A

FOR OFFICE USE ONLY

New Property Identifiers — Additional: See Schedule ☐

Executions — Additional: See Schedule ☐

(1) Registry ☐ **Land Titles** ☐

(2) Page 1 of pages

(3) Property Identifier(s) Block Property — Additional: See Schedule ☐

(4) Consideration

Dollars $

(5) Description This is a: Property Division ☐ Property Consolidation ☐

(6) This Document Contains (a) Redescription New Easement Plan/Sketch ☐ (b) Schedule for: Description ☐ Additional Parties ☐ Other ☐

(7) Interest/Estate Transferred Fee Simple

(8) Transferor(s) The transferor hereby transfers the land to the transferee and certifies that the transferor is at least eighteen years old and that

Name(s)	Signature(s)	Date of Signature Y	M	D

(9) Spouse(s) of Transferor(s) I hereby consent to this transaction

Name(s)	Signature(s)	Date of Signature Y	M	D

(10) Transferor(s) Address for Service

(11) Transferee(s)

	Date of Birth Y	M	D

(12) Transferee(s) Address for Service

Planning Act — OPTIONAL

(13) Transferor(s) The transferor verifies that to the best of the transferor's knowledge and belief, this transfer does not contravene section 50 of the Planning Act.

Signature. . . . . Date of Signature Y M D Signature . . . . Date of Signature Y M D

Solicitor for Transferor(s) I have explained the effect of section 50 of the Planning Act to the transferor and I have made inquiries of the transferor to determine that this transfer does not contravene that section and based on the information supplied by the transferor, to the best of my knowledge and belief, this transfer does not contravene that section. I am an Ontario solicitor in good standing.

Name and Address of Solicitor Signature. . . . . Date of Signature Y M D

Affix Statement by Solicitor for Transferee(s) here if necessary

(14) Solicitor for Transferee(s) I have investigated the title to this land and to abutting land where relevant and I am satisfied that the title records reveal no contravention as set out in subclause 50 (22) (c) (ii) of the Planning Act and that to the best of my knowledge and belief this transfer does not contravene section 50 of the Planning Act. I act independently of the solicitor for the transferor(s) and I am an Ontario solicitor in good standing.

Name and Address of Solicitor Signature. . . . . Date of Signature Y M D

(15) Assessment Roll Number of Property	Cty.	Mun.	Map	Sub.	Par.

(16) Municipal Address of Property

(17) Document Prepared by:

FOR OFFICE USE ONLY

Fees and Tax	
Registration Fee	
Land Transfer Tax	
Total	

FIGURE 21.17 Electronic Transfer

This document has not been submitted and may be incomplete. yyyy mm dd Page 1 of 1

LRO # **Transfer** **In preparation** on **at**

Properties

PIN Estate/Qualifier

Description

Address

Consideration

Consideration $ 0.00

Transferor(s)

The transferor(s) hereby transfers the land to the transferee(s).

Name

Address for Service

I am at least 18 years of age.

This document is not authorized under Power of Attorney by this party.

Name

Address for Service

I am at least 18 years of age.

Transferee(s)	*Capacity*	***Share***
Name	Beneficial Owner	
Date of Birth		
Address for Service		

Calculated Taxes

Retail Sales Tax $0.00

Land Transfer Tax 0.00

FIGURE 21.18 Acknowledgement and Direction

ACKNOWLEDGEMENT AND DIRECTION

Page 1 of 1

TO: ______________________________
{insert lawyer's name}

AND TO: ______________________________
{insert Firm name if applicable}

RE: ______________________________
{insert brief description of transaction}

This will confirm that:

- I/we have reviewed the information set out below, and that this information is accurate;
- You are authorized and directed to register electronically on my behalf the document(s) described in this Acknowledgement and Direction as well as any other document(s) required to complete the transaction described above;
- You are authorized and directed to enter into an escrow closing arrangement substantially in the form attached hereto as Schedule "A" and I/we acknowledge that I/we shall be bound by the terms of that Agreement.
- The effect of the electronic documents described in this Acknowledgement and Direction has been fully explained to me/us and I/we understand that I/we are parties to and bound by the terms and provisions of these electronic document(s) to the same extent as if I/we had signed these documents; and
- I/we are in fact parties named in the electronic documents described in this Acknowledgement and Direction and I/we have not misrepresented our identities to you.

DESCRIPTION OF TRANSFER (for the Transferor(s)):

Properties

PIN Estate/Qualifier
Description
Address

Transferor(s)

Name

Name

Consideration $ 0.00

Dated at ______________, **this** ______________ **day of** ______________, ______________.

Witness: (as to all signatures, if applicable)

______________________________ ______________________________

CHAPTER 22

Preparation for Closing

After the closing documents have been prepared, you must turn your attention to the closing itself. It is at the closing that the purchaser receives title to the property and the vendor receives payment. The purchaser's lawyer wants to make sure that there are sufficient funds on hand to close the transaction and that the purchaser gets exactly what was contracted for. The vendor's lawyer wants to make sure that the appropriate payment is received on behalf of the vendor and that the vendor can deliver title as promised.

ORGANIZATION FROM THE PURCHASER'S PERSPECTIVE

If the purchaser's lawyer and law clerk have been well organized, used checklists, and diarized as they've gone along, there should be very little left to do as the closing date approaches.

Monetary Issues

To prepare for closing, you must know how much the purchaser has to pay to complete the transaction and to whom the money must be paid. You received this information from the statement of adjustments and the direction regarding funds, prepared by the vendor's lawyer. (Both of these documents are discussed in chapter 21, Document Preparation.)

You must also calculate how much the purchaser will have to pay for

- land transfer tax;
- retail sales tax, if any; and
- registration fees.

CALCULATING THE PROVINCIAL LAND TRANSFER TAX

Land transfer tax is calculated using the information in the land transfer tax affidavit (discussed in chapter 21, Document Preparation). Land transfer tax is payable on the amount shown in line (f) — "Value of land, building, fixtures and goodwill subject to Land Transfer Tax."

The land transfer tax rates are

- ½ of 1 percent (0.005) on the first $55,000;
- 1 percent (0.01) on the amount from $55,000.01 to $250,000;
- 1½ percent (0.015) on the amount from $250,000.01 to $400,000;
- 2 percent (0.02) on the amount over $400,000 if the property contains at least one and not more than two single-family residences. Otherwise, the rate remains at 1½ percent (0.015).

As a shortcut, you may do the calculation based on the scale set out below:

- If the consideration is less than or equal to $55,000, simply multiply the amount of the consideration by 0.005.
- If the consideration is greater than $55,000 but is not greater than $250,000, multiply the amount of the consideration by 0.01 and then deduct $275.
- If the consideration is greater than $250,000 but is not greater than $400,000, or the consideration is greater than $400,000 but does not contain at least one and not more than two single-family residences, multiply the amount of the consideration by 0.015 and then deduct $1,525.
- If the consideration is greater than $400,000, and the property contains at least one and not more than two single-family residences, multiply the amount of the consideration by 0.02 and then deduct $3,525.

For example, if the consideration on the sale of a single-family residence is $650,000, the calculation can be done in *either* of the following two ways:

1. For the first $55,000: $55,000 × 0.005 = $275

   For $55,000 – 250,000: $195,000 × 0.01 = $1,950

   For $250,000 – 400,000: $150,000 × 0.015 = $2,250

   For $400,000 – 650,000: $250,000 × 0.02 = $5,000

   Total land transfer tax $9,475

or

2. ($650,000 × 0.02) – 3,525 = $13,000 – 3,525 = $9,475

If the property contained three or more residential units, the rate would not increase again after $400,000.

It is important to advise first-time homebuyers that they are entitled to a rebate of up to $2,000 of the provincial land transfer tax.

CALCULATING THE MUNICIPAL LAND TRANSFER TAX

If the property is located in the City of Toronto, municipal land transfer tax must also be paid. The rates are as follows:

- ½ of 1 percent (0.005) on the first $55,000;
- 1 percent (0.01) on the amount from $55,000.01 to $400,000;
- 2 percent (0.02) on the amount over $400,000.

As a shortcut, you may do the calculation based on the scale set out below:

- If the consideration is less than or equal to $55,000, multiply the amount of the consideration by 0.005.
- If the consideration is between $55,000.01 and $400,000, multiply the amount of the consideration by 0.01, and subtract $275.
- If the consideration is greater than $400,000, multiply the amount of the consideration by 0.02, and subtract $4,275.

First-time homebuyers are exempt from municipal land transfer tax on purchase prices up to $400,000. They have to pay tax on amounts over $400,000.

CALCULATING THE RETAIL SALES TAX

Provincial retail sales tax is payable on the value of the chattels included in the transaction. The calculation of this tax is based on the information contained in the land transfer tax affidavit. To calculate the amount of retail sales tax payable, multiply the amount shown in line (g) "Value of all chattels" by 8 percent.

REGISTRATION FEES PAYABLE ON CLOSING

The purchaser pays to register the transfer and any mortgages other than a vendor take back mortgage. The vendor pays to register any mortgage back and any discharges of mortgage or other documents required to clear the title of encumbrances. At the time of publication, the registration fee was $70.70 for each instrument of any kind; however, registration fees increase regularly.

OBTAINING FUNDS FROM THE CLIENT

You must obtain sufficient funds from the purchaser to cover the balance due on closing, the land transfer tax, the retail sales tax, and the registration fees. In addition, most law firms will want the client to give the firm enough money to cover the legal fees and disbursements for the transaction.

The lawyer will set the amount to be charged for fees. You will need to calculate the total amount of **disbursements**. Disbursements are the out-of-pocket expenses that your firm has paid or will pay with respect to the transaction, such as the costs of a Registry system title search, execution certificate, tax certificate, registration fees, title insurance premium, postage, and courier charges.

disbursements
lawyer's out-of-pocket expenses, or money actually spent on behalf of the client

MORTGAGE PROCEEDS

If the client is financing part of the purchase by way of a mortgage, you will need to know exactly how much the mortgagee will be providing on the closing date. The amount may well be less than the principal amount of the mortgage. For example, if the interest adjustment date is different from the closing date, an amount for interest is deducted from the amount advanced under the mortgage. If the mortgage is a **high ratio mortgage** (a mortgage for more than 75 percent of the value of the property), an amount may be deducted for insurance. The money received from the mortgagee will be applied to the purchase price and will reduce the amount of money to be provided directly by the purchaser.

high ratio mortgage
a mortgage for more than 75 percent of the value of the property

One Week Before Closing

Start your final preparation for closing *at least* one week before the closing date.

REVIEW THE FILE

- Make sure that all preliminary letters, the requisition letter, and any followup letters sent by the law firm have been answered and that the answers are satisfactory.
- Update public utility account and tax information in the case of a long closing or if the original responses revealed arrears that the vendor's solicitor indicated would be paid before closing.

CONTACT THE CLIENT

- You must advise the client of the amount of money to be provided.
- Set up an appointment for the client to deliver the funds and to sign all documents.
- If the closing is electronic, after the client has signed the acknowledgement and direction, the lawyer must sign and fax the document registration agreement (DRA) to the vendor's lawyer for signature.
- Remind the client to arrange insurance coverage for the property as of the closing date. If the purchaser is arranging new mortgage financing, the client will have to provide to the mortgagee particulars of the insurance coverage and a certified copy of the policy at a later date.
- Check that the client has taken all steps necessary for any mortgage approvals, whether there are new mortgages or mortgages being assumed.

PREPARE STATUTORY DECLARATION REGARDING EXECUTIONS

If there are any executions outstanding against a name similar to that of the purchaser, or if the purchaser has a common family name, prepare a statutory declaration regarding executions to be sworn by the client. In the declaration, deal specifically with any executions outstanding at the time the declaration is drafted. If the purchaser's name is a common name, prepare a declaration in blank and make sure that the client is available to deal with the declaration if an execution is found on closing.

CONFIRM ARRANGEMENTS FOR A CONVEYANCER

If the closing is being handled by someone other than you or the lawyer handling the file, and particularly if your firm uses an outside conveyancer, reconfirm the conveyancer's availability and time preferences, and make arrangements for the pickup and delivery of the file.

PREPARE THE CLOSING MEMO

Preparation of the closing memo is discussed below.

The Day Before Closing/Morning of Closing (Registry Office Closing)

If the closing is taking place at the registry office, arrange the specific time for the closing, and exchange the names of the persons attending for the purchaser and vendor.

Make sure you know how the closing cheques are to be payable, requisition or prepare the cheques, and have them signed and certified, as necessary.

PURCHASER'S CLOSING MEMO

The closing memo is a document that sets out all steps to be taken, documents and other things to be exchanged on closing, and registration instructions. If the closing is at the registry office, you will need to prepare a closing memo for the conveyancer. If the closing is electronic, you should prepare a closing memo for yourself in the form of a checklist. The closing memo for an electronic closing will be slightly different because steps in an electronic closing are different. The closing memo for an electronic closing is discussed later in the chapter.

When preparing the closing memo, refer to the requisition letter. If it was drafted properly, it will list all items required on closing.

The closing memo has four main parts:

1. preliminary steps to take;
2. documents and items to get;
3. documents and items to give; and
4. registration instructions.

Preliminary Steps

These steps will be the same in every registry office closing.

UPDATE SEARCH OF TITLE

The closing memo should instruct the conveyancer to subsearch from the last instrument shown in the search.

If a particular instrument was to be registered prior to closing, specify it in the closing memo, with instructions to ensure that it has been registered. Examples include a discharge of mortgage, a mortgage, a mortgage amending agreement, or a release.

Attach the search of title to the closing memo so that it is available, if necessary, to cross-check a recent registration. The search notes also provide the conveyancer with the last instrument number registered in the abstract at the time of the search. This indicates to the conveyancer where to start the subsearch.

UPDATE EXECUTION SEARCH

Set out the details of any executions you are aware of and for which satisfactory arrangements, such as delivery of an affidavit, have been made. If an execution was to be discharged by closing, give particulars in the memo so that the conveyancer can confirm that the execution has, in fact, been discharged.

Documents and Items to Get

Under this heading, list all documents and other items to be obtained from the vendor on closing. This list will be based on the requisition letter. The memo should provide sufficient explanation and copies of draft documents to be obtained.

TRANSFER/DEED OF LAND

The transfer provided on closing must be in the same form as the draft transfer previously submitted by the vendor and approved by the purchaser's lawyer. The memo should instruct the conveyancer to compare the documents, and the draft should be attached.

MORTGAGES TO BE ASSUMED

If a mortgage is being assumed, the conveyancer must obtain

- a mortgage statement for assumption purposes showing a balance outstanding in the same amount as that shown on the statement of adjustments (which should be attached) — the memo should specify what the outstanding principal and interest should be;
- a copy of the mortgage, if not already provided by the title searcher; and
- particulars of the mortgage number and address for payment.

MORTGAGES TO BE DISCHARGED

If a mortgage is to be discharged on or before closing, instruct the conveyancer to make certain either that the discharge has already been registered or that a discharge will be registered before registration of the transfer. The memo must provide full registration particulars of the mortgage to be discharged so that the conveyancer can check the validity of the discharge.

UNDERTAKINGS TO DISCHARGE MORTGAGES

If, by the terms of the agreement of purchase and sale, or otherwise, the purchaser has agreed to accept an undertaking to discharge a mortgage, the memo must instruct the conveyancer to obtain

- a mortgage statement for discharge purposes;
- the vendor's signed direction, and a redirection that the appropriate amount of funds is to be made payable to the mortgagee; and
- the vendor's lawyer's personal undertaking to discharge the mortgage under the terms set out in the agreement of purchase and sale — the memo should set out the precise wording that is acceptable.

EXECUTED COPIES OF DOCUMENTS FORWARDED TO THE VENDOR FOR SIGNATURE

The memo should advise the conveyancer to obtain executed copies of the documents previously prepared by your law firm and forwarded (usually with the requisition letter) to the vendor for execution. These documents include undertakings, warranties, and declarations of possession. Copies of the draft documents should be attached so that the conveyancer can verify that the executed documents are in the proper form.

DOCUMENTS REQUIRED TO ANSWER REQUISITIONS

The closing memo should specify any documents that are required to answer requisitions. These documents may be ascertained by reading the requisition letter, the answers to requisitions, and any followup correspondence. If, as an answer to a requisition, the vendor agreed to provide something, it should be listed so that the conveyancer will obtain it from the vendor on closing.

KEYS

Unless alternative arrangements were made for the delivery of keys to the purchaser, at least one key must be obtained on closing.

DIRECTION REGARDING FUNDS

Before closing, the vendor's lawyer will have advised the purchaser's lawyer of the manner in which closing funds are to be paid and the closing cheques will have been prepared accordingly. The conveyancer should be told to obtain a direction regarding funds in accordance with the cheques provided.

This part of the memo should conclude by instructing the conveyancer to conduct a careful subsearch of the property and to insert the land transfer tax affidavit in the transfer (three copies should be attached).

Documents and Items to Give

Under this heading, list all the documents and other items to be given to the vendor on closing.

MORTGAGE BACK

If this is applicable, the purchaser's lawyer provides the vendor take back mortgage.

CERTIFIED CHEQUES

A certified cheque or cheques made payable as instructed by the vendor should be attached to the memo and particulars of the cheques provided. The conveyancer should be reminded (if instructions have not already been provided) to ensure that the appropriate direction regarding funds is provided by the vendor.

DIRECTION REGARDING TITLE

See chapter 21, Document Preparation, for a discussion of this document.

UNDERTAKING TO READJUST

See chapter 21, Document Preparation, for a discussion of this document.

ADDITIONAL ITEMS

The memo should also specify the additional items delivered with the memo, such as the file and cheques for registration, land transfer tax, and other fees.

Registration

You must specify what documents the conveyancer should register and the required order of registration. If the vendor is to register a discharge, it should be registered before your conveyancer registers anything. If the vendor is registering a vendor take back mortgage, make sure it is registered in the correct sequence with your conveyancer's documents. (If it is a second mortgage, it must be registered after the first mortgage.)

PURCHASER'S CLOSING CHECKLIST (ELECTRONIC CLOSING)

If the transaction is closing electronically, the parties do not meet at the registry office to exchange documents and funds, and register. Instead, the parties exchange documents and closing funds by courier. In some cases it may be possible to wire or transfer funds between branches of financial institutions. You will then update the search and register the documents electronically. The purchaser's checklist reflects these steps.

Documents to Get

With the exception of the transfer, you will receive the same documents as you would in a registry office closing. Instead of receiving them on closing, however, you will receive them by courier in advance of the closing. Your checklist should list all of the documents you will receive and will contain the same information as a registry office closing memo.

Documents to Give

You will give the same documents as you would in a registry office closing. Instead of delivering them on closing, however, you will deliver them by courier in advance of the closing. Your checklist should list all of the documents you will give and will contain the same information as a registry office closing memo.

Subsearch/Executions

It is necessary to conduct a subsearch before registering the transfer, to make sure that title has not changed since the title search was done, except for required registrations such as a discharge of mortgage, a mortgage, a mortgage amending agreement, or a release. If a particular instrument was to be registered, specify it in the checklist. Teraview will automatically search executions against the vendor, unless the vendor is an estate. If the vendor is an estate, you will have to search executions against the deceased. If the purchaser has arranged a mortgage and you are also acting for a mortgagee, you will have to search executions against the purchaser.

Day of Closing

Courier all non-registrable documents and certified cheques to the vendor's lawyer.

ORGANIZATION FROM THE VENDOR'S PERSPECTIVE

Again, if the vendor's lawyer and law clerk have been organized, there should be very little work left to be done.

One Week Before Closing

The following steps should be taken *at least* one week before the closing.

REVIEW THE FILE

Review the file to find out what requisitions have to be answered and to confirm that the documentation necessary to do so is in the file or expected shortly.

CHECK MORTGAGES TO BE DISCHARGED

If there are mortgages to be discharged, make sure that either you have the discharge or arrangements have been made for the mortgagee to attend on closing to provide the discharge. If the mortgagee is attending on closing, check that you have received a mortgage statement for discharge purposes and that you have advised the purchaser to make the appropriate amount of funds payable to the mortgagee. Also check that you have prepared the direction regarding funds.

CHECK MORTGAGES FOR WHICH AN UNDERTAKING TO DISCHARGE WILL BE GIVEN

If an undertaking to discharge a mortgage will be acceptable, check that you have received a mortgage statement for discharge purposes and that you have prepared a direction regarding the payment of the appropriate amount of funds to the mortgagee. Also check that you have prepared the lawyer's personal undertaking to obtain a discharge.

CHECK MORTGAGES TO BE ASSUMED

If the purchaser is assuming a mortgage, you will have to provide a mortgage statement for assumption purposes and a copy of the mortgage. If any steps were required by the purchaser in order to assume the mortgage — for example, obtaining the approval of the mortgagee or executing an assumption agreement — contact the purchaser's lawyer to confirm that these steps have been taken.

CONTACT THE CLIENT

Contact the client to make arrangements for attendance at your office to execute the transfer and other closing documents. Also remind the client to cancel insurance on the premises but only *after* you have called to confirm that the deal has closed.

GET KEYS

Unless alternative arrangements have been made for the transfer of keys to the purchaser, the vendor must provide at least one key for delivery on closing. The remaining keys are usually left in the house.

FINALIZE HOW FUNDS ARE TO BE PAYABLE

Determine how the closing funds are to be payable, (for example, funds may have to be directed to discharge a mortgage or to pay tax arrears) then prepare the appropriate redirection regarding funds. Finally, tell the purchaser's law firm to whom the cheques should be made payable.

CHECK NON-RESIDENT VENDOR REQUIREMENTS

If the vendor is a non-resident, you must make arrangements for payment of the withholding tax and obtain the appropriate certificate.

CHECK EXECUTION SEARCH

If the vendor has a common family name, you should have conducted a search of executions well before closing so that if an execution is disclosed, you can take the appropriate steps in time. In addition, the vendor should complete a statutory declaration with respect to executions, as discussed above with respect to the purchaser.

PREPARE CLOSING MEMO

If the closing is taking place in the registry office, prepare a closing memo that will be the mirror image of the purchaser's closing memo. If there are any documents to be registered, give clear instructions as to the order of registration. Make sure that a key and all relevant documents are attached.

If the closing is taking place electronically, prepare a checklist setting out the closing funds and all the documents you will require from the purchaser before releasing the electronic transfer for registration.

The Day Before Closing/Morning of Closing

If the closing is taking place in the registry office, arrange the specific time for closing and make sure that you give the conveyancer enough money to pay for any registrations.

If the closing is taking place electronically, courier all non-registrable documents and a key to the purchaser's lawyer.

REVIEW QUESTION

1. Tom Cruiser is buying a single-family residence for $505,000. According to the land transfer tax affidavit, the value of the land, building, fixtures, and goodwill subject to land transfer tax is $500,000 and the value of chattels included in the transaction is $5,000. Calculate the land transfer tax and the retail sales tax payable on the transaction.

CHAPTER 23

Acting for the Mortgagee

In most real estate transactions, the purchaser will arrange a charge or mortgage in order to pay for the property. Because the mortgagee is receiving an interest in the land, the mortgagee (just like the purchaser) must be sure that the title to the property is good. The mortgagee will need a lawyer to check the title and to prepare the mortgage documents. The mortgagor pays the mortgagee's legal fees. In order to keep the fees as low as possible, the mortgagee will usually agree to use the mortgagor's (purchaser's) lawyer to do the work. As a result, when you are acting for a purchaser, you will often be doing the legal work for the mortgagee too.

The interests of the mortgagee and the purchaser are similar. As a result, much, although not all, of the work that you will be doing for the mortgagee will also be for the purchaser.

RULES OF PROFESSIONAL CONDUCT

Subrules 2.04(11) and (12) of the Law Society of Upper Canada's *Rules of Professional Conduct* deal with the situation where a lawyer is representing both the lender (mortgagee) and the borrower (mortgagor) in a mortgage transaction. The rules generally prohibit a lawyer from acting for both the borrower and the lender unless

- the lawyer practises in a remote location where there are no other lawyers who could conveniently be retained by either party;
- the borrower is buying property from the lender and the mortgage represents part of the purchase price (a vendor take back mortgage);
- the lender is a bank, trust company, insurance company, credit union, or finance company that lends money in the ordinary course of its business;
- the amount of the mortgage does not exceed $50,000; or
- the borrower and the lender are not at "arm's length" as defined in the *Income Tax Act*.

AN OVERVIEW OF THE PROCESS

The mortgagee will send instructions to your firm, setting out the terms of the mortgage and the mortgagee's specific requirements. Mortgagees will always require

- the lawyer's certification of a good and marketable title (unless title insurance is purchased);
- an up-to-date survey (unless title insurance is purchased);
- proof of adequate insurance on the property;
- a direction to the mortgagee as to how the mortgage funds are to be paid; and
- completion and registration of the charge/mortgage of land.

In addition, mortgagees may require

- life and/or disability insurance (or the mortgagor's waiver of same);
- a sample cheque on the mortgagor's account (to allow for automatic withdrawal of mortgage payments); and
- title insurance.

The mortgagee will usually want to receive a standard-form interim report from your firm stating that these requirements have been met. The mortgagee will then send your firm a cheque in the amount your client is entitled to receive under the mortgage. You will use this money as part of the balance due on closing. When the transaction is completed, the mortgagee will want to receive a standard-form final report.

PRELIMINARY STEPS

You must take certain steps before you can complete the interim report.

Searches and Inquiries

You can rely on the searches and inquiries you are already conducting for the purchaser (see chapter 17, Preliminary Matters) in order to certify title to the mortgagee.

Survey

As indicated in chapter 15, Reviewing the Agreement of Purchase and Sale, the vendor has to give the purchaser any survey in the vendor's possession. As discussed in chapter 15 and in chapter 17, Preliminary Matters, the lawyer needs an up-to-date survey to be able to give an unqualified opinion on title relating to matters such as zoning, encroachments, and rights of way. Accordingly, if the survey is not up to date, the mortgagee may insist that the purchaser have a new survey prepared. This may not apply if title insurance is obtained.

Proof of Insurance

The mortgagee is taking an interest in the property as security for its loan. If the buildings on the property are damaged or destroyed, the value of its security will decrease. Accordingly, the mortgagee wants to make sure that the property is insured to its full insurable value and that the insurance proceeds will be paid to the mortgagee.

You must advise the purchaser to obtain insurance on the property. Get the name, address, and telephone number of the insurance agent. Call the insurance agent to provide the name and address of the mortgagee and ask for an **insurance binder** confirming

insurance binder documented confirmation that a property has been insured

- the name of the insurance company;
- the policy number;
- the amount of the coverage; and
- the inclusion of a standard mortgage clause providing for payment to the mortgagee.

DOCUMENT PREPARATION

There are a number of documents that you will have to prepare.

Charge/Mortgage of Land

The form of the document used will depend on whether or not the property has been automated.

NON-AUTOMATED PROPERTIES

If the property you are dealing with has not been automated, the form used is the standard form used for mortgages under the *Land Registration Reform Act*. It is called a charge/mortgage of land and contains numbered boxes that you must fill in. A blank copy of the form is reproduced as figure 23.1, below.

- Boxes 1, 3, and 5 deal with the legal description of the property. Copy the information from the corresponding boxes in the draft transfer (see figure 21.16).
- Box 4 contains the principal amount of the mortgage. Get the amount from the mortgage instructions and insert it first in words and then in numbers (like a cheque).
- Box 8 is entitled **Standard Charge Terms**. All institutional lenders use certain mortgage terms in all of their mortgages. Under the *Land Registration Reform Act*, these commonly used terms are not included in each mortgage document that is registered on title. Instead, each lender drafts a set of its own standard charge terms and files it with the government, which then assigns a number to it. The actual mortgage

standard charge terms mortgage terms that are used in all mortgages issued by an institutional lender, which are filed with the government and are then assigned a file number

FIGURE 23.1 Charge/Mortgage of Land

Province of Ontario

Charge/Mortgage of Land

Form 2 — Land Registration Reform Act

DYE & DURHAM CFS POLARIS 1995

B

FOR OFFICE USE ONLY

New Property Identifiers — Additional: See Schedule ☐

Executions — Additional: See Schedule ☐

(1) Registry ☐ Land Titles ☐

(2) Page 1 of pages

(3) Property Identifier(s) Block Property — Additional: See Schedule ☐

(4) Principal Amount — Dollars $

(5) Description

(6) This Document Contains (a) Redescription New Easement Plan/Sketch ☐ (b) Schedule for: Description ☐ Additional Parties ☐ Other ☐

(7) Interest/Estate Charged

(8) Standard Charge Terms — The parties agree to be bound by the provisions in Standard Charge Terms filed as number and the Chargor(s) hereby acknowledge(s) receipt of a copy of these terms.

(9) Payment Provisions

(a) Principal Amount $	(b) Interest Rate % per annum	(c) Calculation Period	
(d) Interest Adjustment Date Y M D	(e) Payment Date and Period	(f) First Payment Date Y M D	
(g) Last Payment Date	(h) Amount of Each Payment Dollars $		
(i) Balance Due Date	(j) Insurance Dollars $		

(10) Additional Provisions

Continued on Schedule ☐

(11) Chargor(s) The chargor hereby charges the land to the chargee and certifies that the chargor is at least eighteen years old and that

The chargor(s) acknowledge(s) receipt of a true copy of this charge.

Name(s) Signature(s) Date of Signature Y M D

(12) Spouse(s) of Chargor(s) I hereby consent to this transaction.

Name(s) Signature(s) Date of Signature Y M D

(13) Chargor(s) Address for Service

(14) Chargee(s)

(15) Chargee(s) Address for Service

(16) Assessment Roll Number of Property — Cty. Mun. Map Sub. Par.

(17) Municipal Address of Property

(18) Document Prepared by:

FOR OFFICE USE ONLY

Fees	
Registration Fee	
Total	

document will include only the principal amount, the interest rate, payment provisions, due date, and special additional provisions such as prepayment privileges. The standard charge terms are incorporated into the document by reference to the assigned number. The mortgagor must be given a copy of the standard charge terms, which will be included with your instructions from the mortgagee. To complete box 8, insert the number found on the standard charge terms provided.

- Box 9 sets out the payment provisions of the mortgage. To complete this box, copy the information contained in the mortgagee's letter of instructions as follows:

  (a) *Principal Amount* Insert this amount in numbers only.

  (b) *Interest Rate* Insert the rate in numbers only.

  (c) *Calculation Period* This is the period over which interest is calculated under the mortgage and will usually be "semi-annually, not in advance."

  (d) *Interest Adjustment Date* This is the date from which interest starts to accumulate and, assuming that the mortgage is paid monthly, will be one month before the date of the first payment.

  (e) *Payment Date and Period* This specifies when payments are to be made under the mortgage. For example, if the payments are to be made on the first day of every month, you would insert "1st—monthly."

  (f) *First Payment Date* Insert the date on which the first mortgage payment is to be made.

  (g) *Last Payment Date* Insert the date on which the last payment under the mortgage is to be made.

  (h) *Amount of Each Payment* Insert the amount in words and numbers.

  (i) *Balance Due Date* This is usually the same date as the last payment date. If the mortgage has not been paid in full, the balance of the principal must be paid on this day. Usually the mortgagor will have to renew the mortgage or arrange a new one.

  (j) *Insurance* The common practice is to insert the words "Full insurable value."

- Box 10 sets out any additional provisions not included in the standard charge terms, such as prepayment privileges. If there are any additional provisions, the exact wording is usually provided in the mortgagee's letter of instructions. If the provisions do not fit in the box, insert the words "see attached schedule" and set out the provisions on the schedule. In box 6(b), check "Other."

- Box 11 requires a statement of age and spousal status. You will have to obtain this information from the purchaser. See chapter 21, Document Preparation, for a discussion of the wording of this statement. You must also insert the name of the mortgagor in exactly the same form used in box 11 of the draft transfer/deed of land.

- Box 12 provides a place for spousal consent, if required. This box must be completed only if box 11 states, "I am a spouse. The person consenting below is my spouse."
- Box 13 sets out the mortgagor's address for service. It should be the same address as set out in box 12 of the draft transfer/deed of land.
- Boxes 14 and 15 set out the name and address of the mortgagee.
- Boxes 16 and 17 should be the same as boxes 15 and 16 of the draft transfer/deed of land.

AUTOMATED PROPERTIES

If the property has been automated, the charge will be prepared electronically. The document is completed in much the same way as the electronic transfer discussed in chapter 21, Document Preparation. Teraview will create a separate acknowledgement and direction for the charge/mortgage, which must be signed by the mortgagor to evidence consent and authorization to use e-reg. Print a paper copy of the mortgage document from e-reg to give to the mortgagor together with a copy of any schedules that are attached to the registered document. This is to comply with section 4 of the *Mortgages Act*, which requires that a copy of the mortgage be delivered to the mortgagor.

Direction Regarding Funds

Your law firm will usually want the mortgage proceeds to be made payable to your firm in trust. The purchaser will have to give the mortgagee a written direction to that effect. Figure 21.14 is an example of a direction regarding funds. Make sure that the direction is addressed to the mortgagee and not to the purchaser, is signed by the mortgagor and not the vendor.

Other Forms and Matters

Mortgagees often offer life and/or disability insurance policies to mortgagors. Under these policies, the mortgage will be paid if the mortgagor dies or becomes disabled. The policies are optional, but most mortgagees will want the mortgagor to sign a waiver if the insurance is not desired.

If the mortgage payments will be taken automatically from the mortgagor's bank account, the mortgagee will require a sample cheque. Obtain a cheque from the client with the word "VOID" written across it in large letters.

Interim Report to Mortgagee

Once you have completed all of the preliminary steps and prepared the documents, you must complete the mortgagee's standard-form interim report on title and enclose all of the required documents. Usually, interim reports are faxed to the mortgagee.

PREPARATION FOR REGISTRATION

Review and Execution of Documents

You must arrange to have the mortgagor attend at your office to sign the charge/mortgage and the direction regarding the mortgage funds. This can usually be done at the same time that the client is signing the purchase documents. You or the lawyer handling the file will also have to review the terms of the charge/mortgage and the standard charge terms with the client, to make sure that the client understands the terms and that the terms match the **mortgage commitment** (the client's agreement with the institutional lender when the mortgage was arranged). If you are reviewing the documents with the client and any questions or problems arise, you should turn the matter over to the lawyer handling the file.

mortgage commitment the mortgagor's agreement with the mortgagee when the mortgage is arranged

The Mortgage Funds

You should tell the client how much money the mortgagee will be advancing under the mortgage. Sometimes that amount will be less than the principal of the mortgage because the mortgagee will make deductions.

- *Appraisal fees* The mortgagee may have required the property to be appraised and may charge the mortgagor a fee for the appraisal.
- *An interest adjustment* Monthly mortgage payments are sometimes paid on the 1st or the 15th of each month. If the transaction is closing on another day of the month, the mortgagee will deduct an amount to cover the interest from the closing date to the 1st (or 15th) day of the next month, which is the interest adjustment date.
- *Mortgage insurance fees* If the mortgage is for more than 75 percent of the purchase price, the mortgagee will require the mortgagor to pay for mortgage insurance through the Canada Mortgage and Housing Corporation (CMHC). In that case, the mortgagor will have to pay an insurance application fee and a one-time premium for the mortgage insurance.

If satisfied with your interim report, the mortgagee will give your law firm the mortgage funds, usually by way of a cheque payable to your law firm in trust, in accordance with your client's direction regarding funds. You will have to make arrangements to have the cheque picked up from the mortgagee. Sometimes the mortgagee will arrange to transfer the funds directly into your law firm's trust account. The mortgage funds are payable to the law firm in trust on the understanding that your law firm will not release the money to the vendor until the mortgage has been registered (during the closing of the transaction).

FINAL REPORT TO MORTGAGEE

When the transaction has closed and the mortgage has been registered, you must complete the mortgagee's standard-form final report, which confirms that all its requirements have been met, the charge/mortgage of land has been registered on title, and the mortgagee has a good and valid first (or second, as the case may be) mortgage on the property. You will enclose

- the duplicate registered charge/mortgage of land (or a copy of the electronic charge if the document was registered electronically);
- the insurance binder;
- the mortgagor's direction regarding funds (if not previously forwarded); and
- a copy of the survey (unless previously forwarded or title insurance has been purchased).

REFERENCES

Income Tax Act, RSC 1985, c. 1 (5th Supp.), as amended.

Land Registration Reform Act, RSO 1990, c. L.4.

Mortgages Act, RSO 1990, c. M.40.

REVIEW QUESTIONS

1. Can a lawyer represent both the purchaser and the mortgagee in the purchase of a property? Explain.
2. Why does a mortgagee require an interim report?
3. What is an insurance binder?
4. What is the purpose of standard charge terms?
5. If a mortgage is created electronically, what must the mortgagor sign to authorize the lawyer to use e-reg?
6. Why is the amount that the mortgagee advances sometimes less than the principal amount of the mortgage?

CHAPTER 24

Closing the Transaction

Title is finally conveyed on closing. The lawyer acting for the purchaser must ensure that proper title is obtained because, unless preserved by warranty or undertaking, all rights under the agreement of purchase and sale merge on closing. The lawyer for the vendor must ensure that payment by cash or certified cheque is received before the transfer is registered.

The steps will be different for a registry office closing than for an electronic closing. If the closing memo or closing checklist has been properly prepared, the closing should go smoothly.

PURCHASER'S PROCEDURE FOR A REGISTRY OFFICE CLOSING

Preliminary Steps

The person attending at the closing must be sure to arrive at the land registry office early enough to complete all preliminary steps before the time fixed for closing.

UPDATE TITLE SEARCH

If the property has been entered into POLARIS (Province of Ontario Land Registration Information System), using the PIN (property identifier number), check the title at one of the computer terminals to see if there have been any registrations since that of the last instrument number shown in the search notes. If the property has not been automated, check the abstract book for the property. If a registration is found, you must pull the instrument to determine whether or not it affects the subject property. If it does affect your property, check whether it was an instrument that was supposed to be registered on or before closing, such as a discharge of mortgage or mortgage amending agreement. If you find a document that was not supposed to be registered, you must get instructions from the lawyer handling the file.

UPDATE EXECUTION SEARCH

You must get a new sheriff's certificate to ensure that there are no executions filed against the vendor and, if you are also acting for a mortgagee, against the purchaser.

If the certificate discloses any executions and the closing memo does not mention them, you must obtain instructions from the lawyer handling the file.

LOCATE THE VENDOR'S REPRESENTATIVE

When the time fixed for closing approaches, page the person attending at the closing for the vendor. If you don't know the name of the person, page the name of the vendor's law firm.

Exchange Documents

In an orderly fashion, obtain each item required and check it off against the closing memo. Try to request each item in turn. However, the vendor's conveyancer will often simply hand over all of the documents together. In that case, go through them carefully, checking off each document that is listed.

Hand over and check off all items that are listed to be given. Ideally, you should not hand over closing funds until the documents are accepted for registration. This rule is rarely followed. Instead, the purchaser's conveyancer is usually given the transfer and hands the closing funds to the vendor's conveyancer on the understanding that the vendor's conveyancer will not leave with the funds until registration is complete.

Update Title Search Prior to Registration

You must update your search again just before registering because documents are continually being tendered for registration and you must make sure that nothing has been registered from the time you conducted your subsearch until the time you register.

If the property has been automated, check the computer again for any additional registrations. If the property is not automated, you must check the daily sheets (day book) for any additional registrations. If the property is not automated, documents are placed in a box as they are tendered for registration until a typist can enter them onto the daily sheets by registration number. There is a time lag between the time the documents are tendered for registration and the time the typist enters them on the daily sheets, so you must check the boxes as well.

Register

You must make sure that the documents are registered in the correct order. Look at each document tendered by the vendor for registration before the transfer. Register any discharges first, then the transfer, then the first mortgage followed by any subsequent mortgages. The registration clerk will calculate registration fees and taxes. Once they are paid, the documents will be registered. Make a note of the registration numbers of all documents. Following registration, you should notify the lawyer handling the file and the client that the transaction has closed.

VENDOR'S PROCEDURE FOR A REGISTRY OFFICE CLOSING

The role of the vendor's conveyancer at the closing is quite relaxed. All you have to do is hand over the documents in your possession, register any documents required from the vendor on or before closing, and make sure that the cheques that you receive are in accordance with the direction regarding funds.

If a mortgagee is attending at the closing to provide a discharge, you must page the mortgagee's representative at the time of closing.

PROCEDURE FOR AN ELECTRONIC CLOSING

Prior to closing, both the vendor's and the purchaser's lawyers enter into a document registration agreement (DRA), which sets out the escrow closing procedure to be followed in closing the transaction.

The vendor's lawyer sends **off-title documents** (documents that are not registered) and a key by courier to the purchaser's lawyer. The purchaser's lawyer sends off-title documents and closing funds by courier to the vendor's lawyer. The vendor's lawyer checks the purchaser's documents, and when satisfied that they are acceptable, he accesses Teraview, releases the transfer for registration, and advises the purchaser's lawyer that this has been done. Then the registering party (usually the purchaser's lawyer) logs onto Teraview and conducts a subsearch to verify that title to the property has not changed since the title search was done (or that any required documents have been registered). Teraview will then search executions and register the transfer and any other registrable documents, such as mortgages, released for registration.

off-title documents documents that are required for closing but are not registered on title

When a law firm obtains the Teraview licence and user access, arrangements are made regarding payment of land transfer tax and registration fees. Usually they are debited from the firm's general account. When a document is registered electronically, the registration fees and land transfer tax, if applicable, will be debited at the end of the day.

REVIEW QUESTIONS

1. What steps must a purchaser's conveyancer take to close a transaction in a registry office?
2. What steps must a vendor's conveyancer take to close a transaction in a registry office?
3. What is the purpose of a document registration agreement?
4. What are "off-title documents" in a closing?
5. How is land transfer tax paid in an electronic closing?

CHAPTER 25

Purchaser's Post-Closing Procedure

Once the transaction has closed, you will need to call the purchaser to let him or her know the deal has closed and to make arrangements for the purchaser to pick up the key. You will then need to attend to the post-closing matters that remain outstanding.

MORTGAGES AND OTHER FINANCIAL MATTERS

It may be a while before you send the final reporting letter to the client, and tax installments or mortgage payments may fall due in the meantime. Therefore, immediately after the closing, you should send a letter to the purchaser advising of any payments that must be made in the near future. Give the purchaser enough information to make the payment, such as the mortgage number, the address of the mortgagee, and the amount of the monthly payment.

If there are any mortgages, whether newly arranged or assumed by the purchaser, obtain an amortization schedule for the client. As discussed in chapter 6, Charges/Mortgages and illustrated in figure 6.4, an amortization schedule sets out the breakdown of each mortgage payment between principal and interest and the remaining principal balance after each payment. Most law firms have computer programs that will allow you to print an amortization schedule. If your firm does not have such a program, you can order an amortization schedule from one of several companies that provide them.

UNDERTAKINGS

If your law firm accepted any undertakings on closing, diarize each undertaking for the appropriate period of time. When the time is up, forward reminder letters until all outstanding undertakings have been fulfilled.

INTEREST ON DEPOSIT

Some agreements of purchase and sale provide that the deposit be paid into an interest-bearing account, with interest to be paid to the purchaser on closing. If that is the case, send a letter to the real estate agent requesting a cheque payable either to the purchaser directly or to your law firm. Diarize the letter for a reasonable period of time and follow up with the agent if necessary.

POST-CLOSING LETTERS

Write a letter to the municipal assessment department, with a copy to the tax department, advising of the change in ownership. This is done to make sure that future notices are addressed to the purchaser and not to the vendor. Figure 25.1 is an example of an assessment department letter.

Some firms also notify the utility companies of the change of ownership. Usually, though, the utilities will have amended their records as a result of the pre-closing inquiries made.

REPORTING LETTER

At the end of the transaction, the purchaser's law firm writes a reporting letter to the client. The reporting letter on a purchase is quite long and complex. It summarized the main provisions of the agreement of purchase and sale, describes the procedures on closing, and explains the items in the statement of adjustments. The letter goes on to **certify title** and explains any limitations to the certification. However, if the client has purchased a title insurance policy, certification is not required, and the letter will instead provide particulars about the insurance policy. Finally, the reporting letter contains a statement of the manner in which funds were applied and lists the documents that are enclosed with the letter.

certify title
describe the state of the owner's title, including any limitations

Preparation of a reporting letter is time-consuming, and many lawyers and law clerks are slow to forward one. It is best to deal with the reporting letter as soon as possible because, subject to following up on any undertakings, the file is then completed and may be billed. Also, clients appreciate receiving the reporting letter sooner rather than later.

Figure 25.2 is an example of a reporting letter for a purchase. The precedent includes alternative paragraphs for different situations. When using the precedent, you must choose the paragraphs appropriate to the situation and amend them as required. Do not simply follow the precedent blindly.

Opening Paragraph

The opening paragraph simply confirms that the transaction has been completed.

Agreement of Purchase and Sale

This paragraph specifies the key terms of the agreement of purchase and sale, including the date of the agreement; the vendor's name; the municipal address of the property; and the main financial terms of the contract, such as the purchase price, the amount of the deposit, and the amount of any mortgages to be assumed or given back to the vendor.

Closing

The first paragraph confirms the closing date. If the closing was postponed from the original closing date, the paragraph specifies the original date and the rescheduled one. The next paragraph states where the closing took place and how much money was paid. The final paragraph confirms exactly how the purchasers took title and includes full registration particulars.

If the transaction was completed electronically, the last two paragraphs should provide particulars of the electronic registration (date and registration number).

Land Transfer Tax

This paragraph sets out the amount of land transfer tax (provincial and municipal, if applicable), retail sales tax, and registration fees that were paid on closing.

New First Mortgage Arranged

Use the paragraphs under this heading if a new first mortgage has been arranged. These paragraphs explain the repayment terms of the mortgage, including the principal amount, interest rate, term, and monthly payments. You should also enclose and explain the amortization schedule. Explain any prepayment privileges or other special terms, such as municipal tax payments to be included with the payments of principal and interest.

The letter then provides sufficient information to enable the purchaser to make the monthly payments — the mortgage number, address of the mortgagee, and date of payments, including the date of the first payment.

Following that explanation, the letter reports the registration particulars of the mortgage and confirms enclosure of a copy of the mortgage and the standard charge terms. This group of mortgage paragraphs should conclude with confirmation of the amount of money received from the mortgagee and applied toward the balance due on closing.

New Second Mortgage Arranged

If a new second mortgage has been arranged with a third party, the reporting letter should cover the same matters as for a new first mortgage.

Statement of Adjustments

This paragraph refers to the statement of adjustments enclosed. The entries in the statement of adjustments are explained in the paragraphs that follow.

Deposit

This paragraph confirms the amount of the deposit and that the purchaser was given a credit in that amount in the statement of adjustments.

First Mortgage Assumed

Use the paragraphs under this heading if the purchaser has assumed an existing first mortgage. These paragraphs explain the entry in the statement of adjustments, and the provisions and payment particulars of the mortgage in the same detail as for a new mortgage.

Second Mortgage Back to Vendor

Use the paragraphs under this heading if the vendor is taking back a second mortgage. In that case, the purchaser will be given a credit in the statement of adjustments. The paragraphs explain this adjustment and the provisions and payment particulars of the mortgage in the same detail as for a new mortgage.

Realty Taxes

This paragraph explains the adjustment for realty taxes in the statement of adjustments. It also advises the client that the assessment department has been notified of the change in ownership.

Fuel Oil

Insert this paragraph if the house is heated by oil. It explains the adjustment for fuel oil in the statement of adjustments and reminds the purchaser to check the tank to make sure that the vendor fulfilled the undertaking to leave a full tank.

Water Charges

Insert this paragraph if there was an adjustment for water charges.

Utilities

This paragraph deals with metered utilities. The paragraph confirms that the meters were read before closing, that final bills will be sent to the vendor, and that future bills will be sent to the purchaser.

Balance Due on Closing

This paragraph confirms the amount of the balance due on closing.

Statement of Funds and Disbursements

This statement outlines the receipt and disbursements of closing funds. The statement, also called a trust statement, specifies the source of all funds paid to your firm for the transaction — usually from the purchaser and one or more mortgagees. It also specifies to whom the funds were paid on and after the closing. This statement specifies

- the payees and amounts of all cheques delivered to the vendor's lawyer on closing — cheques may have been payable to a mortgagee, the municipality, or a utility, as well as to the vendor's law firm;

- the amount paid to the Ministry of Finance for land transfer tax, retail sales tax, and registration fees;
- the amount paid to your law firm for legal fees and disbursements; and
- the amount of any balance owing to the client or to your law firm.

Notice that the statement of funds and disbursements is set up in columns. The amount of all funds received is placed in the right-hand numerical column and the amount of all funds disbursed is placed in the left-hand numerical column. These two columns must balance.

Insurance

In your preliminary letter to the purchasers, you advised them to arrange insurance coverage for the property. Before closing, you should have obtained particulars of the insurance policy. This paragraph confirms the information provided by the purchaser or insurance broker.

Survey

There are several paragraphs dealing with the survey to choose from, depending on the circumstances.

The first paragraph is used when the client instructed your firm to have a new survey prepared. The second paragraph is used when the vendor provided you with an existing up-to-date survey. Both of these paragraphs outline the particulars of the survey. The precedent paragraphs state that the buildings are wholly within the lot lines, with no encroachments. If that is not the case, your law firm should have advised the client before the closing, and this paragraph will confirm these earlier discussions and the instructions given by the client at that time. In addition, the title certification will be qualified to reflect this situation and the lawyer handling the file will most likely want to be involved in the drafting of this part of the reporting letter.

The third paragraph is used in the situation where the survey provided by the vendor predates additions or renovations to the buildings and, therefore, the survey is not helpful in determining whether the existing buildings comply with current bylaws. It will be necessary to limit the certification of the title paragraph accordingly. In this situation, the lawyer handling the file should have discussed this matter with the client before closing and should have explained the implications of closing the transaction without an up-to-date survey. The client's instructions to proceed without an up-to-date survey should have been confirmed in writing. The reporting letter should *not* be the first time the client is advised of this situation.

The fourth paragraph is used in cases where no survey was available, and the client instructed your law firm to proceed with the closing without obtaining a survey. The certification of title paragraph will have to be limited accordingly. Again, the client should have had this situation explained, with any instructions to proceed without an up-to-date survey confirmed in writing at that time. The paragraph should confirm these previous instructions.

Municipal Bylaws

This part of the letter describes the results of the building department inquiries. There are two choices. The first paragraph is used when the building department advised your client that the municipal bylaws were complied with.

The second paragraph is used where the survey shows that the location of the buildings does *not* comply with existing bylaws, *but* the property is exempt from the application of the bylaws because the buildings were erected before the passage of the current bylaws and complied with the previous bylaws. (See chapter 8, Government Controls over the Use and Subdivision of Land, for a discussion of the requirements for a legal non-conforming use.)

Restrictions

This paragraph is included if there are any restrictive covenants on title. Under the terms of the standard form agreement of purchase and sale, the purchaser must accept title subject to any restrictive covenants on title so long as they have been complied with. This paragraph therefore specifies the restrictions, states that the client was required to accept title subject to them, and refers to the evidence that was obtained to ensure that the restrictions have been complied with.

Subdivision Agreements

This paragraph is inserted if there are any outstanding subdivision agreements on title. The standard form agreement of purchase and sale requires that the purchaser accept title subject to subdivision agreements provided that the agreements have been complied with or adequate security has been posted.

The paragraph identifies the agreements that are outstanding and states that the terms of the agreement of purchase and sale require the purchaser to accept title subject to them. The paragraph then confirms that the agreements have been complied with or adequate security has been posted.

Easements

If the title was subject to an easement, insert a paragraph setting out the details of the easement. There are two paragraphs to choose from, depending on whether the easement is one the client is required to accept under the agreement of purchase and sale, either as part of the standard terms or by a special paragraph.

If the purchaser is required to accept title subject to the easement, use the first paragraph in the precedent. This paragraph sets out the details of the easement and states that the client is required to accept title subject to it under the terms of the agreement of purchase and sale. The precedent deals with the right of the builder to enter for inspection and repairs. Other common easements are utility easements and easements for access to and from adjoining properties.

On occasion, there will be an easement registered on title that the purchaser decides to accept even though the terms of the agreement of purchase and sale do not require such acceptance. In that case, use the second paragraph in the precedent. That paragraph sets out the nature of the easement and confirms the client's instructions to close notwithstanding the fact that he or she is not required to do so. The reporting letter should *not* be the first time the client hears about this matter. The lawyer handling the file should have discussed this matter with the client before the closing and should have obtained instructions confirming the client's wishes in writing.

If there was an easement registered on title that was discharged before closing, there is no need to make reference to it in the reporting letter.

Family Law Act

You may use this standard paragraph no matter what *Family Law Act* statement was included in the transfer, provided that the *Family Law Act* was complied with. If it was not, the deal should not have closed.

UFFI Warranty

A UFFI warranty should have been obtained on closing, and this paragraph should be inserted in the reporting letter. The wording should reflect the wording found in the standard form agreement of purchase and sale.

Title

This is the paragraph in which your law firm gives a title opinion (certifies title) subject to any limitations referred to in the body of the letter.

The first paragraph summarizes the key searches — title, taxes, and executions. If the tax or execution searches disclosed a problem, it should have been resolved before closing, and the standard wording with respect to executions can still be used. With respect to taxes, the paragraph should set out what the arrears were and the arrangements that were made for their payment.

The second paragraph contains the key words "we are of the opinion that (*name(s) of purchaser(s)*) (*has/have*) a good and marketable title to the said lands in fee simple (*as joint tenants or as tenants in common, if applicable*) and that the title was, at the date of closing, free from encumbrance, save for ..." The paragraph must list any exceptions, such as

- mortgages whether new, assumed, or given back to the vendor;
- subdivision agreements;
- restrictions;
- easements; and
- other title problems, if any exist.

Any exceptions should have been fully discussed earlier in the letter under the appropriate headings.

If the opinion is limited because there was no up-to-date survey or no survey at all, after the words "we are of the opinion that," the following words should be inserted: "subject to any discrepancy that may be shown by an up-to-date survey of the property."

If the client purchased a title insurance policy, this paragraph is not required. Instead, this paragraph should provide particulars about the policy, including

- the company that issued the policy;
- the policy number; and
- exceptions and/or exclusions.

Concluding Paragraph

The concluding paragraph lists the documents enclosed, which should include

- the statement of adjustments;
- the duplicate registered transfer or a copy of the electronic transfer;
- a copy of any mortgage and standard charge terms;
- the survey;
- the title insurance policy (if applicable); and
- any other documents received on closing.

Signature

The reporting letter must be prepared for signature by the lawyer handling the file and must be signed by the lawyer. Law clerks may not sign the reporting letter.

STATEMENT OF ACCOUNT

Prepare a statement of account setting out the fees and disbursements your law firm is charging the client with respect to the purchase transaction. Follow the format used by your firm. Make sure that you retain funds for payment of the account before releasing any funds to the client. The format used for a statement of account varies from law firm to law firm.

CLOSING THE FILE

Do not close the file until all post-closing matters have been completed, including the fulfillment of any undertakings. At that time, follow the standard procedure of your law firm.

REFERENCES

Family Law Act, RSO 1990, c. F.3.

Land Transfer Tax Act, RSO 1990, c. L.6.

REVIEW QUESTIONS

1. Why should you send a letter to the purchaser right after closing, advising him or her of mortgage or tax payments?
2. What is an amortization schedule?
3. What steps must you take after closing if your firm has accepted undertakings on closing?
4. In what circumstances might a real estate broker owe a purchaser money following closing?
5. Why do you write to the assessment and tax departments following closing?
6. What is the function of a reporting letter to the client?
7. When should you close the file?

FIGURE 25.1 Letter to the Assessment Department

Date

Assessment Department
Name of municipality
Address

Dear Sir or Madam:

Re: *Name of transaction*
Address and municipality

Please be advised that as of (*date*), (*purchaser(s)*) (*is/are*) the owner(s) of the above property. Please amend your records and send any future bills and notices to (*him/her/them*) at the above address.

Yours very truly,

cc. Tax Department

FIGURE 25.2 Reporting Letter to the Purchaser

Date

Purchaser's name
Purchaser's address

Re: *Name of transaction*
Address and municipality

Dear (*purchaser's name*):

We are pleased to confirm completion of this transaction and would like to make our report to you.

Agreement of Purchase and Sale

On (*date*) you entered into an agreement with (*vendor's name*) for the purchase of the property municipally known as (*address of property*). The purchase price was $(*purchase price*) and a deposit of $(*deposit*) was paid at that time. [*Where applicable*— You also agreed to assume a first mortgage in the principal amount of $(*principal amount of first mortgage*)]. The balance of the purchase price, after adjustments, was to be paid by cash or certified cheque on closing.

Closing

This transaction closed as scheduled on (*date of closing*), and adjustments were made as of that date.

[*Use this paragraph if the closing was postponed.*]

This transaction was originally scheduled to close on (*date*), but was postponed [*where applicable*— a number of times]. The transaction ultimately closed on (*date of closing*), and adjustments were made as of that date.

[*Use this paragraph if the transaction was not closed electronically.*]

At that time, we attended at the (*name and location of land registry office*) and handed over a (*series of*) cheque(*s*) in the amount of $(*balance due on closing*), being the balance due on closing as set out in the enclosed statement of adjustments. In return, we received a transfer of land endorsed as follows:

PURCHASER'S LAST NAME, first name *purchaser's birthdate (yr-mo-date)*

PURCHASER'S LAST NAME, first name *purchaser's birthdate (yr-mo-date)*

[*where applicable*— as joint tenants.]

This transfer of land was registered in (*name, location, and number of land registry office*) on (*closing date*) as instrument number (*number*).

[*Use this paragraph if the transaction was closed electronically.*]

Prior to closing, we delivered to the vendor a (*series of*) cheque(*s*) in the amount of $(*balance due on closing*) being the balance due on closing as set out in the enclosed statement of adjustments. In return, the vendor released the transfer for registration endorsed as follows:

PURCHASER'S LAST NAME, first name *purchaser's birthdate (yr-mo-date)*

PURCHASER'S LAST NAME, first name *purchaser's birthdate (yr-mo-date)*

[*where applicable*— as joint tenants.]

This transfer was registered electronically on (*closing date*) as instrument number (*number*).

FIGURE 25.2 Continued

Land Transfer Tax

Before closing, you completed (*an affidavit or a statement*) under the *Land Transfer Tax Act*. Based on that document, on closing, we paid provincial land transfer tax in the amount of $(*amount*) and retail sales tax in the amount of $(*amount*) to the Ministry of Finance (and municipal land transfer tax in the amount of $(*amount*) to the Treasurer, City of Toronto, *if applicable*) from the funds deposited to your credit in our trust account. We also paid registration fees of $(*amount*) from the funds deposited to your credit in our trust account.

New First Mortgage [*Use these paragraphs where a new first mortgage is arranged.*]

On your instructions, we prepared a first charge/mortgage in favour of (*name of mortgagee*). This charge/mortgage secures the principal sum of $(*amount*) with interest at (*rate*)% per annum and is repayable by equal monthly installments of $(*amount*) on account of principal and interest. The installments commence on the (*day*) day of (*month*), (*year*) up to and including the (*day*) day of (*month*), (*year*) when the balance, if any, of the principal sum is to be paid.

The monthly installments will be applied first to pay the interest calculated on the principal outstanding from time to time, and the balance of the monthly installments will be applied to reduce the principal.

[*Explain amortization schedule as follows:*] We are enclosing an amortization schedule for this mortgage. The schedule shows how much of each monthly payment is applied to principal and to interest and how much of the principal balance remains outstanding after each payment.

[*Where applicable, include details of any prepayment provisions. Refer to the mortgage for details.*]

[*Where applicable, include details of any tax payment provisions. Refer to the mortgage for details.*]

[*Provide mortgage payment information as follows:*] Your first monthly payment under this charge/mortgage falls due on (*date*) and, if not being taken from your account automatically, should be made payable to (*mortgagee's name*) at (*mortgagee's address*). Please note your mortgage reference number (*number*) on your payments and in any correspondence with the mortgagee.

[*Provide registration particulars as follows:*] This charge/mortgage was registered on title on (*date*) as instrument number (*number*). We enclose a copy of the charge/mortgage together with the standard charge terms.

[*Provide details of mortgage money received as follows:*] Before closing, we received a cheque from (*name of mortgagee*) in the amount of $(*amount*). This cheque was deposited into our trust account and applied to the balance due on closing.

New Second Mortgage [*Use this paragraph if a new second mortgage is arranged.*]

In accordance with the agreement of purchase and sale, we prepared a second charge/mortgage in favour of (*name of mortgagee*).

[*See New First Mortgage for other paragraphs.*]

FIGURE 25.2 Continued

Statement of Adjustments

Before closing, the vendor's lawyer provided us with a statement of adjustments that identified the balance you were required to pay on closing. A copy of the statement of adjustments is enclosed, and the entries and calculations on the statement of adjustments are explained in the following paragraphs.

Deposit

When you signed the agreement of purchase and sale, you paid a deposit of $(*amount*). You were given a credit in that amount on the statement of adjustments.

First Mortgage Assumed [*Use these paragraphs where a first mortgage is assumed.*]

On closing, you assumed a charge/mortgage in favour of the (*mortgagee's name*), securing the principal sum of $(*original principal amount*). At the time of closing, the outstanding principal and interest under that mortgage totalled $(*amount*) as confirmed by the enclosed mortgage statement from the mortgagee dated (*date*). You were given a credit in this amount on the statement of adjustments.

[*Insert paragraph explaining monthly payments — see New First Mortgage.*]

[*Insert amortization schedule paragraph.*]

[*Insert prepayment privilege paragraph where applicable.*]

[*Insert tax payment paragraph where applicable.*]

[*Insert payment information paragraph.*]

We enclose a copy of the charge/mortgage together with the standard charge terms.

Second Mortgage Back to Vendor [*Use these paragraphs if the vendor takes back a second mortgage.*]

In accordance with the agreement of purchase and sale, you executed a second charge/mortgage in favour of the vendor securing the principal amount of $(*amount*). You were given a credit in this amount on the statement of adjustments.

[*Insert paragraph explaining monthly payments — see New First Mortgage.*]

[*Insert amortization schedule paragraph.*]

[*Insert prepayment privilege paragraph where applicable.*]

[*Insert tax payment paragraph where applicable.*]

[*Insert payment information paragraph.*]

[*Insert registration particulars paragraph.*]

Realty Taxes [*This paragraph should explain the realty tax adjustment and must be drafted according to the transaction — for example, if the vendor had paid taxes for the entire year:*]

The realty taxes for (*year*) in the amount of $(*total annual taxes*) have been paid in full by the vendor. Because the vendor's share of the realty taxes was only $(*vendor's share of taxes*), the vendor was allowed a credit for this item on the statement of adjustments in the amount of $(*amount*).

We have advised the assessment department of your purchase of the property and have requested that all future tax and assessment notices be sent to you.

FIGURE 25.2 Continued

Fuel Oil [*Use this paragraph if the property is heated by oil.*]

The vendor agreed to leave a full tank of fuel oil on closing and was given a credit for the cost of the fuel in the amount of $(*amount*) on the statement of adjustments. Please check to make sure that the fuel oil tank is, in fact, full, and advise us immediately if that is not the case.

Water Charges [*If there was an adjustment for water charges, use this paragraph to explain the water charge adjustment — for example, if the vendor had paid more than his or her share:*]

The vendor paid $(*amount*) for water charges for the period from __ to __. Because the vendor's share of the water charges was only $(*vendor's share of water charges*), the vendor was allowed a credit for this item on the statement of adjustments in the amount of $(*amount*).

Utilities

We arranged for the utility meters to be read before closing and for final bills to be sent directly to the vendor. We have also notified the utilities that you are now the owner(s) of the property and that all future utility bills are to be sent to you.

Balance Due on Closing

The balance due on closing as calculated in the statement of adjustments was $(*amount*).

Statement of Funds and Disbursements

The funds to complete this transaction were received and disbursed by us as follows: [*Set out the source of all funds and how the funds were paid out, for example:*]

Received from (*mortgagee*)		$150,000.00
Received from (*client's name*)		131,000.00
Paid to (*vendor's mortgagee*) in accordance with vendor's direction regarding funds (enclosed) re: vendor's first mortgage	$177,818.75	
Paid to (*vendor's law firm*), in trust in accordance with vendor's direction regarding funds (enclosed)	98,390.02	
Paid to the Ministry of Finance for land transfer tax, retail sales tax, and registration of transfer and charge	2,830.00	
Paid to (*purchaser's law firm*) for fees and disbursements	1,225.50	
Balance owing to you	735.73	
	$281,000.00	$281,000.00

Insurance [*Set out the particulars of the client's insurance coverage, for example:*]

We wish to confirm that you made arrangements for insurance with (*name of insurance company*) as policy number (*number*). This policy is for $(*amount*) and expires on (*date*). (*Name of mortgagee*) is shown as first mortgagee.

FIGURE 25.2 Continued

Survey [*Choose one of the following paragraphs.*]

[*When a new survey has been prepared:*]

In accordance with your instructions, we obtained a new survey of the property from [*name of surveyor*], Ontario Land Surveyors. The survey, dated (*date*), indicates that the buildings are located wholly within the lot lines and that there are no other buildings encroaching on or over the property.

[*When an up-to-date survey was provided by vendor:*]

The vendor provided us with a survey of the land and building thereon prepared by (*name of surveyor*), Ontario Land Surveyors, dated (*date*). This survey indicates that the buildings are located wholly within the lot lines and that there are no other buildings encroaching on or over the property. The vendor has confirmed by way of statutory declaration that there have been no changes to land and buildings since the date of the survey.

[*When the survey does not show present location of buildings on the lands:*]

The vendor provided us with a survey prepared by (*name of surveyor*) dated (*date*). As we previously advised you, the survey shows the dimensions of the land but does not show the present location of the buildings on the land. You instructed us to proceed with the transaction notwithstanding this fact. Our opinion on title is therefore subject to any discrepancy that may be disclosed by an up-to-date survey showing the present location of the buildings on the land. [*Under the heading "Title" insert the following words: "subject to any discrepancy that may be shown by an up-to-date survey of the property" after the words "Based on the above searches."*]

[*When no survey is available:*]

We advised you that there was no survey of the property, and you instructed us to proceed with the transaction notwithstanding this fact. Our opinion on title is therefore subject to any discrepancy that may be disclosed by an up-to-date survey showing the location of the buildings on the land. [*Under the heading "Title" insert the following words: "subject to any discrepancy that may be shown by an up-to-date survey of the property" after the words "Based on the above searches."*]

Municipal Bylaws [*Choose one of the following paragraphs, unless a minor variance was or is necessary.*]

[*When property complies with bylaws:*]

We were advised by the building department of (*name of municipality*) that, based on the above survey, the location of the buildings on the property complied with all municipal bylaws at the time of closing.

[*When property is a legal non-conforming use:*]

Based on the above survey, we have been advised by the building department of (*name of municipality*) that the buildings erected on the property do not comply with the zoning bylaw in effect at this time. However, because the buildings were erected before the enactment of the zoning bylaw presently in force, they are exempt from its provisions.

Restrictions [*Set out the particulars of any restrictive covenants — for example, if there were restrictions against altering the grading or drainage.*]

As we discussed before closing, the property is subject to a restriction for a period of seven years from (*day, month, year*), against the alteration of grades, catch basins, or obstruction of drainage. By the provisions of the agreement of purchase and sale, you were required to accept title subject to restrictions, provided that they were complied with. In this regard, on closing, we obtained the statutory declaration of the vendor that, to the best of the vendor's knowledge, the restrictions have been complied with.

FIGURE 25.2 Continued

Subdivision Agreements [*Set out the particulars of any subdivision agreements, for example:*]

At the time of closing, a subdivision agreement between (*name of developer*) and (*name of municipality*) was registered on title as instrument number (*number*). By the provisions of the agreement of purchase and sale, you were required to accept title subject to subdivision agreements provided they have been complied with. We were advised by (*name of municipality*) that the terms and conditions of this subdivision agreement have been complied with to date and that sufficient securities have been deposited with the municipality to ensure the completion of services and of all other obligations of the owner.

Easements [*If there are any easements, choose one of the following paragraphs.*]

[*If the easement is in accordance with the agreement of purchase and sale, set out the particulars — for example, if there is an easement in favour of the builder to enter for repairs:*]

By the terms of the agreement of purchase and sale, you agreed to accept the title subject to the right of the builder to enter upon the land in order to inspect the premises, to carry out the necessary repairs to the building upon the land, and to complete its obligations under the subdivision agreement, this right of re-entry to be for a period of five years from the date of closing.

[*If the easement is not provided for in the agreement of purchase and sale, set out the particulars — for example, if there is a right of way over part of the property:*]

Even though you were not required to do so under the agreement of purchase and sale, you agreed to accept title to the property subject to a right of way over a strip of land 1.23 metres wide by 16.20 metres long in favour of the owners of the property immediately to the east of your property, to provide access to maintain the building on that adjoining property and for the purpose of free and unobstructed access to the rear yard of that adjoining property. This easement is shown on the survey as part 15. In addition, you have a right in the nature of an easement over the property immediately to the west of your property for the same purposes. This easement is shown on the survey as part 14.

Family Law Act

The vendor completed a statement pursuant to the provisions of the *Family Law Act* setting out facts that indicated that there was compliance with the Act.

UFFI Warranty

As provided for in the agreement of purchase and sale, on closing we obtained a warranty from the vendor warranting that, during the time the vendor has owned the property, the vendors has not caused any building on the property to be insulated with insulation containing ureaformaldehyde, and that to the best of the vendor's knowledge, no building on the property contains or has ever contained insulation that contains ureaformaldehyde.

Title

[*Use these paragraphs if title insurance has not been obtained.*]

We have made a full and proper search of the title to this property. We have obtained a certificate from the treasurer of (*name of municipality*) showing that there are no arrears of taxes on the above-mentioned property. We have searched in the office of (*name and location of land registry office*) and have satisfied ourselves that, at the time of closing, there were no executions outstanding affecting the title to the said lands.

FIGURE 25.2 Concluded

Based on the above searches, we are of the opinion that (*name(s) of purchaser(s)*) (*has/ have*) a good and marketable title in fee simple to the said lands [*where applicable* — as joint tenants and not as tenants in common] and that the title was, at the date of closing, free from encumbrance, save for [*list any encumbrances:*]

1.
2.
3.

[*Use this paragraph if title insurance has been obtained.*]

In accordance with your instructions, your title to the property is protected under a title insurance policy issued by (*name of company*) as policy number (*number*). Schedules identifying the property and the insured, and listing additional exceptions as well as affirmative assurances relating to matters not covered, excluded, or excepted, are attached to the title insurance policy. Your copy of the policy, including schedules, will be forwarded to you shortly. Should you ever be required to file a claim, it is important that you follow the procedures set out in the policy.

Because this transaction is now completed, we enclose the following documents:

1. statement of adjustments;
2. duplicate transfer/deed of land number (*number*);
3. copy of charge/mortgage of land number (*number*), together with standard charge terms;
4. vendor's undertaking;
5. UFFI warranty;
6. direction regarding funds [*where applicable* — and redirection of funds];
7. statutory declaration;
8. bill of sale;
9. survey;
10. (*other*);
11. (*other*).

We also enclose our statement of account, which we trust will meet with your approval.

This completes our report to you. If you have any questions in connection with this transaction, please do not hesitate to contact us. We are pleased to have assisted you in this matter.

Yours very truly,

(*Purchaser's lawyer*)

Encls.

CHAPTER 26

Acting for the Vendor

The previous chapters have mostly covered the residential real estate transaction from the perspective of the purchaser. This chapter examines the transaction from the vendor's point of view.

In a residential real estate sale, the vendor's law firm will

- open and organize a file;
- review the agreement of purchase and sale;
- gather information about the property and the state of title;
- prepare the statement of adjustments;
- receive and respond to the purchaser's requisition letter;
- prepare or review the necessary closing documents;
- prepare for the closing;
- ensure that the vendor properly executes all documents;
- close the transaction;
- fulfill any undertakings given on closing; and
- provide the client with a reporting letter.

OPENING AND ORGANIZING THE FILE

The first step is to open and organize a file for the sale transaction. Obtain or prepare a checklist and insert it in the file. Figure 26.1 is an example of a sale checklist.

After reviewing the agreement of purchase and sale, diarize any outstanding condition dates, the requisition date, and the closing date. As the file progresses, diarize the dates on which you expect responses to any letters that you send out. See chapter 14, Opening and Organizing a Real Estate File, for a discussion of this topic.

REVIEWING THE AGREEMENT OF PURCHASE AND SALE

Review the agreement of purchase and sale to determine what matters you will need to attend to and what documents you will have to prepare to close the deal. See chapter 15, Reviewing the Agreement of Purchase and Sale, for a discussion of this topic.

GATHERING INFORMATION ABOUT THE STATE OF TITLE

Ask your client to provide you with the following:

- transfer;
- survey;
- reporting letter the vendor received when the property was purchased;
- details of outstanding mortgages;
- any declarations of possession;
- receipted tax bills;
- information about how the property is heated;
- information about spousal status; and
- information about residency status.

PREPARING THE STATEMENT OF ADJUSTMENTS

See chapter 21, Document Preparation, for a discussion of the statement of adjustments.

RECEIVING AND RESPONDING TO THE REQUISITION LETTER

See chapter 18, Requisitions: An Overview, and chapter 20, The Requisition Letter, for a discussion of requisitions.

PREPARING OR REVIEWING CLOSING DOCUMENTS

See chapter 21, Document Preparation, for a discussion of closing documents.

PREPARATION FOR CLOSING

You must arrange for the vendor to come to your office so that you can

- explain all the necessary documents and have them signed by the vendor;
- explain the statement of adjustments;
- discuss how the closing funds are to be disbursed; and
- arrange for delivery of the keys.

Determine how the closing funds are to be payable, and advise the purchaser's lawyer. Prepare the appropriate redirection regarding funds. See chapter 21, Document Preparation, for a discussion of these matters.

Prepare a closing memo. See chapter 22, Preparation for Closing, for a discussion of this topic.

CLOSING

See chapter 24, Closing the Transaction, for a discussion of closing procedures on behalf of the vendor.

VENDOR'S POST-CLOSING PROCEDURE

There are a number of matters that the vendor's firm has to attend to after the closing of the transaction.

Mortgages and Financial Undertakings

If the firm gave an undertaking to discharge any mortgages, forward the discharge funds to the mortgagee as soon as possible, preferably on the day of closing. Interest on the mortgage continues to accrue each day until the funds are actually received by the mortgagee. If the law firm delays in delivering the discharge funds to the mortgagee, your firm may have to pay the extra interest.

Retain enough money in the law firm's trust account to cover any undertakings provided on closing for payment of utility or tax arrears.

Forward Funds to the Client

After covering the law firm's fees and disbursements, forward the balance of the closing funds to the client as soon as possible. Obtain your client's instructions — your client may want to pick up the cheque, have it delivered, or have it deposited directly into a bank account. Proceeds of sale are generally very large, and the client will not want to lose interest on the money. If you delay in forwarding the money to the client, your firm may have to pay the client for any interest lost.

Real Estate Commission

The deposit will ordinarily have been paid to the vendor's real estate broker, and, once the transaction has closed, it is used to pay the real estate commission on the transaction. If the deposit is not enough to cover the real estate commission, you will have to pay the balance of the commission from the closing proceeds. It is not usually necessary to calculate the amount of the commission because you will likely receive a letter from the broker setting out the amount owed.

If the deposit is greater than the amount of the commission on the transaction, forward a letter to the broker asking that the excess amount be sent immediately to your client. Diarize a date approximately two weeks later to call your client to determine whether the payment was received.

Follow Up on Undertakings

Take steps to follow up on all undertakings given personally by the law firm. Diarize to ensure that a mortgagee provides or registers a discharge of mortgage, or that outstanding property taxes or utility arrears have been paid. Remind the client of any undertakings he or she must fulfill — for example, to pay the final water bill.

Assessment Department

Write to the municipal assessment department and forward a copy to the tax department, advising them to change their records to show the purchaser as the new owner. Even though a similar letter will likely be sent by the purchaser's law firm (see figure 25.1), you want to ensure that the vendor is no longer billed for taxes. Some firms send similar letters to the various utility companies.

Reporting Letter

Although a reporting letter to the vendor is not as long and detailed as a reporting letter to the purchaser, there is still a tendency to delay its preparation. Clients appreciate receiving one sooner rather than later.

The letter specifies key terms in the agreement of purchase and sale, summarizes the closing procedure, and explains the statement of adjustments. It concludes by explaining how funds were received and disbursed. Figure 26.2 is a precedent reporting letter to the vendor.

PREAMBLE

The opening paragraph confirms completion of the transaction.

AGREEMENT OF PURCHASE AND SALE

This paragraph sets out the date of the agreement, the name of the purchaser, the address of the property, the sale price, and the amount of the deposit.

CLOSING

This paragraph confirms the closing of the transaction, sets out the amount of money received, and confirms that, in exchange, your firm handed over a transfer of land to the purchaser. If the transaction was completed electronically, this paragraph will state that the transfer was released for registration.

MORTGAGES

The reporting letter covers any mortgages assumed by the purchaser and explains the adjustment in the statement of adjustments. Make sure you confirm in the letter that, although the purchasers have assumed your client's mortgage, the client is still responsible for all payments under the mortgage until it is discharged, if the purchaser fails to make any payments. (The client should have been advised of this obligation before closing.)

If the vendor took a mortgage back, the paragraph sets out the principal amount of the mortgage and states that the purchaser was credited with that amount on the statement of adjustments. Payment particulars are also set out, and an executed copy of the mortgage, the standard charge terms, and an amortization schedule are enclosed. Identify any special provisions in the mortgage, such as prepayment privileges.

REALTY TAXES

This paragraph explains the municipal realty tax adjustment on the statement of adjustments.

FUEL OIL

This paragraph explains the fuel oil adjustment on the statement of adjustments and confirms that the vendor filled the tank prior to closing.

WATER

This paragraph explains any adjustment for water on the statement of adjustments if water is not metered.

OTHER ADJUSTMENTS

There should be a paragraph, under the appropriate heading, explaining any other item on the statement of adjustments. For example, there may be an adjustment for rental payments if there are tenants living on the property.

MORTGAGE DISCHARGED

This paragraph describes the steps taken if the vendor had an outstanding mortgage that was required by the agreement of purchase and sale to be discharged.

REAL ESTATE COMMISSION

The agreement of purchase and sale directs the vendor's solicitor to pay any remaining balance outstanding on the real estate commission. The deposit will already have been applied against the commission and is usually sufficient. If the deposit is insufficient, the reporting letter should set out the deficiency and state that it has been paid from the proceeds of the sale. If the deposit is greater than the amount of the commission, the reporting letter should state that you have asked the real estate broker to forward the excess amount directly to the vendor.

STATEMENT OF FUNDS AND DISBURSEMENTS

The statement covering receipt and disbursement of funds shows receipt of the balance due on closing and how those funds have been applied.

The amount of the balance due on closing appears in the right-hand numerical column and the amount of all payments your firm made from the proceeds appears in the left-hand numerical column. Payments from the proceeds might include

- the balance of the real estate commission;
- money paid to discharge a mortgage;
- money paid on account of utility or other arrears;

- money retained in trust on account of other undertakings that has not yet been disbursed — for example, money held back on account of work orders that have to be cleared; and
- your law firm's fees and disbursements.

The sum remaining after deducting these items is the net proceeds.

NET PROCEEDS

Include a paragraph stating how the net proceeds have been dealt with. Although the reporting letter may not be prepared for a while, vendors almost always want to receive the proceeds on the day of closing. Accordingly, the proceeds will likely have been paid to the vendor by cheque or deposited into a bank account before the preparation of the reporting letter.

CONCLUDING PARAGRAPH

The concluding paragraph lists the documents being enclosed. Generally, there are few documents following a sale. Although the vendor signed a number of documents that were delivered to the purchaser, in most cases there is no need to provide copies of them. Once the property has been sold, they are of little interest to the vendor. Generally, the only documents enclosed are the statement of adjustments, the statement of account, and an executed copy of any mortgage given back to the vendor, together with the standard charge terms.

SIGNATURE

The reporting letter must be prepared for signature by the lawyer handling the file and must be signed by the lawyer. It may not be signed by a law clerk.

Statement of Account

Prepare a statement of account setting out your firm's fees and disbursements on the sale transaction. The law firm will have kept sufficient funds to pay the account before releasing the closing funds to the client.

Closing the File

Do not close the file until all post-closing matters have been completed, including performance of any undertakings. At that time, follow the standard procedure of the law firm.

REVIEW QUESTIONS

1. What dates should you diarize if you are acting for the vendor?
2. If there is a mortgage being paid off, what document do you prepare to advise the purchaser's lawyer how funds are to be payable?
3. If a mortgage is being discharged, why is it important for the vendor's lawyer to deliver funds to the mortgagee as soon as possible after closing?
4. The purchaser's deposit is usually made payable to the real estate broker in trust. When the transaction closes, the broker can take the deposit from the trust account and apply it to the real estate commission.
   a. What if the deposit is not enough to cover the commission?
   b. What if the deposit is more than the commission?
5. Does the vendor's lawyer's reporting letter contain a legal opinion?
6. What is the purpose of the vendor's lawyer's reporting letter?

FIGURE 26.1 Sale Checklist

SALE TRANSACTION

VENDOR(S) __________	PURCHASER(S) __________
SPOUSE __________	PURCHASER'S SOLICITOR__________
ADDRESS __________	ADDRESS __________
__________	__________
PHONE BUS __________	__________
RES __________	PHONE __________
NEW ADDRESS __________	
__________	
__________	

CLOSING DATE __________	REQUISITION DATE__________
RESPONSIBLE SOLICITOR__________	REQUISITIONS SUBMITTED __________
	REQUISITIONS ANSWERED__________

- ❑ Letter to client
- ❑ Letter to purchaser's lawyer
- ❑ Receive from client: tax bill, old title documents, annual mortgage information letter, mortgage & SCT, survey, oil bill, etc.
- ❑ Receive & review requisition letter (including title direction) — amend documents enclosed
- ❑ Prepare statement of adjustments
  - ❑ check if water metered or billed semi-annually (in old city of Toronto)
  - ❑ oil heat — remind client to order last fill & confirm size of tank & current price for oil
- ❑ Reply to requisition letter
  - ❑ forward amended documents prepared by purchaser's solicitor or prepare & send own form of undertaking/warranty/bill of sale & declaration
- ❑ Order mortgage statement for discharge purposes
- ❑ Receive & review discharge statement
  - ❑ check prepayment penalty & provisions in mortgage (only 3 months if mortgage over 5 years old)
  - ❑ discharge to be registered by mortgagee
  - ❑ discharge amount set out in statement $ __________
  - ❑ send to purchaser's lawyer
- ❑ Send survey to purchaser's lawyer
- ❑ Sign & send LSUC form of e-reg agreement to purchaser's lawyer if not received
- ❑ Prepare transfer and acknowledgement & direction for registration of transfer
- ❑ Get commission statement from realtor
- ❑ Send commission statement & discharge statement to client for review
- ❑ Prepare & send estimated account
- ❑ Prepare direction re: funds and redirection re: funds
- ❑ Undertaking to discharge — to be signed by lawyer
- ❑ Arrange meeting with client to sign & review closing documents
- ❑ Get photocopy ID
- ❑ Prepare closing memo to agent
- ❑ Prepare letter to mortgagee sending money & requesting acknowledgement of receipt
- ❑ Prepare letter to realtor sending balance of commission or advising of closing & requesting balance to be sent to client

POST-CLOSING

- ❑ Undertakings complied with (list on file cover)
- ❑ Report to client & statement of account

FIGURE 26.2 Reporting Letter to the Vendor

Date

Vendor's name
Vendor's address

Re: *Name of transaction*

Dear (*Vendor's name*):

We are pleased to confirm completion of this transaction and would like to make our report to you.

Agreement of Purchase and Sale

On (*date of agreement*) you accepted the offer of (*purchaser's name*) to purchase (*address of property*). The agreement of purchase and sale provided for a sale price of $(*amount*). A deposit of $(*amount*) was paid, with the balance of the purchase price to be paid by certified cheque on closing, subject to adjustments.

Closing

[*Use this paragraph if the closing was not completed electronically.*]

On (*date of closing*), we received [*a certified cheque/a series of certified cheques*] in the amount of $(*balance due on closing*) being the balance due on closing calculated in accordance with the enclosed statement of adjustments. In exchange, we handed over a transfer endorsed in favour of the purchasers.

[*Use this paragraph if the closing was completed electronically.*]

Prior to the closing, we received a (*series*) of cheque(*s*) in the amount of $(*balance due on closing*) being the balance due on closing calculated in accordance with the enclosed statement of adjustments. In exchange we released the transfer for electronic registration.

Mortgage Assumed [*Use this paragraph if there was a mortgage assumed by the purchaser.*] On closing, the purchaser assumed a first mortgage in favour of (*name of mortgagee*) on which there was the outstanding sum of $(*amount*) for principal and interest from (*date of last payment*) to (*date of closing*) in the amount of $(*amount*). The purchaser was credited with both of these amounts on the statement of adjustments.

As we previously advised you, should the purchaser fail to make a payment or payments, you may be responsible for the mortgage until it is discharged.

Mortgage Taken Back

In accordance with the agreement of purchase and sale, you took back a second charge/mortgage securing the principal amount of $(*amount*). The purchasers were given a credit in this amount in the statement of adjustments.

The charge/mortgage was registered on title on (*date of closing*) as instrument number (*number*). We enclose an executed copy of the charge/mortgage together with the standard charge terms.

This charge/mortgage secures the principal sum of $(*amount*) with interest at (*rate*)% per annum and is repayable by equal monthly installments of $(*amount*) on account of principal and interest. The installments commence on the (*day*) day of (*month*), (*year*) up to and including the (*day*) day of (*month*), (*year*) when the balance, if any, of the principal sum is to be paid to you.

FIGURE 26.2 Continued

The monthly installments will be applied first to pay the interest calculated on the principal moneys from time to time outstanding, and the balance of the monthly installments will be applied in reduction of the principal.

[*Explain amortization schedule as follows:*]

We are enclosing an amortization schedule for this mortgage. The schedule shows how much of each monthly payment is applied to principal and to interest and how much of the principal balance remains outstanding after each payment.

[*Where applicable, include details of any prepayment provisions — for example:*]

The purchaser has the privilege, at any time when not in default under the mortgage, to prepay all or any part of the outstanding principal balance without notice or bonus.

Realty Taxes [*This paragraph should explain the realty tax adjustment — for example, if the vendor paid the realty taxes in full:*]

The realty taxes for (*year*) in the amount of \$(*total annual taxes*) were paid in full by you. Because your share of the realty taxes was only \$(*vendor's share of taxes*), you were allowed a credit for this item on the statement of adjustments in the amount of \$(*amount*).

Fuel Oil [*Insert this paragraph if the property is heated by oil:*]

You left a full tank of fuel oil on the premises and were therefore allowed a credit of \$(*amount*) for this item on the statement of adjustments.

Water Charges [*If there was an adjustment for water charges, insert a paragraph to explain this adjustment — for example, if the vendor paid more than his or her share of the water charges:*]

You paid \$(*amount*) for water charges for the period from __ to __. Because your share of the water charges was only \$(*vendor's share of water charges*), you were allowed a credit for this item on the statement of adjustments in the amount of \$(*amount*).

Utilities

Arrangements were made for the utility meters to be read before closing. Final bills will be forwarded to you. Please pay them promptly upon receipt.

Mortgage Discharged [*Use this paragraph if a mortgage was discharged on closing.*]

At the time of closing, there was an outstanding mortgage in favour of (*name of mortgagee*). By the terms of the agreement of purchase and sale, you were required to discharge this mortgage. A mortgage statement obtained from (*name of mortgagee*) showed an outstanding balance of \$(*amount*) owing as of the date of closing. Accordingly, we delivered a cheque in the amount of \$(*amount*) to (*name of mortgagee*) and have arranged for the mortgage to be discharged.

Real Estate Commission

We have paid the balance of the commission due to (*real estate broker*) in the amount of \$(*amount*).

FIGURE 26.2 Concluded

Statement of Funds and Disbursements

[*Set out the balance due on closing and how the funds were paid out — for example:*]

The following is the manner in which the closing funds were received and disbursed in this transaction:

Balance due on closing		$271,554.60
Paid (*name of mortgagee*)	$172,359.14	
Paid (*name of broker*) balance of real estate commission	2,500.00	
Our fee and disbursements	987.50	
Net proceeds	95,707.96	
	$271,554.60	$271,554.60

Net Proceeds [*Insert one of the following paragraphs.*]

[*If proceeds were picked up by client:*]

We wish to confirm that on (*date*) you came to our office and picked up our trust cheque in the amount of $(*amount of net proceeds*).

[*If proceeds were delivered to client:*]

We wish to confirm that on (*date*) we delivered to you our trust cheque in the amount of $(*amount of net proceeds*).

[*If proceeds were deposited into client's bank account:*]

On your instructions, on (*date*), we deposited the sum of $(*amount of net proceeds*) to your credit into (*bank account and branch*).

As this matter is now complete, we enclose the following documents:

1. statement of adjustments;
2. our statement of account;
3. [*list any other documents enclosed*].

This completes our report to you. If you have any questions in connection with this transaction, please do not hesitate to contact us. We are pleased to have assisted you in this matter.

Yours very truly,

(*Vendor's lawyer*)

Encls.

PART IV

More Complicated Transactions

CHAPTER 27

Purchase of a New Home

Buying a newly built home is different from buying a resale home. While a resale home is a finished product that can be inspected prior to closing, a new home is typically purchased before construction has even begun, based on a model home or the builder's plans. For this reason, the agreement of purchase and sale will address various risks and issues associated with the construction of a new home. Because of these differences in the agreement of purchase and sale, there are additional concerns that arise for lawyers acting on such a transaction. This chapter examines these concerns.

OVERVIEW

The builder or vendor and the purchaser approach the issues from different perspectives. Generally, builders want to be protected from the uncertainties beyond their control that are inherent in the building process. Some examples of events that could delay or compromise completion of the deal as promised include bad weather, unavailability of construction materials, and labour disruptions. Builders want some flexibility with regard to completion dates and delays, and the ability to substitute construction materials if necessary.

The purchaser, on the other hand, wants the home to be completed on time, to be of the quality promised, and to be free from any defects. The purchaser wants some protection against unlimited delays and extensions of closing dates, and against improper substitution of construction materials. The purchaser also wants some warranty against defective materials or construction that will extend beyond the closing date.

THE NEW HOME AGREEMENT OF PURCHASE AND SALE

The agreement of purchase and sale for a new home is typically drafted by the builder and therefore tends to be one-sided in the builder's favour. There is a standard form of agreement created by the Greater Toronto Home Builders' Association (GTHBA form). This form was introduced in 1987 and has been updated several times, most recently in 2001. It was specifically designed to be easier to understand and to be fairer to purchasers than the forms often used by builders. In practice, however, most builders continue to use their own form of agreement of purchase and sale. Although there are some warranty protections that new home builders are legally required to provide and cannot contract out of, builders can and do draft agreements that provide them with a great deal of flexibility.

ONTARIO NEW HOME WARRANTIES PLAN ACT

The *Ontario New Home Warranties Plan Act* is the governing legislation dealing with new home purchases. It outlines the extensive warranty protection provided to purchasers and sets out the responsibilities of new home builders.

The Act applies to all new homes sold in Ontario and is administered by Tarion Warranty Corporation, formerly the Ontario New Home Warranty Program (ONHWP). Tarion is a private company that regulates new home builders and protects the rights of new home buyers by

- registering new home builders and vendors;
- enrolling new homes for warranty coverage;
- investigating illegal building practices;
- resolving warranty disputes between homeowners and builders; and
- educating new home buyers about their rights.

Under the Act, every builder or vendor of a new home must register with Tarion. In addition, the builder or vendor must enroll the new home in the warranty program before construction commences. Builders typically pass the enrollment fees on to the purchaser in the agreement of purchase and sale.

Every new home agreement of purchase and sale must include an addendum prescribed by the regulations under the Act. This mandatory addendum contains important information about the new home transaction that will be of particular concern to the purchaser. For example, the addendum

- clarifies the rights of the vendor;
- provides registration and enrollment details under Tarion of the builder and the home;
- contains provisions dealing specifically with extensions and delays;
- advises purchasers to seek legal advice before signing the agreement of purchase and sale; and
- provides the builder's contact information.

If there is any conflict between provisions in the addendum and the agreement of purchase and sale, the provisions in the addendum will prevail.

Tarion maintains a guarantee fund that is financed entirely by registration, renewal, and enrollment fees. If a builder fails to complete the purchase agreement or breaches any statutory warranty obligations, Tarion will use this fund to pay the claims of any purchasers.

New Home Warranties

Under Tarion, every vendor of a new home provides warranties for the following items:

1. deposit protection;
2. defects in work and materials;
3. major structural defects;
4. substitution of materials; and
5. delays in completion.

Warranty coverage begins as soon as the purchaser is in possession of the new home and remains in effect until the warranty period expires, even if the property is resold. The total maximum coverage for each home is $300,000, for homes with a possession date on or after July 1, 2006.

DEPOSIT PROTECTION

The purchaser's deposit on a new home is protected up to a maximum of $40,000 per home. If the sale is not completed, through no fault of the purchaser, the purchaser can make a deposit claim.

Any deposit moneys paid in excess of this amount are not protected. If the agreement of purchase and sale provides for a deposit greater than $40,000, the purchaser should ensure that the excess amount is payable to the vendor's solicitor in trust, to be released only when the transaction closes.

DEFECTS IN WORK AND MATERIALS

New home purchasers have two warranty protections against defects in work and materials. The builder warrants that for the year immediately following possession, the home

- is properly constructed, in accordance with the Ontario *Building Code Act*;
- is free of defects in materials; and
- is fit for habitation — in other words, is ready to live in.

The builder also warrants that for the two years immediately following possession, the home is free from

- water penetration through basement or foundation walls;
- water penetration into the building envelope that is caused by defects in materials or work such as caulking, windows, and doors;
- defects in materials or work related to the electrical, plumbing, and heating systems;
- defects in materials or work that cause exterior cladding (brickwork, or aluminum or vinyl siding) to detach, displace, or deteriorate; and
- violations of the Ontario *Building Code Act*'s health and safety provisions.

MAJOR STRUCTURAL DEFECTS

The builder warrants that for seven years immediately following possession, the home is free from any major structural defects, which are defined in the *Ontario New Home Warranties Plan Act* as any defect in materials or work that

- results in the failure of a load-bearing part of the home's structure or materially and adversely affects its load-bearing function; or
- significantly and adversely affects the use of the building as a home.

The Act provides some exceptions to this coverage. These include major structural defects resulting from

- flood damage;
- dampness that is not caused by the failure of a load-bearing portion of the building;
- damage to drains or sewers;
- damage to finishes;
- damage arising from acts of God, acts of the owner, acts of the owner's tenants and/or guests, or acts of war; or
- malicious damage.

SUBSTITUTION OF MATERIALS

The agreement of purchase and sale typically provides the builder with the right to substitute materials if those originally specified are not available. While this makes practical sense from the builder's point of view, purchasers need assurance that they will not end up with a significantly different home with respect to quality and appearance.

Tarion offers protection to the purchaser against improper substitution of materials by the builder. The builder is not permitted to substitute for items of construction or finishing that the purchaser is entitled to select without the purchaser's written consent. For example, if the purchaser has personally selected tiles, cabinets, bathroom fixtures, or paint colours, the purchaser must consent if substitutions are to be made. The purchaser must be notified in writing of the builder's inability to provide the purchaser's selection. The purchaser is then given seven days to make another selection, failing which the builder may substitute materials of equal or better quality.

For items that the purchaser is entitled to receive under the agreement but is not entitled to choose, the builder can only substitute items of equal or better quality. For example, if the purchaser is entitled to a certain model of washing machine, which is unavailable, the builder must provide a washing machine of equal or better quality.

DELAYS IN COMPLETION FOR AGREEMENTS SIGNED BEFORE OR ON JUNE 30, 2008

The builder is required to take all reasonable steps to build the new home without delay. Under most new home agreements, the home is sufficiently completed for closing if it is finished enough to permit lawful occupancy in accordance with the building code, even though aspects such as landscaping are not yet finished. If the builder must extend the closing date, the procedure set out under the Act and included in the addendum to the agreement of purchase and sale must be followed.

If a builder requires additional time for construction, the closing date may be extended as follows:

- For a delay of more than 15 days, the builder must notify the purchaser of the new closing date in writing at least 65 days before the original closing date. The extended closing date cannot exceed 120 days.
- For a delay of less than 15 days, the builder must notify the purchaser of the new closing date in writing at least 35 days before the original closing date. If there has already been a delay of more than 15 days, the combined delay cannot exceed 120 days.
- For a delay of up to 5 days, the builder does not need to notify the purchaser in advance.

If the builder complies with these requirements, the purchaser will not be entitled to claim compensation for any costs incurred as a result of the delay. If the delay does not meet the above requirements, the purchaser will be entitled to claim compensation in the amount of $100 a day, up to a maximum of $5,000. If the delay is in excess of 120 days, the purchaser also has the right to terminate the agreement between day 121 and day 130. If the purchaser does not terminate the agreement during this time, the builder is entitled to additional delays to a maximum of 120 days. If the home is still not ready for occupation after 120 days and the builder and the purchaser cannot agree on a new closing date, the agreement will automatically terminate and the deposit will be returned, with interest, to the purchaser.

There is no compensation for delays caused by the purchaser or by events beyond the builder's control, such as strikes or floods.

DELAYS IN COMPLETION FOR AGREEMENTS SIGNED AFTER JUNE 30, 2008

Agreements signed after June 30, 2008 must contain a Tarion addendum that outlines closing details, including a Statement of Critical Dates, which sets out the expected closing date and the latest possible dates allowed for extensions. The addendum also contains important information about the property being purchased, such as when construction is likely to start; whether water and sewer services are available; and if there are any conditions precedent in the agreement, which, if not met, would result in early termination of the agreement. (Only certain early termination conditions are permitted, and most involve obtaining external approval, or the occurrence of an external event. Examples of such conditions are consent to the creation of a lot; obtaining a certificate of approval of a septic system; and completion of services such as roads, water lines, and sewer lines for the property or surrounding area.)

Firm Closing Date

When a builder is fairly sure of completing a house by a specific date, he or she will provide a firm closing date in the Statement of Critical Dates, and an outside closing date, which is 365 days after the firm closing date, and is the latest possible closing date.

Tentative Closing Dates

When a builder is unsure of the exact date that the home will be completed, the builder may provide two tentative closing dates, a firm closing date, and an outside closing date in the Statement of Critical Dates. This allows the builder to extend the closing date twice, each by up to 120 days, without paying compensation. The first tentative closing date is the date by which the builder expects to complete the home. The second tentative closing date adds up to 120 days to the first tentative closing date. The firm closing date extends the second tentative closing date by up to 120 days.

If the builder has to delay beyond the first tentative closing date, the builder must give the purchaser written notice of the delay at least 90 days before the first tentative closing date; otherwise, the first tentative closing date becomes the firm closing date. Similarly, if the builder has to delay beyond the second tentative closing date, the builder must give written notice of the delay at least 90 days before the second tentative closing date; otherwise, the second tentative closing date becomes the firm closing date. The outside closing date is 365 days after the earlier of the second tentative closing date and the firm closing date. For example, a builder might provide a Statement of Critical Dates as follows:

First tentative closing date	November 15, 2008
Second tentative closing date	March 15, 2009
Firm closing date	July 13, 2009
Outside closing date	March 15, 2010

If the closing date is going to be delayed beyond November 15, 2008, the builder must give the purchaser notice of the delay no later than August 17, 2008 (90 days before November 15). If there is a further delay beyond March 15, 2009, the purchaser must receive notice of the delay by December 15, 2008 (90 days before March 15).

Delayed Closing Dates

In both the above cases, if the home is not completed by the firm closing date, the builder must set a delayed closing date, and the purchaser is entitled to "delayed closing compensation" for living expenses of $150 per day for each day of delay, until the delayed closing date or termination of the agreement, up to a maximum of $7,500. Receipts are not required. Compensation is also payable for costs incurred, such as extra moving or storage expenses, but receipts for those expenses must be provided.

Delayed closing compensation is not payable if the delay was due to any extraordinary circumstance that was not the fault of the vendor or the purchaser. Such extraordinary circumstances would include a strike, fire, explosion, act of God, civil insurrection, act of war or terrorism, or a pandemic. In these cases, the builder is obligated to advise the purchaser of the delay and keep him or her informed as to its length.

If the home is not completed by the outside closing date, the purchaser has 30 days from the outside closing date to terminate the agreement and is entitled to delayed closing compensation and a refund of all deposits paid, plus interest.

More information on delayed closing warranties can be found on the Tarion website at www.tarion.com.

Pre-Delivery Inspection

When the home is complete, the purchaser must arrange for a pre-delivery inspection (PDI) to be conducted before he or she moves in. During this inspection, the purchaser should identify any unauthorized substitutions as well as any items that are damaged, missing, incomplete, or not working properly. All deficiencies are noted on a special PDI form, which provides a written record of the condition of the home as it existed before the purchaser moved in.

During the PDI, the purchaser will sign a certificate of completion and possession. This certificate confirms the official date of possession and activates the warranty coverage for the new home. The purchaser will also confirm receipt of a homeowner information package. This package explains the rights and responsibilities of the new home buyer under the Act. It also explains the procedure to be followed by the purchaser when requesting warranty service. The homeowner information package can be found on the Tarion website at www.tarion.com under "Resources."

ADDITIONAL CONCERNS AND STEPS

A lawyer acting for the purchaser of a new home will have the same concerns, and must take the same steps, as those involved in the purchase of a resale residential property. There are some additional concerns and steps as well.

Special Concerns Regarding Searches

There are special concerns at the search and inquiry stage of a new home purchase.

MORTGAGES

The search of title may disclose a **blanket mortgage** on the entire development for millions of dollars. Usually the agreement of purchase and sale will require the purchaser to accept the builder's undertaking to provide a partial discharge of the mortgage within a reasonable period of time after closing.

blanket mortgage
a mortgage creating a lien against more than one property; developers use blanket mortgages when subdividing large parcels of land into many separate lots; a blanket mortgage is spread over the entire parcel of land, rather than applied to each individual lot

RESTRICTIONS ON TITLE

As is the case in resale agreements, the purchaser of a new home must take title subject to any registered restrictions, easements, and agreements. The new home agreement will usually also require the purchaser to accept future and potential easements, restrictions, and agreements entered into by the vendor between the time the agreement is entered into and the closing date. It is very important for the purchaser to check the "permitted encumbrances" clause in the new home agreement to determine the nature and scope of any potential title restrictions.

TARION SEARCH

In addition to the usual searches and letter inquiries, a lawyer acting on the purchase of a new home must contact Tarion to ensure that the builder or vendor has, in fact, registered with Tarion and that the new home has, in fact, been enrolled in the new home warranty program.

Adjustments on Closing

The statement of adjustments in a new home purchase will be different from that for a resale home, primarily because the agreement of purchase and sale of a new home generally allows the builder to pass a number of expenses on to the purchaser.

ENROLLMENT FEES

The agreement of purchase and sale may provide that the cost of enrollment under Tarion will be added to the purchase price. The cost depends on the purchase price of the property.

UTILITY CONNECTIONS

The agreement of purchase and sale of a new home usually allows the builder to pass on to the purchaser any charges paid to a utility for the connection of services or the installation of meters.

GOODS AND SERVICES TAX (GST)

GST of 5 percent is payable on new homes, but purchasers usually qualify for a rebate of up to 2.5 percent of the GST payable. Most new home agreements of purchase and sale assume that the purchaser qualifies for this rebate, and therefore the purchase price will reflect the discounted GST amount. If it turns out that the purchaser does not qualify for the rebate, the purchase price will be increased by way of an adjustment in the vendor's favour.

REALTY TAXES

For resale properties, the adjustment of realty taxes on closing is based on actual taxes assessed. For new homes, before construction is complete, taxes are calculated on the basis that the land is vacant; therefore, they do not provide an accurate indication of what the taxes will be once the construction has been completed and the property separately assessed. Accordingly, on closing, the taxes are adjusted as if they had been assessed on the completed property and as if the vendor had paid them in full at this higher rate. By adjusting taxes in advance, the vendor avoids having to go after the purchaser for any additional taxes owing after closing. Once a supplementary tax bill is issued, the vendor will pay the taxes and the taxes will be readjusted, if necessary, in accordance with the undertakings to readjust that are exchanged on closing. If the vendor has overestimated the new taxes, the vendor will refund money to the purchaser. If the vendor has underestimated the new taxes, the purchaser will have to pay the difference.

REFERENCES

Ontario *Building Code Act*, SO 1992, c. 23, as amended.

Ontario New Home Warranties Plan Act, RSO 1990, c. O.31.

REVIEW QUESTIONS

1. What is the *Ontario New Home Warranties Plan Act*?
2. How is the *Ontario New Home Warranties Plan Act* administered?
3. What should a purchaser of a new home do to protect his or her statutory warranty rights?
4. What is an "addendum"?
5. What happens if a builder fails to fulfill the purchase agreement or breaches any statutory warranty obligations?
6. For what items does a vendor of a new home provide warranties?
7. When does warranty coverage begin and end?
8. What can a purchaser of a new home do if the builder delays completion without complying with the Act?
9. What takes place during the pre-delivery inspection?
10. How are realty taxes adjusted on the closing of a new home purchase?

DISCUSSION QUESTIONS

1. Sally is purchasing a new home. The builder is registered with Tarion, and the home has been enrolled in the program. The builder's form of agreement of purchase and sale provides for a deposit of $50,000. The agreement also provides that the builder can substitute materials if necessary.
    a. Sally is nervous about giving so much money as a deposit. What advice should Sally's lawyer give her?
    b. Sally is excited about being able to choose some of the items in her new home (lighting and plumbing fixtures, cabinets, carpets, tiles, and paint colours) and is concerned about the builder being able to make changes. She is worried that she will not like the quality or appearance of substitutions that are made by the builder. What advice should Sally's lawyer give her?
2. Peter is a new home builder, registered with Tarion. He signed an agreement of purchase and sale for a new home that is scheduled to close on May 15, 2008.
    a. If Peter needs to delay closing for a month, what must he do and by when must he do it?

   b. If Peter needs to delay closing for two weeks, what must he do and by when must he do it?

3. Ramona purchased a new home that is enrolled in the warranty program and had a firm closing date of September 30, 2008. On July 25, the builder sent Ramona a letter notifying her that the closing date was being extended to October 25 because of a shortage of bricks. Ramona is very upset about these delays and wants to know whether she is entitled to any compensation. Explain your answer.

CHAPTER 28

Purchase of a Condominium

If the client is purchasing a condominium, the steps and procedures for the transaction are mostly the same as those for the purchase of a residential property owned in fee simple. This chapter discusses the main differences, which arise because of the nature of condominium ownership. As discussed in chapter 10, Condominiums, the purchaser will become the sole owner in fee simple of the interior of the condominium unit and a part owner (tenant in common with all of the other unit owners) of the common elements of the condominium corporation. The purchaser will also become a member of the condominium corporation that manages and administers the condominium property.

PURCHASE OF A RESALE CONDOMINIUM

Agreement of Purchase and Sale

The standard form of agreement of purchase and sale for a resale condominium is different from the one used in the purchase of a resale residential property owned in fee simple. Both the Ontario Real Estate Association (OREA) and the Toronto Real Estate Board (TREB) have a standard form of agreement to be used for the purchase of a resale condominium. In addition to the usual clauses in an agreement of purchase and sale, the vendor agrees to give the purchaser copies of the key condominium documentation, and the vendor makes representations about the amount of the common expenses and the financial status of the condominium corporation. (See the discussion below under the heading "Status Certificate.")

A copy of the OREA form of agreement of purchase and sale for a condominium resale is reproduced as figure 28.1.

Title Search

The title search of a condominium property is different from the search for a property owned in fee simple. All condominiums are registered in the Land Titles system. The nature of the search will depend on whether the property has been converted to POLARIS and is therefore automated.

If the property has not been converted to POLARIS, you must check the following four registers when searching title:

Property Parcel Register
register that contains the description of the property including any easements and the original encumbrances that affect the entire condominium property

Constitution Index
register that contains the declaration, description, and bylaws of the condominium

Common Elements and General Index
register that contains a description of the common elements and any easements and encumbrances that affect all the units

Unit Register
register that shows ownership of each unit and any mortgages, liens, and leases relating to the unit

- the **Property Parcel Register**, which shows the state of title of the property at the time the condominium development was registered;
- the **Constitution Index**, which contains the declaration, description, and all bylaws of the corporation;
- the **Common Elements and General Index**, which records all instruments affecting the common elements, such as blanket mortgages and construction liens; and
- the **Unit Register**, which records all instruments affecting title to the individual unit. If the parking unit or locker is treated as a separate unit, the unit register for each of these units must be searched as well.

It is necessary to examine all four registers in order to verify the state of title to the unit being purchased.

Most condominium properties have been converted to POLARIS, in which case there is only one register or index for each unit in the condominium. All of the instruments previously recorded in the above four registers are combined and recorded in each unit's separate parcel register.

Execution Search

The execution search in a condominium resale differs from the usual execution search for a Land Titles property. In addition to the usual search against the vendor, you should also search for executions against the condominium corporation. If there is a judgment against the corporation, then the unit owners may be liable for a portion of the judgment.

Status Certificate

status certificate
certificate from the condominium corporation that includes, among other things, financial information, directors and officers, and the declaration

In addition to the above searches, the purchaser of a condominium unit must obtain a **status certificate** from the condominium corporation. The status certificate will contain the following information:

1. the amount of common expenses for the unit and whether or not the vendor is in default of payment of common expenses;
2. whether the common expenses will be increased and, if so, the reason for the increase;
3. whether or not assessments have been levied against the unit and, if so, the reason for the assessments;
4. whether or not there are any judgments against the condominium corporation, including the status of any legal actions to which the condominium corporation is currently a party;
5. the address for service of the corporation, including the names and addresses for service of all directors and officers of the corporation; and
6. a copy of the current declaration.

Pursuant to section 76(6) of the *Condominium Act, 1998*, the status certificate will bind the corporation "as of the date it is given or deemed to have been given, with respect to the information that it contains or is deemed to contain, as against a purchaser or mortgagee of a unit who relies on the certificate."

The condominium corporation must also provide a copy of the following documents:

- the last annual financial statements of the corporation;
- the corporation's current budget;
- the condominium's current declaration, bylaws, and rules;
- the property management agreement; and
- the current insurance certificates.

It is important that the lawyer in charge of the file review all of these documents with the client prior to closing.

Requisitions on Title

In addition to the requisitions that might arise on any residential purchase, you may have requisitions that arise from your review of the status certificate and condominium documentation if the information provided differs from that in the agreement of purchase and sale.

Statement of Adjustments

In addition to the usual adjustments, there will be an adjustment for the monthly common expense payment, which is generally payable on the 1st of the month and covers the month that follows.

PURCHASE OF A NEW CONDOMINIUM

As in the case of other types of newly constructed homes, the agreement of purchase and sale for a new condominium is often signed before construction of the condominium has started. In fact, in many agreements, the builder is not even obligated to start construction of the condominium until a specified number of units are sold. This is because most banks will not provide financing for construction unless a specified number of units are presold. However, in the case of a new condominium, the agreement of purchase and sale is not binding on the purchaser until the vendor, referred to as the **declarant** (or as the **proposed declarant** until such time as the declaration and description are registered on title to create the condominium) delivers a **disclosure statement** to the purchaser. This document, which must be given to every purchaser of a new condominium unit, includes a description of the property and its amenities; a copy of the declaration, bylaws, and rules; construction dates (if not completed); a description of contracts involving the corporation; a copy of the budget for the year of registration; and a copy of the insurance trust agreement. The purchaser has a 10-day **cooling-off period** from the later of (1) the

declarant
upon registration, the person who owns the land described in the description and who registers the declaration and description that create the condominium plan

proposed declarant
prior to the registration of the declaration and description, the person who owns the land described in the description

disclosure statement
document given to every purchaser of a condominium unit that includes details pertaining to the physical, legal, and financial aspects of the condominium corporation

cooling-off period
10-day period during which the purchaser can back out of the purchase

receipt of the disclosure statement and (2) receipt of an executed copy of the agreement of purchase and sale, during which time the purchaser may withdraw from the agreement. In order to withdraw, the purchaser must give the proposed declarant written notice, which must be received by the proposed declarant within the 10-day period. If there are subsequent material changes to the disclosure statement, the proposed declarant must give the purchaser an amended disclosure statement, and the purchaser has another 10-day cooling-off period.

Deposits

All deposits that a purchaser pays must be held in trust by the proposed declarant's lawyer or a designated trustee until title is transferred to the purchaser, unless the proposed declarant provides security for the deposits. The first $20,000 of a deposit is secured under the *Ontario New Home Warranties Plan Act*. The proposed declarant must pay interest on any deposits up to the interim occupancy closing date.

Two-Stage Closing

Often a condominium is built and ready for occupancy before the description and declaration are registered. Title cannot be transferred to the purchaser until these are registered and so the final closing is delayed. Most agreements of purchase and sale require the purchaser to occupy the unit as soon as it is ready, even if the purchaser cannot get title to the property at that time. The date of occupancy is called the **interim occupancy date**.

interim occupancy date date on which the purchaser takes possession prior to final closing and transfer of title

Tarion has a delayed occupancy warranty for condominiums, based on both firm and tentative occupancy dates, that is similar to the delayed closing warranty (based on both firm and tentative closing dates), discussed in chapter 27. It applies to agreements of purchase and sale signed after June 30, 2008. For more information, see the Tarion website at www.tarion.com.

On the interim occupancy date, the purchaser will have to pay any amounts required by the agreement of purchase and sale. The parties will enter into an interim occupancy agreement, which sets out the rights and obligations of the parties during the time between occupancy of the unit and the transfer of title to the purchaser at the final closing.

The *Condominium Act* allows the proposed declarant to charge monthly interim occupancy fees during the interim occupancy period. These fees can be no greater than the total of

- the monthly interest on any unpaid balance of the purchase price, the interest rate being based on the Bank of Canada rate for a one-year mortgage;
- a reasonable estimate of the unit's portion of municipal taxes, on a monthly basis; and
- the projected monthly common expenses for the unit.

Once the description and declaration have been registered, the declarant can provide the purchaser with a transfer, and the final closing can take place. The purchaser will have to pay the balance of the purchase price, subject to adjustments, at this time.

REFERENCES

Condominium Act, 1998, SO 1998, c. 19.

Ontario New Home Warranties Plan Act, RSO 1990, c. O.31.

REVIEW QUESTIONS

1. How do you conduct a title search of a condominium property?
2. How does an execution search for a condominium resale differ from the usual execution search for a Land Titles property?
3. What information is contained in the status certificate?
4. When does an agreement of purchase and sale for a new condominium become binding on the purchaser?
5. What is an interim occupancy agreement?

DISCUSSION QUESTIONS

1. Sunita recently signed an agreement of purchase and sale for a new condominium. She now thinks that she made a huge mistake and wants to back out of the deal. She has not yet received any documents from the vendor/builder. Can she withdraw from the agreement?
2. Betty signed an agreement of purchase and sale for a new condominium unit. The disclosure statement that she received two months ago indicated that the condominium was providing a games room and a health club. Betty has just been informed that these facilities will no longer be included in the condominium. What, if anything, can Betty do?
3. Last year, Sam signed an agreement of purchase and sale for a new condominium unit before construction of the building had even begun. Sam has just been told that although he won't get title to the property yet, his unit will be ready for occupancy next month.
    a. Is Sam obligated to occupy the unit before he gets title?
    b. What amount will Sam be required to pay to the vendor/builder when he moves in?

FIGURE 28.1 OREA Agreement of Purchase and Sale — Condominium Resale

OREA Ontario Real Estate Association

Agreement of Purchase and Sale
Condominium Resale

Form 101
for use in the Province of Ontario

This Agreement of Purchase and Sale dated this.................................. day of .... 20........

BUYER,..., agrees to purchase from
(Full legal names of all Buyers)

SELLER,.., the following
(Full legal names of all Sellers)

PROPERTY:
a unit in the condominium property located at...
in the...being
Unit No. .... Level No. .... Condominium Plan No. ....
Building No. .... known as .... No. .... together with ownership
(Apartment/Townhouse/Suite/Unit)

or exclusive use of Parking Space(s) ...., together with ownership or exclusive use of
(Number(s), Level(s))

Locker(s) ...., together with Seller's proportionate undivided tenancy-in-common interest
(Number(s), Level(s))
in the common elements appurtenant to the Unit as described in the Declaration and Description including the exclusive right to use such other parts of the common elements appurtenant to the Unit as may be specified in the Declaration and Description: the Unit, the proportionate interest in the common elements appurtenant thereto, and the exclusive use portions of the common elements, being herein called the "Property".

PURCHASE PRICE: Dollars (CDN$)..

....Dollars

DEPOSIT: Buyer submits ....
(Herewith/Upon Acceptance/as otherwise described in this Agreement)

.... Dollars (CDN$).......................................

by negotiable cheque payable to.. "Deposit Holder" to be held in trust pending completion or other termination of this Agreement and to be credited toward the Purchase Price on completion. For the purposes of this Agreement, "Upon Acceptance" shall mean that the Buyer is required to deliver the deposit to the Deposit Holder within 24 hours of the acceptance of this Agreement. The parties to this Agreement hereby acknowledge that, unless otherwise provided for in this Agreement, the Deposit Holder shall place the deposit in trust in the Deposit Holder's non-interest bearing Real Estate Trust Account and no interest shall be earned, received or paid on the deposit.

Buyer agrees to pay the balance as more particularly set out in Schedule A attached.

SCHEDULE(S) A...**attached hereto form(s) part of this Agreement.**

1. **IRREVOCABILITY:** This Offer shall be irrevocable by .... until .... a.m./p.m. on
(Seller/Buyer)
the .... day of .... 20........., after which time, if not accepted, this Offer shall be null and void and the deposit shall be returned to the Buyer in full without interest.
2. **COMPLETION DATE:** This Agreement shall be completed by no later than 6:00 p.m. on the .... day of ...., 20......... . Upon completion, vacant possession of the property shall be given to the Buyer unless otherwise provided for in this Agreement.
3. **NOTICES:** Seller hereby appoints the Listing Brokerage as Agent for the purpose of giving and receiving notices pursuant to this Agreement. **Only if the Co-operating Brokerage represents the interests of the Buyer in this transaction,** the Buyer hereby appoints the Co-operating Brokerage as Agent for the purpose of giving and receiving notices pursuant to this Agreement. Any notice relating hereto or provided for herein shall be in writing. This offer, any counter offer, notice of acceptance thereof, or any notice shall be deemed given and received, when hand delivered to the address for service provided in the Acknowledgement below, or where a facsimile number is provided herein, when transmitted electronically to that facsimile number.

FAX No. .... (For delivery of notices to Seller) FAX No. .... (For delivery of notices to Buyer)

INITIALS OF BUYER(S): ( ) **INITIALS OF SELLER(S):** ( )

 Form 101 2007 **Page 1 of 5**

FIGURE 28.1 Continued

4. **CHATTELS INCLUDED:**..
....
....

5. **FIXTURES EXCLUDED:**..
....

6. **RENTAL ITEMS:** The following equipment is rented and **not** included in the Purchase Price. The Buyer agrees to assume the rental contract(s), if assumable: ....
....

7. **COMMON EXPENSES:** Seller warrants to Buyer that the common expenses presently payable to the Condominium Corporation in respect of the Property are approximately $..............................per month, which amount includes the following:...
....

8. **PARKING AND LOCKERS:** Parking and Lockers are as described above or assigned as follows:..............................
.... at an additional cost of:..

9. **GST:** If this transaction is subject to Goods and Services Tax (G.S.T.), then such tax shall be .... (included in/in addition to) the Purchase Price. If this transaction is not subject to G.S.T., Seller agrees to certify on or before closing, that the transaction is not subject to G.S.T.

10. **TITLE SEARCH:** Buyer shall be allowed until 6:00 p.m. on the .... day of..................................., 20......., (Requisition Date) to examine the title to the Property at Buyer's own expense and until the earlier of: (i) thirty days from the later of the Requisition Date or the date on which the conditions in this Agreement are fulfilled or otherwise waived or; (ii) five days prior to completion, to satisfy Buyer that there are no outstanding work orders or deficiency notices affecting the Property, and that its present use (...) may be lawfully continued. If within that time any valid objection to title or to any outstanding work order or deficiency notice, or to the fact the said present use may not lawfully be continued, is made in writing to Seller and which Seller is unable or unwilling to remove, remedy or satisfy or obtain insurance in favour of the Buyer and any mortgagee, (with all related costs at the expense of the Seller), and which Buyer will not waive, this Agreement notwithstanding any intermediate acts or negotiations in respect of such objections, shall be at an end and all monies paid shall be returned without interest or deduction and Seller, Listing Brokerage and Co-operating Brokerage shall not be liable for any costs or damages. Save as to any valid objection so made by such day and except for any objection going to the root of the title, Buyer shall be conclusively deemed to have accepted Seller's title to the Property. Seller hereby consents to the municipality or other governmental agencies releasing to Buyer details of all outstanding work orders or deficiency notices affecting the Property, and Seller agrees to execute and deliver such further authorizations in this regard as Buyer may reasonably require.

11. **TITLE:** Buyer agrees to accept title to the Property subject to all rights and easements registered against title for the supply and installation of telephone services, electricity, gas, sewers, water, television cable facilities and other related services; provided that title to the Property is otherwise good and free from all encumbrances except: (a) as herein expressly provided; (b) any registered restrictions, conditions or covenants that run with the land provided such have been complied with; (c) the provisions of the Condominium Act and its Regulations and the terms, conditions and provisions of the Declaration, Description and By-laws, Occupancy Standards By-laws, including the Common Element Rules and other Rules and Regulations; and (d) any existing municipal agreements, zoning by-laws and/or regulations and utilities or service contracts.

12. **CLOSING ARRANGEMENTS:** Where each of the Seller and Buyer retain a lawyer to complete the Agreement of Purchase and Sale of the Property, and where the transaction will be completed by electronic registration pursuant to Part III of the Land Registration Reform Act, R.S.O. 1990, Chapter L4 and the Electronic Registration Act, S.O. 1991, Chapter 44, and any amendments thereto, the Seller and Buyer acknowledge and agree that the exchange of closing funds, non-registrable documents and other items (the "Requisite Deliveries") and the release thereof to the Seller and Buyer will (a) not occur at the same time as the registration of the transfer/deed (and any other documents intended to be registered in connection with the completion of this transaction) and (b) be subject to conditions whereby the lawyer(s) receiving any of the Requisite Deliveries will be required to hold same in trust and not release same except in accordance with the terms of a document registration agreement between the said lawyers. The Seller and Buyer irrevocably instruct the said lawyers to be bound by the document registration agreement which is recommended from time to time by the Law Society of Upper Canada. Unless otherwise agreed to by the lawyers, such exchange of the Requisite Deliveries will occur in the applicable Land Titles Office or such other location agreeable to both lawyers.

13. **STATUS CERTIFICATE AND MANAGEMENT OF CONDOMINIUM:** Seller represents and warrants to Buyer that there are no special assessments contemplated by the Condominium Corporation, and there are no legal actions pending by or against or contemplated by the Condominium Corporation. The Seller consents to a request by the Buyer or the Buyer's authorized representative for a Status Certificate from the Condominium Corporation. Buyer acknowledges that the Condominium Corporation may have entered into a Management Agreement for the management of the condominium property.

14. **DOCUMENTS AND DISCHARGE:** Buyer shall not call for the production of any title deed, abstract, survey or other evidence of title to the Property except such as are in the possession or control of Seller. Seller agrees to deliver to Buyer, if it is possible without incurring any costs in so doing, copies of all current condominium documentation of the Condominium

INITIALS OF BUYER(S): ( ) **INITIALS OF SELLER(S):** ( )

 Form 101 2007

FIGURE 28.1 Continued

Corporation, including the Declaration, Description, By-laws, Common Element Rules and Regulations and the most recent financial statements of the Condominium Corporation. If a discharge of any Charge/Mortgage held by a corporation incorporated pursuant to the Trust And Loan Companies Act (Canada), Chartered Bank, Trust Company, Credit Union, Caisse Populaire or Insurance Company and which is not to be assumed by Buyer on completion, is not available in registrable form on completion, Buyer agrees to accept Seller's lawyer's personal undertaking to obtain, out of the closing funds, a discharge in registrable form and to register same, or cause same to be registered, on title within a reasonable period of time after completion, provided that on or before completion Seller shall provide to Buyer a mortgage statement prepared by the mortgagee setting out the balance required to obtain the discharge, and, where a real-time electronic cleared funds transfer system is not being used, a direction executed by Seller directing payment to the mortgagee of the amount required to obtain the discharge out of the balance due on completion.

15. **MEETINGS:** Seller represents and warrants to Buyer that at the time of the acceptance of this Offer the Seller has not received a notice convening a special or general meeting of the Condominium Corporation respecting; (a) the termination of the government of the condominium property; (b) any substantial alteration in or substantial addition to the common elements or the renovation thereof; OR (c) any substantial change in the assets or liabilities of the Condominium Corporation; and Seller covenants that if Seller receives any such notice prior to the date of completion Seller shall forthwith notify Buyer in writing and Buyer may thereupon at Buyer's option declare this Agreement to be null and void and all monies paid by Buyer shall be refunded without interest or deduction.
16. **INSPECTION:** Buyer acknowledges having had the opportunity to inspect the Property and understands that upon acceptance of this offer there shall be a binding agreement of purchase and sale between Buyer and Seller. **The Buyer acknowledges having the opportunity to include a requirement for a property inspection report in this Agreement and agrees that except as may be specifically provided for in this Agreement, the Buyer will not be obtaining a property inspection or property inspection report regarding the property.**
17. **APPROVAL OF THE AGREEMENT:** In the event that consent to this sale is required to be given by the Condominium Corporation or the Board of Directors, the Seller will apply forthwith for the requisite consent, and if such consent is refused, then this Agreement shall be null and void and the deposit monies paid hereunder shall be refunded without interest or other penalty to the Buyer.
18. **INSURANCE:** The Unit and all other things being purchased shall be and remain at the risk of the Seller until completion. In the event of substantial damage to the Property Buyer may at Buyer's option either permit the proceeds of insurance to be used for repair of such damage in accordance with the provisions of the Insurance Trust Agreement, or terminate this Agreement and all deposit monies paid by Buyer hereunder shall be refunded without interest or deduction. If Seller is taking back a Charge/Mortgage, or Buyer is assuming a Charge/Mortgage, Buyer shall supply Seller with reasonable evidence of adequate insurance to protect Seller's or other mortgagee's interest on completion.
19. **DOCUMENT PREPARATION:** The Transfer/Deed shall, save for the Land Transfer Tax Affidavit, be prepared in registrable form at the expense of Seller, and any Charge/Mortgage to be given back by the Buyer to Seller at the expense of the Buyer.
20. **RESIDENCY:** Buyer shall be credited towards the Purchase Price with the amount, if any, necessary for Buyer to pay to the Minister of National Revenue to satisfy Buyer's liability in respect of tax payable by Seller under the non-residency provisions of the Income Tax Act by reason of this sale. Buyer shall not claim such credit if Seller delivers on completion the prescribed certificate or a statutory declaration that Seller is not then a non-resident of Canada.
21. **ADJUSTMENTS:** Common Expenses; realty taxes, including local improvement rates; mortgage interest; rentals; unmetered public or private utilities and fuel where billed to the Unit and not the Condominium Corporation; are to be apportioned and allowed to the day of completion, the day of completion itself to be apportioned to the Buyer. There shall be no adjustment for the Seller's share of any assets or liabilities of the Condominium Corporation including any reserve or contingency fund to which Seller may have contributed prior to the date of completion.
22. **TIME LIMITS:** Time shall in all respects be of the essence hereof provided that the time for doing or completing of any matter provided for herein may be extended or abridged by an agreement in writing signed by Seller and Buyer or by their respective lawyers who may be specifically authorized in that regard.
23. **TENDER:** Any tender of documents or money hereunder may be made upon Seller or Buyer or their respective lawyers on the day set for completion. Money may be tendered by bank draft or cheque certified by a Chartered Bank, Trust Company, Province of Ontario Savings Office, Credit Union or Caisse Populaire.
24. **FAMILY LAW ACT:** Seller warrants that spousal consent is not necessary to this transaction under the provisions of the Family Law Act, R.S.O. 1990 unless Seller's spouse has executed the consent hereinafter provided.
25. **UFFI**: Seller represents and warrants to Buyer that during the time Seller has owned the Property, Seller has not caused any building on the Property to be insulated with insulation containing ureaformaldehyde, and that to the best of Seller's knowledge no building on the Property contains or has ever contained insulation that contains ureaformaldehyde. This warranty shall survive and not merge on the completion of this transaction, and if the building is part of a multiple unit building, this warranty shall only apply to that part of the building which is the subject of this transaction.
26. **CONSUMER REPORTS: The Buyer is hereby notified that a consumer report containing credit and/or personal information may be referred to in connection with this transaction.**
27. **AGREEMENT IN WRITING:** If there is conflict or discrepancy between any provision added to this Agreement (including any Schedule attached hereto) and any provision in the standard pre-set portion hereof, the added provision shall supersede the standard pre-set provision to the extent of such conflict or discrepancy. This Agreement including any Schedule attached hereto, shall constitute the entire Agreement between Buyer and Seller. There is no representation, warranty, collateral agreement or condition, which affects this Agreement other than as expressed herein. For the purposes of this Agreement, Seller means vendor and Buyer means purchaser. This Agreement shall be read with all changes of gender or number required by the context.

INITIALS OF BUYER(S): ( ) **INITIALS OF SELLER(S):** ( )

 Form 101 2007 Page 3 of 5

FIGURE 28.1 Continued

28. **SUCCESSORS AND ASSIGNS:** The heirs, executors, administrators, successors and assigns of the undersigned are bound by the terms herein.

SIGNED, SEALED AND DELIVERED in the presence of: IN WITNESS whereof I have hereunto set my hand and seal:

(Witness) (Buyer) (Seal) DATE

(Witness) (Buyer) (Seal) DATE

I, the Undersigned Seller, agree to the above Offer. I hereby irrevocably instruct my lawyer to pay directly to the Listing Brokerage the unpaid balance of the commission together with applicable Goods and Services Tax (and any other taxes as may hereafter be applicable), from the proceeds of the sale prior to any payment to the undersigned on completion, as advised by the Listing Brokerage to my lawyer.

SIGNED, SEALED AND DELIVERED in the presence of: IN WITNESS whereof I have hereunto set my hand and seal:

(Witness) (Seller) (Seal) DATE

(Witness) (Seller) (Seal) DATE

SPOUSAL CONSENT: The Undersigned Spouse of the Seller hereby consents to the disposition evidenced herein pursuant to the provisions of the Family Law Act, R.S.O.1990, and hereby agrees with the Buyer that he/she will execute all necessary or incidental documents to give full force and effect to the sale evidenced herein.

(Witness) (Spouse) (Seal) DATE

CONFIRMATION OF ACCEPTANCE: Notwithstanding anything contained herein to the contrary, I confirm this Agreement with all changes both typed and written was finally accepted by all parties at..................a.m./p.m. this.......................................day of..., 20.......... .

(Signature of Seller or Buyer)

INFORMATION ON BROKERAGE(S)

Listing Brokerage.. Tel.No.(................)................

Co-op/Buyer Brokerage.. Tel.No.(................)................

ACKNOWLEDGEMENT

I acknowledge receipt of my signed copy of this accepted Agreement of Purchase and Sale and I authorize the Agent to forward a copy to my lawyer.

(Seller) DATE

(Seller) DATE

Address for Service..

........................Tel.No.(...........)........................

Seller's Lawyer..

Address..

(..........)........................ (..........)........................
Tel.No. FAX No.

I acknowledge receipt of my signed copy of this accepted Agreement of Purchase and Sale and I authorize the Agent to forward a copy to my lawyer.

(Buyer) DATE

(Buyer) DATE

Address for Service..

........................Tel.No.(...........)........................

Buyer's Lawyer..

Address..

(..........)........................ (..........)........................
Tel.No. FAX No.

Property Manager:........................ (Name) (Address) (Tel No.,FAX No.)

FOR OFFICE USE ONLY

COMMISSION TRUST AGREEMENT

To: Co-operating Brokerage shown on the foregoing Agreement of Purchase and Sale:
In consideration for the Co-operating Brokerage procuring the foregoing Agreement of Purchase and Sale, I hereby declare that all moneys received or receivable by me in connection with the Transaction as contemplated in the MLS® Rules and Regulations of my Real Estate Board shall be receivable and held in trust. This agreement shall constitute a Commission Trust Agreement as defined in the MLS® Rules and shall be subject to and governed by the MLS® Rules pertaining to Commission Trust.

DATED as of the date and time of the acceptance of the foregoing Agreement of Purchase and Sale. Acknowledged by:

(Authorized to bind the Listing Brokerage) (Authorized to bind the Co-operating Brokerage)

 Form 101 2007

FIGURE 28.1 Concluded

OREA Ontario Real Estate Association

Schedule A

Agreement of Purchase and Sale – Condominium Resale

Form 101
for use in the Province of Ontario

This Schedule is attached to and forms part of the Agreement of Purchase and Sale between:

BUYER,..., and

SELLER,...

for the purchase and sale of ....

.... dated the .... day of ...., 20......... .

Buyer agrees to pay the balance as follows:

This form must be initialed by all parties to the Agreement of Purchase and Sale.

INITIALS OF BUYER(S): ( ) **INITIALS OF SELLER(S):** ( )

 Form 101 2007 **Page 5 of 5**

CHAPTER 29

Purchase of a Rural Property

If the client is purchasing a rural property such as a cottage or farm property, the steps and procedures to complete the transaction are largely the same as those for the purchase of an urban residential property. There are, however, a number of additional concerns. This chapter highlights only some of those concerns. It is not intended to be an exhaustive study of rural conveyancing.

WATER

Most rural properties are not connected to municipal water systems. They obtain their water from wells located on the property, and their water is discarded by way of septic systems.

If the property has a well, it is important to verify that the water is potable. The purchaser can do so by obtaining a sample of the water and sending it to the local health unit to be tested.

If the property has a septic system, you will have to write to the local health unit to find out whether it was installed according to the regulations in effect at the time of installation. If it was not, the purchaser's lawyer should submit a requisition that the system be reinstalled pursuant to the regulations. If it is an older system, the health unit may not have any record of the installation. Most agreements of purchase and sale for rural properties contain a warranty by the vendor that to the best of his or her knowledge the septic system was properly installed and has operated satisfactorily during his or her occupancy. The purchaser will have to rely on that warranty if no records are available.

ACCESS

A number of issues may arise with respect to access to rural properties.

Property Fronting on a Provincial Highway

If the property fronts on a provincial highway, you will have to write to the Ministry of Transportation to make sure that the entrance to the road from the property has been approved.

In addition, there are restrictions on what can be built or placed near a highway without a permit, so you must check section 34(2) of the *Public Transportation and Highway Improvement Act* to determine when a permit is required. If the property fronts on a controlled access highway, you should write to the Ministry of Transportation to find out whether or not a permit is required and, if so, whether or not one has been issued pursuant to section 38 of the Act.

Property Abutting an Unopened Road Allowance

Some properties abut unopened road allowances, which do not look any different from the rest of the property. On occasion, owners of rural property assume possession of the road allowance property and build on it. If that is the case, the municipality (which still owns the road allowance) can insist that any buildings be demolished.

It is therefore important to check the plan of survey to make sure that there are no structures located on an unopened road allowance. If structures have been built on the road allowance, the purchaser should requisition the vendor to apply to the municipality to have the road allowance conveyed to the vendor prior to closing.

Access by Right of Way

If access to the property is by right of way over other private or government property, the client should be aware that the right of way is not maintained by the municipality and maintenance of it will be an added expense to the client. Often there are cottage associations that attend to the maintenance of rights of way through membership fees.

Access by Water

If there is no road access to the property and access is only by water, the purchaser should make inquiries as to what boat launching and mooring and parking facilities are available, and what costs are associated with these.

WATERFRONT PROPERTIES

Other than issues of access as noted above, there are a number of other issues that may arise with respect to waterfront properties.

66-Foot Reservation

Some rural waterfront properties do not go right to the waterline. There may be a 66-foot strip between the lot line and the waterline that is owned by the Crown or the local municipality. The landowner has the right to cross over the strip, but not to build on it or pipe water across it without municipal permission. Ownership of the strip can be determined by checking Registry Office records.

Shoreline Ownership

Purchasers of shoreline property should be aware that they cannot alter the shoreline in any way or build anything over the water, such as a dock or a boathouse, without obtaining permits from the Ministry of Natural Resources and the Ministry of Transportation.

Conservation Authority

Properties near or on a watercourse may be governed by the *Conservation Authorities Act*. Section 28 of the Act gives a conservation authority the right to require its approval before any building is erected or fill is placed on land within its jurisdiction. Thus, a purchaser may be restricted in what can be done with the property.

ZONING

If the client intends to use the property year-round, you should make sure that the property is not zoned "seasonal," because municipal services may not be provided year-round to properties with this zoning.

REFERENCES

Conservation Authorities Act, RSO 1990, c. C.27, as amended.

Public Transportation and Highway Improvement Act, RSO 1990, c. P.50, as amended.

REVIEW QUESTIONS

1. How are most rural properties supplied with water, and how do they dispose of waste water?
2. If there is a well on the property, how can a purchaser be sure that the water is potable?
3. If the property abuts an unopened road allowance, can the owner build a structure on the road allowance?
4. What rights does the owner of a waterfront property have over the 66-foot strip between the lot line and the waterline?

DISCUSSION QUESTIONS

1. Frank has just purchased a cottage on a lot that extends to the shoreline of Lake Simcoe. As soon as the deal closes, he plans on building a boathouse. What should Frank be aware of before he goes ahead with his plan?
2. Alice loves the outdoors and wants to purchase a rural property that she can use year-round. She has found a property that is close to both a beautiful lake and a ski resort. She thinks it's perfect and wants to make an offer. What should Alice do before she makes an offer?

CHAPTER 30

Purchase of a Property Under Power of Sale

In chapter 6, Charges/Mortgages, we discussed mortgages from the perspective of the mortgagor. As stated in that chapter, a charge or mortgage is a loan secured against land. If the mortgagor (the borrower) defaults under the mortgage, usually by failing to make payments on the loan when due, the mortgagee (the lender) has the right to realize on the security of the land by seizing and selling it. This chapter discusses mortgages from the perspective of a purchaser buying the land from a mortgagee selling under the power of sale contained in the mortgage and examines the special conveyancing concerns that arise on such a purchase.

THE POWER OF SALE

As discussed in chapter 6, virtually every mortgage contains power of sale provisions that allow the mortgagee to sell the mortgaged property and use the proceeds from the sale for payment of the mortgage debt. A mortgagee can take steps to sell the mortgaged property if the mortgagor is in default for at least 15 days. The mortgagee is entitled to enter into an agreement of purchase and sale 35 days after proper notice of the sale has been given. As a practical matter, mortgagees rarely act this quickly and provide warnings before taking such action.

Pursuant to sections 35 and 36 of the *Mortgages Act*, the purchaser of a property under power of sale will obtain good title to the mortgaged property, free and clear of the mortgagor's interest in the property, provided that the notice of sale was proper and was given in "professed compliance" with the Act. If the notice of sale is defective, however, the sale may be declared invalid and the purchaser's title will be tainted. Accordingly, it is essential for the lawyer acting for the purchaser to ensure that the mortgagee has fully complied with the notice of sale provisions contained in the Act.

Pursuant to section 35, there will be conclusive evidence of compliance with the notice of sale provisions of the Act if the mortgagee (or the mortgagee's solicitor or agent) delivers the following statutory declarations at the time of registration of the transfer:

- a statutory declaration confirming default under the mortgage;
- a statutory declaration proving service of the notice of sale, together with copies of the post office registration receipts, if any; and
- a statutory declaration that the sale complies with the Act.

Examples of these three declarations are provided in figures 30.1, 30.2, and 30.3.

Although the mortgagor or any other person who suffers as a result of the sale may have a remedy against the person who exercised the power of sale, pursuant to section 36, a notice given in "professed compliance" with the Act cannot be challenged on the basis that the provisions of the Act were not, in fact, complied with. As a result, even a defective notice of sale may be enough to give good title to the purchaser if it was given in professed compliance with the Act. The courts have interpreted "professed compliance" to mean that the notice

> must be such as to enable the parties to whom the notice is required to be given to protect their interest. It must, in other words, identify the mortgage, stipulate the amount due thereon for principal, interest and costs and state that unless the sum is paid by a specified date the property will be sold. (*Re Botiuk and Collison et al.*)

As long as the notice provides this required information, it will not be struck out if it contains a minor omission or typographical error.

CONVEYANCING CONSIDERATIONS

The lawyer acting for the purchaser in a power of sale transaction must take steps to ensure that the provisions of section 35 of the *Mortgages Act* have been complied with.

The Agreement of Purchase and Sale

Ordinarily, the agreement of purchase and sale will include an acknowledgement by the purchaser that the property is being sold by the mortgagee under power of sale.

The Title Search

In addition to the usual searches and inquiries, the lawyer for the purchaser should review the mortgage under which the property is being sold to ensure that its power of sale provisions have been complied with.

Closing Documentation

The documentation differs depending on whether the property is registered in the Registry or the Land Titles system.

PROPERTY IN THE REGISTRY SYSTEM

If the property is registered in the Registry system, the usual practice is for the mortgagee to deliver the three declarations referred to in section 35 of the *Mortgages Act* for deposit on title at the time of closing, by registration of a document general to which the declarations are attached. Figure 30.4 is an example of the document general for the power of sale referred to in figures 30.1, 30.2, and 30.3. In addition, the transfer will include recitals that refer to the registration of the mortgage, the power of sale provisions in the mortgage, details of the notice given, and the mortgagor's continued default. Figure 30.5 is an example of the transfer.

Prior to closing, the purchaser's lawyer must carefully review the declarations, including the notice of sale and registration receipts, to ensure that the sale, in fact, complies with the Act.

PROPERTY IN THE LAND TITLES SYSTEM

When property in the Land Titles system is sold under power of sale, the mortgagee/chargee must register "evidence specified by the Director of Titles" in order to transfer good title to the purchaser.

If the closing is not electronic, the evidence will be in the form of statutory declarations, referred to as "sale papers," in a format similar to that required in the Registry system. The sale papers must be approved by the land registrar prior to closing and are then attached to the transfer. The mortgagee sends a draft of these sale papers to the purchaser's lawyer, advising him or her that they are also being sent to the Director of Titles for pre-approval. Although the purchaser's lawyer reviews the sale papers, since the property is in Land Titles, the lawyer will ultimately rely on the land registrar to ensure that they are correct.

Figure 30.6 is an example of Land Titles sale papers, and figure 30.7 is an example of a Land Titles transfer.

If the closing is electronic, the parties have the choice of electronically registering the transfer without compliance with law statements, in which case the sale papers must be filed separately at the Land Titles office, or including the following compliance with law statements in the electronically registered transfer:

- that the sale is authorized under the *Mortgages Act* and under the mortgage;
- that money was advanced under the mortgage;
- that the mortgage was in default when the notice of sale was given and continues be in default;
- that the sale complies with the mortgage and the *Mortgages Act* (and other acts, where applicable);
- identification and particulars of instruments registered after the mortgage;
- identification and particulars of writs of execution filed subsequent to the mortgage; and
- identification of spousal status for each person whose interest may be deleted upon registration of the transfer and whose spouse was not served with a notice of sale.

GENERAL CONCERNS

Whether the property is registered in the Land Titles or the Registry system, the lawyer for the purchaser must do the following:

- review the mortgage to ensure that it contains a power of sale clause;
- review the declarations to make sure that the registration particulars of the mortgage are stated correctly;

- review the declarations to confirm that the mortgage was in default for the appropriate period of time before the notice of sale was served and that the property was sold only after the expiry of the required notice period;
- review the search of title for subsequent encumbrancers and execution creditors to confirm that the appropriate parties were served with the notice of sale;
- review the mortgage to determine whether it contains addresses for service for any of the parties and then review the declaration regarding service to ensure that the parties were in fact served at those addresses;
- review the declaration of service to confirm that the post office receipts match the addresses set out; and
- review the notice of sale to confirm that
  - there are no errors in the names of the parties, the legal description of the property, or the statement of arrears;
  - the notice was properly signed; and
  - the specified redemption period has passed.

These steps are required notwithstanding the fact that section 36 of the *Mortgages Act* protects the purchaser's title, because the purchaser will lose the protection if it can be shown that there was notice of the invalidity of the notice of sale.

EFFECT OF A POWER OF SALE

When the sale is completed, the mortgagee will have no further interest in the property. The sale will also extinguish the interests of the mortgagor, and of any subsequent encumbrancers, who must satisfy their claims from any surplus remaining after the mortgagee's loan and related expenses have been paid out of the sale proceeds. The purchaser's title will be subject only to any prior registered encumbrances.

REFERENCES

Botiuk and Collison et al., Re (1979), 26 OR (2d) 580, 103 DLR (3d) 322 (CA).

Mortgages Act, RSO 1990, c. M.40.

REVIEW QUESTIONS

1. Does the purchaser of a property under power of sale get good title to the mortgaged property, free and clear of the mortgagor's interest in the property?
2. What constitutes conclusive evidence of compliance with the notice of sale provisions of the *Mortgages Act*?
3. When searching title to property being purchased under power of sale, what steps, in addition to the usual searches and inquiries, should the purchaser's lawyer take?
4. If the property being purchased is registered in the Registry system, what additional information should be included in the transfer?
5. If the property being sold under power of sale is registered in the Land Titles system and the closing is electronic, what is required in order to transfer good title to the purchaser?
6. What information is the purchaser's lawyer confirming when reviewing the notice of sale documents prior to closing?
7. When a power of sale is completed, what effect will this have on both the mortgagor's and the mortgagee's interest in the property?

FIGURE 30.1 Declaration Regarding Default

Declaration Regarding Default (Registry)

PROVINCE OF ONTARIO JUDICIAL DISTRICT OF TORONTO	) IN THE MATTER OF TITLE to) Lot 26, Plan 329, in the City of) Toronto
	) AND IN THE MATTER of a sale) thereof contained in a mortgage) dated February 1, (*year*), made by) David Defaulter and Donna) Defaulter, as mortgagor, and Secure) Trust Company, as mortgagee and) registered in the Land Registry) Office for the Registry Division of) the City of Toronto (No. 64) as) Instrument No. 987654
	) AND IN THE MATTER of a sale of) of the above-noted lands and) premises by Secure Trust Company

TO WIT:

I, ALVIN ADMINISTRATOR, of the City of Toronto, do solemnly declare that:

1. I am the Chief Financial Officer of Secure Trust Company, and as such have personal knowledge of the matters herein deposed to.

2. Pursuant to the mortgage dated February 1, (*year*), and registered in the Land Registry Office for the Registry Division for the City of Toronto (No. 64) on the 3rd day of February, (*year*) as Instrument No. 987654 (the "Mortgage"), David Defaulter and Donna Defaulter mortgaged the above-noted lands and premises to the mortgagee.

3. The Mortgage has been in default since the 5th day of October, (*year*), and has remained in default to the date hereof.

4. The Mortgage remained in default at the time when the mortgagee entered into the agreement of purchase and sale of the above-noted lands and premises to Peter Purchaser.

5. There is presently owing on the Mortgage for the principal money, interest, taxes, insurance premiums, appraisal fees and costs in excess of the sum of $71,250.00 and the costs and expenses of the above-noted sale.

6. The mortgagee has not, nor has any other person or persons on its behalf or as agent, received the moneys referred to in paragraph 5 hereof, or any security for the same, other than the Mortgage.

FIGURE 30.1 Concluded

7. So far as I am aware, the mortgagee has not received any written notice of any statutory lien against the above-noted lands and premises in favour of the Crown or any other public authority, and, so far as I am aware, the mortgagee has not received actual notice in writing of any other interest in the above-noted lands and premises other than those served with the notice of sale herein.

8. No action for foreclosure of the mortgagor has been commenced by the mortgagee.

AND I MAKE this solemn declaration conscientiously believing it to be true and knowing that it is of the same force and effect as if made under oath.

DECLARED BEFORE ME at the City of Toronto,	)	
In the Province of Ontario	)	______________________
	)	Alvin Administrator
this day of , (*year*)	)	
______________________________	)	
A Commissioner, etc.	)	

FIGURE 30.2 Declaration of Service

Declaration as to Service (Registry)

PROVINCE OF ONTARIO JUDICIAL DISTRICT OF TORONTO	)))	IN THE MATTER OF TITLE to Lot 26, Plan 329, in the City of Toronto
	))))))))))	AND IN THE MATTER of a sale thereof contained in a mortgage dated February 1, (*year*), made by David Defaulter and Donna Defaulter, as mortgagor, and Secure Trust Company, as mortgagee and registered in the Land Registry Office for the Registry Division of the City of Toronto (No. 64) as Instrument No. 987654
	)))	AND IN THE MATTER of a sale of of the above-noted lands and premises by Secure Trust Company

TO WIT:

I, CAROL CLERK, of the City of Toronto, do solemnly declare that:

1. I am a law clerk at the law firm of Susan Smart, solicitor for Secure Trust Company, and as such have knowledge of the matters herein deposed to.

2. I did on the 1st day of April, (*year*), serve by prepaid registered mail David Defaulter, Donna Defaulter, the Spouse of David Defaulter, and the Spouse of Donna Defaulter, with a notice of sale under mortgage, a true copy of which is attached hereto and marked as Exhibit "A" to this declaration, in accordance with the *Mortgages Act.*

3. The original certificate of post office registration in support is attached and marked as Exhibit "B" to the declaration.

AND I MAKE this solemn declaration conscientiously believing it to be true and knowing that it is of the same force and effect as if made under oath.

DECLARED BEFORE ME at the City of Toronto, In the Province of Ontario this day of , (*year*) ____________________ A Commissioner, etc.	))))))	____________________ Carol Clerk

FIGURE 30.2 Continued

EXHIBIT "A"

Notice of Sale Under Charge

TO: David Defaulter & Donna Defaulter
123 Picket Fence Drive
Toronto, Ontario
M2B 4L7

AND TO: The Parties shown on Schedule "A" attached hereto.

TAKE NOTICE that default has been made in payment of the moneys due under a certain charge dated the 1st day of February, (*year*) made

BETWEEN:

DAVID DEFAULTER & DONNA DEFAULTER

Chargor

- and -

SECURE TRUST COMPANY
a trust company incorporated under
the laws of the Province of Ontario,

Chargee

on the security of ALL AND SINGULAR that certain parcel or tract of land and premises situate, lying and being in the city of Toronto and being composed of the whole of Lot 26, according to Registered Plan 329 registered in the Land Registry Office for the Registry Division for Metropolitan Toronto (No. 64) which charge was registered on the 3rd day of February, (*year*) in the Land Registry Office for the Registry Division for Metropolitan Toronto (No. 64) as Instrument No. 987654 (the "Charge").

AND Secure Trust Company hereby gives you notice that the amounts now due on the Charge for principal money, interest and costs, respectively, are as follows:

Principal money	$65,000.00
Interest as of April 1, (*year*)	5,250.00
Cost of these proceedings	1,000.00
TOTAL	$71,250.00

AND UNLESS the said sums, together with interest thereon at the rate of 12% per annum calculated half-yearly, not in advance and any further costs and disbursements incurred in these proceedings, are paid on or before the 6th day of May (*year*), Secure Trust Company shall sell the property covered by the said Charge under the provisions contained in it.

THIS NOTICE is given to you as you appear to have an interest in the charged property and may be entitled to redeem the same.

DATED at Toronto, Ontario, this 1st day of April, (*year*)

SECURE TRUST COMPANY

By its solicitor and authorized agent,
Susan Smith, Barrister & Solicitor
456 Bay Street
Toronto, Ontario, M5G 8D3

per: ____________________
S. Smart

FIGURE 30.2 Concluded

SCHEDULE "A"

DAVID DEFAULTER
123 Picket Fence Drive
Toronto, Ontario
M2B 4L7

DONNA DEFAULTER
123 Picket Fence Drive
Toronto, Ontario
M2B 4L7

SPOUSE OF DONNA DEFAULTER
123 Picket Fence Drive
Toronto, Ontario
M2B 4L7

SPOUSE OF DAVID DEFAULTER
123 Picket Fence Drive
Toronto, Ontario
M2B 4L7

FIGURE 30.3 Declaration of Compliance with the Mortgages Act

Declaration of Compliance with the *Mortgages Act* (Registry)

PROVINCE OF ONTARIO	)	IN THE MATTER OF TITLE to
	)	Lot 26, Plan 329, in the City of
JUDICIAL DISTRICT OF TORONTO	)	Toronto
	)	AND IN THE MATTER of a sale
	)	thereof contained in a mortgage
	)	dated February 1, (*year*), made by
	)	David Defaulter and Donna
	)	Defaulter, as mortgagor, and Secure
	)	Trust Company, as mortgagee and
	)	registered in the Land Registry
	)	Office for the Registry Division of
	)	the City of Toronto (No. 64) as
	)	Instrument No. 987654
	)	AND IN THE MATTER of a sale of
	)	of the above-noted lands and
	)	premises by Secure Trust Company

TO WIT:

I, SUSAN SMART, of the City of Toronto, do solemnly declare that:

1. I am the solicitor for Secure Trust Company, and as such have knowledge of the matters herein deposed to.
2. Pursuant to a mortgage dated the 1st day of February, (*year*) and registered in the Land Registry Office for the Registry Division for the City of Toronto (No. 64) on the 3rd day of February, (*year*) as Instrument No. 987654 (the "Mortgage"), David Defaulter and Donna Defaulter mortgaged the above-noted lands and premises to Secure Trust Company.
3. I have read over the material in connection with the sale of the above-noted lands and premises under the power of sale contained in the Mortgage, and I am of the opinion that it complies with Part III of the *Mortgages Act*, and this statutory declaration is delivered pursuant to section 35 of the said Act.

AND I MAKE this solemn declaration conscientiously believing it to be true and knowing that it is of the same force and effect as if made under oath.

DECLARED BEFORE ME at the City of Toronto,	)	
In the Province of Ontario	)	______________________
	)	Susan Smart
this day of , (*year*)	)	
______________________	)	
A Commissioner, etc.	)	

FIGURE 30.4 Document General for Declarations

Province of Ontario

DYE & DURHAM CO. INC.—Form No. 985
Amended NOV. 1992

Document General

Form 4 — Land Registration Reform Act

D

FOR OFFICE USE ONLY

New Property Identifiers — Additional: See Schedule ☐

Executions — Additional: See Schedule ☐

(1) Registry ☒ **Land Titles** ☐

(2) Page 1 of 5 pages

(3) Property Identifier(s) Block Property 12345-6789 Additional: See Schedule ☐

(4) Nature of Document DEPOSIT under s. 106(1) of the Registry Act

(5) Consideration Dollars $

(6) Description

Lot 26,
Plan 329
City of Toronto

Registry Division for the City of Toronto
(No. 64)

(7) This Document Contains: (a) Redescription New Easement Plan/Sketch ☐ (b) Schedule for: Description ☐ Additional Parties ☐ Other ☐

(8) This Document provides as follows:

I, Susan Smart, of the City of Toronto here deposit with and require you to take into your Custody, pursuant to Part II of the Registry Act, the following documents:

Description of Documents	Names of all Parties	Any Other Particulars or Subject of Certificate, Affidavit, Etc.
Statutory Declaration	Carol Clerk	Re: service of notice of sale
Statutory Declaration	Alvin Administrator	Re: default under mortgage
Statutory Declaration	Susan Smart	Re: compliance with Mortgages Act

Continued on Schedule ☐

(9) This Document relates to instrument number(s)

(10) Party(ies) (Set out Status or Interest)

Name(s)	Signature(s)	Date of Signature Y M D
SMART, Susan, Solicitor	Per: Susan Smart, Solicitor	
456 Bay Street		
Toronto, Ontario M5G 8D3		

(11) Address for Service 456 Bay Street, Toronto, Ontario M5G 8D3

(12) Party(ies) (Set out Status or Interest)

Name(s)	Signature(s)	Date of Signature Y M D

(13) Address for Service

(14) Municipal Address of Property

123 Picket Fence Drive
Toronto, Ontario
M2B 4L7

(15) Document Prepared by:

Susan Smart
Barrister and Solicitor
456 Bay Street
Toronto, Ontario
M5G 8D3

FOR OFFICE USE ONLY

Fees and Tax	
Registration Fee	
Total	

FIGURE 30.5 Registry System Transfer Under Power of Sale

Province of Ontario

DYE & DURHAM CO. INC.—Form No. 970 Amended NOV. 1992

Transfer/Deed of Land

Form 1 — Land Registration Reform Act

A

FOR OFFICE USE ONLY

New Property Identifiers — Additional: See Schedule ☐

Executions — Additional: See Schedule ☐

(1) Registry ☒ Land Titles ☐ (2) Page 1 of 2 pages

(3) Property Identifier(s) Block Property 12345-6789 Additional: See Schedule ☐

(4) Consideration Three Hundred Thousand Dollars $ 300,000.00

(5) Description This is a: Property Division ☐ Property Consolidation ☐

Lot 26
Plan 329
City of Toronto

(6) This Document Contains (a) Redescription New Easement Plan/Sketch ☐ (b) Schedule for: Description ☐ Additional Parties ☐ Other ☒

(7) Interest/Estate Transferred Fee Simple

(8) Transferor(s) The transferor hereby transfers the land to the transferee and certifies that the transferor is at least eighteen years old and that

Name(s) SECURE TRUST COMPANY

Signature(s) Per: Alvin Administrator, Chief Financial Officer

Date of Signature Y M D

(9) Spouse(s) of Transferor(s) I hereby consent to this transaction
Name(s) Signature(s) Date of Signature Y M D

(10) Transferor(s) Address for Service 86 King Street West, Toronto, Ontario, M4H 5D2

(11) Transferee(s) PURCHASER, Peter — Date of Birth Y 1965 M 06 D 24

(12) Transferee(s) Address for Service 123 Picket Fence Drive, Toronto, Ontario M2B 4L7

Planning Act — OPTIONAL

(13) Transferor(s) The transferor verifies that to the best of the transferor's knowledge and belief, this transfer does not contravene section 50 of the Planning Act.
Date of Signature Y M D Signature .... Date of Signature Y M D Signature ....

Solicitor for Transferor(s) I have explained the effect of section 50 of the Planning Act to the transferor and I have made inquiries of the transferor to determine that this transfer does not contravene that section and based on the information supplied by the transferor, to the best of my knowledge and belief, this transfer does not contravene that section. I am an Ontario solicitor in good standing.
Name and Address of Solicitor — Signature .... Date of Signature Y M D

Affix Statement by Solicitor for Transferee(s) here if necessary

(14) Solicitor for Transferee(s) I have investigated the title to this land and to abutting land where relevant and I am satisfied that the title records reveal no contravention as set out in subclause 50 (22) (c) (ii) of the Planning Act and that to the best of my knowledge and belief this transfer does not contravene section 50 of the Planning Act. I act independently of the solicitor for the transferor(s) and I am an Ontario solicitor in good standing.
Name and Address of Solicitor — Signature .... Date of Signature Y M D

(15) Assessment Roll Number of Property

Cty.	Mun.	Map	Sub.	Par.
01	25	023	076	00024

(16) Municipal Address of Property
123 Picket Fence Drive
Toronto, Ontario
M2B 4L7

(17) Document Prepared by:
Susan Smart
Barrister and Solicitor
456 Bay Street
Toronto, Ontario
M5G 8D3

FOR OFFICE USE ONLY — Fees and Tax

Fees and Tax	
Registration Fee	
Land Transfer Tax	
Total	

FIGURE 30.5 Concluded

Province of Ontario

DYE & DURHAM CO. INC.—Form No. 288
Amended NOV. 1992

Schedule
Land Registration Reform Act
Recitals for Deed Under Power of Sale (Registry)
(Attach to Form 1)

S

Page 2 of 2

WHEREAS:

1. By a Mortgage dated the 1st day of February (year) and registered in the Land Registry Office for the Registry Division for the City of Toronto (No. 64) as Instrument No. 987654 on the 3rd day of February (year) ,

David Defaulter and Donna Defaulter

as Mortgagor

did mortgage the lands herein to

Secure Trust Company

as Mortgagee

for securing payment of the sum of SIXTY THOUSAND---------------------------------
--------------------------($60,000.00)------------------------------------ DOLLARS
and interest as therein mentioned.

2. The Mortgagee, on default of payment under the said Mortgage for fifteen days is entitled on thirty-five days' notice to sell the said lands.

3. Such default has been made in payment of the principal and interest secured by the said Mortgage and notice of exercising the power to sell the said lands has been duly given by the Mortgagee to all persons entitled thereto.

4. Such default has not been remedied and the time set forth in the notice of sale has expired.

5. Statutory Declarations setting forth the particulars of such default, the service of notice of sale and the sale proceedings have been deposited and registered in the said Land Registry Office as Instrument No. 987654

AND THEREFORE under and by virtue of the powers of sale contained in the said Mortgage, the said lands were sold to the Transferee.

In construing this document, the words "Mortgagor", "Mortgagee" and "Transferee" and all personal pronouns shall be read as the number and gender of the party or parties referred to herein requires and all necessary grammatical changes, as the context requires, shall be deemed to be made.

FOR OFFICE USE ONLY

FIGURE 30.6 Land Titles System Sale Papers

STATUTORY DECLARATION OF CHARGEE

IN THE MATTER OF Parcel 26-1, Section M-329, City of Toronto

AND IN THE MATTER OF a sale thereof under the power of sale contained in Charge No. 987654 made by David Defaulter and Donna Defaulter to Secure Trust Company, dated February 1, (*year*) and registered in the Land Registry Office for the Land Titles Division of Toronto (no. 66) on February 3, (*year*).

I, ALVIN ADMINISTRATOR, of the City of Toronto, do solemnly declare that:

1. I am the Chief Financial Officer of Secure Trust Company, the registered owner of Charge No. 987654, and as such have personal knowledge of the matters herein deposed to.
2. To the best of my knowledge and belief, money or money's worth was actually advanced or supplied under the said Charge without my having actual notice of any encumbrance registered or filed subsequent to the Charge.
3. To the best of my knowledge and belief, subsections 78(2) and 78(5) of the *Construction Lien Act* do not give priority to any lien under the *Act* over Charge No. 987654.
4. Default entitling the chargee to sell the land was made in respect of payment of Charge No. 987654 on October 5, (*year*), and the charge remained in default at the time a sale under the said charge was made.
5. The charge remains in default as of the date hereof.

AND I MAKE this solemn declaration conscientiously believing it to be true and knowing that it is of the same force and effect as if made under oath.

DECLARED BEFORE ME at the City of Toronto,	)	
In the Province of Ontario	)	______________________________
	)	Alvin Administrator
this day of , (*year*)	)	
________________________________	)	
A Commissioner, etc.	)	

FIGURE 30.6 Continued

STATUTORY DECLARATION OF SERVICE OF NOTICE OF SALE UNDER CHARGE

IN THE MATTER OF Parcel 26-1, Section M-329, City of Toronto

AND IN THE MATTER OF a sale thereof under the power of sale contained in Charge No. 987654 made by David Defaulter and Donna Defaulter to Secure Trust Company, dated February 1, (*year*) and registered in the Land Registry Office for the Land Titles Division of Toronto (no. 66) on February 3, (*year*).

I, CAROL CLERK, of the City of Toronto, do solemnly declare that:

1. I am a law clerk at the law firm of Susan Smart, solicitor for Secure Trust Company, the registered owner of Charge No. 987654, and as such have knowledge of the matters herein deposed to.
2. I did on the __________day of____________________, (*year*), serve by prepaid registered mail David Defaulter, Donna Defaulter, the Spouse of David Defaulter, and the Spouse of Donna Defaulter, with a notice of sale under charge, a true copy of which is attached hereto and marked as Exhibit "A" to this declaration, in accordance with the *Mortgages Act.*
3. The original certificate of post office registration in support is attached and marked as Exhibit "B" to the declaration.

AND I MAKE this solemn declaration conscientiously believing it to be true and knowing that it is of the same force and effect as if made under oath.

DECLARED BEFORE ME at the City of Toronto,	)	
In the Province of Ontario	)	____________________
	)	Carol Clerk
this day of , (*year*)	)	
______________________________	)	
A Commissioner, etc.	)	

FIGURE 30.6 Concluded

STATUTORY DECLARATION OF CHARGEE'S SOLICITOR

IN THE MATTER OF Parcel 26-1, Section M-329, City of Toronto

AND IN THE MATTER OF a sale thereof under the power of sale contained in Charge No. 987654 made by David Defaulter and Donna Defaulter to Secure Trust Company, dated February 1, (*year*) and registered in the Land Registry Office for the Land Titles Division of Toronto (no. 66) on February 3, (*year*).

I, SUSAN SMART, of the City of Toronto, do solemnly declare that:

1. I am the solicitor for Secure Trust Company, the registered owner of Charge No. 987654, and as such have knowledge of the matters herein deposed to.
2. I have made or caused to be made a thorough search in the Land Registry Office for the Land Titles Division of the City of Toronto (No. 66) and found no persons entitled to receive notice of exercising the power of sale other than the following who were served with the notice as required by the *Mortgages Act.*

   DEFAULTER, David
   DEFAULTER, Donna
   The Spouse of David Defaulter
   The Spouse of Donna Defaulter
3. In my opinion, the sale proceedings carried out by Secure Trust Company, in exercise of the power of sale contained in Charge No. 987654 are in compliance with Part III of the *Mortgages Act*, the terms of the charge, the *Planning Act*, and other relevant requirements of law.

AND I MAKE this solemn declaration conscientiously believing it to be true and knowing that it is of the same force and effect as if made under oath.

DECLARED BEFORE ME at the City of Toronto,	)
In the Province of Ontario	) ______________________
	) Susan Smart
this day of , (*year*)	)
______________________________________	)
A Commissioner, etc.	)

FIGURE 30.7 Land Titles System Transfer Under Power of Sale

Province of Ontario

DYE & DURHAM CO. INC.—Form No. 970 Amended NOV. 1992

Transfer/Deed of Land

Form 1 — Land Registration Reform Act

A

FOR OFFICE USE ONLY

New Property Identifiers — Additional: See Schedule ☐

Executions — Additional: See Schedule ☐

(1) Registry ☐ Land Titles ☒

(2) Page 1 of 1 pages

(3) Property Identifier(s) Block Property — 12345-6789 — Additional: See Schedule ☐

(4) Consideration — Three Hundred Thousand Dollars $ 300,000.00

(5) Description This is a: Property Division ☐ Property Consolidation ☐

Parcel 26-1, Section M-329
Lot 26, Plan M-329
City of Toronto

(6) This Document Contains (a) Redescription New Easement Plan/Sketch ☐ (b) Schedule for: Description ☐ Additional Parties ☐ Other ☐

(7) Interest/Estate Transferred — Fee Simple

(8) Transferor(s) The transferor hereby transfers the land to the transferee and certifies that the transferor is at least eighteen years old and that

This transfer is pursuant to a power of sale contained in Charge No. 987654 under Part III of the Mortgages Act.

Name(s)	Signature(s)	Date of Signature Y	M	D
SECURE TRUST COMPANY	Per:			
	Alvin Administrator			
	Chief Financial Officer			

(9) Spouse(s) of Transferor(s) I hereby consent to this transaction

Name(s)	Signature(s)	Date of Signature Y	M	D

(10) Transferor(s) Address for Service — 86 King Street West, Toronto, Ontario, M4H 5D2

(11) Transferee(s)

Name	Date of Birth Y	M	D
PURCHASER, Peter	1965	06	24

(12) Transferee(s) Address for Service — 123 Picket Fence Drive, Toronto, Ontario M2B 4L7

Planning Act — OPTIONAL

(13) Transferor(s) The transferor verifies that to the best of the transferor's knowledge and belief, this transfer does not contravene section 50 of the Planning Act.

Signature .... Date of Signature Y M D — Signature .... Date of Signature Y M D

Solicitor for Transferor(s) I have explained the effect of section 50 of the Planning Act to the transferor and I have made inquiries of the transferor to determine that this transfer does not contravene that section and based on the information supplied by the transferor, to the best of my knowledge and belief, this transfer does not contravene that section. I am an Ontario solicitor in good standing.

Name and Address of Solicitor — Signature .... Date of Signature Y M D

Affix Statement by Solicitor for Transferee(s) here if necessary

(14) Solicitor for Transferee(s) I have investigated the title to this land and to abutting land where relevant and I am satisfied that the title records reveal no contravention as set out in subclause 50 (22) (c) (ii) of the Planning Act and that to the best of my knowledge and belief this transfer does not contravene section 50 of the Planning Act. I act independently of the solicitor for the transferor(s) and I am an Ontario solicitor in good standing.

Name and Address of Solicitor — Signature .... Date of Signature Y M D

(15) Assessment Roll Number of Property

Cty.	Mun.	Map	Sub.	Par.
01	25	023	076	00024

(16) Municipal Address of Property

123 Picket Fence Drive
Toronto, Ontario
M2B 4L7

(17) Document Prepared by:

Susan Smart
Barrister and Solicitor
456 Bay Street
Toronto, Ontario
M5G 8D3

FOR OFFICE USE ONLY

Fees and Tax	
Registration Fee	
Land Transfer Tax	
Total	

Glossary

abstract/abstract book
book in the Registry system that records registered interests in land; record of all registrations affecting a parcel of land

abstracting
process of examining and summarizing into search notes the contents of all registered documents that affect title

accelerate
demand immediate payment

acceleration clause
clause permitting the chargee to demand immediate payment of the full amount of the loan in the event of default

acknowledgement and direction
document signed by parties to a real estate transaction authorizing their respective lawyers to sign and release the documents electronically on their behalf

adjoining land
property that shares a common boundary with the property being searched

advanced
given or provided

adverse possession
valid title to land through open, visible, and uninterrupted possession of that property, without the owner's permission, for a period of at least 10 years

adversely
without the owner's permission

affidavit of spousal status
affidavit attached to a deed (in use after 1978 until the *Land Registration Reform Act* came into force) that provided evidence of the marital status of the grantors or transferors

agreement of purchase and sale
contract created once an offer of purchase and sale has been accepted

amortization period
length of time it takes to repay a loan in full following the schedule of monthly payments in the charge

amortization schedule
schedule setting out the breakdown of each monthly blended payment between principal and interest and the remaining principal balance after each payment

annexation
attachment

arrears of rent
unpaid rent that is owed to a landlord

assignment
arrangement whereby a tenant transfers tenancy to another person for the remainder of the tenancy's term

assumed charge
existing charge taken over by the purchaser, who pays the vendor the purchase price of the property minus the outstanding balance of the charge

Automated Registry
computerized abstract listing all registered documents, including those registered prior to automation

balance due on closing
exact amount the purchaser pays to the vendor when the real estate deal closes

balloon payment
final payment for the amount of principal that remains unpaid at the end of the term of a charge

blanket mortgage
a mortgage creating a lien against more than one property; developers use blanket mortgages when subdividing large parcels of land into many separate lots; a blanket mortgage is spread over the entire parcel of land, rather than applied to each individual lot

blended payment
charge payment combining principal and interest into equal monthly payments

block
area of land created during the remapping of property under POLARIS

block number
five-digit number assigned to a block; the first part of the PIN

bona fide purchaser for value
purchaser of property who gives valuable consideration for the property and is acting in good faith

bonus interest
penalty of interest for a period of time, for early payment of a loan

building permit
document that grants legal permission to start construction of a "building"

buyer
purchaser of the property

bylaw (municipal)
law that is passed by a municipality

bylaws (condominium)
rules governing the internal operation of the condominium corporation

capital gains tax
federal tax levied on the profit realized when capital property, other than a principal residence, is sold

caveat emptor
Latin term meaning "let the buyer beware"

certificate of action
certificate of the court verifying that a statement of claim has been filed in a construction lien action

certify title
describe the state of the owner's title, including any limitations

chain of title
list of all owners within the 40-year search period

charge taken back
another name for vendor take back charge

chargee
lender

chargee in possession
chargee who takes possession of the charged property after default by the chargor

chargor
borrower and owner

chattels
movable possessions not attached to the real property

Children's Lawyer
government official charged with protecting the best interests of children in the province

closed charge
charge that prohibits repayment of the loan before the expiry of the term

closing date
day on which a real estate transaction is completed and title is transferred

commit waste
destroy, abuse, or make permanent undesirable changes to a property

committee of adjustment
independent body appointed by a municipality with the authority to grant consent to conveyances that result in a severance

common elements
areas of the condominium development owned as tenants in common by all of the individual unit owners

Common Elements and General Index
register that contains a description of the common elements and any easements and encumbrances that affect all the units

common expenses
monthly fees paid by unit owners to cover the condominium corporation's obligations

compliance with law statements
statements in which a lawyer confirms that all necessary legal requirements have been met

concession
large parcel of land created during the original division of land in Ontario resulting from the creation of east–west road allowances in a township

condominium corporation
corporation that comes into existence upon registration of the condominium plan

condominium unit
unit that is part of a condominium development

consent to variance
committee of adjustment approval of a building or use of a property when it does not conform to a current bylaw and is not a legal non-conforming use

Constitution Index
register that contains the declaration, description, and bylaws of the condominium

construction lien
lien against land that may be claimed by a person providing labour, services, or materials to a construction project

construction pyramid
illustration of the contractual relationships between parties in a typical large construction project

cooling-off period
10-day period during which the purchaser can back out of the purchase

counteroffer
offer tendered by the original offeree as an alternative to the original offer; also known as a sign-back

covenant
promise

Crown patent
grant of land by the Crown (the government) to the first owner

damages
financial compensation for losses arising out of a breach of contract

day book
record listing recent registrations not yet entered into the abstract book

declarant
upon registration, the person who owns the land described in the description and who registers the declaration and description that create the condominium plan

declaration
document stating that the property is governed by the *Condominium Act, 1998* and providing the consent of all mortgagees of the property, setting out the percentage of common elements associated with each unit and the percentage of common expenses that each unit owner will be required to pay, providing the address of the condominium corporation, and designating exclusive use common elements

deed
document that transfers ownership of land

deemed
accepted as conclusive of a certain state or condition in the absence of evidence or facts usually required to prove that state or condition

default
breach of one or more of the obligations contained in the charge; most commonly, the failure to remit principal and interest payments when due

deposit
document registered on title that verifies or clarifies facts related to the title; part of the purchase price prepaid when the contract is entered into and applied against the purchase price

description
document containing a plan of survey of the condominium property, architectural plans of the buildings, specification of unit boundaries, unit diagrams, and the certificates of the architect and land surveyor

diarize
record on a calendar the dates by which work must be completed

digital signature
unique digital identifiers comparable to a password or bank PIN used by lawyers when documents are registered electronically

disbursements
lawyer's out-of-pocket expenses, or money actually spent on behalf of the client

discharge of charge
a document given by the chargee to the chargor confirming that the loan has been paid in full and extinguishing the chargee's interest in the property

discharge of lien
document registered on title that discharges a construction lien

disclosure statement
document given to every purchaser of a condominium unit that includes details pertaining to the physical, legal, and financial aspects of the condominium corporation

distress
the right of a commercial landlord to seize and dispose of a tenant's property

document registration agreement
agreement entered into by the lawyers for the parties dealing with the procedures for electronic registration and the escrow closing arrangement

dominant tenement
land that benefits from an easement

dower
entitlement of a widow to a one-third life interest in the total value of any land that her husband owned during their marriage

due on sale clause
provision in a charge permitting the chargee to accelerate full payment of the loan in the event that the chargor sells the property and the chargee does not approve the purchaser

e-reg
electronic registration

easement
right to use a portion of someone else's land for a specific purpose, without requiring the owner's permission

easement implied by law
creation of an easement when the only way to gain access to a property is by crossing over another property

encroachment
building or structure intruding upon someone else's land

encumbrances
charges, claims, liens, or liabilities attached to a property

escheat
reversion of property to the Crown

escrow closing
exchange and holding of funds, keys, and documents by the lawyers pending registration of the electronic documents

estate
interest in land that provides the right to exclusive possession

exclusive possession
sole possession of the land; denial of possession to all others

exclusive use common elements
areas of the condominium development owned by all unit owners but used only by designated unit owners

execution
signing of a document; also a short name for a writ of execution or a writ of seizure and sale

express grant
creation of an easement by written document from the owner of the servient tenement to the owner of the dominant tenement

expropriation
reacquisition of land, with compensation, by the Crown for public purposes

extinguish
bring to an end

fault grounds
grounds for termination based on conduct or behaviour of the tenant or a guest of the tenant

fee simple
the right to exclusive possession and the right to dispose of the land for an indefinite period of time

first charge
charge registered first and thus taking priority over subsequently registered charges

fixed interest rate
rate of interest that remains the same for the term of the charge

fixed-term tenancy
tenancy that has a specified beginning and end date and can be for any period of time, from months to years

fixtures
chattels that have become attached or affixed to the real property; immovable possessions attached to the real property

flip
resale of property before the closing of the original purchase

foreclosure
court action whereby the chargee obtains legal title to the property after default by the chargor

forfeit
lose the right

grant
document that transfers ownership of land

***habendum* clause**
clause in a deed (old form) that indicates that ownership is subject to reservations, limitations, provisos, and conditions expressed in the original Crown grant

high ratio mortgage
a mortgage for more than 75 percent of the value of the property

holdback
sum of money required to be deducted by the payer and held for a specified period of time from the amount owing to a payee in a construction contract

improvement
changes made to real property, including construction, alteration, repair, installation, erection, and demolition

in escrow
holding of funds or documents by a third party to be released only on certain specified conditions

institutional lender
a lender other than an individual, including a bank, trust company, credit union, or insurance company

insurance binder
documented confirmation that a property has been insured

interest
amount added to the principal amount of the loan in return for the right to obtain and use the money advanced

interest adjustment date
date on which an adjustment is made for interest that accumulates between the date the loan was advanced and the charge payment date for the following month; assuming that charge payments are being made monthly, this date will be one month before the date of the first regular payment

interest rate
rate charged for the use of borrowed money, calculated as a percentage of the amount of the loan

interests
rights to land that are not estates and do not confer a right to exclusive possession of the land

interim occupancy date
date on which the purchaser takes possession prior to final closing and transfer of title

joint tenants
two or more people owning property where on the death of one, the survivors inherit the deceased's share

judgment creditor
party to whom a court awards the payment of money

judgment debtor
party against whom a court awards the payment of money

judicial sale
sale of charged property ordered and administered by a court

Land Titles Absolute (LT Absolute)
properties originally in the Land Titles system prior to POLARIS; corporate existence and *Planning Act* compliance are not guaranteed

Land Titles Assurance Fund
fund established under the *Land Titles Act* to compensate a person wrongfully deprived of an estate or interest in land as a result of an error regarding title

Land Titles Conversion Qualified (LTCQ)
properties originally in the Registry system and converted to the Land Titles system as a result of POLARIS; *Planning Act* compliance and corporate existence are guaranteed for the period prior to the date of conversion; properties remain subject to any pre-existing mature claims for adverse possession, prescription, or misdescription

Land Titles Plus (LT Plus)
properties upgraded from LTCQ with the additional guarantee against any mature claims for adverse possession

Land Titles system
land registration system in Ontario governed by the *Land Titles Act*

land transfer tax
provincial (and possibly municipal) tax on the purchase of land

latent defect
defect of which the vendor of a property was aware but which the purchaser did not know about and could not have discovered upon reasonable inspection of the property

Law Society of Upper Canada (LSUC)
professional body governing the activities of lawyers in Ontario

Lawyers' Professional Indemnity Company (LAWPRO)
insurance company controlled by the Law Society of Upper Canada that insures lawyers against errors and omissions and administers TitlePLUS, a title insurance product

leasehold estate
right to exclusive possession of property for a specified period of time in return for the payment of rent

legal description
description of land that is used in documents creating an interest in land; describes the land with reference to recorded maps, surveys, or plans

legal non-conforming use
status of a building or use of a property that does not conform to the current municipal bylaw but is acceptable because the building or use existed before the passing of the bylaw and has not subsequently been altered or discontinued

lien
charge for payment of a debt that allows the land to be sold to satisfy the debt

life estate
right to exclusive possession of the property for the length of a particular lifetime

lot
200-acre parcel of land created during the original division of land into concessions; also, a parcel of land created by a plan of subdivision

matrimonial home
defined under the *Family Law Act* to include every property in which a person has an interest and that is (if the parties are still married) or was (if the parties have separated) at the time of separation occupied by the spouses as their family residence

maturity date
date on which any outstanding balance of a charge is to be paid

metes and bounds description
written description of the boundaries and dimensions of a parcel of land in relation to lot lines; enables a sketch of the parcel to provide a picture of the area of land

monthly tenancy
a periodic tenancy that renews automatically at the end of each month until terminated by the landlord or the tenant

mortgage commitment
the mortgagor's agreement with the mortgagee when the mortgage is arranged

mortgagee
lender

mortgagor
borrower and owner

mortmain licence
licence to own land in Ontario that a corporation was required to obtain if it was incorporated in a jurisdiction other than Ontario, Quebec, or Canada

municipality
form of urban organization including cities, towns, and villages

natural environment
air, land, and water, or any combination or part thereof

new charge
arrangement by the purchaser for a new loan by way of charge for the purchase of property

no-fault grounds
grounds for termination unrelated to the conduct or behaviour of the tenant or a guest of the tenant

non-blended payment
charge payment that does not blend or combine principal and interest into equal payments; the amount of principal repaid each month is a fixed amount and the amount of interest is calculated on the outstanding principal at the time

notice of sale
document used in a power of sale setting out the particulars of the default and the amounts owing under the charge

offer
proposal from one person to another that, when accepted, becomes a contract

offeree
person to whom an offer is made

offeror
person who makes an offer

official plan
statement of planning principles prepared for a municipality by the local planning board

off-title documents
documents that are required for closing but are not registered on title

open a file
start a file

open charge
charge that permits repayment of the loan before the expiry of the term

parcel register
book in the Land Titles system that records all registered interests in land

Parcelized Day Forward Registry (PDFR)
computerized abstract listing only the most recent transfer prior to automation and those documents registered after the property was automated

part lot control
government control over transactions involving part of a subdivision lot

per diem
per day; for each day; daily

perfect
ensure that a preserved lien does not expire by commencing an action to enforce the lien and registering a certificate of action against title to the property

periodic tenancy
a tenancy that renews automatically at the end of the relevant period until terminated by either the tenant or the landlord, the period being defined by the frequency of rental payments

personal property
chattels; property that is not real property

phase I environmental assessment
assessment of property conducted to determine the likelihood that one or more contaminants have affected all or part of the property

phase II environmental assessment
assessment of property conducted to determine the location and concentration of contaminants on the property; follows completion of a phase I assessment

plan of subdivision
registered plan illustrating the measurements and boundaries of all lots and streets created by the division of concession lots into many smaller lots

plan of survey
schematic sketch showing boundaries of property and location of all fences, structures, and rights of way

POLARIS
Province of Ontario Land Registration Information System; computerized land information system

possession
control or occupancy of land regardless of ownership

power of attorney
document authorizing someone to deal with land or other property on the owner's behalf

power of sale
power to exercise the remedy of sale in case of default under a charge

pre-population
electronic process of copying information from a database into a document

prescription
means by which an interest is acquired in another's land after a period of open and uninterrupted use

preserve
ensure that lien rights are protected and do not expire by registering a claim for lien against title to the property on which work was performed within 45 days of completion of the work

principal
amount of money borrowed under a loan

priority
rank or status of a registered interest in land as determined by the date of registration of that interest

profit à prendre
interest created when mineral rights are acquired in the land of another person

property
term used to describe area of land created by the division of blocks during the remapping of land under POLARIS

property identifier number (PIN)
unique nine-digit number for each property created by combining the block and property number for that property

property number
four-digit number assigned to a property; the second part of the PIN

Property Parcel Register
register that contains the description of the property including any easements and the original encumbrances that affect the entire condominium property

proposed declarant
prior to the registration of the declaration and description, the person who owns the land described in the description

public utility
system that provides to the public water, sewage, fuel (including natural gas), energy (excluding electricity), heating, cooling, or telephone supplies or services

purchaser
buyer of the property

real property
land, including everything that is attached to it

realize on the security
seize and/or sell the charged property

recital
statement that sets out facts on which a document is based

redeem
release or free land from a claim against it by paying the amount owing under the charge

reference plan
registered survey prepared to illustrate the boundaries of a parcel of land

Registry system
land registration system in Ontario governed by the *Registry Act*

reporting letter
letter signed by the lawyer, outlining what was done in the transaction

requisition
request made to the vendor to clear up problems revealed by the title search and other inquiries

requisition date
deadline by which the purchaser (buyer) must submit any title requisitions to the vendor (seller)

requisition going to the root of title
requisition based on a defect that calls into question the legal enforceability/validity of the title

requisition on conveyance
requisition that requires the vendor to produce an effective conveyance, assuming that the vendor has the ability to do so

requisition on matters of contract
requisition for specific things that the purchaser is entitled to receive under the contract

requisition on title
query of directives made by the purchaser that asks the vendor to remedy problems with title

reserve fund
covers costs of major repairs to and replacement of common elements

restrictive covenant
promise by an owner of land to refrain from doing something on the property

retail sales tax
provincial tax on the purchase of chattels

right of survivorship
automatic vesting of an interest in the surviving joint tenant or tenants when one joint tenant dies

right of way
right to use a portion of another's land for access purposes

riparian rights
rights to the use of a watercourse running through or adjacent to the property

root of title (root deed)
first conveyance of the fee simple estate (a deed or transfer) registered after the commencement date of a title search

ruled off
the land registrar's drawing of a line through the entry in the abstract book of a mortgage that has been discharged

search notes
summary of the contents of all registered documents affecting title; reveals the state of the title including any encumbrances

search the title
conduct an investigation into the status and history of title to land

searching behind the plan
examining the abstract book for the original concession lot of which property was a part prior to the registration of the plan of subdivision

second charge
charge registered after the first charge and thus having subsequent priority to the first

seller
vendor of the property

servient tenement
land over which an easement runs

severance
division of land into smaller parcels

sign-back
offer whereby the original offeree changes some of the terms in the original offer, initials the changes, then submits it to the original offeror

simultaneous conveyance
two abutting parcels of land conveyed at the same time to two different people

specific performance
court order requiring a transaction to be completed; a type of remedy for breach of contract

spousal consent
consent of the spouse of the owner on title to the transfer or mortgage of a matrimonial home, required under the *Family Law Act*

standard charge terms
mortgage terms that are used in all mortgages issued by an institutional lender, which are filed with the government and are then assigned a file number

statement of adjustments
statement that outlines the various credits and debits against the purchase price and specifies the exact amount to be paid on closing

status certificate
certificate from the condominium corporation that includes, among other things, financial information, directors and officers, and the declaration

statutory declaration
sworn statement given by a person that attests to a given set of facts

subdivision agreement
agreement between a municipality and a builder setting out the terms under which the builder is allowed to subdivide the land

subdivision control
government control over the division of land into smaller parcels

sublet
arrangement whereby a tenant moves out of a rental unit for a period of time and allows another person to reside in the unit until the tenant returns at a specified future date

subsearch
a brief examination of title records to update an earlier search

tenancy agreement
written, oral, or implied agreement between a landlord and a tenant that creates the tenancy

tenants in common
two or more people owning property where on the death of one, the deceased person's share passes to his or her heirs rather than the other owners; no right of survivorship

tender
presentation of executed copies of all closing documents or funds to the other party in a real estate transaction

Teraview
software used to access the electronic land registration system in Ontario

term
period of time within which the chargor has agreed to repay the loan in full

termination for cause
termination by the landlord on fault grounds

title
legal right to the ownership and possession of property; evidence showing such a right

title opinion
lawyer's statement as to whether or not the purchaser has good title to the property

title requisition
request made to the vendor (seller) to clear up a problem found during the search of title

transfer
document that transfers ownership of land

UFFI
ureaformaldehyde foam insulation

Unit Register
register that shows ownership of each unit and any mortgages, liens, and leases relating to the unit

vacant possession
free or empty of all people and chattels

vacated
removed from title by registration of a court order that vacates or annuls the certificate of action

variable interest rate
rate of interest that fluctuates with changing market conditions during the term of the loan

vendor
seller of the property

vendor take back charge
charge created when the vendor of a property agrees to lend the purchaser money toward the purchase price and the purchaser gives the vendor a charge on the property as security for the loan

vest
to provide an immediate right to present or future ownership or possession

whiteprint
copy of the plan of survey of a plan of subdivision that shows the dimensions of individual building lots

will
document stating how a person's property will be dealt with upon death

writ of execution
judicial order addressed to the sheriff requiring the enforcement of a judgment

writ of possession
court order giving the chargee the right to take possession of the property

zoning
classification of permitted land use that includes categories such as residential, commercial, industrial, and agricultural

zoning bylaws
bylaws enacted by a municipality to regulate the use of land

Index